Inside the Undergraduate Experience

Inside the Undergraduate Experience

The University of Washington's Study of Undergraduate Learning

Catharine Hoffman Beyer
Gerald M. Gillmore
Andrew T. Fisher

University of Washington

ANKER PUBLISHING COMPANY, INC.
Bolton, Massachusetts

Inside the Undergraduate Experience
The University of Washington's Study of Undergraduate Learning

ISBN 978-1-933371-26-9

Composition by Jessica Holland
Cover design by Borges Design

Anker Publishing Company, Inc.
563 Main Street
P.O. Box 249
Bolton, MA 01740-0249 USA

www.ankerpub.com

Library of Congress Cataloging-in-Publication Data

Beyer, Catharine Hoffman.
 Inside the undergraduate experience : the University of Washington's study of undergraduate learning / Catharine Hoffman Beyer, Gerald M. Gillmore, Andrew T. Fisher.
     p. cm.
Includes bibliographical references and index.
ISBN 978-1-933371-26-9
1. University of Washington. 2. Education, Higher--Washington (State)--Longitudinal studies. 3. Education, Higher—Washington (State)—Case studies. 4. College students—Washington (State)—Case studies. I. Gillmore, Gerald M. (Gerald Millard), 1941- II. Fisher, Andrew T. III. Title.

 LD5753.B49 2007
 378.797—dc22

                                    2006101314

*This book is dedicated to the 304 participants
in the University of Washington's Study of Undergraduate Learning.*

*We are grateful that they let us walk with them through their coursework,
important times with friends and families, world travels, job searches, and
changing understanding of who they were, what they cared about, and what they
wanted to do in their lives. We thank them for sharing their ideas, experiences,
stories, dreams, and selves with us so openly. We wish them every good thing
as they continue on their life paths.*

Table of Contents

List of Figures and Tables

Tables

Figures

About the Authors

Catharine Hoffman Beyer is a research scientist in the University of Washington's Office of Educational Assessment, where she directs the University of Washington Study of Undergraduate Learning (UW SOUL) and assists faculty and departments as they develop learning goals and the methods to assess them. For the last 20 years, she has taught writing courses linked with courses across the curriculum in the university's Interdisciplinary Writing Program, receiving the English department's distinguished teaching award for that work in 1997. She codirected a series of three writing assessment studies for the UW and later served as dean for assessment and institutional effectiveness at a local community college. She received her M.A. in English from the University of Michigan in 1970 and has taught English and writing at the high school, community college, university, and graduate-school levels in Michigan, Oregon, and Washington. Her poetry has appeared in a number of literary magazines, as well as on Seattle city buses.

Gerald Gillmore is director emeritus of the University of Washington's Office of Educational Assessment. He served as the UW's coordinator of assessment from 1988 until 2001. In this capacity, he worked with departments across the university on assessing their curricula, developed a system of student and alumni surveys, led statewide assessment efforts in writing and quantitative reasoning, and represented the university at the state level. Dr. Gillmore developed the UW's Instructional Assessment System for collecting students' course evaluations, a system that is currently used at more than 60 colleges across the nation, as well as at the UW. He also developed and directed the State of Washington academic placement testing program. Dr. Gillmore received his Ph.D. in psychology in 1970 from Michigan State University. His research interests and areas in which he has published include measurement theory, faculty evaluation, and assessment of student learning.

Andrew T. Fisher began his work on the UW SOUL in fall quarter 2000 as an undergraduate researcher, and he was hired to continue working with the study as a research assistant. He earned his B.A. in the comparative history of ideas in 2001 with a thesis on critical thinking. While an undergraduate, he began a group called Agora to serve as a meeting place for comparative history of ideas majors to discuss issues associated with their program and earned a Mary Gates Leadership Grant for this work. After traveling to Brazil and China, he left the UW in 2004 to build a house with his father, and he is currently working in San Francisco. His many interests include how and why people change their minds, the role of the personal in academic learning, and conflict resolution.

Foreword

When I was a junior at Haverford College in 1968, a classic longitudinal study on students at that institution was published by Douglas Heath. Titled *Growing Up in College,* it exemplified a widespread genre of single-institution case studies of student development that constituted much of the source material for such student development classics as *Education and Identity* (Chickering, 1969). Sadly, this genre was going out of fashion by the mid-1980s, when one of its best examples came out—a multi-method longitudinal look at a single class at Stanford University through its four years of enrollment (Katchadourian & Boli, 1985). What largely replaced such studies in the literature on college student development were multi-institutional, heavily quantitative analyses seeking to establish generalized effects—the kinds of studies so ably summarized by Pascarella and Terenzini (1991, 2005). But frequently lost in the myriad of statistics was the authenticity of student voices and experiences. Catharine Beyer, Gerald Gillmore, and Andrew Fisher have found them again at the University of Washington.

Inside the Undergraduate Experience thus revives and updates a great tradition. From a conceptual standpoint, it benefits especially from the insights of constructivism and cognitive science—emphasizing the many ways students "make meaning" of their experiences in unique and unpredictable ways. From a methodological standpoint, it benefits from many years of refinement in assessment technique, directly examining student *learning* as well as growing up in college through such approaches as amassing and analyzing portfolios of actual student work as well as direct assessment. The result is emphatically *not* in search of generalized effects. Indeed, the authors are frequently critical of too-quick applications of such well-known "staged" theories of college student development as those of Chickering (1969) and Perry (1970). They prefer instead to emphasize the many differences among student paths to learning and, indeed, how attaining mastery may happen differently across different areas of knowledge or skill, and at different times in a college career, for even the same student. And although quantitative research tools are ably employed throughout, so are fully developed individual student stories, told in their own words. Purely empirical multi-institutional studies in search of generalized effects typically explain at most 35% of the variance on any criterion variable. This book is essentially about the nearly two-thirds that are missing.

This is not to say that general lessons are absent. Indeed, many of the major findings of this work are highly consistent with what others have found across different settings. One is the dominance of disciplines and the distinctiveness of student experience within the majors. The authors emphasize that the kinds of cross-cutting skills frequently claimed as products of "general education"—effective writing, critical thinking, and quantitative skills—are distinctively manifested in different disciplinary settings—so much so, in fact, that they can be claimed to be different abilities entirely. Echoing the findings of many studies, moreover, the authors find that each major constitutes a distinctive social and intellectual environment, which differentiates students far more than university-wide socializing experiences and events occurring elsewhere can bring them together.

Another familiar finding is the vast gap between high school and college with respect to academic expectations and assuming responsibility for learning. On the first, students are particularly eloquent in their testimony about the sheer amount of writing they were required to do in their first year of college, and how little prepared they were for such a workload. With respect to quantitative skills, moreover, they were used to formulaic "plug-and-chug" approaches that required little genuine understanding of mathematical concepts. More important, first-year students frequently found it difficult to transition from the relatively structured academic environment of high school to an academic culture in which managing one's own learning on one's own is the norm. Lack of early feedback on academic performance until mid-terms often misled some into postponing their academic work, occasionally with disastrous consequences. It is for very good reasons that Beyer, Gillmore, and Fisher call this time "the Hammering."

But there are also revealing patterns of student attitudes toward learning and learning behaviors that have been less subject to treatment elsewhere. Information literacy is a good example, as how college students learn about the process of inquiry and the modes they use to conduct it have not been as frequently assessed as things like writing and critical thinking. Here again, the authors maintain that disciplines condition everything and students diverge rapidly by major in how they seek and find information. At the same time, they use the Internet to "research" everything and are frequently less than critical about what they find there. Although somewhat more frequently treated in the wider literature, diversity is another example. The authors report that students arrive at the University of Washington with surprisingly high expectations about the benefits of interacting with peers drawn from different backgrounds, but that this falls off strikingly as their college careers progress. While their *knowledge* of diversity increases—together with their recognition of what constitutes appropriate behavior—their actual *experience* with diversity diminishes steadily. As the authors point out, this is also the case for academic skills like critical thinking: Individual *dispositions* to act in certain ways may decisively govern whether and how a given ability is deployed, even if it is theoretically mastered. It is in treating such matters that this book is at its best, because multiple methods and authentic voices allow the empirical complexity of what is going on to begin to emerge. Interestingly, when they reflect on their learning and development, students attribute few of the many areas of growth that they report to the university. They attribute them instead to their own attitudes and actions—sometimes with amazing frankness. Where they have not progressed, by their own admission, they take full responsibility. And they are quite comfortable with the levels of mastery they have achieved (though their faculty members frequently are not). Even the definition of "good grades" varies across students and circumstances and, despite the current mythology that today's college students consider them all-important, concerns about earning good grades are largely confined to the freshman year. The resulting bottom line on learning, the authors conclude, is that students *do* learn a lot in college. But exactly what they learn is uneven across individuals and subjects, and depends critically on the ways they choose to engage.

Above all, this book is an antidote to currently popular critiques of residential student behaviors like John Merrow's recent PBS special *Declining by Degrees*. The portrait it paints of the current undergraduate is complex and richly nuanced, avoiding stereotypes and needless theorizing that mask the individual struggle of all students to make sense of what they see, hear, read, and do in college. That they rise to the occasion so often—albeit in distinctively different ways—is both moving and reassuring. These stories vividly recreate the "awe" of collegiate learning. They remind us all in the academy of why we do this stuff.

Peter Ewell
National Center for Higher Education Management Systems (NCHEMS)
September 2006

REFERENCES

Chickering, A. W. (1969). *Education and identity.* San Francisco, CA: Jossey-Bass.

Heath, D. H. (1968). *Growing up in college: Liberal education and maturity.* San Francisco, CA: Jossey-Bass.

Katchadourian, H. A., & Boli, J. (1985). *Careerism and intellectualism among college students.* San Francisco, CA: Jossey-Bass.

Pascarella, E. T., & Terenzini, P. T. (1991). *How college affects students.* San Francisco, CA: Jossey-Bass.

Pascarella, E. T., & Terenzini, P. T. (2005). *How college affects students: A third decade of research.* San Francisco, CA: Jossey-Bass

Perry, W. (1970). *Forms of intellectual and ethical development in the college years: A scheme.* New York, NY: Holt, Rinehart & Winston.

Acknowledgments

Studies like the University of Washington's Study of Undergraduate Learning (UW SOUL) cannot occur without significant administrative and emotional support. The study has been housed in its entirety in the Office of Educational Assessment (OEA) at the University of Washington, and we express our gratitude to our colleagues. They supported us and our efforts with comments, encouragement, love, food, and extra hands when needed. We are especially grateful to Nana Lowell, director of OEA after Gillmore, who gave the study significant financial support, accommodated the needs of students as they came and went from the office, was a caring and generous listener, and gave us the time to work on this book and the freedom to determine its direction and goals.

In addition, we are grateful to Fred Campbell, George Bridges, and Christine Ingebritsen, deans and vice provosts of undergraduate education during the years of the study. Each of them provided us with significant financial and personal support for the project from its inception. We also thank Kim Johnson-Bogart, assistant dean of undergraduate education at the time of the study, for her contribution, both to our lives and our work. Her wisdom, insight, and advocacy for providing rich experiences for undergraduates guided us, and her willingness to read drafts of the book helped us immeasurably.

In addition to administrative help, the UW SOUL had the support of an advisory committee of gifted faculty and staff. This group of busy, highly respected scholars and teachers provided feedback on study design questions, commented on drafts of reports, and helped us think through findings that were confusing. We are grateful for the input of this committee, whose members included:

- Pete Dukes, Business

- Mike Eisenberg, Information School

- Sandra Eyres, Nursing

- Joan Graham, Interdisciplinary Writing Program

- Michaelann Jundt, Carlson Center for Leadership and Public Service

- Laura Little, Psychology

- Don Marshall, Mathematics

- Joel Migdal, Jackson School of International Studies

- Ratnesh Nagda, Social Work

- Johnny Palka, Zoology and Program on the Environment

- Mark Patterson, English

- Uta Poiger, History

- James Riley, Mechanical Engineering

- Betty Schmitz, Curriculum Transformation Project

- Sam Wineburg, Education

- Don Wulff, Center for Instructional Development and Research

- Anne Zald, Geography/UWired Librarian

We received significant hands-on assistance from researchers who worked on the study for short periods of time. We are grateful for the work of Patti Neff, who helped us design the study and take it through its first year. In addition, we thank Jessica Beyer whose results from her interviews with faculty on the nature of academic research are included in Chapter 8 of this book and who served as a temporary assistant to the study, conducting interviews with students in 2002. We are grateful, as well, to Gayla Shoemake, who volunteered short-term but gave us invaluable assistance with project management, and Rebecca Hartzler, who used her sabbatical to help us understand quantitative reasoning at the UW. In addition, we thank Matthew Baronowski, our extraordinary data manager who made it possible for us to analyze results; Joanna Loss, Melinda Marks, Jessica Hamburg, Cyndy Snyder, Warren Brown, and Emily Beyer for their help in analyzing students' responses; and Stephen Gillmore for his creative web site. We thank those who read an early draft of several chapters and gave us clear direction for the book's revision. Those who are not mentioned elsewhere in this acknowledgement include Joe and Cheryl Piha and Adrianne and Marty Shorb.

Regarding hands-on assistance, we extend deepest gratitude to the undergraduate students who served as research assistants for the UW SOUL. Over the course of the study, we worked with eight undergraduate assistants who helped us understand the undergraduate experience by analyzing qualitative data (and, they would say, "reanalyzing and reanalyzing it!"), by presenting it to faculty and others, and by sharing their own experiences with us. We could not have completed the study without the generous, intelligent, funny, dedicated, and unpaid help of the following undergraduates:

- Oluwatope Fashola, Sociology and American Ethnic Studies
- Andrew Fisher, Comparative History of Ideas
- Tula Habb, Sociology
- Wendy Huynh, Sociology
- Angela Kao, Applied and Computational Math/Sciences
- Amy Lu, Art
- Naomi Panganiban, Sociology and Portuguese
- Idrus Rudies Sayed, Economics

We are proud to be part of an institution that supports undergraduate research, and we are grateful to have been a small part of the undergraduate education of these fine students.

Finally, we personally acknowledge the help of our family and friends. Catharine Beyer acknowledges with gratitude the help in drafting and revising provided by her husband, Richard, and more important, the amazing light that he is in her life. In addition, she is grateful to her daughters, Jessica and Emily, for stepping in to help with the project when asked and for the grace with which they move through their days. She thanks her parents, Arthur and Lucia Hoffman, for celebrating question-asking and for making her feel cherished. She thanks her sisters, Micky Grooters and Dorothy Schlientz, and all her friends, who listened to stories about students and to the agonies and ecstasies of the research process for six years.

Gerald Gillmore wishes to express his gratitude to his wife, Professor Paula Nurius, for insightful comments about various ideas in the book, for pressing us for precision in method and language, for ever-present love, encouragement, and confidence in our abilities, and for the joy she brings to everyone around her.

Andrew Fisher acknowledges with gratitude his parents for providing a safe and loving place from which to wander, his sisters, Brita and Leah, for their companionship and understanding, and the posse for the joyfulness they shared. He is grateful that the OEA let a freewheeling student join the team.

Finally, the authors thank each other for making this study a journey of the heart as well as the mind and for keeping the process fun.

Introduction

Education is something you do, not something you get. [1]

The University of Washington's Study of Undergraduate Learning (UW SOUL) was a four-year study conducted from fall 1999 to spring 2003. The study tracked 304 students[2] as they moved through their college experience and focused on six areas of their learning: writing, critical thinking/problem solving, quantitative reasoning, information literacy, understanding and appreciating diversity, and personal growth. The purpose of this book is to share with faculty, administrators, students, and others what the UW SOUL participants told us about their learning through four years of interviews, surveys, focus groups, and submissions of coursework. Our hope is that the book will convey what we learned and what colleges and universities can learn by listening closely and in a number of ways to a sample of students over time.

The study had several purposes. First, we wanted to know what students learned and where they learned it in their undergraduate programs. Second, because our focus was assessment, we wanted to identify what helped students learn, as well as the obstacles or challenges to learning that they faced. Third, like most undergraduates attending most colleges and universities, our students are rarely asked to evaluate their own experience in depth, and we wanted to hear what students would say when asked to do this kind of reflection. Fourth, we wanted to learn what we could about students' personal development and the role that the university experience plays in that growth. Finally, we wanted to keep together a group of students whose opinions on University of Washington (UW) initiatives or current issues could be polled.

In addition to these purposes, we wanted to create a study that could maintain enough flexibility in its design to respond to ideas, questions, and directions set by faculty and staff. If a faculty member, for example, had a question that fell within our study purposes, we wanted to be able to accommodate her. In fact, we were able to do this, asking study participants questions that came from UW faculty, regents, and department chairs, as well as from faculty at community colleges.

The UW SOUL has allowed us to see students' experiences in two ways: close up, focused tightly on individuals, and from a distance, giving us an aggregate view of the group. These two views gave us the opportunity to look and marvel at how students become participants in fields of knowledge, how they grow and meet challenges, how they display amazing insights at the same time that they may be repeating previous mistakes, and how they learn about themselves and their world, even from thin sources.

Jeremy's Path

The longitudinal view, student by student, made clear the unique path each student took, and throughout this book we share some of these rich stories. We begin with Jeremy Nolan's story.[3] In September 1999, Jeremy Nolan became one of the 12 million undergraduates enrolled in colleges and universities across the country (U.S. Census Bureau, 1999), one of 4,515 new freshman to enter the University of Washington, and a participant in the UW SOUL. Jeremy entered the UW planning to enroll in one of the largest majors on campus—business—so that he could become a stockbroker.

Jeremy's career choice was influenced by his search for ways to invest his inheritance after his father had committed suicide, and after the bitter probate battle that he and his brother went through. Jeremy said:

> A family friend knew a good stockbroker, and I asked questions about everything. I started exploring it, finding out more about it, and I thought "I could do this." I wanted a 9 to 5 job, a suit and a tie in a downtown office building. So I thought being a stockbroker was it.

But by the time he graduated, Jeremy's passion for the suit, the tie, and the stockbroker's license had cooled, and the world of business and downtown offices was more than a jungle away.

What happened to Jeremy Nolan between the day he entered the UW, certain that he would collect his business degree, and the day during his senior year, when, sitting in an island jungle far away from Seattle, Washington, he wrote the following list of the 11 things that he most wanted to do?

- Work in Antarctica (sp?)

- Capuchin field site in Costa Rica

- Teach English in foreign country

- Trek through Africa/climb Mt. Kilaminjaro

- Scuba instructor in Thailand

- Ph.D.

- EMT

- Skydive

- Bungee jump

- Snowboard

- See Mt. Everest (possibly climb...?)

Jeremy's path through the UW was marked by several major turns. We know, for instance, that in his first quarter at the UW, Jeremy took a popular, large lecture class, Psychology 101. While waiting outside his teaching assistant's office one day, he saw a flyer for the Indonesian Field Study Program 2000. Jeremy decided to apply. "I applied not thinking I would get accepted, because it seemed like a rigorous program meant only for upperclassmen. But I wanted the experience of applying. Remember, I was the high school student who had applied for 58 scholarships."

Contrary to his expectations, Jeremy was accepted into the program. In the summer after his freshman year, Jeremy went to Tinjil Island in Indonesia to study monkeys. There on the island, Jeremy's ideas about his future changed. As he described it in an interview:

> There I was in the middle of the Indian Ocean on this tiny island. White sand beaches surrounding me. The island surrounded by coral reefs. Beautiful fish everywhere. Immaculate sunsets every night. The island was a jungle—plants and vines you've never seen before. All around you are these sounds you've never heard before—insects, birds, monkeys, snakes—critters. One day, I was walking along and there were monkeys in the trees overhead and on the ground, monkeys swinging from branch to branch, and I said to myself, "Okay, I'm in

Indonesia. I'm in a jungle. There are monkeys all around me. I could probably do this for the rest of my life."

Later, Jeremy would write of his time on Tinjil Island: "I can describe my experience as nothing short of life changing." The close group of friends Jeremy developed during his time on the island was also "very inspirational," and so after Jeremy's path had taken him to Tinjil Island, it made another turn, taking him away from the business major to a major in primatology.

In addition to the field experiences that led him to focus on primatology, Jeremy told us about some of the courses that helped him decide on this field. He took a course the following year, for example, that taught him how to write like a scientist, as he learned how to measure infant monkeys for a study on infant primate development.

But Jeremy's life as a college student contained more than a sudden love of primates. Among an exhausting array of activities and interests, Jeremy was an active member of a fraternity and a summer employee for a computer company. The summer after his idyllic moment on Tinjil Island, this computer company sent Jeremy to its New York office. He told us about setting out to make a delivery at the World Trade Center on September 11 and, instead, finding himself suddenly working as a volunteer for the Red Cross.

The experience blocked the direct path he seemed to be taking to a Ph.D. in primatology. "I felt totally helpless," he said. "When I came back to school fall quarter, I had no motivation." While he continued to do well in his courses, Jeremy began to drift, as he sorted through his experience in New York on 9/11.

During his junior year, Jeremy continued his work in primatology, and his research paper on captive orangutans received attention from scholars in his field. The summer after his junior year, Jeremy traveled alone through Singapore, Saigon, Cambodia, and Bangkok on his way to his second research experience on Tinjil Island. This time his research focus on the island was on ecology—the effects the monkeys had on the environment. Two excerpts from Jeremy's Tinjil Island journal during his second visit capture some of his experience there:

> Thursday, 8 August 2002. So there I was, 100 meters south of the SH trail with a troop of monkeys passing as if I wasn't there. I know, I know, this happens everyday at base camp, but this was different, this was the jungle. Monkeys were out of the trees on the ground, walking within inches of me, like I wasn't there. I looked east and walking towards me was Big Mamma, a huge pregnant female. We made eye contact and she just continues walking right up behind me. I wanted to

step out of the way and say, "Pardon me, Ma'am," but that would have scared her into the trees.

Monday, 12 August 2002. I guess my first mistake was to start a relationship with the girl that Abba, the beta male, was head over heels for. Female 863 walked into my life two years ago and she's been in my heart ever since. Because 863 is so special to me, I'd always keep a banana or two for her and she would sit right next to me and eat her treat. Lately, 863 has been receptive (in estrus) and Abba has taken a special liking to her. He'd follow her everywhere, and I assume he was jealous of me. I don't think she digs Abba as much as she digs me. When he tries to inspect her, she sits; when he moves closer, she moves. As she was sitting near me today and out of the corner of my eye, I see Abba begin to lunge at me. His weight on the branch brings him down to eye level. Oh shit, he's about three feet away from me and wants to fight. I stand up and show how big I am compared to him, and he lunges. I step back in just enough time to miss his teeth. I look down at Abba on the ground and he lunges again, catching me off guard, but misses. I scream like a 6-year-old girl at the haunted house and jump back. I pull out my machete and swing to get distance. Finally, he backs off, and I check my boxers for any messes. None. Good. Back to work.

When Jeremy returned, he decided to add a second major, biology, to his undergraduate program, postponing graduation by another year. He was back on the primatology track but, with his list of the 11 things that he wished to do in hand, he was not sure that he would pursue a Ph.D. after his undergraduate degree. When asked in his fourth year about how he had changed since high school, Jeremy said, "I've done this reversal since high school, maybe because I have experienced so many more things than when I was working at Safeway, trying to pay off my truck."

Close to the end of UW SOUL data collection in 2003, Jeremy applied for a leadership training grant to support a project he initiated in March of that year. In the short term, Jeremy hoped to get children interested in conservation. About this goal, he wrote in his application, "nonhuman primates are among the most imperiled fauna. Primates are large, charismatic mammals, and consequently, they are a powerful flagship species for conservation efforts." In the long term, Jeremy hoped to inspire an interest in college in these young students. Jeremy also wrote that the project was an important way he hoped to give something back to a broad community that he felt had supported him in his own growth. However, he did not get the grant.

Jeremy Nolan graduated at the end of winter quarter, 2004, with degrees in biology and psychology and minors in anthropology and quantitative science. He was a published author, had done research with scholars at other institutions, and at the end of that quarter was deciding what to do next on his list of 11 things.

Other Individual Paths

Not all students at the UW and in the UW Study of Undergraduate Learning walked a path as serendipitous as Jeremy's. Michael Rodriquez, for example, came to the UW hoping to put his fascination and experience with computers together with a business degree. He applied to and was rejected by majors four times—twice by the business major and twice by informatics—because his GPA was below their cut-offs for admission to the major. Finally, Michael was accepted into the geography major. Going through those rejections was both depressing and worrisome, but in a focus group during his senior year, Michael said this about the major he landed in after working hard to get into others:

> My major, geography, has opened my eyes to the inequalities around us. Geography has changed how I think. I was open to poverty before, especially since I came from the Philippines. But before I came here, I was interested in making money. Geography changed this. I am still interested in [computers and technology], but now I have this desire to change the world. I am interested in teaching, and after I graduate, I am going to do Teach for America. I want to help empower people with education.

Some students did not make it to their senior year. Nicole Gamborino, for example, dropped out after her first year at the UW. Nicole's grades plummeted after one of her closest friends was shot and killed on the busy street that borders the university in a widely publicized incident. She was already struggling financially to stay in college, and these financial and academic difficulties suddenly seemed impossible in the wake of her friend's violent death. As Nicole described it:

> He was my best friend. He was the type of person who, you would walk into a room, and he would be smiling for no apparent reason. He was always enthused about everything he did—even eating a taco. It wasn't just a normal taco, but the

best one he ever ate. He was around me every day, and it was hard for me to go back to that environment without him in it and concentrate and focus on anything. His girlfriend, my best girlfriend, left college after that too, so I didn't have anything that I had when I came.

Kate McDonald also left the UW, but her leaving turned out to be temporary. In her first interview, Kate's comments about what she wanted to learn at the UW showed great enthusiasm for being there:

I want to learn about life in the city, about science. I want to pick a field and become knowledgeable about it. I want to learn about the community, how it works. I want to learn about living with a person. The roommate experience is totally new to me. I want to learn how to compromise, to work together, how to be a better leader, how to ride the Metro bus system, where all the cool places to hang out in Seattle are, what it feels like to live somewhere where it rains more than nine inches a year, how it feels to work with a professor who is on the cutting edge of knowledge and is passionate about what he is doing. I want to become more passionate about things.

But after two years, Kate was disappointed with her education, unsure about the science major she had selected, and lonely. Kate transferred to another public university closer to her home town and took classes in religion and communication. She returned to the UW and the science major she had left behind after a year away, saying that the courses she had taken during that time were "wonderful classes, and I felt like I had a break and learned some of the stuff I wanted to learn without having to relate it to my degree." In thinking about the decisions to leave and then to come back, Kate said:

I felt that I was able to take hold of things and make decisions to get out of a bad situation at both times. It felt good to make a decision to change things in a big way. It helped me to have some physical and emotional distance from the situation I was in, so I could look back at it and say, "Is this what I want? What can I change and what will remain the same?"

Some students' paths through the UW were easier than others. All of them had sweet moments and traumas. The UW SOUL allowed us to learn about such moments for many students. To share what we learned about individual paths, we have included case studies and many quotations from study participants in this book.

Shared Paths

The second view the study afforded was collective. In addition to a view of the unique paths of individual students that we observed, we have seen similarities in the experiences shared by many of the students and by subgroups of students. To provide this collective view, we analyzed qualitative data in ways that allowed us to aggregate results whenever possible. We also applied statistical analyses to student responses to scaled survey items, looking for systematic changes over time and differences by genders, ethnic groups, and areas of major. This approach showed us, for example, that for most of the students much of the first year at college is about becoming independent, in every sense of that word. We also have seen how being "humbled" in some way, whether at the hands of introductory calculus or from rejection by a roommate, is very much a part of the first-year experience and that finding a clear direction is part of the second year's process for most students. To give readers a sense of the shared paths students walked, we present similarities among students within subgroups, most notably in disciplinary areas where students tend to show different patterns of learning even before they have chosen a particular area of study. We also present broader similarities in the chapters that follow.

Impetus for the Study

The impetus for the UW SOUL came from three related directions, listed here and detailed in subsections that follow. First, we felt that theories on student development in college did not capture the full chaotic complexity of that development. Second, we wanted to bring assessment attention back to students and their experiences as learners, after a time when it has felt as though the assessment movement in our state, as elsewhere, was in danger of being replaced by the requirement for accountability measures. These measures are aimed at evaluating institutions in areas such as retention and graduation efficiency, aspects of performance that can be described with a number. Our desire to refocus attention on student learning was articulated beautifully in fall 1999, just as we were starting the study, by Pat Hutchings and Lee Shulman in their article, "The Scholarship of Teaching," published in *Change* magazine:

> Imagine . . . a kind of institutional research that asks much
> tougher, more central questions: What are our students really

learning? What do they understand deeply? What kinds of human beings are they becoming—intellectually, morally, in terms of civic responsibility? How does our teaching affect that learning, and how might it do so more effectively? These are, in fact questions that the assessment movement . . . put into the picture at some campuses, but they're hardly questions we've finished with. If we reconceived "institutional research" to be about such questions, in the service of its faculties, led by faculty members, then the scholarship of teaching would not be some newly conceived arena of work, or a new route to tenure, but a characteristic of the institution that took learning seriously. (p. 15)

We photocopied those words and literally kept them in front of us as we began the UW SOUL. The words of Hutchings and Shulman bring us to the third impetus: our personal paths to the study of undergraduate student learning.

Theories of Student Development in College

Much has been written in the last 30 years about students' progress through college, and a number of well articulated and well tested theories have been proposed. We decided, however, not to design our study as a measure of theoretical premises. First, ours was an assessment study, and, like Richard Light's (2001) book that reports results of 10 years of interviews with Harvard seniors, our particular interest was in learning what happened to students as they moved through the University of Washington's academic environment. With such specificity, we hoped to be able to offer faculty, staff, and others ideas about what students said worked well in their experience at the UW and what needed improvement, while also generating information that might be useful to other institutions. Our focus was on learning and not primarily on college student development, although our data have given us a number of insights on development that we share in this book.

A second reason that we did not structure the study to test a theory on student development in college was that we could not find a theory that we felt fully represented the complex messiness students described in speaking about that experience. As Pascarella and Terenzini (1991) have noted, the early theories concerning college student development are almost all psychological. The psychosocial theories of the development of traditionally college-aged adults—beginning with Erik Erikson's (1968) theory of the relationship between crisis and identity response and Arthur Chickering's (1969) seven vectors leading to students' development of integrity—as well as the cognitive-structural theories—such as William Perry's (1970, 1981) nine stages of college student development and Kitchener and King's (1981) theory of the development of reflective judgment—are rooted in stage-based assumptions about student change. These theories assume that college students develop along a linear and progressive path, rather than paths that, while they share some broad features, are also iterative, dynamic, chaotic, and bumpy, as our interactions with students seemed to suggest.

Furthermore, though they argue that the contexts in which students find themselves matter, the psychosocial and cognitive theories never fully address the ways that an environment might, for example, toss a student backward into an earlier stage. Also, as Dannefer (1984) points out, neither do these theories address the very specific ways the environment might launch a student toward the next level of her development. As an assessment study, our focus was not so much on where students landed as it was on how they got there. As Banta, Lund, Black, and Oblander (1996) noted, the assessment of teaching and learning processes that lead to learning are as important as a focus on whether outcomes have been met.

In addition to assumptions about students' linear progress and lack of specificity about the relationship of environment to change (out of necessity, given the scope of these models), the psychosocial and cognitive models suggest that all students proceed along the same path. This argument was challenged more than 20 years ago on the basis of gender by Gilligan (1982) and Belenky, Clinchy, Goldenberger, and Tarule (1986), and later by Baxter Magolda's (1992) luminous book, *Knowing and Reasoning in College.* Cross-cultural scholars and scholars who study race and ethnicity have also raised questions about the universalist assumption apparent in most developmental theories (Cross, 1991; Tatum, 1997). Finally, scholars who have noted the ways that academic disciplines shape students' learning experiences raise questions about the "one-path" theories, most notably Bransford, Brown, and Cocking (2000), Biglan (1973), Bazerman (2000), Wineburg (1991), Donald (2002), and Shulman's (1986, 1987) work on teacher education.

Our own conversations with students suggested that while they may experience broad changes at similar times in their college years, their paths were also unique. Also, it seemed obvious that a student could simultaneously occupy several of Perry's stages of cognitive development—one in her chemistry course, another in her Asian American studies class, and yet another in her thinking about whom to vote for in the next election—all in a given academic term. In addition, students seemed sometimes to reverse direction—moving away from a more relativist perspective to a more black-and-white view on, say, the causes of cultural change among the Kung!. And one student's movement might be quite different from his movement on another issue, as well as quite different from another student's movement. Race, gender, socioeconomic status, age, residence, and other factors noted by environmental theorists and others certainly seemed to play a role in determining those differences.

However, for the students we could see up close, we felt that degrees of difference among them were even finer than broad demographic categories could account for. For one thing, what they knew and how they grew seemed shaped by their academic majors to a great extent, which meant that their intellectual development was uneven and "domain specific" (Fisher, Beyer, & Gillmore, 2001; Shulman, 2002). A student majoring in computer science and engineering, for example, might think in highly sophisticated and complex ways about concepts and issues in that field, but she might think about politics dualistically. Also, what students learned seemed equally dependent on who they were when they came in and what kinds of experiences they came from. Jeremy Nolan applied to go to Tinjil Island as a freshman, even though it seemed clear that the program was for advanced psychology majors, because he had a history of applying for things. We saw students' pasts acting on their present experiences again and again. As Bransford et al. (2000) state:

> They come to formal education with a range of prior knowledge, skills, beliefs, and concepts that significantly influence what they notice about the environment and how they organize and interpret it. This background, in turn, affects their abilities to remember, reason, solve problems, and acquire new knowledge. (p. 10)

These problems with the psychosocial and cognitive models of student development seemed to suggest that we could more readily embrace interactionist theories of student development in college. Interactionist theories focus on points of impact in college, such as Astin's (1993a) "I-E-O" model. Astin's descriptive model argues that input, or what the student brings to college, is acted upon by a wide range of influences in the college environment, such as interactions with faculty, peers, and clubs, to bring about what the student is when she leaves college—or the "output." In his study, Astin uses data from the annual Cooperative Institutional Research Program (CIRP) survey to answer the question of what value college adds to students' learning, among other things. His findings show the importance of the level of students' involvement in academic and nonacademic activities. Tinto's model (1987, 1993), which focuses on student attrition, argues that the intentions and commitments that students bring to college are constantly changed by the interactions students have with the people and experiences they encounter in college. Further, Tinto argues that college students who form early personal connections with a faculty or staff member are more likely to stay in school than those who do not make such connections. Lending support to this argument, Pascarella and Terenzini (1991) found that research showed that advising, orientation, and academic support programs were often correlated with student retention and graduation.

These environmental arguments fit better with our sense of student development than the psychosocial or cognitive-structural theories, but the environmental theories also seemed aimed too broadly for our specific questions. CIRP data give one an astronaut's view of students' experience, and results seem sometimes to rest on assumptions about what students mean and how well their definitions of terms agree when completing the CIRP survey. A student at the UW who checked the "very satisfied" box about his "general education or core curriculum," for example, might have had a radically different experience from that of a student at a comparable institution who also checked the "very satisfied" box—so what do we know when we learn that students at research universities are "very satisfied" with their general educations? When students check the box that indicates that their professors frequently provided them with "intellectual challenge and stimulation," what does that mean their professors actually did?[4] Perhaps even more important, how can such results lead to institutional improvement? While we laud the contribution CIRP (and particularly Astin's [1993a] tracking of it) has made to broad understandings of students' experiences, we were interested in a closer view that might point the way to improvement.

Finally, with regard to Astin's (1993a) model, we wondered whether the inputs could reach into his output, spinning him off in an unexpected direction, or whether the college environment could be invaded by external times, places, and events, and, consequently, be altered by it. Jeremy Nolan is a perfect example of the messiness and the backward-forward motion that environmental models have a hard time capturing. In the words of Peter Ewell (1997), "the learner is not a receptacle of knowledge, but rather creates his or her learning actively and uniquely . . . Learning is about making meaning for each individual learner by establishing and reworking patterns, relationships, and connections" (p. 3).

Ewell's words and research on how people learn, presented by Bransford et al. (2000) for the National Research Council, suggest a constructivist perspective. Our own experiences inside academia, as well as our questions, led us to those perspectives that argue that learning and knowledge are created in very particular social contexts. As members of an institution arranging itself into communities (academic departments) that create distinct ways of doing similar things, we believe that social constructivist arguments mirror a reality we see every day. However, we also agree with scholars such as Tsoukas (2000) and

Block (1999), who argue that a belief in social construction does not contradict belief in realities that exist separate from individuals' creations. Searle (1995) argues that social constructions are the result of collective intentionality and tacit or explicit agreement, a characteristic that seemed to apply well to some of the knowledge and practices created in and by academic disciplines, but not to everything equally. As Block (1999) points out, "Leukemia is not a social construction or creation" (p. 200), and neither are the treatments designed in and by academic disciplines to cure it. Our understanding of where realism ends and construction begins in the wide range of academic disciplines at the UW is limited. Therefore, while UW SOUL findings sometimes supported constructivist perspectives, we did not set out to validate them.

Of all the theories we reviewed, we felt most strongly connected to the sociological argument about emerging adulthood put forth by Arnett (2000). Arnett argues that the previous markers of adulthood—school completion, marriage, a permanent residence, parenthood, and others—no longer effectively indicate the beginning of adulthood, because 18–25 year olds are now delaying those activities. Furthermore, Arnett's earlier study (1997) of 18–25 year olds showed that, except for parenthood, 18–25 year olds do not believe that those markers are valid criteria for their entry into adulthood. In contrast, their own criteria for adulthood include accepting responsibility for themselves, making independent decisions, and becoming financially independent.

Arnett argues that some cultures better foster a prolonged period of identity and role exploration than others. The cultural context in the U.S. is tolerant of such exploration. Indeed, it seems clear that cultural changes in the last 20 years have made a wide range of experiences possible for college-aged men and women. For example, young people in this group have access to easy travel opportunities as well as a shared value for traveling as a way of learning; a wide range of ways to take college courses; the possibility and practice of having multiple romantic partners, perhaps related to the relative freedom from the fear of pregnancy; and a wide range of athletic possibilities that range from back-country snowboarding to local Frisbee golf teams for women as well as for men. Furthermore, access to information about these experiences, including access to information provided by people as they are experiencing them, is only a "Google search" away.

It seemed to us that inside U.S. culture, no culture is more tolerant of exploration than colleges and universities in general. Students attending large, public research universities have easy access to an especially bewildering array of experiences and opportunities. For example, students in the UW SOUL joined the cycling team; learned to white-water kayak and began competing in that sport; traveled to Italy, South Africa, Madagascar, Brazil, England, Ireland, Spain,

Germany, India, China, Japan, and Indonesia; worked as volunteers in rural Washington, in the Seattle public school system, and with refugees learning to read; met the love of their lives; broke up with long-time lovers; experimented sexually; gave poetry readings; passed as the opposite sex; changed jobs; joined and quit gyms; went backpacking for the first time; taught snowboarding; and acted in plays. While not unique to university students nor equally accessible to them, these experiences and others like them mentioned by our UW SOUL participants suggest that college campuses offer young people unusual ranges of choices for change and exploration.

As Arnett (2000) describes this period:

> Emerging adulthood . . . is a period characterized by change and exploration for most people, as they examine the life possibilities open to them and gradually arrive at more enduring choices in love, work and worldviews. . . . As scholars, we can characterize emerging adulthood as a period when change and exploration are common, even as we recognize the heterogeneity of the period and investigate this heterogeneity as one of emerging adulthood's distinguishing characteristics. (p. 480)

This book embraces Arnett's idea of a period of heterogeneity; of exploration that spills over academic boundaries and blurs distinctions between what is learned in Anthropology 101 and what is learned in Solstice, a local coffee shop; of developmental paths that move forward and back and forward again, and of a culture that actively fosters variety.

Assessment as a Driving Force for the Study

While we were interested in ideas about college student development, the UW Study of Undergraduate Learning primarily grew out of the authors' long-term experience with assessment in higher education and our concern about the direction in which assessment seemed to be heading. In the mid- to late-1980s when state governments first required public universities to be more publicly accountable through assessment, the call was for standardized testing. One of this book's authors, Gerald Gillmore, was a key participant in a State of Washington research project that evaluated standardized achievement tests of rising juniors and included the participation of students and faculty from two- and four-year institutions of higher education throughout the state (Washington Council of Presidents and State Board for Community College Education, 1989). This research has national implications because it demonstrated the ineffectiveness of a one-size-fits-all standardized testing approach to assessment. The study showed that standardized tests for critical thinking, quantitative reasoning, and writing were insensitive to what students actually learned in college and that faculty found the results neither valid nor useful in planning instruction.

In 1989 the Washington state legislature gave every public two- and four-year institution of higher education budgets for assessment, and at the UW, as well as nationally, the next phase of assessment became focused on campus-specific activities. Those of us working in assessment greatly admired the work at Alverno College and a few other colleges that wove assessment into the fabric of their curricula, but the size and hands-off culture of our large research institution made such fully integrated approaches daunting. Therefore, we began by working on assessment projects with the faculty and programs most open to assessment, as well as by performing some institution-wide surveying of students. Our early emphasis was influenced by the thinking of assessment leaders who emphasized classroom-based assessment, such as Angelo and Cross (1993), and we designed and used various strategies to help us understand and increase student learning, with little generalization possible beyond particular classes.

It was at this point that another of this book's authors, Catharine Beyer, along with her colleague, Joan Graham, initiated a series of studies on writing (Beyer & Graham, 1990, 1992, 1994a, 1994b; Beyer, 1997). At the time, Beyer was a faculty member in the Department of English's Interdisciplinary Writing Program, a program Graham has directed since 1978 that links writing courses with courses in the disciplines.[5] The purpose of their studies was assessment of college-level writing, and the three qualitative studies they conducted tracked the writing experience of large samples of students through their undergraduate coursework.

The years between 1989 and 1997 were marked at the UW by a number of rich assessment projects. In addition to the studies on student writing, we worked with projects focusing on large lecture courses and academic programs, including nursing and psychology. These studies became important touchstones for the UW SOUL. Assessment of academic programs suggested that departments had differing methods for determining whether their students had learned, as well as differing goals for that learning. These differences came back to us, as we analyzed data from UW SOUL participants. In addition, the writing studies conducted from 1989–1997 showed us the wealth and depth of data that qualitative methods could provide, and we designed our methods for UW SOUL accordingly.

Toward the end of this creative and productive era, the State Higher Education Coordinating Board identified four areas of learning that all institutions were required to assess: writing, critical thinking, quantitative reasoning, and information literacy. These areas were broad enough to cover at least some aspect of every disciplinary context in two- and four-year institutions of higher education.

Then the state legislature changed its focus from assessment of student learning to accountability. State legislatures (and the federal government) rightly wish to hold public educational institutions accountable for their performance. While there may be a natural affinity between assessment and accountability, there are unfortunately some differences between the two. For one, the accountability movement seeks quantifiable measures of successful academic performance, such as graduation rates, because such measures allow for easy comparisons to performance standards across campuses. Thus, for the most part, accountability operationalizes performance as something that can be captured with a number or two. In contrast, while assessment also makes use of quantifiable data, its focus is on learning. Learning is complex. It cannot often be captured with a single number or even a single set of measures. Assessment recognizes this complexity, and seeks both to understand and preserve it.

Another difference between accountability and assessment is that accountability indicators are almost always imposed from outside, while assessment indicators are almost always developed from within. This means that accountability measures must, by definition, be general, while assessment measures can take into account the unique cultures and practices of the places where learning occurs. In addition, assessment focuses on improvement. In contrast, accountability often leads to punitive action (although it no longer does in our own state), and punitive action can impede improvement. In *Our Underachieving Colleges,* Bok (2006) speaks eloquently about the inability of punitive action to effect improvement, noting, among other things, the strangeness of rewarding schools that are already doing well by giving them more resources and of punishing schools that are doing poorly by removing resources from them that they could have used to improve their work.

Inevitably, if an institution is required to focus primarily on accountability, it loses some or all of its focus on assessment. This loss is at least partially the result of scarce resources—time *and* energy. As accountability was beginning to dominate the many state legislative conversations about public education at the end of the nineties, Thomas Angelo (1999) wrote these words about assessment and accountability in higher education:

> Today, most faculty and faculty administrators have finally, if
> reluctantly, come to accept that dealing with both [assessment
> and accountability] is a political and economic inevitability.
> Nonetheless, most of us think assessment should be first and
> foremost about improving student learning and secondarily

about determining accountability for the quality of learning produced. In short: Though accountability matters, learning still matters most. (p. 3)

At the same time that accountability was becoming a focus of state legislatures, assessment was becoming a force in accreditation. In the early to midnineties, accrediting bodies for professional schools, such as nursing and engineering, required programs to identify learning goals for students and to demonstrate that they were assessing them. Also at this time, regional associations of schools, colleges, and universities required academic institutions to respond in their accreditation self-studies to Standard 2B, which asked institutions how they were measuring the learning of all their students. In effect, accrediting agencies adopted an assessment model for evaluating the effectiveness of institutions' undergraduate programs, just at the time when state legislatures were focusing on other models.

However, as powerful as those accrediting agencies are, their new standards were not bringing about rapid educational change. In their excellent overview of the assessment movement from a national perspective, Lazerson, Wegener, and Shumanis (2000) note a study conducted by Celia Lopez, associate director of the North Central Association of Schools, Colleges, and Universities, which showed that the 320 institutions that went through the North Central accreditation process between 1997 and 1999 were all only at the beginning stages of their assessment processes.

In early 1999 when we began seriously discussing the possibility of a longitudinal study of student learning, we could see that the value of assessment was making inroads throughout many academic communities at the UW. For example, more of the faculty truly understood the difference between teaching goals and learning goals. More often than in the early days of assessment, we saw faculty trying to change their instruction in accordance with information they were gathering formally and informally about what students were and were not learning in their classes. Departments had developed capstone courses for their majors, which had the potential to provide evidence for whether the stated or unstated goals of the major were being met. And goals and assessment/evaluation plans were being demanded for new programs.

Even so, we felt the promise of the assessment movement and its focus on student learning outcomes was not being fulfilled. As Ewell (1997) asserts, nationally these efforts were "attempted piecemeal"—done by a scattering of courses and programs but never systematically across an institution—and that was true at the UW as well. While the piecemeal efforts clearly had an impact on our campus culture, and especially on the cultures of some departments, they did not result in broad institutional change. We understood that higher education moves at a glacial pace, and we also knew intimately that the extended period of diminishing or certainly not expanding resources was taking a toll.

Nonetheless, we asked ourselves what was lacking. Why were we feeling dissatisfied? Our belief in the importance of careful assessment of student learning as driving instructional and curricular decision-making remained unshaken. Admittedly, this dissatisfaction partly came from the fact that the impact of assessment is so often indirect and mingled with many other forces for change. This disappointment was felt nationwide, and it, in part, launched the scholarship of teaching movement in the assessment field.

Most troubling, perhaps, was that we saw that faculty in two- and four-year institutions, whose enthusiasm about assessment had thrust them into campus leadership positions, were experiencing burnout from hard work with little reward. Many were dropping out of assessment work and were not being replaced in equal numbers by new faculty. Fullan (1997) illuminates this problem among those engaged in educational reform, arguing that "a deepening malaise among educators" has been caused, at least in part, by the fact that none of the efforts for reform has resulted in major change and that emotion and hope had been "either ignored or miscast" in reform efforts. At the same time, Ewell (1997) speaks about the failure of the assessment movement to bring about educational reform. The national story told by Lazerson, Wegener, and Shumanis (2000) describes a similarly disappointing path, which captured our local experience almost perfectly.

Here in Seattle in 1999, after 10 years of state funding for assessment, we felt it was time to regroup. Luckily for our institution, we had some Carnegie fellows among our faculty who were spreading the word about the scholarship of teaching and learning. We had an active Center for Instructional Development and Research, as well as discipline-based instructional centers such as the Center for Engineering Learning and Teaching and the Physics Education Group. We also were working with other baccalaureate-granting public institutions in the state on interesting writing and information literacy assessment projects. From our perspective, however, it seemed clear that the move to accountability had in some ways limited what assessment could be and do on our campus.

We also wondered how the structure of university undergraduate education limited the way in which assessment must operate within that structure. One might think of a university as a large supermarket, in which the cereal section is the political science department and the coffee section is comparative literature. On the left are fresh fruit and vegetables (engineering) and on the right are dairy products (biology). Each student moves through, choosing certain cereals and vegetables (courses), and at the time of graduation, a checker records the various bar codes associated with what is in the grocery cart and determines whether the right assortment exists for the student to leave the store—in other words, to graduate. The bill has been paid in advance, and the student attains alumna status and goes on her way. Of course, we hope that through the course of four or more years that the student has moved from selecting Sugar Corn Pops to choosing low-fat, organic granola, and from iceberg lettuce to Belgian endive.

This analogy may be a reach, and we do not in any way wish to imply that we view the student as a consumer of higher education, nor do we want to suggest that curriculum planning does not occur. Our point is that a college education tends to be *thought of* as a linear series of loosely related events—mainly classes—and this view does not adequately recognize how students really learn. Departmental curricula are structured to lead the student through a logical progression of learning, but not much attention has been paid to how students progress through that curriculum.

Talking to students makes it clear that learning does not proceed in a wholly linear fashion, and it does not all take place within classes, as many scholars, most faculty members, the majority of parents, and all students know. Rather, learning is iterative. We learn; we forget. We learn a second time, perhaps from a different orientation, perhaps emphasizing a different facet. We learn from other students, sometimes in the class, sometimes in a discussion or argument outside class, maybe even over a beer. Sometimes concepts are learned from textbooks, but sometimes they are cemented on bus trips. Some learning—such as early learning in math—is sequential. Other kinds of learning—such as learning to become a skilled writer or painter—are not so much sequential processes as they are deepening processes, where students' understanding of key concepts becomes richer, physical, and multifaceted. Most of the time, our institutions of higher education pay more attention to the basket full of groceries, to an analysis of what is in the cart and what should be, rather than to the human being pushing the cart. If the focus is on the cart, we will never see how the choices that an individual made were affected by other choices, by world events, and by total transformations resulting from a pause beside the cauliflower display. If the focus is on the cart, we miss Jeremy Nolan's moment on Tinjil Island when monkeys were accompanying him along a jungle path and Kate McDonald's reasons for leaving the UW, as well as her reasons for coming back.

We wanted to be able to walk with students like Jeremy and Kate in order to assess student learning on our campus. In large part, our own history in assessment and the movement to accountability in our state and in the nation led us to design a longitudinal study of undergraduate learning.

Personal Reasons for the Study

In addition to the grand backdrops for a study such as the UW SOUL, we each had our own smaller reasons for wanting to follow a large sample of students through college. As director of the UW's Office of Educational Assessment between 1980 and 2001, Gillmore participated in all phases of the assessment movement in higher education since its inception. In his years as the assessment coordinator for the UW campus, he implemented a program to survey entering students, seniors, and graduates of the UW one year, five years, and 10 years after graduation. He sat on faculty committees to design research on writing and quantitative reasoning, and he was often the one who conducted this research. He worked with departments to design studies to assess the extent to which students were meeting their outcomes.

Looking back, there was one compelling problem with all of this experience. All of his research had been cross-sectional and aggregated. Gillmore felt that he had missed individual students and their particular paths. Long before, he had dreamt of convening annual panels of students who would respond to surveys on matters of contemporary campus interest. This idea slowly expanded into the desire to do a deep study of the learning and development of the members of a cohort. Gillmore continues to see validity and generalization as hallmarks of worthy research. Nonetheless, this study served as a welcomed opportunity to take a much closer look at the trees that make up the forest of a college education.

Beyer came to the study with many desires. She wanted to hear what students' experiences were in their own words. Distrustful of using any single measure—the broad brush of national surveys, for example, or an in-depth analysis of a case or two—to understand the undergraduate experience, Beyer wanted to ask questions and listen to answers from a large number of students. Also, as a faculty member in the Interdisciplinary Writing Program for many years, she had taught writing courses that were linked with courses in the disciplines, and had observed changes that many of the faculty members incorporated into their teaching over time. Through her observations and conversations about teaching with faculty across the curriculum, she learned that even at an institution as large as the UW, faculty cared deeply about their teaching and worked, sometimes heroically, to be good at it. Therefore, another motivating desire for Beyer was to be able to help faculty improve their teaching. While there is a wealth of information available to faculty on how to improve instruction, Beyer wanted to start with what students had to say.

Finally, Beyer's experience suggested that what Maki (2002) described as "institutional curiosity" about learning had been building at the UW, manifesting itself in many departments and programs across campus. In Maki's words:

Institutional curiosity seeks answers to questions about which students learn, what they learn, how well they learn, when they learn, and explores how pedagogies and educational experiences foster student learning. When institutional curiosity drives assessment, faculty and professional staff across the institution raise these kind of questions and jointly seek answers to them, based on the understanding that students' learning and development occur over time both inside and outside the classroom. (p. 8)

Beyer wanted, therefore, to create a study that would include institutional input and tell an institutional story about undergraduate learning.

Unlike Gillmore and Beyer, Fisher came to the study "haphazardly"—his word. In his final year of undergraduate work, he felt a vague need for an internship experience. As a comparative history of ideas major, his studies focused on issues in pedagogy and critical theory, and his continual interest was exploring how the self is engaged in and influences thinking. In his senior thesis, he developed a notion of critical thinking as an ongoing, personal investigation, so it was only fitting that his quest for an internship experience landed him at the UW SOUL in the area of critical thinking and problem solving. Interestingly, his analysis of the critical thinking and problem-solving data provided a compelling answer to a tension he struggled with in his thesis: intellectually, he believed in his own conception of critical thinking, yet he suspected it was all wrong. However, overcoming his own intellectual bias was extremely difficult. The process only began because as he listened to students' descriptions of their critical thinking and problem-solving experiences, the disciplines resisted abstraction and could not be ignored. The answer was eventually quite simple: generic models of critical thinking, including his own, are misleading. After Fisher's transformation during his analysis of critical thinking and problem solving comments, he became a passionate advocate for listening, for vigilance about one's own biases and theories during both design and analysis stages of the study, and for the role of the researcher as a learner. These perspectives made him an excellent mentor for the undergraduates who worked on the study.

These personal paths led us to design this longitudinal study of student learning based on students' own written and spoken descriptions of that learning, as well as on systematic surveying and on looking at actual student products from their courses. We were able to do in this study what most educators would love to do, had they the time: watch a fairly large number of students traverse the entire university. In doing this, we learned a great deal, and the goal of this book is to pass on what we have learned.

Study Design

As a result of these three streams of influence—the literature on development, the progress of assessment, and our own personal paths—we designed the UW SOUL to use both quantitative and qualitative methods to gather information about and to assess the undergraduate program at the UW. The study was exploratory and discovery based, rather than hypothesis driven, although it was focused around our identified aims and priorities. We were interested in casting a big net and seeing what we might find, in discerning nuances in students' learning processes and practices, and in gathering information that might generate "small-t" theories that would be useful to others doing assessment work. As Merriam (1998) stated, however, no qualitative study is theory free, because some coherent set of ideas frames the questions being asked. This statement is clearly true of quantitative and mixed method studies, too. As stated previously, social constructivist theory broadly framed our study, and we were particularly guided by Arnett's (2000) theory of emerging adulthood. As we analyzed data, our findings led us to theories of learning that focus on the ways disciplines shape knowledge and knowledge acquisition (Bazerman, 2000; Biglan, 1973; Donald, 2002; Wineburg, 1991).

Given our broad goals, in designing this study, we felt we needed to make use of both quantitative and qualitative methods, hoping that the findings of each method would enrich rather than contradict the other. Our study has made greater use of qualitative methods for the following reasons:

> [Qualitative research] is an effort to understand situations in their uniqueness as part of a particular context and the interactions therein. This understanding is an end in itself, so that it is not attempting to predict what may happen in the future necessarily but to understand the nature of that setting—what it means for participants to be in that setting, what their lives are like, what's going on for them, what their meanings are, what the world looks like in that particular setting—and in the analysis to be able to communicate that faithfully to others who are interested in that setting…The analysis strives for depth of understanding. (Patton, 1985, as cited in Merriam, 1998, p. 6)

We describe our research methods in more detail in Chapter 2.

Central Argument

Our findings led us to understand that at the UW, and we believe at most institutions, the academic disciplines shape students' educational experience in every way.[6] What students learn about diversity, critical thinking, writing, quantitative reasoning, information literacy, and technology —including how these terms are defined—is mediated by the disciplines, as are the best pedagogical strategies to teach students these skills.

This mediation is not only true for students' third and fourth years in college, as many people might assume, but for the first two years as well. Therefore, the "fact" of general education, in the sense of it being a shared experience by all or nearly all students, is largely a myth (Gillmore, 2003), particularly for institutions, such as ours, that have what Astin (1993a) calls a "distributional" model of general education. A student taking a 100-level history course in her first quarter will be expected to write papers that a historian would recognize as thoughtful, well supported, and clear, whether or not the student has ever written a history paper before or has received any instruction in how to write such a paper in any history course. The same is true for first-year chemistry labs. In other words, faculty teaching these courses use the standards and practices of their disciplines in their work with these students, just as they do in their work with juniors and seniors. Furthermore, faculty teaching these freshmen and sophomore level courses have been immersed so fully and for so long in the practices, purposes, frameworks, and research of those disciplines that they are often unable to step outside those perspectives to explain them—even if they wish to, even if they believe they ought to.

We have learned, and we argue here, that there is no such thing as an undergraduate education; instead, we have many undergraduate educations filtered through the lenses of particular disciplines—a reality also noted by Pike (2004) in speaking about student engagement. For this reason, generic approaches to assessment or approaches that attempt to measure learning at the institutional level are doomed to capture little information that matters about students or their learning. Therefore, when we think about improving undergraduate education or increasing learning, even in broad areas (for example, writing, critical thinking, information technology and literacy, and quantitative reasoning chosen for assessment by the State of Washington), we need to keep our focus on majors and disciplines, as a necessary first step in assessing the undergraduate curriculum. Departments define learning, and departments should measure it for their majors.

This argument comes at an interesting time in our country's educational policy history. Our book does not address no-child-left-behind testing currently underway in K–12 institutions across the country. However, we believe that our findings bolster the positions of K–12 educators and researchers who argue that high-stakes standardized testing cannot measure student learning. In contrast, our book is a direct challenge to arguments in a recent *New York Times* article (Arenson, 2006), put forward by the Spellings Commission on Higher Education, that standardized testing such as that underway in K–12 should be extended to students in higher education. We argue, here, that such testing could never accurately measure student learning, and our evidence supports our earlier state study on the use of standardized tests to assess learning (Washington Council of Presidents and State Board for Community College Education, 1989). Standardized assessment approaches would require a huge investment in time, money, and energy—just as the K–12 experiment has required—and, because they could not capture the unique learning students acquire from the disciplines of their majors, standardized tests would reveal nothing about student learning that faculty and departments could use to improve their work.

While the information we collected and analyzed strongly shows the central role of disciplines in college students' growth as learners, a second argument underlies every chapter in the book. That argument is that self-reflection is a mode of learning. Bransford et al. (2000) speak eloquently of the contribution of metacognition to students' learning, and the importance of self-reflection and assessment to successful work performance has been a subject of research. Yet one might ask where students learn how to assess their own performances accurately. Self-assessment is rarely built in to courses at large public research institutions such as our own; we rarely ask students to speak or write about their learning and almost never deliberately teach them to assess their own progress. Instead, most of us who teach, hope that students will pick up ways to look critically at their learning and thinking by paying attention to how *we* look at it, putting our faith in modeling as a way of instruction, in osmosis—a through-the-skin transmission of how to evaluate one's own ideas. This approach is decidedly different from that at Alverno College, the premier assessment institution in the U.S., which makes teaching students to be effective at self-assessment a deliberate part of its work.

In talking with students over the four years of the UW SOUL, we have learned that there are big pay offs for students and for institutions in asking students what they hope to learn, what they actually learned, and how what they learned did or did not change them. We believe that these pay offs are evident in many of the quotations we include in each chapter and in every case study we include. In addition, we speak more directly of what students' perceive as the benefits of such reflection and institutional benefits in the last chapter of the book.

Organization

This book's purpose is to share with faculty, staff, administrators, parents, and students involved in higher education what we learned about students' learning from UW undergraduates.

To achieve this purpose and to mine the richness of the information that the study has yielded, we present the data in several ways, including ways that blur distinctions among individual students' paths. However, we try not to stray too far from actual student voices. For this reason, we include many student quotations[7] throughout the book, and we begin each chapter with one or more extended case studies that illustrate aspects of the learning we discuss in the chapter. Even so, many of the case studies that we present spill over the containers of their chapters. We believe that this spillover effect is important, because it accurately represents our experience in talking with students. Learning happened messily rather than in the neat packages we set out to examine, and students always reported more than we could capture.

The rest of the book is divided into the following chapters:

- Chapter 2, "Research Process," provides an overview of the UW SOUL's research questions and methodology, as well as a description of the study's sample and its representativeness.

- Chapter 3, "Personal Growth," presents results that focus broadly on students' academic and personal experience. It considers students' comments on how they changed as they moved through their university experience, and what they felt contributed to those changes.

- Chapter 4, "Understanding and Appreciating Diversity," gives students' responses to questions on diversity that show students' attitudes toward diversity and associated behavior when they entered UW and how those attitudes and behavior changed over time.

- Chapter 5, "Critical Thinking and Problem Solving," argues that students' descriptions of critical thinking and problem solving support the idea that critical thinking is "domain-specific" (the phrase of Sam Wineburg at Stanford), and it reports critical thinking challenges in seven broad disciplinary categories. Chapter 5 also includes faculty descriptions of critical thinking in their fields.

- Chapter 6, "Writing," closely paralleling Chapter 5, tracks what students said about their writing experience over time. It includes information about how much writing students did at the UW and where they did that writing, as well as descriptions of the writing that students considered their most challenging. In addition, the chapter discusses the gap between writing in high school and writing in college.

- Chapter 7, "Quantitative Reasoning," describes the kinds of quantitative reasoning tasks students found challenging, as well as providing comments from faculty on the kinds of quantitative reasoning necessary to do the work of their disciplines. This chapter illuminates the ways that disciplines are or are not infused with quantitative tasks.

- Chapter 8, "Information Technology and Literacy" shows that the way students gathered and used information technologies varied radically across disciplines, making institutional assessment of information technology and literacy challenging. This chapter also includes results of an interview study with faculty on how they define *research*—another word for "finding and using information."

- In Chapter 9, "General Learning," students note what helped and hindered their learning while in college. Their comments on what faculty can do to communicate they care about student learning and on what advances their own learning confirm research on how people learn.

- Chapter 10, "Summary and Last Words," focuses on the effects of the study on student learning, pulls together our conclusions and recommendations, and provides follow-up information on the student case study included in this introduction—Jeremy Nolan.

Guiding Principle

In conducting this study and analyzing its results, our guiding principle has been to respect the students' words, always letting those words generate whatever categories we were sorting them into while recognizing the individual voices among them. Our guiding principle was always to focus on what the students said. With this in mind, combined with the fact that much of this book describes students in the aggregate, we feel that it is important to note that after reading and listening to thousands of statements from UW SOUL participants, we learned that there is no "general" UW story. Each student's path was as unique as Jeremy Nolan's and Kate McDonald's, and this is surely true of students at any other college, as well. This book cannot recreate those paths, but we hope that it gives the reader a sense of both their sameness and their variety.

Endnotes

1) Quotations that begin these chapters come from the interviews and email of student participants in the UW SOUL (except in Chapter 4).

2) We tracked students until they left the study, left the UW, graduated, or reached the end of the fourth year in college. See Chapter 2 for further information on the study population.

3) All students' names have been changed.

4) See www.gseis.ucla.edu/heri/css_survey.html for information on CIRP and the survey.

5) See http://depts.washington.edu/engl/iwp/ for information on the UW's Interdisciplinary Writing Program.

6) When we speak of "disciplines" in this book, we include interdisciplinary and transdisciplinary majors as disciplines. We believe that most of these programs, such as the UW's Women Studies Department or the Program on the Environment, operate in many of the same ways that disciplines operate. They have agreed-upon values and pedagogical approaches, and they also often have learning goals for students, which can serve as criteria for assessing student learning. Also, as do traditional academic disciplines, they have connections with other inter- and transdisciplinary programs like themselves across the country, publish in their own academic journals, and participate in national conferences in their fields. In contrast to traditional disciplines, inter- and transdisciplinary majors embrace a wide range of methodologies, as well as a broad range of questions, which means that assessment can be more challenging in these departments than it is for the traditional areas. Furthermore, faculty in inter- and transdisciplinary majors usually come from traditional disciplines, which complicates assessment of students who are asked to demonstrate more integrated kinds of thinking using a broader range of tools than those assessing them have learned. While there are crucial and interesting differences between inter/transdiscplinary majors and majors in the traditional academic disciplines, we believe that the similarities are such that we include the inter/transdisciplinary majors as disciplines when we say that learning is a disciplinary act.

7) Quotations have been shortened and slightly edited in some cases. When edited, distracting phrases, such as "you know" and "like" were often removed. However, for the most part, quotations are exactly as students spoke or wrote them.

2

Research Process

The second step, putting all of the responses into broader categories, is the most annoying part. Trying so hard to not lose the meaning of what the respondents are saying—it's just difficult for me for some reason. After redoing those categories about 50 times, then comes the written draft of the data in report form.

—Oluwatope Fashola, Undergraduate Researcher

This chapter summarizes the processes and methods we used in conducting the UW SOUL. In designing the study, we began with the assumption that students' college educations are lived processes experienced in multiple ways. Our goal was to understand both the nature of those experiences and their meanings from the students' perspectives, with the expectation that we would encounter "multiple realities" (Merriam, 1998). Given this goal, we felt that a mixed methodology was necessary. We used quantitative methods primarily to gather information on how many classes required students to do certain tasks and to ask for students' assessments of their attitudes and learning. We used qualitative methods to help us track four of Maxwell's five purposes (in Bickman & Rog, 1998) for which qualitative or interpretive studies are particularly useful, as follows:

- Understanding the meaning participants make of their experience

- Understanding the context(s) in which participants are situated and the influence of the context(s) on their actions

- Identifying unexpected influences and generating grounded theories about them

- Understanding the processes that lead to outcomes

Maxwell's fifth purpose for qualitative studies, "developing causal explanations" (p. 75), was not one of our primary motivations for conducting the study. We hoped that information gathered quantitatively would clarify and extend information gathered qualitatively, and vice versa.

In designing the UW SOUL, our intention was to provide an assessment of undergraduate education for faculty and administrators at our own institution. However, as we analyzed our results, we realized that what we learned may have wide applicability to other campuses as well.

The following sections in this chapter describe our research processes and strategies:

- Rationale for a longitudinal study

- Recruitment and the student participants

- Generalizability: information about the UW, demographic information, and representativeness of sample

- Focusing the study: the research questions

- Data sources and methods of analysis

- Staffing

Rationale for a Longitudinal Study

Because we hoped to identify areas where the UW excelled in its work with undergraduates and where it needed improvement, our focus was necessarily on how students changed while at the university and why. As noted in Chapter 1, we were equally interested in how individual students changed and in what those changes meant to them. Indeed, even as we began the study, we suspected what we have now come to know—that generalizations about students obscure important and intriguing variations. These goals led us to focus on a longitudinal study, rather than a cross-sectional approach to gathering information.

As is well known, it is a dangerous business to infer change from cross-sectional data (Campbell & Stanley, 1971). The problem with such inference is that one cannot disentangle the effects of change within individuals, preexisting differences in groups, contemporaneous events, and changing cultural standards. For example, inferring change from cross-sectional data might lead us to conclude erroneously that people's taste in music changes from love of hip hop to love of big-band music as they advance from their teenage years to old age. Because we wanted to track change, therefore, we needed a longitudinal study.

But there is another reason why we needed a longitudinal study to address our particular issues. By taking cross-sectional cuts, we could not have observed individual change. For example, we could not have known what moved Jeremy Nolan (see Chapter 1) from his initial desire to be a stock broker to graduating with a focus in primatology.

Critical in our longitudinal approach was taking the same measures at multiple points in time (Willets, 1988). We resisted the urge to revise repeating instruments, although we occasionally added or deleted questions. We administered nearly identical surveys via the Internet at the end of every academic quarter except summers. Diversity surveys that repeated the same rounds of questions were administered three times during the four years of the study. In addition, we interviewed students during their first quarter at UW, and after that we used protocols that repeated a core set of questions in interviews conducted every subsequent spring quarter. These instruments can be viewed and downloaded from our web site: www.washington.edu/oea

Recruitment and the Student Participants

Projecting a 10% acceptance rate, we invited 1,660 students who had completed the UW's Entering Student Survey (ESS) to participate in the study. We invited these students based on a few constraints. First, we eliminated Entering Student Survey takers who were under 18 years old because of human subjects regulations. Second, we invited all entering underrepresented minority students to participate, whether or not they had completed the ESS. We oversampled this group because past research indicated lower volunteer rates and higher attrition rates among these students, and we wanted to see if we could identify differences in the experience of underrepresented and majority students.[1] Third, because 40%–50% of graduating seniors at the UW are transfer students, we divided the ESS takers into freshman and transfer student populations, and invited 60% of the invitees randomly from the freshman population, and 40% randomly from the population of incoming transfer students. We soon learned that extracting our sample from the group of students who took the Entering Student Survey led to a selection bias[2] in our sample that is discussed in the "Generalizability" section of this chapter. Based on our past experience with longitudinal studies and after much deliberation, we settled on $300 per year as a modest amount to offer this sample of invitees to do the following:

- Participate in an entry interview and annual interviews

- Participate in annual focus groups

- Respond to open-ended email questions each quarter

- Complete web-based surveys each quarter

- Submit pieces of the work they had done for some of their courses each year in a portfolio

- Write and submit a reflective essay about the work in their portfolios annually

Instead of our anticipated 10% volunteer rate, more than 800 students accepted the invitation—a response rate of about 50%. Apparently, $300 was more than a modest amount to college students! We sent all respondents email messages, informing them that we had miscalculated the potential response rate. Then we accepted into the study all the underrepresented minority students who responded, and drew the remaining students randomly—60% from the freshman respondents and 40% from the transfer students who had accepted the initial invitation. A total of 142 of those students joined the study as Group 1.

One month later, additional funding from the office of Undergraduate Academic Affairs allowed us to add a second group to the study. This group would be paid $100 per year to:

- Respond to open-ended email questions each quarter

- Complete web-based surveys each quarter

To create this group, we randomly selected 170 of the students who had agreed to participate in the study as Group 1 members but whose names had not been selected to join the study. We invited these students to participate as Group 2 members. Of those we invited, 162 agreed to participate in the study at this level. Thus, we began with 304 UW SOUL participants in fall 1999.[3]

Table 2.1 shows how many of the 304 students who began the study left the study before it was concluded, how many dropped out of the UW, how many graduated by the end of the study, and how many were still enrolled at the study's end.[4] As the table shows, the attrition rate was 29.3%. Of these, 12.5% dropped out of the university and 16.8% continued at UW but dropped out of the study. At the end of four years, 53.3% of the sample had graduated and 17.4% were still enrolled.

Because we had less contact with students in Group 2 than those in Group 1, we compared attrition, graduation, and continued enrollment for both groups. Table 2.1 shows that Group 2 students had a higher four-year gradua-tion rate and withdrew at a lower rate than did UW SOUL participants in Group 1; however, none of these differences was significant.[5] While differences among Group 1 and Group 2 students were not statistically significant, we wondered why they appeared to be different. We knew that underrepresented minority students withdrew at higher rates than Asian and Caucasian students. As stated previously, we oversampled underrepresented minority students in Group 1, so in order to understand if the underrepresented minority population was affecting the difference in graduation rates between Group 1 and Group 2 students, we removed the underrepresented students from the analyses. When we did so, the differences in the withdrawal rates for the two groups disappeared and the difference in the graduation rate decreased, as displayed in Table 2.2.

Table 2.1. *UW SOUL Attrition and Retention Rates*

	Group 1	Group 2	Total (N and %)
Withdrew	**43 (30.3%)**	**46 (18.4%)**	**89 (29.3%)**
Withdrew from Study	23 (16.2%)	28 (17.3%)	51 (16.8%)
Withdrew from UW	20 (14.1%)	18 (11.1%)	38 (12.5%)
Remained in Study	**99 (69.7%)**	**116 (71.6%)**	**215 (70.7%)**
Graduated by 8/2003	69 (48.6%)	93 (57.4%)	162 (53.3%)
Still enrolled 2003	30 (21.1%)	23 (14.2%)	53 (17.4%)

Table 2.2. *UW SOUL Attrition and Retention Rates Without Underrepresented Minority Students*

	Group 1	Group 2	Total (N and %)
Withdrew	**30 (28.6%)**	**41 (26.9%)**	**71 (27.6%)**
Withdrew from Study	19 (18.1%)	25 (16.4%)	44 (17.1%)
Withdrew from UW	11 (10.5%)	16 (10.5%)	27 (10.5%)
Remained in Study	**75 (71.4%)**	**111 (73.0%)**	**186 (72.4%)**
Graduated by 8/2003	57 (54.3%)	91 (59.9%)	148 (57.6%)
Still enrolled 2003	18 (17.1%)	20 (13.1%)	38 (14.8%)

Generalizability: Information About the UW, Demographic Information, and Representativeness of Sample

This section describes characteristics of the UW so that other institutions can determine how well our findings might fit their situations. It also describes the UW SOUL sample and discusses how well that sample represented the general UW population.

The University of Washington

The University of Washington is a large, public, Research I institution. It includes three campuses in the Puget Sound region; however, the UW SOUL studied only students on the UW's Seattle campus, which is the largest and oldest. The campus is located well within the city limits, offering students access not only to a vibrant and beautiful metropolitan city, but to the Cascade and Olympic mountain ranges and to two beautiful waterways—Lake Washington and the Puget Sound, gateway to the Pacific Ocean. This rich urban and natural environment offers students many possibilities for discovery, fun, and learning away from campus.

As a major research institution, the UW receives much of its total funding from research grants and contracts. Since 1974, it has been the number one public university in America in receiving federal support for research and training. Research plays the most significant role in faculty tenure and promotion decisions, although teaching success and service are also factors in those decisions. As have other universities, the UW has made a conscious effort to parlay its research emphasis into an enhancement of undergraduate education in part by developing research opportunities for undergraduates.

While Astin (1993a) argued that it is "virtually impossible" to maintain strong focuses on research *and* on students, the UW is institutionally invested in effective teaching and undergraduate learning, as well as in research. The office of Undergraduate Academic Affairs (UAA) is led by its own dean, who also serves as a vice provost. The UAA advocates for undergraduate education and offers a wide range of experiential learning opportunities for students. The UW also supports several undergraduate study/tutorial centers, including the math study center; general and disciplinary writing centers; the Center for Learning Undergraduate Education (CLUE), a study center that is open five nights a week; and the Instructional Center, an award-winning multidisciplinary tutoring center primarily for underrepresented students.

In addition to sites for student learning, the UW offers faculty annual training opportunities that focus on integrating writing, technology, and active learning techniques into teaching. These have included the Provost's Fall Workshops, the Large Class Colloquium, the Institute for Teaching Excellence, and the Faculty Fellows Program, which provides all new faculty with instruction in pedagogy and information from and about university resources. The UW also supports several centers whose common purpose is to improve teaching, including the Center for Instructional Development and Research, the Center for Engineering Learning and Teaching, and the Physics Education Group.

When the UW SOUL students arrived on campus in the fall of 1999, the undergraduate student body numbered 26,638, along with 8,212 graduate students and 1,731 professional students. Admission to the undergraduate program was competitive. The average freshman entered UW with a high school GPA of 3.65 and an SAT score of 1155. About 43% of the entering UW freshmen were in the top 10th percentile of their high school graduating class. About 89% of the undergraduate students were residents of Washington State, and about two-thirds entered UW directly from high school. Two-thirds of the undergraduates were from the Seattle metropolitan area and nearly 80% were from the Puget Sound basin. While many students lived on or around campus in dorms, fraternity/sorority housing, and apartments, a substantial number commuted to families and/or jobs. Based on past years, we expected about 40% of the freshman entrants to graduate in four years, 65% in five years, and 70% in six years.

In 1999, 23% of the students were Asian or Pacific Islanders; 4% were Hispanic; 2% were African-Americans; and 1% were Native Americans. Females slightly outnumbered males and the average age of the undergraduates was 21.

In general, students seem satisfied with their undergraduate educations. The UW consistently maintains a first-to-second-year retention rate of 90% or more. First-to-second-year retention of underrepresented minority students is slightly lower than that for Caucasian and Asian students, averaging around 86% for underrepresented students who entered in 1999.[6] These first-to-second-year retention rates are considered good for public universities such as the UW. In addition to retention, alumni surveys indicate general student satisfaction with their experience at the UW. These surveys, conducted one, five, and 10 years after graduation, regularly find that about 89% of the students would choose to attend the UW if they had the chance to go back and make the choice again.

Students from the UW SOUL may not be perfectly comparable to those from other institutions, but we believe that institutions of any size can learn from our results. For example, while UW students may not be comparable to community college students who do *not* transfer to four-year colleges and universities, more than a third of the students in our sample were transfer students—most of whom came from community colleges. We gathered quite a bit of information on the transfer experience and how it differs from that of incoming freshmen.

Regarding generalizability, another point of difference that some may note between the UW and other institutions is the UW's level of selectivity. Our level of selectivity is moderate, typical of most major research universities. It is likely less selective than elite private schools, and more selective than some smaller state universities. However, differences in selectivity may not prohibit comparison. In Pascarella and Terenzini's (1991) review of research on students in higher education, they concluded:

> There is little consistent evidence to indicate that college selectivity, prestige, or educational resources have any important net impact on students in such areas as learning, cognitive and intellectual development, other psychosocial changes, the development of principled moral reasoning, or shifts in other attitudes or attitudes and values. Nearly all of the variance in learning and cognitive outcomes is attributable to individual aptitude differences among students attending different colleges. Only a small and perhaps trivial part is uniquely due to the quality of the college attended. (p. 592)

Another concern about generalizability may be geographical. The UW's location in a metropolitan area with a number of appealing geographical features certainly affected the number and shape of experiences available to student exploration. One of the UW SOUL participants was a snowboarding instructor, for example, an opportunity not available to students at the University of Texas or at Scottsdale Community College in Arizona. However, our findings suggest that the lure of the city and mountains played a small role in students' experience. More important were interactions in and outside class with faculty and peers, as well as college-supported experiential learning opportunities, organizations, and informal meeting places.

In addition to arguments about geography and generalizability, some might argue that the UW's position as a major research university contrasts with institutions whose major function is teaching, where the pressure to publish is less strong. However, this difference, once again, may not be a barrier between our findings and the experiences of institutions that seem different from our own. Contrary to common conceptions, Astin (1993a) concluded in his landmark research as follows:

> This study has shown that neither the institution's overall level
> of resources, nor the type of institution per se (for example,
> liberal arts, university), has much direct effect on any student
> outcomes, once the effects of the specific educational practices
> . . . are taken into account. (p. xiii)

While it is true that any one-institution study creates issues of generalization, many wonderful research studies, including Light's (2001) and Baxter Magolda's (1992) were limited to one place, one kind of institution, and, therefore, one kind of student culture. Even with the particular characteristics of the UW, we believe that the students in the UW SOUL were more like students at other colleges and universities than they were unlike them. Thus, we believe that a longitudinal study such as this one at *any* institution or group of institutions would be likely to reveal a similar range of experience and attitudes in its undergraduate population. We feel safest, of course, in claiming generalization to other urban research universities with similar student demographics and a "distributional" approach to general education (Astin, 1993a). Nonetheless, research on educational outcomes in relation to institutional characteristics does not indicate any major obstacles to generalization, with intelligent caution, to other settings.

Finally, regarding generalizability, the UW SOUL included methods, detailed in this chapter, that strengthen external validity, such as use of standard sampling procedures, of multiple cases to study the same issues, of predetermined questions that repeated from year to year, of multiple methods for gathering similar data, and of specific procedures for coding qualitative data; also, we frequently treated qualitative data quantitatively (Merriam, 2001). Therefore, we believe that readers from other colleges and universities will find insights and ideas in our results that they can judiciously apply to their own environments.

Representativeness of the Sample

To view the representativeness of the UW SOUL sample, we compared its characteristics with those of all remaining students who entered UW in fall of 1999 as undergraduates. In addition, we compared some of our sample's characteristics with those of others who took the Entering Student Survey (ESS). The total number of students in the population was 6,621. Knowing that about 85% of entering students attended orientation in 1999, where they were asked to fill out the ESS, we erroneously expected that we would be sampling from nearly 85% of the entering students. However, as reported earlier in this chapter, the ESS was completed and turned in by about 46% of the freshmen entrants and about a third of the transfer entrants.

And the ESS-takers were different from the non-ESS takers. As is usually the case with survey takers and study volunteers, more women than men and fewer members from underrepresented minority groups than from majority groups took the survey. In addition, fewer transfer students completed the survey. Another difference, stated previously in this chapter, was that the students who took the ESS had significantly higher high school and transfer GPAs and admissions test scores than those who did not turn in completed surveys (McGhee, 2000). Thus, there was already some selection bias in the population from which we sampled, and much of that bias was reflected in our own UW SOUL study population.

Gender and Ethnicity

The percentage of women in the UW SOUL sample (54.9%) was nearly equivalent to that in the remaining population (53.4%). Similarly, the percentage of transfer students in the UW SOUL sample (36.8%)[7] was nearly equivalent to that in the remaining population (35.5%). As Table 2.3 shows, because we purposely oversampled underrepresented minorities in Group 1, the resulting percentages for African-Americans, Hispanic, and Native American students were larger in Group 1 than Group 2 and larger in the entire UW SOUL sample than in the population. In contrast, a larger percentage of students in the non-SOUL population designated themselves as "Other" than did students in the UW SOUL.

Table 2.3. *Ethnic Group Membership (Percentage of Total)*

	Group 1	Group 2	Total SOUL	Total UW
White	77 (54.2%)	113 (69.7%)	190 (62.5%)	3800 (57.4%)
Asian American	22 (15.5%)	34 (21.0%)	56 (18.4%)	1429 (21.6%)
African-American	13 (9.2%)	3 (1.9%)	16 (5.3%)	136 (2.1%)
Hispanic	15 (10.6%)	6 (3.7%)	21 (6.9%)	224 (3.4%)
Native American	9 (6.3%)	1 (0.6%)	10 (3.3%)	60 (0.9%)
Other	6 (4.2%)	5 (3.1%)	11 (3.6%)	972 (14.7%)

Academic Performance

A comparison of academic variables is presented in Table 2.4. As the table shows, averages for the UW SOUL sample were statistically significantly higher than those for other students on all academic variables except total transfer credits.[8]

Relative to the averages of non-UW SOUL students, participants in the study came to UW with higher average high school or transfer GPAs and higher average admissions test scores. Similarly, at the end of the four years of the study, UW SOUL students had higher UW GPAs and, for the subset who had graduated, higher degree GPAs than did the non-UW SOUL students. As the table also shows, GPAs and scores of students who took the Entering Student Survey but were not in the UW SOUL (Non-SOUL ESS Taker) were nearly always lower than those of UW SOUL students, but higher than those of the non-SOUL, non-ESS-taking population.

These results indicate that the averages of the sample of students who took the ESS were statistically significantly higher on the academic variables tested than those who did not take the survey. Moreover, the averages of the sample of UW SOUL participants were significantly higher than those of the sample of ESS takers and, of course, significantly higher than those of the entire non-UW SOUL population. This result was obtained even though we were able to randomly sample from about 50% of all those taking the ESS. Nonetheless, when dealing with volunteer samples of higher education students, it is not unusual to find selection bias in the direction of more academically successful students.

Differences can be statistically significant but not meaningfully different, especially when dealing with large samples and populations. To determine the strength or magnitude of these differences, we also computed eta-squared values for each comparison. This statistic measures the strength of relationships by indexing the percentage of the total variance in a variable that is attributable to the differences among groups (Becker, 1999; Kirk, 1982). In the comparisons

Table 2.4. *Mean Comparisons Between UW SOUL and Non-UW SOUL Students on Academic Variables*

		SOUL	Non-SOUL ESS Taker	Non-SOUL Non-ESS Taker	All Non-SOUL		SOUL vs Non-SOUL ESS	SOUL vs Non-SOUL	Non-SOUL ESS vs No ESS
HSGPA	N	192	1684	2229	3913	*t*-Val	2.86	4.02	5.15
	Mean	3.71	3.65	3.61	3.63	Signif	0.005	0.0001	0.0001
	Std Dev	0.26	0.27	0.30	0.29	Eta Sq	0.4%	0.4%	0.7%
TR GPA	N	114	562	1665	2226	*t*-Val	0.45	1.84	3.61
	Mean	3.43	3.41	3.34	3.36	Signif	NS	NS	0.0001
	Std Dev	0.36	0.37	0.42	0.41	Eta Sq	0.0%	0.%	0.6%

Table 2.4 (continued). *Mean Comparisons Between UW SOUL and Non-UW SOUL Students on Academic Variables*

		SOUL	Non-SOUL ESS Taker	Non-SOUL Non-ESS Taker	All Non-SOUL		SOUL vs Non-SOUL ESS	SOUL vs Non-SOUL	Non-SOUL ESS vs No ESS
SAT-VERB	N	251	2018	3065	5081	*t*-Val	3.36	4.54	4.16
	Mean	592.87	572.85	562.02	566.29	Signif	0.001	0.0001	0.0001
	Std Dev	88.56	89.04	91.34	90.60	Eta Sq	0.5%	0.4%	0.3%
SAT-MATH	N	251	2018	3065	5081	*t*-Val	2.25	3.44	4.22
	Mean	604.22	591.34	581.01	585.12	Signif	0.05	0.001	0.0001
	Std Dev	85.76	85.32	85.82	85.77	Eta Sq	0.2%	0.2%	0.3%
ACT	N	97	590	790	1380	*t*-Val	1.83	2.75	2.97
	Mean	25.68	24.90	24.25	24.53	Signif	NS	0.01	0.005
	Std Dev	3.51	3.95	4.03	4.01	Eta Sq	0.5%	0.5%	0.6%
TRANS CREDITS	N	304	2333	3987	6318	*t*-Val	4.16	0.21	12.86
	Mean	32.04	22.67	36.68	31.51	Signif	0.0001	NS	0.0001
	Std Dev	40.70	36.39	44.70	42.37	Eta Sq	0.7%	0.0%	2.6%
UWGPA 06/03	N	304	2333	3987	6316	*t*-Val	4.58	5.61	3.43
	Mean	3.28	3.10	3.05	3.07	Signif	0.0001	0.0001	0.001
	Std Dev	0.45	0.64	0.65	0.64	Eta Sq	0.8%	0.5%	0.2%
UWGPA 06/05	N	304	2333	3987	6318	*t*-Val	4.53	5.54	3.31
	Mean	3.28	3.11	3.06	3.08	Signif	0.0001	0.0001	0.001
	Std Dev	0.45	0.63	0.64	0.63	Eta Sq	0.8%	0.5%	0.3%
Degree GPA03 *GRADS* only	N	187	1105	1926	3029	*t*-Val	1.97	3.09	3.52
	Mean	3.41	3.35	3.31	3.32	Signif	0.05	0.0025	0.0001
	Std Dev	0.33	0.33	0.36	0.35	Eta Sq	0.3%	0.3%	0.4%
Degree GPA05 *GRADS* only	N	253	1765	2860	4623	*t*-Val	2.97	4.22	4.00
	Mean	3.37	3.30	3.25	3.27	Signif	0.005	0.0001	0.0001
	Std Dev	0.34	0.36	0.38	0.37	Eta Sq	0.4%	0.4%	0.4%

among academic variables, shown in Table 2.4, the eta-squared values for comparing UW SOUL students with non-UW SOUL students are no larger than one-half of 1%. In other words, for none of these variables do the differences among means account for more than 0.5 % of the total variance of the variable. Viewed from this perspective, differences between UW SOUL students and non-UW SOUL students were not substantial, and selection bias should not create an appreciable limit on generalization to the entire UW undergraduate population.

Four-Year Graduation and Attrition

In addition, we compared four-year graduation and attrition rates among several populations. First, we compared four-year graduation and attrition for UW SOUL and non-SOUL students who entered the UW in 1999. This comparison presented a challenge: we were unsure how best to treat the group of 51 students who left the study but remained at the UW. (Thirty-eight additional students withdrew from the study *and* UW.) Of these 51 students, 29 graduated by the end of the study (spring 2003) and the remaining 22 were still enrolled. Sixteen of these had graduated by spring 2005.

The treatment of study dropouts was particularly problematic, because some students left the UW SOUL as early as the first quarter of the study, while others left the quarter before they would have graduated. The decision of how to treat this group of students was important not only for the issue of representativeness of the sample but also for questions about the intervening effects of the study. To look at representativeness of our sample, we decided to compare four-year graduation and attrition for UW SOUL participants and nonparticipants in two ways. First, we simply compared the graduation and attrition rates of UW SOUL and non-SOUL students by including all of the students who were initially in the study. The second way we looked at the two groups was to begin with the assumption that if a student dropped out of the study, many of the analyses we conducted and the conclusions we drew would not include her data; therefore, we could not determine effects of the study. Using this assumption, we took the 51 students who dropped out of the study out of the analysis altogether. The results of these comparisons are found in Table 2.5.

For both comparisons, UW SOUL students graduated at a higher rate, while non-UW SOUL students withdrew and remained enrolled in higher percentages. A chi-square analysis comparing the students who were in the UW SOUL at "some time" with students who were never in the study showed a significant difference between UW SOUL and non-SOUL students with respect to attrition, four-year graduation, and still enrolled status ($\chi^2 = 14.8$, df = 2, p < 0.0001). Similarly, a comparison of students who were in the UW SOUL either until they graduated or the study ended and those who were never in UW SOUL showed a similar result (χ^2 = 12.3, df = 2, p < 0.002).[9]

We believed that our oversampling of underrepresented minority students may have influenced the results shown in Table 2.5, because as a group, underrepresented minority students at the University of Washington have somewhat lower four-year graduation and retention rates than do other groups of students. Therefore, we also compared UW SOUL participants' four-year graduation and attrition rates with those of nonparticipants without including underrepresented minority students. The results of this comparison are found in Table 2.6 for students who were in UW SOUL "at some time" and students who were in UW SOUL either until they graduated or the study ended. The four-year graduation rate for UW SOUL students, regardless of how long they were in the study, was higher than the graduation rate of students who had never been in the study. These differences were statistically significant.[10] With or without the inclusion of underrepresented minority students in our analysis, the UW SOUL participants had a higher four-year graduation rate than the non-SOUL students.

Table 2.5. *Four-Year Graduation and Attrition Rates*

	In UW SOUL at Some Time	In UW SOUL until They Graduated or the Study Ended in 2003	Never in UW SOUL
Withdrew from UW	38 (12.5%)	38 (15.1%)	1219 (19.3%)
Graduated by 2003	193 (63.5%)	162 (64.0 %)	3336 (52.8%)
Still Enrolled	73 (24.0%)	53 (20.9%)	1762 (27.9%)

Chi-square analysis showed no significant differences between the graduation and attrition rates of Group 1 and Group 2 students. However, the differences in four-year graduation and retention rates for UW SOUL students and the Entering Student Survey takers who did *not* participate in UW SOUL were statistically significant. Regarding the non-SOUL ESS takers, 47.6 % graduated within four years, 36% were still enrolled, and 16.6 % had dropped out. We discuss these results further in Chapter 10.

Table 2.6. *Four-Year Graduation and Attrition Rates Without*
Underrepresented Minority Students

	In UW SOUL at Some Time	In UW SOUL until They Graduated or the Study Ended in 2003	Never in UW SOUL
Withdrew from UW	27 (10.5%)	27 (12.7%)	1134 (19.1%)
Graduated by 2003	177 (68.9%)	148 (69.5%)	3158 (53.1%)
Still Enrolled	53 (20.6%)	38 (17.8%)	1652 (27.8%)

Conclusions About Generalizability

As previously stated, we believe that our methods and results may be of interest to any other college or university engaged in asking similar questions about how and where students learn. Regarding the self-selection bias evident in the academic variables, it is good to remember that selection bias plagues most research that is dependent on a voluntary sample. Our decades of experience with survey research with voluntary samples of students have consistently found that respondents exhibit consistently higher averages on academic variables as a group than do nonrespondents. Thus, the bias in our sample was expected and likely unavoidable. Even so, the selection bias we found was small. We are confident that results can be generalized to the UW population and to populations at institutions similar to the UW, because students in the UW SOUL sample overlapped considerably more (more than 99%) with their peers on entry than they differed and because students at other institutions are likely to be similar to those at UW.

Graduation status and final UW GPA require special mention. Differences between UW SOUL and non-UW SOUL students are likely to be attributable in part to initial selection bias—students who begin college with higher scores on academic variables are likely to perform somewhat better, on average. But it is also possible that the act of participating in the study could have affected academic decisions and performance, which we discuss further in Chapter 10.

Focusing the Study: The Research Questions

As stated in Chapter 1, in the 1990s the state of Washington mandated that all baccalaureate-granting institutions assess student learning in the areas of writing, critical thinking, quantitative reasoning, and information literacy. We decided, therefore, to focus our assessment questions on these four areas, as well as on two others: understanding and appreciating diversity and personal growth. Some of our findings on student learning failed to fit neatly into these areas; hence, we have included an additional chapter on general learning. Our rationale for the six areas of focus and some of our early research questions follow.

Personal Growth

The overarching question we addressed under personal growth was whether and how students changed in their years of college. Prior surveys of our students, as well as research on college students (Pascarella & Terenzini, 1991) showed that students made gains in areas outside those we typically think of as classroom-driven learning. We hoped that by incorporating a focus on personal growth into the UW SOUL we might learn more about how students' experiences inside and outside the classroom shaped their sense of themselves and helped them meet their goals for their own learning.

Understanding and Appreciating Diversity

While not entirely separate from questions about personal growth, we were also interested in how students' attitudes and knowledge about cultural and ethnic diversity may or may not change as a result of their college experience. We were intrigued by an earlier UW study, conducted by Nagda, Gillmore, Schmitz, and Silas (1997), that showed that UW undergraduates who took four courses with diversity-related content had more positive attitudes about diversity than students who took no such courses. This result was interesting in the light of gains that most UW students reported in understanding and appreciating diversity when completing senior and alumni surveys. In addition, we knew that being able to work with people from diverse backgrounds and experiences was a skill employers value in the workplace. With the value that colleges, students, and employers placed on diversity, and as the UW campus experienced decreases in the diversity of its student body as a result of the passage of I-200,[11] it seemed critical that we explore questions about students' learning and attitudes in the area of "understanding and appreciating diversity."

Critical Thinking and Problem Solving

Faculty often speak of critical thinking and problem solving abilities as important outcomes of instruction. On our alumni surveys, students consistently rated the ability to define and solve problems, as well as the ability to critically analyze written information, as areas in which they had learned a great deal.

Furthermore, according to our alumni surveys, these are areas that graduates identified as particularly important to the work they were doing after they graduated. In the UW SOUL, we hoped to determine how students talked about the critical thinking they were asked to do, what kinds of problems they had to think about and solve in courses across the curriculum, and whether we were teaching students to self-assess.

Writing

The ability to write effectively is essential to student success. Writing is a way of thinking and a way of demonstrating thought; writing both creates and shares knowledge. Learning to write is a complex, dynamic process, intimately linked to methodologies and purposes in the disciplines in which it occurs. Surveys of students who came to the UW as freshmen, and of students who transferred to the UW, have indicated that students felt that they made significant gains in their ability to write effectively by the time they were seniors. Yet two pilot studies of student writing across the state, as well as writing studies conducted by the Office of Educational Assessment from 1989–1996, suggested that UW students needed to improve writing skills. In the UW SOUL, we hoped to follow up on those earlier writing studies, identifying how much and what kinds of writing students were required to complete as undergraduates and how they experienced those writing demands.

Quantitative Reasoning

In surveys that the UW administers one, five, and 10 years after graduation, alumni have consistently ranked quantitative reasoning (QR) as low in importance. Furthermore, senior surveys indicate that students believe they have not made significant gains in their ability to think quantitatively while they were here. Yet quantitative reasoning is an essential skill for survival in a world that increasingly uses numbers to justify policy and products. Furthermore, ability in this area extends beyond itself into other kinds of thinking. Therefore, we hoped to learn where in their undergraduate experience students were asked to do QR and what kinds of QR they found challenging.

Information Technology and Literacy

Surveys from students who graduated from the UW showed that "locating information needed to help make decisions or solve problems" was the workplace skill most valued by students after they graduated. In addition, entering freshmen and transfer students reported significant gains in this area when they responded to questions on senior surveys. While information literacy crosses areas such as writing and critical thinking, we realized that this area is most closely aligned with the research that students were asked to perform in classes. In addition, we wondered if they were finding and using information for their own purposes. Therefore, in the UW SOUL we looked at where students found information and how they used it.

Data Sources and Methods of Analysis

The UW SOUL used a variety of methods to explore the research questions. We were committed to looking deeply at students' individual experience while still being able to generalize confidently about that experience, even though many argue that one cannot generalize from qualitative data. The latter goal made triangulation of data and prestructured methods of data collection important. We structured our methods before the study began, in order to be able to track data across time and students, and to ensure that researchers were consistent in their conduct of the study. However, while we created our instruments before the study began, we were able to allow one method to inform another, particularly early in the study, and we were able to add questions to our survey, interview, and email instruments throughout the study. Focus groups conducted with students in their second quarter, for example, identified items that we needed to include on our surveys. In addition, we conducted member checks on results that we felt needed clarification, such as some of the results on diversity and on personal growth.[12]

Alias Creation

At the beginning of the study, each student signed a consent form and created an alias following prescribed rules. All data were stored under those aliases to ensure students' privacy. Email responses were coded with students' aliases but were not added to the database. Similarly, names were removed and aliases added when papers and other work were turned in.

Structured Interviews

We conducted 60–90 minute interviews with participants in Group 1 during autumn quarter of the first year of the study (1999) and in each of the four spring quarters after that. The entry interview focused on students' prior experience at their high schools or transfer institutions. The four annual spring interviews questioned students about their experience during the preceding academic year. All interviews were structured to ensure consistency across interviewers and comparability of results over time, and through the course of the four years, the interview protocol remained largely constant. The interview questions focused on the six

major areas of inquiry (writing, critical thinking/problem solving, quantitative reasoning, information literacy, personal growth, and understanding/appreciating
diversity), in addition to general questions about learning. Over time, a few items
were discarded and a few items were added based on input from other data
sources, as well as on information requested by faculty and staff.

The number of students interviewed declined over time because students
graduated, left the study, or left the UW for reasons other than graduation. We
interviewed 143 students in fall 1999, 134 of those students in spring 2000, 112
in spring 2001, 88 in spring 2002, and 63 in spring 2003. Students were asked
an average of 30 questions per interview. Students were given the option of
interviewing in person or by telephone; most chose face-to-face interviews.

At the start of each interview, we gave students a copy of their transcripts to
help them remember their course-taking history as they answered questions
about the year they had just completed. If students were interviewed by phone,
we dictated their full transcripts to them over the phone before we began asking
interview questions. Using students' aliases as identifiers, interviewers entered
students' responses to questions directly into a database during interviews, preserving students' actual words as much as possible. The primary interviewers had
typing speeds of more than 90 words per minute.

Constant Comparison Method

Most of the interview responses were analyzed with an inductive process that
included no preestablished categories. Researchers were given all students'
responses to a question or question set. They tabulated the data that were easily
countable, including numerical information (such as how many courses had
required quantitative reasoning) and responses to yes/no questions (such as
whether a student had taken a course that year that required research).

Analysis of the discursive part of participants' responses took longer.
Researchers wrote brief summaries of each discursive response next to the original, preserving the students' language when possible. The researcher then identified themes in a constant comparison method and coded the responses
accordingly. These steps involved an iterative process, first identifying themes,
merging some of them, redefining others, checking the original responses to be
sure that the categories were appropriate, and then repeating the process.
Researchers eventually arrived at categories of responses for any given question,
while still preserving responses that were idiosyncratic. As we coded, we also
identified quotations that illuminated emergent categories of response.

Variation

We varied this method of analysis for some interview questions. Early in our analyses, one researcher attempted to use the constant comparison method to analyze students' descriptions of their most challenging critical thinking experience (discussed in Chapter 5). When he tried to use this method to identify critical thinking "moves" that students described, the method quickly became unworkable. He noticed that the themes he was identifying obscured the fact that the same words often had quite different meanings in different disciplinary contexts. For example, Table 2.7 shows examples of four students' descriptions of critical thinking and problem solving challenges. Parts of these responses were at first labeled under the general category of "learning new concepts."[13] However, as the table shows, the concepts the students reported having learned included, among others, supply and demand, derivatives, aspects of database models, and the behavior of light. Not only were these concepts very different, but so were the methods used to engage them. In this first analysis, we saw that these significant differences and others would be lost if we grouped all responses like these under a general label that paid no attention to context.

Therefore, we decided to try to categorize the courses that students were discussing according to seven or eight broad disciplinary contexts as a first step, and then analyze students' descriptions within those contexts as a second step, using the constant comparison method. In the case of critical thinking, those disciplinary contexts included architecture and urban planning, the arts, business, engineering, humanities, math, science, and social sciences.[14]

Our sense of why we needed to categorize students' responses within these broad disciplinary groupings was later bolstered when we conducted 17 interviews with UW faculty regarding critical thinking. Those conversations revealed wide-ranging definitions of critical thinking and problem solving across disciplines.

This approach was so useful in analyzing students' qualitative responses to learning critical thinking and problem solving skills that we tested it with students' responses to a question about their most challenging writing. We had already analyzed students' first-year writing responses to this question using the constant comparison method. We reanalyzed those responses by first dividing them into the disciplinary areas assigning the papers the students described; then we used the constant comparison method to identify recurring themes. In this second analysis, significant differences in the meaning of terms popped out. For example, we could see disciplinary differences in what students meant when they said that research made the paper they had written particularly challenging (see Chapter 6, Table 6.4). Students came to the university with a shared language in writing that they did not have about critical thinking, so identifying what students meant by terms such as *structure* and *evidence* was critical to

Table 2.7. *Learning New Concepts*

Economics	New concepts, new topics. The instructor asked us to look at certain supply and demand curves this way. We had to look at these different markets, see how they related to one another and how they differed.
Math	Just getting the derivatives is the main part of calculus and never having been exposed to that before, it was pretty tough for me to learn how to do it. We never went over that in precalculus. So we were totally introduced to it in 124.
Business	I had to set up a database model, make sure that it works, make sure that it has proper connections. We didn't get good instruction in there so it was challenging, and the ideas were all new to me.
Physics	Dealing with the geometry of a light wave or a light beam and how it acts changing mediums. Certainly the math involved in these is hard. There are a lot of ideas in the class that are similar to each other, so not getting them confused is hard and seeing how they relate and their differences is hard, too.

understanding the actual work they had done in their writing. We used this approach again when we analyzed descriptions of challenging thinking in quantitative reasoning and questions in information literacy.

Checking Each Other's Work

As with any qualitative analysis that attempts to quantify results, one challenge is to identify categories of response without blurring the distinctions among what students say. Therefore, data were analyzed more than once, and categories and coding were cross-validated among researchers. The conversations as we checked each other's work were fascinating. We helped each other identify the ways we were inappropriately reading into results what we hoped was there or what we assumed was there. These conversations made us highly reflective about the work we were doing, and we became somewhat evangelical about using the students' actual words whenever possible.

Importance of Student Agreement in Qualitative Data

In line with any analysis of qualitative data, we could assume that agreement in the responses among even a small number of students would reflect agreement among greater numbers of students if their attention was directed to that particular issue—through a survey item, for example. For this reason, we reported categories described by small, as well as larger, groups of students.

Surveys

All students were asked to fill out detailed, web-based surveys each quarter. The purpose of these surveys was to track what students did in their courses and in course-related learning experiences, as well as to discover how much students perceived they had learned in the six areas of focus. Survey questions remained mostly constant throughout the entire four years, with the exception that a few items were added over time as new needs and important omissions were noted. We occasionally tacked a few questions onto a single survey in service of particular campus needs. For example, the English department wanted to know if students might be interested in a writing minor, and we were able to put that question on one of our surveys.

The major categories of survey questions and the number of items in each category were as follows:

- 21 items about the level of challenge posed by courses

- 33 items on what students did in their courses each quarter (number of courses in which certain activities were performed)

- 26 items on how much students learned each quarter

- 36 items on what helped students' learning

- 36 items on what hindered students' learning

- 8 items about involvement with faculty and participation in research, service-learning, and internships

The number of students who completed surveys each quarter and the number who completed at least one survey each year are listed in Table 2.8. In analyzing the data from the quarterly surveys, we often restricted analysis to the 153 students who completed at least one survey each year. This restriction allowed us to view the characteristics of a full four years of college education and to look at trends over the four years. To determine four-year averages for each student, we averaged ratings across the surveys for each year, and then across the four years.

Table 2.8. Number of Students Completing Quarterly Academic Surveys

Academic Year	Fall	Winter	Spring	Total
1999–2000	282	279	271	304
2000–2001	252	250	235	256
2001–2002	190	186	182	190
2002–2003	151	143	128	153
Total completing at least one survey each year, 1999–2003			153	

Overall, the 153 students completed over 95% of the 12 possible surveys. The limitation this approach imposed was that very few transfer students were included in our analyses of survey responses, because most of them graduated in two or three years.

For a set of 33 items that asked students what they did in their courses each quarter (number of courses in which certain activities were performed), we sometimes restricted attention to those 135 students who had completed all 12 surveys (92) or had completed 11 of the 12 (43). Our rationale for this choice was to be able to arrive at a view of entire student college careers. Some of these 135 students also attended quarters in summers when we did not administer surveys, or completed a fifth year of undergraduate study after the UW SOUL had concluded. Thus, our data likely still underestimate the actual numbers of classes in which various activities occurred.

In addition to the end-of-quarter surveys, students were asked to complete three surveys on diversity. The first of these was administered in students' first quarter at the UW (fall 1999) and was completed by 290 students. The other two surveys were attached to the end-of-quarter surveys sent to students in their sixth quarter (spring 2001), completed by 230 students, and again to students in their twelfth quarter (spring 2003), completed by 130 students. The first-quarter survey asked a few questions about diversity at students' prior academic institutions, while the second and third diversity surveys asked these same questions relative to the UW. Otherwise, all three surveys were identical.[15]

When a survey became available for completion, usually in the last week of the academic quarter, each student was sent an email message giving him a personal URL linked to his alias that took him to the survey. Results were stored by alias. For quantitative analyses, we created SPSS flat files from relevant Microsoft Access tables. Creating specific-purpose SPSS files relevant to the question under investigation allowed us to avoid huge and ever-expanding files. This means of data reduction was important, because we collected more than 2,000 items of raw quantitative information from each four-year participant.

Structured Focus Groups

Focus groups were conducted annually throughout the four years of the study. Half the students in Group 1 participated in groups in the first year and the other half participated in focus groups the next year. The number of students studying abroad, working, and having complex schedules made it difficult to schedule 90 minute conversations, so by the third and fourth years, we asked all members of Group 1 to participate in the focus groups if they could. Table 2.9 shows how many participants were involved in focus groups in the four years of the study. As the table shows, an average of 53 students participated in 9–10 focus groups each year. Most of the questions in the focus groups were repeated, although there was some variation over the years.

Table 2.9. *Focus Groups, 2000–2003*

Year	# Students	# Focus Groups
2000	58	10
2001	51	9
2002	57	9
2003	47	10

The input of one of the UW SOUL faculty advisors, John Palka, then a zoology professor and cochair of the Program on the Environment, influenced us to center the focus groups primarily on students' values as the following email exchange illustrates. This focus included personal values, values around public issues, and educational values.

Johnny Palka Email

On Thu, 4 Nov 1999, C. Beyer wrote:
Dear John,

Today in the meeting, you asked me if we were going to try to learn anything in our study about how students' values develop over time. I have been thinking about that since the meeting, and I wondered if you would take a few minutes to let me know what you had in mind when you asked that question.

I think that when you asked me that, I kind of skittered away from it in my own mind, because directly confronting how students' university experience contributes to the development of their values seems hard. But remembering my own undergraduate experience, I realized that a huge part of my own values system was shaped by that experience. And that made me think that if I continue to skitter away from this, I may miss something huge. So, would you mind helping me think about this a little more?

Cathy

Date: Thu, 4 Nov 1999 16:47:20 -0800 (PST)
Hi, Cathy -

Well, you never know when a comment will strike a chord in someone, do you? Here's what I was thinking.

If we measure only what our students have learned in the way of intellectual skills, we may miss a second and, to me equally important, aspect of education. That aspect is multifaceted, but I was using "values" as a code word for it. I think of it in a rather rudimentary way. For example, we can talk all we want about population ecology and how it bears on conservation biology, but if we do not actually value the natural world we will never act on its behalf: we will not vote funds for conservation, we will not alter our own behavior, and so on and so forth. Effective action in most any arena is the outcome of some combination of what we understand with our minds and what we feel somewhere inside. It seems to me that good education impacts both the intellectual understanding and the inner sense of what is valuable, honorable, and worthy of our best efforts.

I am quite thrilled that you took me up on my query, whether or not it turns out to lead to something concrete in your study!

Johnny

Focus groups were conducted by two researchers. One introduced the process, asked the questions, and made sure that all members of the focus group responded to all questions. The second researcher entered students' responses as they gave them. As with the interviews, the success of this method for recording responses relies on the note taker's speed and commitment to recording students' comments nearly verbatim.

To analyze focus group responses, we used the group as our unit of analysis. As with interview responses, we analyzed focus group responses inductively. Researchers first read through every group's responses to all the questions. Then, we analyzed all groups' responses to the same question in a step-by-step process, noting unit themes first. When two or more members of a focus group agreed on a response—for example, that their families were what they valued most—the researchers counted that as a unit theme. We then noted unit themes that crossed groups and counted them. In addition, we noted when single members of a focus group identified a theme that was a unit theme in other groups.

As a result, our findings included both the number of groups and the number of lone individuals who identified a particular theme. For example, our analyses might note that four groups and single participants in two additional groups (noted as "4+2") reported that what they valued most were their families. This level of analysis allowed us to see how much agreement there was about values across units and how much individual support there was for various categories of response. Once we had coded the focus groups, we identified quotations that represented the most frequently identified values.

Open-Ended Email Questions

Each quarter, all students were asked to respond to one or more open-ended questions via email. In addition, we sent seniors a list of three questions as they were about to graduate. Responses to these questions gave us a rich set of data and kept us current on which students were in school and in the study, and which had left one or the other. Unlike other areas, email questions were not planned in advance, but they allowed us to focus on areas of current interest. Questions were sometimes personal, such as what surprised students the most in their first year at the UW; were sometimes related to study findings, such as member checks that asked students to clarify results; and were sometimes institutional, such as questions about the meaning of UW course evaluation results. A complete list of the questions we asked students is included on our web site with other UW SOUL instruments (www.washington.edu/oea).

Email questions were analyzed in the same manner as responses to interview questions, except that all analyses had to be done by hand with legal pads, sticky tabs, highlighters, and, in the case of one student researcher, scissors and envelopes. This analysis process was made more challenging by the fact that the students from Groups 1 and 2 responded to the email questions, which meant that, overall, we gathered and analyzed about 4,000 discursive responses to email questions over the four years of the study.

Academic Records

We had full access to student transcripts and other official university academic records through the student database. We were able to use these records to determine course-taking patterns, academic success, enrollment status, and graduation status.

Portfolios

At the end of each spring quarter, students in Group 1 turned in portfolios that included some of the work that they had completed for their courses during the year, as well as a three-to-five-page reflective essay on the pieces they included. Table 2.10 lists the portfolio requirements for each year. As the table shows, the list includes items from each of the study's academic areas of focus, as well as essays that explain each of the items included in the portfolios. At present, only samples of the portfolios have been analyzed, and reflective essays have only been reviewed cursorily. In the future, we hope to gather groups of faculty together to review portfolios of students in their disciplines. We have not included an analysis of the portfolios in this book.

Staffing

Due to the expense of paying participants, the UW SOUL was always understaffed. Staff included two full-time equivalent research positions and a portion of the time of a database manager. Analyzing qualitative date is time intensive, and the UW SOUL included approximately 16,050 open-ended responses to interview questions, 4,000 email responses to open-ended questions, and responses from a total of 213 students in 38 focus groups to about 48 questions.

To help us analyze the qualitative data, we offered 1–4 general studies credits to students who wanted an undergraduate research experience. We were fortunate to have had exceptional undergraduate students working with us during the study's second, third, and fourth years. (Fisher began working on the study in this capacity.) We trained undergraduates to do qualitative analysis and supervised them carefully in their work. They analyzed open-ended responses, drafted reports, and made presentations. They were extremely competent and insightful. Without their help, we would still be buried under the data, and our work lives would have been less fun.

Table 2.10. Annual Portfolio Requirements

Year	Requirements
1999–2000	• The best piece of writing students had written that year • The worst piece of writing they had written that year • The item that represented the most complex thinking they had done that year (or a description of it, if they could not include it) • A 3–5 page reflective essay explaining the above three items
2000–2001	• The best piece of writing students had written that year • An example of a piece of writing or a project they had completed that had required them to do research • The item that represented the most complex thinking they had done that year (or a description of it, if they could not include it) • A 3–5 page reflective essay explaining the above three items
2000–2002	• The best piece of writing students had produced that year • Their most challenging quantitative reasoning assignment over the three years they had been at the UW • The item that represented the most complex thinking they had done that year (or a description of it, if they could not include it) • A 3–5 page reflective essay explaining the above three items
2002–2003	• The best piece of writing students had produced recently • A piece of writing the students had produced early in their time at the UW • The item that represented the most complex thinking they had done that year (or a description of it, if they could not include it) • A 3–5 page reflective essay explaining the above three items

Endnotes

1) Regrettably, although we identified a few experiential differences between under-represented minority students and other populations of students, we were ulti-mately unable to answer our question about attrition with this study.

2) In 1999, 45.6% of the freshman class completed the ESS, while 33.1% of the transfer students did. A study of the representativeness of students who filled out the survey showed that freshmen ESS respondents exhibited academic achievement that was higher than the average for the general freshman population, while trans-fer respondents were very similar to their overall population. See McGhee (2000).

3) We counted students as participants if they completed the entry interview and at least one survey.

4) All information about students in the UW SOUL and UW students in general is from the UW's student database.

5) We made three comparisons: Group 1 and Group 2 students who left the study and those who remained in the study for all four years or until graduation (χ^2 = 1.05, d.f. = 1, ns); Group 1 and Group 2 students who left the study with regard to whether they remained at UW or not (χ^2 = 0.0012, d.f. = 1, ns); and Group 1 and Group 2 students who remained in the study with regard to whether they graduated or not (χ^2 = 3.75, d.f. = 1, ns).

6) By the second year, this gap widens, with the cumulative retention rate for Asian students entering in 1999 at about 87%; the rate for Caucasian students at about 82%; and the rate for underrepresented minority students averaging about 76%.

7) Determining a definition of transfer students was more challenging than we had anticipated. Running-start students—those who attend community colleges and receive credit that counts toward both high school graduation and college—enter the university as freshmen. These students enter with a wide-range of credits— some having taken one college course and others having completed two years of college when they enter as freshmen. We invited students to participate who were defined as transfer students by our admissions office, but we recounted transfers at the beginning of the second year, at this point including the running-start students who had transferred 30 or more quarter credits in that number. Students who transferred with fewer than 30 credits were counted as freshmen entrants.

8) Differences between Group 1 and Group 2 averages were negligible on these variables.

9) After six years (spring 2005), 83.2% of the initial sample of UW SOUL students had graduated, compared to 73.2% of the non-UW-SOUL fall 1999 entrants.

10) χ^2 = 25.6, p < 0.0001 and χ^2 = 22.1 , p < 0.0001 for "some time" in SOUL and until graduation or study's end in SOUL, respectively.

11) Designed to model California's Proposition 209, Washington's Initiative 200 called for the elimination of minority "preferences" in state and municipal hiring and recruitment to the state university system. The initiative passed in 1998.

12) All instruments can be downloaded from our web site: www.washington.edu/oea

13) While some may think "learning new concepts" is too simple to identify as critical thinking or problem solving, the student responses indicated otherwise. Our role was to report what students said, not to judge what *should* count.

14) These categories shifted somewhat depending on the skill we were analyzing, because we based them on the range of students' responses. For example, sometimes math and sciences were combined into one category.

15) Because we used differing criteria for inclusion for diversity and end-of-quarter survey analyses, the number of students within areas of major may differ somewhat across tables.

3

Personal Growth

My university experience has changed how much I believe in myself. I am going to come away from here with a lot more confidence in what I can do. I had these pre-conceived notions about coming to the UW. It was larger than the city I was born in. I was overwhelmed by the system, the requirements. The confidence I have gained over the last two years was dealing with and overcoming those large institutional hurdles. The grades I have received in the classes have shown me that I am as potentially sharp as everyone else in the room. My small town experience hasn't negatively affected me, and in fact, it allowed me to bring things into the conversation that others may not have thought about. I guess I feel like if I can tackle these problems here—I feel like the world is my oyster. I think anything I want to do is accessible, and I can do it with confidence.

People who work in academic institutions are not only in the knowledge-creation business; they are also in the life-changing business. Every single day, faculty and staff at institutions of higher education magically connect with some yearning, some latent interest, some intellectual need or idea, or some personal quality in individual undergraduate students, and this connection changes those students, and sometimes faculty and staff. In addition to the role that faculty and staff play in that transformation, students learn ideas, perspectives, ways of being, and values from each other, and that also changes them.

The UW SOUL found what Pascarella and Terenzini (1991) concluded in their extensive review of previous studies: Students were changed, often profoundly, by their college experience. College transforms students intentionally and accidentally, providing a time and space where students are safe to experiment with ideas about themselves and their world, where they can fail and recover, where they meet people who are unlike themselves and their childhood friends, and where they can work out what they believe and know—in short, a time and space where they can transform themselves. As one student put it, undergraduates "get the opportunity to change their minds about a lot of things without punishment." The students we studied found that they had intellectual capabilities they did not imagine, and they developed relationships, discovered interests, and identified goals that surprised them.

While all students changed, students' development as learners was uneven within individuals as well as across them. As the case study that we have included in this chapter demonstrates, students can and did lose ground or tread water in some areas of their learning while they advanced in others. Difficulty and challenge, as the case study also shows, pushed students to higher levels of learning, but they also stopped students in their learning tracks. How students responded to difficulty and challenge depended a great deal on who the student was, what past experience told her about dealing with difficulty, what she had to draw on for help, and how much the challenge mattered to her—the "I" in Tinto's (1993) input-environment-output model.

While we believe that students who do not go to college also change during this time in their lives, we think that the combination of coursework and personal exploration in a relatively safe place—a college campus— in the company of generally bright and interesting people provides students with unique opportunities to grow.[1] In his argument about emerging adulthood, Arnett (2000) argues that some cultures actively foster a prolonged period of identity and role exploration. The campuses of most colleges and universities function as such cultures.

Inside this culture, students took many paths as they sought to learn who they were, what they believed in, what was fun, and what they hoped to do with their lives. Students in the UW SOUL traveled and did coursework in Italy, South Africa, Madagascar, Brazil, England, Ireland, Spain, Germany, India, China, Japan, and Indonesia. They joined the swim team, created robots, wrote and acted in plays, started literary magazines, tutored high school kids in math and college students in economics, and taught new immigrants to speak English. They had internships that took them all over the country, participated in service-learning activities, and did research with nationally recognized scholars. They worked at nearly every kind of job—from positions in high-powered accountants' offices to pizza delivery. They met future husbands and wives, had sex for the first time, got married and divorced, and became parents. They struggled to get jobs and lost them, started jogging for exercise, and taught science labs. Some stopped eating or started throwing up to stay thin. Many learned they could live for six weeks on ramen noodles. Some sent money home to parents. They tried new sports, learned how to explore the city on a bus, and watched drama students put on midnight improv performances. And they did these things while taking approximately 15 credits each quarter and maintaining grade point averages that were a little above a B, on average.

In addition to the kinds of exploration students chose to have, they suffered a variety of explorations they would not have chosen. Among the students in our study, two lost parents to cancer, and one student in the study was diagnosed with cancer herself. One student had to drop out of school because of severe depression; two others finally sought treatment for depression after trying to handle it themselves for three years. One student in the study learned his father was having an affair. One student's parents cut her off financially when she told them she was a lesbian, so she had to get a full-time job to stay in college. Another student had brain surgery to repair an aneurysm. Three students attended grandparents' funerals, and all of them, grieving the time they had not spent with those grandparents, committed themselves to more balanced lives. One study participant's roommate tried to commit suicide. One student flunked out. One lost all sensation in his hands. One student had a father who left Lake Tahoe and disappeared into thin air. One was publicly ejected by a professor from a required class because she arrived a day late from spring break. One was falsely accused of sexual harassment and cleared. These experiences and many others more mundane comprised the selected and unselected parts of individual students' individual journeys.

We hope to have it both ways in this chapter, asserting that subtle changes in the small ecosystem that each student inhabits in college bring about big changes in that student, but also identifying some larger-scale trends that many students reported experiencing in the bigger college environment. In general, our findings on personal growth corroborate Pascarella and Terenzini's (1991) findings in their review of the research on growth in college students:

> In the vast majority of studies conducted, upperclassmen, as compared to freshmen, tend to be less authoritarian or dogmatic and more open and flexible in their perceptual processes, more autonomous and independent of authority imposed through social institutions, more tolerant and understanding of others, and more interpersonally sensitive and skilled. (p. 338)

This chapter argues that personal growth happens and that it is in the direction of more openness in students' thinking, greater independence in all aspects of their lives, increased self-understanding, and the confidence that accompanies these other changes. The chapter is organized into three main sections. First, we present the case of Fiona O'Sullivan. Her story is not particularly dramatic, but her experience in college was quite dramatic to her life as she lived it. Furthermore, Fiona's experience foreshadows later chapters in the book that address how students learn to think critically, write effectively, and reason quantitatively. Next, we describe some of the shared perceptions and experiences that speak to students' personal growth. Finally, we present conclusions and teaching and assessment implications that emerged from what the students told us.

Fiona's Path

Fiona O'Sullivan grew up in a Washington community noted for its fine public school system. She received top grades in high school, arriving at the UW with a 3.9 high school GPA, a swimming scholarship, and a love of math and photography. In her first conversation with us, Fiona said that she hoped to become more confident:

> I would like to have more confidence in myself in general. I really want to figure out what I love to do and do that. I would also like to be more understanding—loosen up a little bit. I have high expectations of myself, which isn't all that bad, but if it doesn't go that way, then I get crushed. I would rather just take it kind of in stride. And I would like to meet some people that I really connect with.

Within the first few hours of being at the UW, Fiona began to progress toward meeting that last goal, discovering that her roommate was "awesome."

In her first year at the UW, instead of becoming more confident, Fiona lost confidence. She took the first of UW's three-part calculus sequence and struggled with it. A "straight-A student in math my entire high school years," Fiona loved math because it was "systematic and everything works out in puzzles." However, after a few weeks in calculus, she noted significant differences between the math she had loved in high school and the math she was taking in college:

> In high school, it was generally just the problems. You would work it out. Here, it is translating it from word problems and figuring out which method to use from the word problems. I have always had trouble translating from word problems to the equations. Once I have the equations, I am fine. I don't think math questions in high school really stretched your thinking, but here they really stretch you to think. I'm not taking [the second quarter of calculus]. I've been putting a lot of effort into it, and I don't think I really have what it takes. Coming in, I thought I would minor in math. Now I figure that I'm not good enough.

Also in her first year, Fiona took a communication course taught by a dynamic professor, and because she loved that class, she decided to major in that field. That year she took a speech communication course that prompted her to have her first conversation with a professor, a couple of comparative literature classes that she did not enjoy, a basic chemistry course, and an introduction to geology. As Fiona described it, her path through her first year in college was marked by growing independence in the many senses of that word. In her second quarter, for example, Fiona talked about the ways she had been changed by her first quarter's experience:

> I believe that my last quarter here did change me in some ways. I learned to trust myself more and figure things out, relying on myself. I had to deal with learning how to live with another person and work out differences. I think I also matured some, in the sense that I realized a lot of patterns that my life was taking that I didn't like, and changed them, or at least tried.

Later that first year, reflecting on her experience in math, Fiona talked about becoming responsible for her own learning.

> In high school, it is not that essential to be able to do this, but here you have to figure things out for yourself or work with other people to figure them out. You can't just go to mom or dad. In high school, sometimes you can worm your way out of things. Here you are taking your education into your own hands.

In response to an email message we sent students at the beginning of the second year, asking them to tell us what they hoped would happen for them in their second year in college, Fiona wrote:

> This year, I would like to challenge myself more to apply myself and find something that I love to do, and take a chance with it. I am for the first time in my life beginning to crave learning. There is so much I want to learn about the world.... I am hoping that I can find out about the study abroad programs and get myself out there in the world. I hope the university can help me with that.

And interestingly, Fiona largely accomplished what she set out to do in her second year. A history course that focused on labor studies, which she enrolled in during the winter quarter of that year, became a landmark. Fiona described that class as the most difficult, the most time consuming, and the most engrossing class that she had ever taken:

> I didn't know anything about labor studies, unions, or anything like that. I was freaking out in the beginning, because I

> had no clue what all the acronyms meant. [For the take-home exam] we had to trace labor throughout history, whether it had to do with immigration, for example—how peaks of immigration affected labor or labor laws. . . . It was so much to try to pack in. I seriously spent 15 hours on that exam. It was kind of exciting, though, because I felt that I knew stuff and could put it into the paper. That history class really stepped it up a level for me. Now I kind of know what I can do. I know I can work hard. I figured out that you can learn it, if you work hard enough at it.

By the end of her second year, Fiona was a history major. She had also gotten the "lowest grade I have ever gotten on a paper" in her second history class—a 1.8.[2] Fiona asked her teaching assistant (TA) how to write better history papers and went to her previous history TA, the one she had in the labor studies course, for help. She ended up getting a 3.5 on her last paper in that class.

In addition to figuring out how to fight back from a 1.8 on a paper and to discovering she wanted to major in history, Fiona was deciding whether to quit the swim team or not. She talked about this decision in her end-of-the-year interview, saying:

> My entire college career, I have scheduled my life around [swimming]. I am also realizing that it has held me back from things. I kind of feel that school is not the main thing on my plate, and it should be.

Last but not least, by the end of her second year, Fiona had decided to spend a semester studying in Ireland the following year.

Fiona's experience shows that she put into play all the things she "hoped would happen to her" in her second year. It was as though she had written a blueprint for herself in the email response she sent us at the beginning of that year. She challenged herself to apply herself more fully in her labor studies class; she found something she loved to do—history; and she checked out study abroad programs, enrolling herself in a program in Ireland. At the end of that year, we asked Fiona if her beliefs, plans, or sense of herself had changed in any way. Her answer suggested that she was continuing her move toward independence:

> [I learned that] you are the only one who can make decisions for yourself. You can't always listen to what other people think for you. You have to make your own mistakes. I have always looked to other people to tell me what I should do—what I

should take that will look good on my transcript and so on.
This last quarter, I have realized that I have to figure out how
to do it. It is my life. I have to figure out what makes me
happy and I have to do that myself. If something is right for
me, I have to make that decision.

Fiona's third year was a time of consolidation and exploration. She dropped
out of swim team, took an intermediate expository writing class, a speech class,
and another history course in fall quarter. Her history class that quarter taught
her something about what it means to be a student of history, foregrounding her
place as a participant in the discipline. She said:

> It was challenging to come up with an argument [for my 300-
> level history course], when I thought I had learned the informa-
> tion. I thought, "This is history; these are the facts." I think that's
> not how historians look at it anymore, and they were trying to
> get us to see that—that everyone has his own take on stuff.

In Ireland, Fiona studied 20th-century fiction and "Women in Irish Society."
She worked as a bouncer in an Irish pub. She was hired for the job because in
Ireland only women are allowed to physically remove other women from pubs,
and—tall and athletic—Fiona could handle that.

Her work as a bouncer and her course on the status of women in Ireland
raised some questions about diversity for Fiona. In speaking of the course on
women, Fiona said:

> We talked about the difference between the gypsies and the
> "travelers" and Irish women. We also talked about differences
> between women in other European countries and in America.
> It seems as though women in Ireland have had a completely
> different path than we have. They are in a more submissive
> role than we are, but they have made significant progress.

As one might guess, by the end of her third year in college, Fiona said that
her study abroad experience had given her confidence that she could go off to
another place, make her own life, meet people, and be successful there. Also, as
one would expect, her time in Ireland made her want to travel more, perhaps to
South or Central America to "have my Spanish become fluent again," or to
Scotland after graduation.

As a senior, Fiona immersed herself in her major, taking two history classes
each quarter. She learned in her last year how to read primary documents, for
which she was grateful:

I'm a history major, and I never took a class that taught us about primary documents! We didn't even look at primary documents until History 301. I didn't know how to read primary documents for that class, so this class [History 376] was very helpful.

That year Fiona also wrote a paper that earned a 3.9, and her TA gave it to the professor as an example of an excellent response to his assignment.

As it is for many students, Fiona's senior year was a time of looking both forward and back, of wondering and worrying about what she would do next. Her plans for her immediate future included a return to Ireland. Looking back over her four years at the UW, Fiona had this to say:

My four years have taught me so much in so many different areas, I am not exactly sure where to start. I think in the last year, I have really begun to appreciate this incredible opportunity I have had to learn. Since my classes have become smaller and my direction a little more focused, I really have started looking forward to class. School used to just be a place where I was so focused on my grades that I really wasn't learning anything. It has been a freeing and enlightening experience to learn that life isn't about the grades. I finally have come to the realization that yes, grades are necessary, but they really tell you nothing about a person's knowledge and who they are. That may seem like a stupid statement or something that is incredibly obvious—take your pick—but my first two years here, all I did was get by. I was swimming and I managed to get everything done, but as I came to the summer before my junior year, I looked back and realized I had learned nothing. Yeah, my GPA was a 3.7—very good—but I couldn't remember what I had learned the quarter before.

That was probably the number one thing I learned—the most important thing I could have learned at the UW—that I am here on this earth to experience life, not just get through it. What a concept. I quit [swimming], and it was like all the curtains lifted. I could jump out of this box of my own making. Doors opened that I never knew were there. That is what college taught me, that is what the university… taught me— there is so much out there to learn and if you open yourself up to it you can reap the benefits. There is nothing more worthwhile than that. It has been inspiring to have professors who are so passionate about what they teach. There is nothing more fulfilling than walking away from a class thinking, "Wow, I never knew that," or "Wow, I would love to learn more about that." For me, the most important thing has been the change I have made within myself and what I outlined (not very clearly, sorry) above.

Fiona O'Sullivan came to college hoping to develop greater confidence in herself, to figure out what she loved to do, and to "loosen up a little bit." At the end of her four years, she had grown in all three areas. Fiona did, in fact, go to Ireland the summer after graduation. She got a job at the hostel she had stayed in during her previous trip and spent about six months making the beds and cleaning the toilets of others who were visiting Galway. This time, her journey to Ireland was marked by loss and challenges, including the breakup of her first serious romance. Just before she came back to Seattle, she sent us a letter from a train on its way through Wales, and the letter showed another stage in Fiona's emerging adulthood—the stage of knowing when to let go. From Fiona's letter dated November 27, 2003:

> So right about the time I got your email, I went for a trip by myself, out to the Aran Islands (Inis Mor) for a night away from everyone and to get out of Galway for a bit. Ironically enough, as I biked to catch the bus to the ferry dock, it poured like it hadn't for months. I was absolutely drenched, but I was determined to go. I boarded the bus looking like a drowned rat, made it to the ferry, and when I reached the island, it was still miserably raining. I got out for one little walk, but got soaked again on my way back to my hostel. Luckily, I had a room to myself and I did a lot of thinking. By the end of the night, I came to a decision: I wanted to go home. It wasn't that I wanted to leave Ireland, but it was what I needed to do. It took me a while to realize how intense this [time in Ireland] has been emotionally. It has basically been a bit of a slap in the face—but one I would NEVER take back. It felt like no matter what I did, I was swimming against the tide, and just when I tried to get up, something would knock me back down.
>
> The next morning, I woke to the most beautiful and serene morning. Pink and orange sunrise over the harbor and clean fresh air. The storm had completely blown over. It was as if the weather had been mirroring my inner turmoil.

Fiona's path illustrates the movement of a single student through college and into her first postcollege experience. That path was not always easy. She stumbled in her calculus class and gave up math. She stumbled in writing, but sought help until she finally understood how to improve her own work. She learned what it meant to think, write, and do research in history. She had to deal with the loss of swim team friends, and with the challenges of moving away from the guidance of her parents toward self-reliance. But in the end, she got some of what she came to college for—greater self-confidence, more openness and flexibility, ideas about what she loved to do.

What Students Said About Their Personal Growth

Taken together, the results in this section give us a picture of what Arnett's (1997) theory of emerging adulthood looks like on the ground. One limitation of our results on personal growth is that we do not identify nuanced differences in personal growth, particularly across gender or ethnicity. We do, however, report such differences where we found them. We have organized results into the following subsections:

- Change in the first year

- Change in the second year

- Values: the focus group results

- Beliefs, plans, and sense of themselves

- Turning points

- Regrets

The story these subsections tell is one of change—change in values, beliefs, confidence, and direction—that is initiated in a variety of ways. What brings about this change varies, but one theme that seems to dominate is the way the diverse community of people, cultures, practices, and ideas that is the university call on students to think about who they are, what they believe, and what they value.

Change in the First Year

If college is a transforming experience for students, much of the groundwork for change, as well as much change itself, occurs in the first year. Students we interviewed in fall 1999, particularly those who entered as freshmen, tended to be exuberant, excited, scared, confused, ill-informed, optimistic, and goofy. The energy these often conflicting feelings generated, plus the sheer relief that many students said they felt because they were no longer in high school, made conversations with them fascinating. One year later the same students were competent, focused, and seemed about 20 years older. Our results suggest that students' first year was colored by the many goals that students had for their learning when they arrived at the university—goals that called on them to explore, be more open with peers than they previously had been, take social risks, experiment with classes and majors, and challenge the identities they carried through high school and at their community colleges. Furthermore, after joyful exploration, as well as sometimes painful intellectual challenges in the first year, students' focus began to shift from the present to the future—a shift that became more dramatic over time.

Students' Goals for Their Own Learning

The goals that students carried with them to college directly informed their personal growth, and these goals were complex. As Fiona's case illustrated, students appeared in many ways to lay out their goals when they entered the UW and go about meeting them while they were there. In our entry interviews with students, we asked them what the most important things they hoped to learn were and what social skills or abilities, if any, they were interested in developing. One student responded to the question about learning goals with these words:

> I want to learn about life in the city, about science. I want to pick a field and become knowledgeable about it. I want to learn about the community, how it works. I want to learn about living with a person. The roommate experience is totally new to me. I want to learn how to compromise, how to work together, how to be a better leader, how to ride the Metro bus system, where all the cool places to hang out in Seattle are, what it feels like to live somewhere where it rains more than nine inches a year, how it feels to work with a professor who is on the cutting edge of knowledge and is passionate about what he is doing. I want to become more passionate about things.

This student's quotation is illustrative, carrying in it many of the eight themes that emerged in students' responses to the first quarter question that asked them to talk about the most important things they wanted to learn. Those themes, the percentage of students who mentioned them,[3] and quotations that illustrate them follow.

Knowledge in a specific field. About 34% of the incoming students said that they hoped to gain knowledge in a specific area. However, their responses often suggested that they did not know how those fields operated at the university. It seemed clear, for example, that they were not aware of how departments and disciplines functioned to identify and create boundaries around what was studied and, more importantly, around *how* topics were studied. These two students' quotations—the first from a transfer student and the second from a freshman—illustrate this category of response and some of these issues:

> How to save the planet. That is my overall goal with the department that I am going into. It is a daunting task, but I can't think of a better way to say it. I want to clean up wetlands and dirty soil and use all the science classes I am taking to do that.

> I honest-to-God want to study artificial intelligence. I want to create it. So what I want to learn is anything that will help me in this school. I want to learn biology, archaic languages, the whole gamut. Anything that can be remotely connected with AI that will help me benefit my goal.

Broad-based knowledge—"Everything!" When asked what the most important things they wanted to learn at the UW were, 21% of the students said some version of "everything." The quotation below, as well as the one that began our discussion of students' goals, illustrates this set of responses:

> This sounds really cheesy, but kind of an appreciation of all different levels of education, all different subjects. I would like to be well-rounded when I leave here, so if I major in English, I want to know chemistry and biology for example. I want to have an appreciation and enjoyment of learning, so I can pick up a paper and read about politics and then go to the opera and then come home and derive equations. I just want to be well rounded in all different areas so I can enjoy life. I want to know about everything.

Skills that will pay off in the job market. About 20% of the students who responded to the interview question focused on learning the skills they would need to get a good job after college. Sometimes these students had specific skills in mind; sometimes their focus on work skills was financially motivated; often it was stated as a broad, ill-defined concern. Interestingly, even as they entered the UW, many students' comments about work after college took on a spiritual dimension, focusing more on a "calling" than a career—something that they could care deeply about because it connected to their beliefs and passions. This theme recurred in the focus group discussions, and it appeared in other places in interviews as well. The following quotation illustrates this type of response:

> Academically I'm not sure yet. I'm not sure what I want to major in. I would like to have a job in a secure market. I want a degree where I can actually get a job in something where I can be financially stable and support a family with and something that I have a passion about. I don't want to just get a degree in something because I'm going to make money in it; that isn't the most important thing. So the most important goal I have here is trying to sort all that out.

A direction; A major. About 12% of the interviewees, more of them freshmen than transfer students, said they hoped they would learn a direction for their studies or their lives. For example:

> [I want to learn] what I want to do with my life. I'm right now deciding if I want to be here next quarter or go to school in California. I'm trying to figure out what I want to do and where I want to be and how that relates to me as a person.

Students who already had direction but hoped to be able to further those visions through their studies were a variation on this theme, as this quotation illustrates:

> I want to develop. I feel like I have ideas in my head that are the seedlings of really good ideas, but they are not fully developed. I don't think I know enough to have these really well thought out, blossoming ideas that can do good things for this planet. I am not sure what I need to learn to develop these ideas, but I am hoping that will happen. I am hoping that by focusing on these two fields—anthropology and botany—I am hoping I will be able to develop these ideas more fully. Also I hope that I will know what to do, and that I will have a network to help me get funding or go and do those things.

Increased understanding of human interaction and behavior. Interviewees (12%) also said that they wanted to learn more about people and why they behave as they do. Sometimes students' desires to learn about people brought them to a specific major, as the following quotation spoken by a transfer student illustrates:

> One of the things I've been exploring and want to learn is how the family works. I am really interested in that. I come from a completely broken house, and I have never had an idea of how family works. In the sociology department, I am kind of on that track of becoming a counselor or a teacher.

Better writing skills. Some students—about 8%—said that they wanted to improve their writing ability. This was the only specific skill area that a number of students identified. As one freshman said:

> I want to improve my writing. I have improved a lot. I am taking English composition now, and my first paper I wrote, I got a 2.0 on. I would have gotten a 4.0 on it in high school. I rewrote it and got a 3.6.

Increased understanding of diverse people/cultures. About 7% of the students we interviewed said that they hoped to increase their understanding of diversity. For some students, that focus was primarily cultural awareness, as this student's quotation exemplifies:

> Cultural differences are important to me—being able to understand where other people are coming from because of their differences and not being so focused on the way my culture is but understanding that they are responding to the way their culture is.

How to be independent and self-aware. When asked about what they hoped to learn at the UW, about 7% of the UW SOUL participants interviewed said that they hoped to learn how to be independent or to be more aware of who they were. As one freshman put it:

> I want to learn to take care of myself, not to have to run home all the time—just be self-reliant and independent.

In addition to asking students about their goals for their learning, we asked students if they had personal abilities or skills that they hoped to develop while in college. Four students answered "no" to this question, and many of the students' responses were too idiosyncratic to categorize. However, in spite of the large number of unique responses, six themes emerged, which sometimes overlapped with themes we identified for the question about learning.

Make friends/be more outgoing. About one in five students said that they hoped to make new friends and become more outgoing in college. Most of these students were freshmen, and for many of them, improving their social skills represented a break between their high school selves and the selves they hoped to become. However, some transfer students also expressed the desire to make more friends. The following quotations, the first from a freshman and the second from a transfer student, illustrate this category of response:

> I think I am a very good student—getting my work done, studying for tests, etc. But a lot of times I think I need to go out and meet new people, and I want to work hard in that area. Being more welcoming to more people.

> I would like to be better at making friends. I have a hard time with failure. Like if I put myself out to be friends with somebody and they just brush me off. Just getting along with people better.

Communication skills. About 15% of the students interviewed said that they hoped to improve their communication skills, including talking one-on-one with people, speaking in public, and writing. The following quotation illustrates this group of responses:

> I want to be really good at communicating with people. I used to be really good at getting my point across, but I have noticed that I am not so well able to do that. Maybe I realize that there are more people who are really good at expressing their feelings, and that makes me shy away a little bit. But I have good ideas in my head that I can't spit out.

Time management/self-discipline. Several students (10%) mentioned the need to develop better time management skills or improve their self-discipline. This aspect of personal development often came up again in the question on learning as "independence." The merging of time management with independence was also a theme in responses to other questions on personal growth. The following quotation illustrates this theme:

> [I want to develop] independence—financial independence from my family. I want to be able to know that I am totally fine by myself. Also, I want to develop self-motivation and time management, which are both connected to independence.

Learn/understand diverse viewpoints. About 8% of the students said that they hoped to understand viewpoints different from their own. A relative newcomer to the U.S. said:

> It is a big country, so I can learn about how to think about my thinking widely in my world. In Korea, it is a small country—one country, one Asian. Here there are Asians from different countries. Here I can learn how to think about other people, how to be with them. From the diversity in the UW, I can think more widely.

Become more well rounded. Another 8% of the students we interviewed said that they wanted to develop personal strengths in a wide range of areas. Two students' comments illustrate this category, and, as they demonstrate, "well-rounded" is a phrase that means different things to different people:

> Just become a more well-rounded person in the areas like community service and diversity and friendships. Just to be better prepared for the world outside school.

> I hope to be a more well-rounded person and to gather every experience that I possibly can and to use it to my fullest. I basically want options in the world as a person. That is something I can't get back home. I just want the option to be the person I want to be without having to conform to everyone else's standards. And being around such diversity, I am allowed to do exactly that—explore and express who I want to be.

Students' responses to these two questions about their academic and personal development goals demonstrated three things. First, they showed that students had wide-ranging academic and personal goals when they came to the university. Their definitions of learning were complex, and distinctions between personal and academic goals were often unclear. Second, the range of students' responses revealed that sometimes students' goals, particularly those of freshmen, were in conflict. For example, a freshman choosing between studying for an economics exam and going bowling with people from his dorm floor would be choosing between two goals that matter to him—one academic and the other personal. The range of students' goals might partially account for the lower grades students experience in their freshman year than they experience later, for it seemed clear that first-year students—particularly freshmen—spent a good deal of time and emotional energy gathering a group of friends around themselves, establishing some kind of community, and experiencing/exploring wide-ranging social options—in other words, meeting their social and personal goals while trying to do well in school. Third, students' responses underscored differences in the university's goals for them and their goals for themselves. Faculty and staff work hard to help students meet academic goals, but we often pay little attention to students' social goals or to their goals related to self-awareness and understanding.

Students' Perceptions of Change After Their First Quarter

Students felt themselves changing as they moved through their first year, primarily in the directions of greater independence—in every sense of that word—and greater social comfort. As students began their second quarter at the university, we sent an email message to 142 participants. We asked them if they felt that their experience in their first quarter had changed them in any way and to explain their response. Only 8% said that they had *not* changed as a result of their first-quarter experience; 92% reported that they had changed in some way. In discussing their changes, most students talked about what they had learned. By far, the most frequent response students gave (44%) was that they had learned to be independent, particularly in the area of managing their own time, as this response illustrates:

> I have become a bit more resourceful and self-dependent. For example, I had no car starting fall quarter and learned how to navigate Seattle on the wonderful Metro Bus System using my U-Pass (a wonderful offer for university students, by the way). I learned how to coordinate trips to the grocery store with a big backpack and umbrella in hand. The large and academically intimidating libraries were soon conquerable as well. I just had to put one foot in front of the other and go and do so. Overall, I can say that I became more self-reliant, self-trusting, forward, and resourceful, and in those ways, I grew up a little bit over the course of my first quarter.

Another frequently mentioned direction of change was learning how to study, with about one in four of the students giving that response. For example:

> It has changed me in my habits of studying. I can no longer get by with just cramming before the test. The program that I am in is quite challenging, and with 16–17 credits per quarter, I barely have time to breathe. But all in all, it has made me aware of my previously bad study habits.

In addition, about 20% of the study participants said that they had learned to deal with people in new situations, such as dealing with roommates, and 17%

said that they had learned more about what college is like—or how to "do" college. This student's response illustrates both of those categories:

> I now know what to expect from the professors, how to ration homework, what to eat and not to eat in the residence hall cafeterias, how to deal with a roommate, and what I need to do to get into my major.

Along these same lines, 13% of the students reported that they had made a lot of friends, and the same number reported that they had learned from the diversity of people at the university, as this student said:

> This quarter has helped me learn what I value as I compare myself to the other people I have met so far. And I have enjoyed the fact that everyone here seems to be willing to accept everyone's unique values. People are strong in certain areas but need work in others. I believe the same goes for me. Just hanging around both sexes together for really the first time in my life is helping me understand what the differences between men and women are. I didn't get that kind of diversity in my old high school.

In addition to these most frequently mentioned categories of response, smaller numbers of students said that they had:

- Learned to use resources at the UW, such as TA and professors' office hours, activities, and other opportunities (11%)

- Become more self-confident (11%)

- Become more friendly and outgoing (8%)

- Missed and realized the importance of family and old friends (6%)

- Learned specific skills, such as writing, art, problem solving, and math (6%)

Perhaps the most interesting aspect of the changes that students reported is that 10 of the 11 categories of response focused on aspects of personal growth and development, rather than on the development of academic skills or the acquisition of knowledge. In addition, students' responses show that by the second quarter of college, students had already made progress on the goals they had set for themselves when they arrived.

The Hammering

Another kind of change that students experienced was not connected with goals they set for themselves. This is the experience that we came to call "the hammering." Many students reported going through at least one experience in their first year that painfully called their intellectual identities into question. We did not ask them a question about this experience; rather, it came to light by itself through responses to other questions. In understanding the significance of the hammering, it is important to remember that most of the students who go to universities have experienced success in their high schools and community colleges. Many have been told all their lives that they were gifted and intelligent. Often college students have impressive achievements on their resumes, including being the valedictorians and salutatorians of their high school classes and winning honors and awards at high schools, community colleges, and on the job. Because many of them come from such esteemed positions at their previous institutions, often just the way large universities do business—collecting first and second-year students into large classes where the professor does most or all of the talking and does not even know their names—can hammer students' sense of who they are and how valuable their contributions might be. As one student said, "It is disheartening to look out over a class of 300 and think that you mean anything to the instructor."

For some students, the hammering was less dramatic than for others. The sudden awareness that every student in the 300-person lecture hall was as smart as the others could sometimes call a student's intellectual gifts into question. For many students, however, the hammering occurred when they faltered in courses in which they expected to do well. Fiona O'Sullivan's calculus class, as well as her 1.8 paper grade are examples of this kind of hammering. These two students' comments were typical:

> The first quarter was almost shocking, because there are so many really intelligent people at the UW, and I am just not used to all that competition. It was intimidating. Working with other students, getting quizzes and tests back, seeing the class curve and where I would be falling—those things made me aware of the other students' abilities. It made me kind of give up a little bit. When I was in high school, I didn't have to work hard to do well.

> I feel as if I have learned my limitations. I know what I can reasonably do and beyond that I do not have extraordinary expectations of myself. This is a very difficult lesson to learn

and barrier to overcome, especially when your grades come
back as a 2.9 and you were valedictorian of your high school.

Other ways of experiencing the hammering included students failing to get
into majors they had planned on entering for years, or placing into much lower
levels of math than they expected.

For many students, the hammering was simply doing badly in a class for the
first time in their lives. And almost all students in their first year felt that they
had done badly in at least one class; 77% of the UW SOUL transfer students
and 88% of the students who entered as freshmen said that they had done badly
in at least one of their classes in their first year at the UW. Most of them defined
"doing badly" as getting a low grade, and the average grade they considered bad
was a 2.6. However, the range of bad grades students reported was 0.8 (which is
really bad) to 3.9 (which most students would be ecstatic to receive). Students
largely blamed themselves for failing to do well, a practice that we discuss later
in this chapter and also in Chapter 9.

Whatever form it took, the hammering was not a pleasant experience for
students, and they had to recover from it in order to continue. At our institution, evidence that most of them do recover is found in first-to-second-year
retention rates in the 90% range. Furthermore, some might argue, notably
Erikson (1968), that identity formation is a response to crisis, and, therefore,
that some kind of hammering experience might be necessary for students to
grow and to succeed. This argument makes some sense. The assumptions that
one is "the best" and that one's performance must be "perfect" can be counter-
productive over time, and some might argue that the hammering many students
experience in their first year in college opens the door for students to do exactly what Fiona O'Sullivan did when she received a 1.8 on her first paper: challenge themselves to take responsibility for their own intellectual growth, use the
resources available, and advance to the next level of awareness, understanding,
or performance.

It is important to remember that the hammering can have other effects as
well. For better or worse, it often propels students out of one path and into
another—from majoring in biology to majoring in art, for example. This effect
actually may be fortuitous for the student's own personal and academic growth,
but often it is costly for institutions, because such changes can add years to students' time-to-graduation.

A more profound effect of the hammering than institutional costs is that it
can permanently change how students think of themselves and their abilities.
Again, Fiona serves as an example. When she learned that she was not as competent in math as her high school experience had led her to think she was, Fiona

stopped taking math. We do not know what makes students stop in the face of such experiences and what makes them push forward, but we suspect that this decision has to do with both past and present events in students' lives. Fiona had newly fallen in love with history, and she knew she would need to be able to write to be successful there. The goal of improving writing was, therefore, braided with the goal of learning more about history, while improvement in math was only connected with itself. This is, of course, only speculation. It is just as possible that Fiona believed she *could* improve in writing, but that she did not believe she could improve in math.

Sense of Accomplishment in the First Year

In general, students felt they had accomplished what they set out to do in their first year in college. In the spring of their first year, we asked UW SOUL participants if they had accomplished what they had set out to do. Of the 134 students we interviewed, 58% said that they had done so; 31% said that they had accomplished some of what they had set out to do; and 10% said that they had not accomplished their goals. One percent of the students said that they had not set out to accomplish anything.

When asked what they felt they had accomplished, 63% said that they had accomplished some of their academic goals, including doing well in their courses and getting good grades, finding a direction or a major for their academic careers, and having learned in the courses they took. About 30% of the students said that they had accomplished social goals. Most of this group said that they had hoped to meet new people and they had done that. Several students in this group said that they felt they had finally found a place where they "fit in." In addition, 25% of the students talked about accomplishing goals related to their own personal awareness and growth. Some of these students were happy to have made it through the year; others said that they had moved in the direction of becoming more independent, as this student said:

> Mostly I wanted independence and I've done that. I feel I have grown up through my interaction with people. In some respects it has been a challenging thing but it has taught me more to think for myself and definitely be more independent.

Finally, about 17% of the students said that they felt they had accomplished extracurricular goals, such as taking a yoga class or learning to sail.

A follow-up interview question asked students why they felt they had met or failed to meet their goals. Table 3.1 lists reasons students gave in order of frequency, and both sets of responses show the extent to which students in their

Table 3.1. *Reasons for Success or Failure in Accomplishing Goals*

Reasons for Success	Reasons for Failure
• I have grown/matured. • My goals were realistic. • I had outside support (friends/family). • I have a focus/direction. • I have learned to balance social goals with academic goals.	• I didn't do well in my classes. • I procrastinated or I didn't try hard enough. • My goals were unrealistic. • I had/have bad study habits. • There are too many outside demands on my time and attention. • I was worried about finances. • I had lost/not yet found a direction.

first year felt responsible for their success or failure. As the table shows, students credited themselves, time, and external support for their success. They mostly blamed themselves for their failures.

As was clear by responses to both questions on entry and exit interviews in students' first year, students came to the university with a wide range of goals—academic, social, and personal. However, when they talked about the goals they had accomplished in their first year, most of them singled out academic goals. It is possible that the dominance of academic goals in students' responses to this interview question said more about ease of assessing this kind of accomplishment than it said about what students actually accomplished. However, it is also possible that by the end of the first year, students were more focused academically than they had been when they arrived. Perhaps the dominant values of the environment in which they were immersed had focused their attention.

Regardless of why students' goals seemed to shift to a stronger focus on academic success by the end of their first year, students' responses to this question showed us that, for the most part, they had accomplished many of the goals they had set for themselves. Furthermore, they credited themselves, as well as family and friends, with helping them accomplish those goals. Finally, when students failed to accomplish their goals in their first year, they tended to blame themselves. What was noticeably missing from both sides of the list in Table 3.1 were references to classes, faculty, or TAs. We believe that this omission indicates a belief that many young people have in the "power of one" and perhaps some naiveté about the place they have entered. In reality, academic institutions can be characterized as complex webs of interaction and interdependency, with people willingly and accidentally assisting others in knowledge creation and personal growth. Students did not seem completely aware of that network in their first year, but later, they did.

Change in the Second Year

The second year was marked by a shift in focus to the future—on finding a direction and pursuing it. As they began their third year, we sent an email message to all UW SOUL participants, asking them in what ways, if any, they felt that they were different than they were when they first came to the UW. We also asked them to tell us what role being a student had played in any change they noted. Only two of the 195 respondents indicated that they had not changed in any way over the two years. Six major areas of change emerged from our analysis of students' responses.

Clearer Focus/Better Direction

About 36% of the students reporting change said that they were more focused or had a better sense of their own direction. For example, one student said:

> I am less inclined to take classes that will "broaden my horizons." I've found an area of knowledge that I am REALLY interested in, and I enjoy the time that I spend working in that area.

Self-Confidence

About a third of the respondents said that their level of self-confidence had increased as they began the third year of college. For example:

> I am more confident. Papers, big assignments, tests do not phase me. I know that these are part of the process of earning my degree. I chose to be here, so there is no reason to complain or stress too much about school work. It will get done.

Adjustment to Academic Life

In addition, about a third of the students said that they were better adjusted to college life and academic demands, as this student's quotation illustrates:

> Being a student here has played a big role in my change. When I first came here, I didn't really like to ask questions in my classes because they were big. I think I was a little more intimidated by my surroundings than I let on. But once I adjusted, I was more willing to volunteer in class. Since this is such a big university, the only way to get help is to ask for it.

Independence

A fourth major area of change that students noted in their email responses was independence. About 20% of the students who responded noted this change. One student's comment illustrates this group:

> I also find myself more independent and more self-driven. I do things because I want to, not necessarily because someone else says I should.

Sense of Academic Responsibility

Another frequently given response was that students had become more responsible. About 18% of the students who said they had changed gave this response, as illustrated by this student's quotation:

> After having experienced all the parties and the fun times, and having figured out my major, I feel more inclined to sit down and study. I still feel the social aspect of college is very important; however, I realize I am here to learn and that takes first priority.

Personal Identity

Finally, about 16% of the students reported that some aspect of their personal identity had changed. For example:

> Coming out of high school, I am sure that I had a huge interest in what and who was "cool." Then, living in the fraternity for two years, I realized that the people who were "cool" in there—many of them I disliked, not because of the way they treated me, but because of the way they treated others.

Students' sense of how great a role the university played in these changes varied with the changes they described. Table 3.2 lists the change and the percentage of students who felt that the UW had played a role in that change. As the table shows, students felt that the university played a more significant role in changes in who they were and in their focus and direction than it played in the other four areas of change they noted. Interestingly, not even half of the students felt that change they experienced in responsibility and adjustment to college came from a role the institution played.

Table 3.2. Role of UW in Self-Reported Changes

Change	% of Those Reporting Change Who Said UW Played a Role
Changes in self/identity	100
Better focused/sense of direction	96
Independence	64
Confidence	58
Better adjusted to UW	44
Responsibility	41

When the university played a significant role in how they had changed, students identified three major pathways for change. First, they spoke of the classes they took and the faculty who taught those classes as having a powerful impact on their personal development. As one student said:

> Educationally, I give my thanks to an amazing staff here. I have had so many inspiring teachers that have indirectly forced me to understand myself. Their knowledge, not only of the "textbook material," but of human nature constantly surprises me. Even more than the professors, the TAs have had a personal role with the students—forcing us outside of the box. The diversity of classes I have taken (astronomy, art, history, psychology) have all helped to develop the kind of person I want to be. Honestly, I don't want college to end. There is too much left I want to learn!

A second frequently cited avenue for change was through the diversity of people and viewpoints students had experienced. This student's quotation illustrates this group:

> Being a student at the UW means being part of a very large and diverse community, and being able to hear different voices and ideas. That really helped me to expand my mind beyond my scope.

Third, students described opportunities that came through their connections with UW clubs, internships, ROTC, and campus talks and events.

In addition to crediting the university with providing the impetus for change, students also attributed change to areas of their lives outside university life. These were, in order of frequency:

- Living on their own

- Friends and family

- Getting older, more mature

- World events (such as 9/11)

Member Check on Changes in the First and Second Years

In order to check results from the first two years, we sent an email question to all students in the study at the end of their third year at the UW informing them that our results suggested they had changed by becoming more independent in their first year and more self-confident, focused, directed, and better adjusted to university life in their second year. We asked them if those results seemed accurate to them, and if not, to explain why.

Approximately 180 students responded to the email question. The majority agreed that these two changes characterized their experience. While we had significantly fewer transfer students still enrolled in the third year than we had in the first two years of the study, we were able to compare responses of transfer students with those of students who entered as freshmen. As might be expected, transfer students reported less change in *personal* independence in their first year than students who entered as freshmen. However, transfer students reported growth in *intellectual* independence similar to that which freshmen reported. Several students—both those who entered as freshmen and those entering as transfer students—pointed out that, even though there may have been spikes in independence in the first year and self-confidence in the second, the paths to both continued throughout all three years, as did clarity of direction. The following two quotations—the first from a student who entered as a freshman and the second from a transfer student—illustrate these responses:

> The first year was very difficult because of the independence. Not having a curfew, a parent telling you what to do, or anyone telling you to go to class make the first year overwhelming. I got poor grades due to my slacking off, based on my freedom, and I have been working hard since then to get my GPA back up. I think that you finally get into the swing of things by the spring of your freshman year, because you have realized that, yes, you do have freedom, and, yes, it is great, but you need to get the good grades again. The essence of my second year here at UW was gaining a better understanding of who I was, what I want to do for a career, and just feeling

comfortable with my decision. This was the year that I went full force with ROTC, because I realized that being a pilot was attainable, and it was something that I wanted to do.

Well, during my first year at the UW I did feel more independent and capable to make decisions about my education. I felt equipped and able to negotiate the systems in place at the university, such as financial aid, registration, degree requirements, course work requirements, the library system, computer labs, etc. Ethical decisions . . . I feel I entered the UW with a set of beliefs from which I could make decisions. I found, however, that I was challenged and compelled to question my belief system and to evaluate my decision-making apparatus. This has been such a gift. While I did feel very independent, I also felt very supported by the professors, TAs, and other students in my major—the comparative history of ideas. I felt independence with a net, an experience—and another gift—for which I am most grateful. During my second year, my self-confidence did blossom. I did have a clearer sense of the direction and purpose of my education. However, upsets in my personal life had the effect of eroding some of my self-confidence, independence, and belief in my abilities to make sound decisions for my education and my future.

Values: The Focus Group Results

Four years of focus group results showed that many students' values changed over time and some did not, but all students experienced challenges to their values as they moved through college. As described in Chapter 2, we conducted focus groups every winter quarter with a randomly selected subset of students in Group 1. Questions for the focus groups primarily addressed students' values—both personal and educational. We also used focus groups as a way to gather information on students' perceptions of what helped and hindered their learning, which we discuss in Chapter 9.

Personal Values

Each year we asked students what mattered to them, including personal relationships, public issues, and social causes. In all four years, family, friends, and romantic partners were what most groups agreed mattered to them. Beyond those two constants, what mattered to students changed over time. As Table 3.3

shows, in the first year, students cited acceptance of diversity; personal attributes, such as honesty and integrity; free time; and education as the values they held after family and friends. By the second year, "balance"—keeping other aspects of their lives in balance with academic demands—became a significant value, as did students' faith. Free time, personal attributes (different qualities in the second year than in the first), and happiness were mentioned frequently by students, although there was less agreement on particular values than the previous year. In the third year, students said they valued being happy and having free time, after the primary value they placed on family and friends. Students in the fourth year added "learning" and finding work that allowed them to make a contribution to society to the usual items—"family and friends" and "free time."

One interesting result shown in Table 3.3 is that students spoke of valuing education only twice, once in the first year and again in the fourth. All other values they noted can be characterized as "personal" values. In addition, social issues or causes rarely appeared in students' responses to this question. They were mentioned so infrequently, in fact, that we began to ask them specifically whether there were any social or public causes or issues that mattered to them after they had given their initial responses to this question. We sometimes asked them about specific issues or events, the environment, or the effects of September 11, but we noted no strong trends in their responses.

After we asked students what mattered to them, we asked them if their values had been affected or shaped in any way by their time at the UW. Students' responses to this question changed over time. In the first year, students in nine of the ten focus groups said that their beliefs and values had been challenged or reinforced, but not changed. By the second year, students in most of the focus groups said that their beliefs and values had been changed by their college experiences, while students in two groups said that their values and beliefs remained unchanged. In the third year, students in every focus group said that their values had been changed by their experience in college. But the last year, nine out of 10 of the focus groups agreed that their beliefs and values had been changed by their college experience, while students in one group agreed that their values had been reinforced. These responses clearly show the impact of college and college life on students' values. In the first year, values were challenged; by the fourth year, values had been changed.

Students' responses to a question we posed in the fourth year focus groups also spoke to the shift in values. We posed the following question for them:

> Think about yourself now in relation to what you imagine you
> would be like if you hadn't gone to college—How do you think

Table 3.3. Focus Group Responses—What Matters to You?
(Number of Groups Citing Each/Total Number of Groups in Parentheses)

2000	2001	2002	2003
Family (5/10)	Friends and romantic partners (6/9)	Friends and romantic partners (7/9)	Family and friends (8/10)
Friends and romantic partners (5/10)	Family (5/9)	Family (4/9)	Learning, the opportunity to be a college student (2/10)
Acceptance of diversity (5/10)	Balance (3/9)	Being happy (4/9)	Finding work that allows me to make a contribution (1/10 + frequent individual mention in other groups)
Specific values, including honesty, integrity, and motivation (5/10)	Faith (2/9)	Free time (2/9)	Free time (1/10 + frequent individual mention in other groups)
Free time (4/10)	Free time (1/9 + frequent individual mention in other groups)		
Education (3/10)	Specific values, including respecting others and self-discipline (1/9 + frequent individual mention in other groups)		
	Happiness (1/9 + frequent individual mention in other groups)		

you would be different in regard to your values? Your interests?
How you think about things? Your hopes and dreams?

Students in five of the ten groups agreed that their values would have been different, noting that their values had broadened because of exposure to people with values unlike those with which they had grown up. They also said that their values had been challenged, and, as a result, they felt they better understood these values. In the remaining five focus groups, there was little agreement about whether values would differ had students not attended college. In contrast, most groups (eight of the ten) agreed that current interests would be different had they not gone to college, noting that exposure to new ideas, areas of study, the possibility of travel, potential career paths, and people had added new passions to their former interests.

Regarding their hopes and dreams, students in most of the groups (six of ten) believed that their current hopes and dreams were further-reaching and more ambitious than they would have been if they had not gone to college. Finally, regarding changes in thinking, students in six of the groups agreed that their thinking would be different if they had not gone to college. They said that they questioned and challenged more than they would have if they had not come to college. Also, they said that they thought more independently and analytically than they had before college. Two groups and several individuals mentioned that they thought more about global issues and world politics than they would have had they not come to college.

Educational Values

We asked focus group participants questions about their educational values. One of the questions we asked each year was how students personally defined college success. Table 3.4 shows the responses of focus groups to this question over the four years of the study. As the table shows, students' definitions of success were multifaceted, reminding us of the complexity of the learning goals they brought with them to college.

The table shows that students' views moved away from the present and toward the future in their second year, a shift that we saw in students' interviews and email responses earlier in this chapter. Also, when students talked about that path beyond college, they focused on finding something they *loved* to do, rather than on something they might make a great deal of money doing. Across all years, only one student brought up potential earnings in focus group discussions, saying, "Carats on the wrist and plaques on the wall—that's what it's all about for me." For the majority of students, the path they were looking for would engage them in something they could commit themselves to, something they "felt good about going to on Monday."

The table also shows the relative unimportance of grades in students' ideas about college success. After the first year, no one talked about getting good grades. This struck us as so odd that for the first three years, we deliberately asked them how they defined good grades. Once again, students refused to give simple definitions, and there was remarkable consistency over the three years in how students defined "good grades." Definitions included grades as "keys" to the next step in students' plans; as relative to the challenge and interest level of the course they were given in; and as related to effort, learning, and confidence. As was the case with the question on college success, students saw good grades as multidimensional, rather than as representing one idea, and they did not array these dimensions hierarchically. In all groups, for each of the years we asked this question about grades, we tried to force students to tell us what grade a good grade actually was, and except for the "not a 2.0" response in the second year (i.e., a good grade is not a bad grade), students refused to link what constituted a good grade with an actual grade. Earlier in this chapter in discussing the hammering, we noted that in their first year, students had linked "not doing well" in a class with grades, but that the range of grades they described was 0.8–3.9, a finding that is consistent with students' focus group responses about what grades mean.

Another question we asked to get at students' educational values—this time only in the third and fourth years of the study—was "what does it mean to be educated?" Table 3.5 shows students' responses to this question over the two years. As the table shows, equal numbers of focus groups agreed on the first two definitions of what it meant to be educated in the third and fourth years. In both years, students said that being educated meant openly entertaining others' perspectives and maintaining a questioning stance when confronted with information and ideas. Regarding that questioning stance, one student put it this way:

> To be educated is to question the truth. Whose truth is it?
> Why should that truth be my truth? What we are learning in
> college is to question.

Other responses in the third year included knowing how to deal effectively with people and situations—again that social goal coming forward in students' responses—and being able to think critically. The "critical thinking" response was different in nature from the "questioning information and ideas" response, in that students often were speaking of critical thinking as academic problem-solving activities and processes, while "questioning" applied more broadly to a general stance one took.

Table 3.4. *Focus Group Responses—How Do You Define College Success? (Number of Groups Citing Each/Total Number of Groups in Parentheses)*

2000	2001	2002	2003
Getting good grades (9/10)	Gaining knowledge and skills—both as an end in itself and as a means to a job or grad school (4/9)	Discovering and doing what I want to do in my life (5/9)	Graduating (3/10)
Gaining experiences (9/10)	Finding something I love to do (3/9)	Being prepared for what's next (4/9)	Finding an area of study, a direction, a path that you have passion for (2/10)
Developing social skills (7/10)	Social skills/making friends (3/9)	Reaching goals/graduating (3/9)	Having learned to think/having learned something (2/10)
Gaining and applying knowledge (6/10)	Learning about oneself (3/9)	Taking advantage of opportunities (2/9)	Having a diversity of experiences (2/10)
Learning about oneself (4/10)	Setting and reaching goals (2/9)	Learning about oneself (2/9)	
Getting a degree (3/10)	Getting a good job (2/9)		
	Taking advantage of opportunities (2/0)		

In contrast, in the fourth year, students focused on having wide-ranging experience as well as academic knowledge, a value that takes us back to students' goals when they entered the university, as well as to the ways they defined college success in the focus groups (Table 3.4). In addition, two focus groups said that being able to find knowledge, which they saw as the key to "lifelong knowledge," contributed to what it meant to be educated.

Table 3.5. *Focus Group Responses—What Does It Mean To Be Educated?*
(Number of Groups Citing Each/Total Number of Groups in Parentheses)

2002	2003
Being open-minded (4/9)	Being able to listen to others' perspectives, to look at own beliefs from different perspectives. (4/10)
Questioning information, ideas (3/9)	Questioning information, ideas, "truths" (3/10)
Knowing how to deal with people and situations (2/9)	Someone who has both wide-ranging experience as well as "book knowledge" (or "streetsmarts and booksmarts") (2/10)
Being able to think critically (2/9)	Lifelong knowledge, being able to find knowledge—knowing where to go to learn more. (2/10)

What the Focus Groups Told Us About Change

Focus group results on students' personal values revealed what was both change-less and changing in students' lives as they moved through college. In general, what students held most dear all four years were family and friends. Another area of no change were the ways students hoped to be transformed by learning. Focus group responses to questions about educational values were just as complex over all four years of the study as the goals students described for their learning when they entered the university. What changed were values around balance and happiness, which became more important over time. Furthermore, students pointed out that their experience in college reinforced and challenged their values, and finally caused them to change their values in the direction of more openness and greater possibilities, as Pascarella and Terenzini (1991) would have predicted. Students pointed to people, values, and opportunities that differed from those they might have experienced in the places where they grew up as contributing to these changes.

Beliefs, Plans, and Sense of Themselves

Each year in the annual interviews, we asked students if their beliefs, plans, or sense of themselves had changed that year. Table 3.6 tracks students' most frequently given responses over time. As the table shows, in each year, the majority of students felt they had undergone change in beliefs, plans, sense of themselves, or all of the three.

Changes in Beliefs

Regarding changes in beliefs, even small agreement among students in their open-ended responses to broad questions can be significant, and we find numbers of students remarking on changes in their religious beliefs or spirituality in all four years of the study noteworthy (Table 3.6), echoing Richard Light's (2001) findings at Harvard University. Light's interviews with seniors found that they were actively engaged in exploring their beliefs about God and spirituality and were interested in learning what their peers believed as well. Two UW SOUL students' comments on changes in their religious beliefs—each in a different year of the study—show us different directions for such change:

> *First year:* Actually I went back to church toward the beginning of spring quarter. There were a lot of reasons I went back, not one in particular. I wanted to go back for support and for my own personal reasons. Just being so far away from home, you need somewhere to go.

> *Fourth year:* Beliefs—there has been a general progression throughout college. I have moved away from religion quite a bit. It doesn't make my mom happy but she accepts it. I became disillusioned with it. I think the people I have come in contact with as well as my own research and reading and looking at the world changed me.

As Table 3.6 shows, in their third and fourth years in college, students reported changes in their political beliefs and in the breadth of their beliefs in general in those same two years. Students commented on becoming more open to others' ideas and to entertaining challenges to their own thinking in these years. This student's comment illustrates the latter change:

> I've opened my mind up to more stuff, including my roommate's conservative opinions that I mentioned in the diversity section.

By the fourth year of the study, in addition to changes in religious and political beliefs and a movement to more tolerance in general, students noted changes in their sense of the importance of family and friends, as this student's response illustrates:

> My sense of family has gotten stronger just because of the loss of my aunt. I have been spending time with my parents and realizing that you can't control time, it's going by fast. It is

Table 3.6. Changes in Students' Beliefs, Plans, and Sense of Themselves over Time

Change	2000	2001	2002	2003
None	19%	13%	10%	17% Two of these repeat from 2002
Beliefs				
In spirituality	10% • About a third of these lost faith. • 2/3 noted strengths in faith.	10% • Most reported that they had gained in faith.	14% • About half of these students said that their spiritual beliefs had become stronger. • A little less than half reported becoming more uncertain about their spiritual beliefs.	13% • About half of these students said that they were still trying to figure out their spiritual beliefs. • About half either broadened or lost their spiritual beliefs.
In political views			8%	6%
Beliefs have been challenged or broadened			14%	13%
Learning is more valuable than grades				6%
Relationships are as important as academic or career concerns				10%

Table 3.6 (continued). *Changes in Students' Beliefs, Plans, and Sense of Themselves over Time*

Change	2000	2001	2002	2003
Plans Changes in thinking about majors, career plans, or direction.	31% • More than half of these students decided on a career, major, or direction. • About a quarter of them changed major or direction. • Close to 30% of these students said they were actively seeking a direction.	34% • About two out of five of these students decided on a career, major, or direction. • Close to one in five changed majors or direction. • About a quarter of them were still thinking about these issues.	88% • About 58% of the students who mentioned changes in their career plans, majors, or direction focused on their careers. • About 18% spoke of changes in major. • About 12% talked about planning to apply or to delay application to graduate school.	77% • About 38% talked about changes in thinking about careers. • 38% talked about decisions to pursue advanced degrees in the coming year—about half deciding to go and a third deciding not to go. • 10% focused on plans for graduating in a year or two. • 8% were deciding where to locate after college.
Sense of Self More open-minded	23%	8%	3%	
More independent	19%	6%	9%	17% For all but one of these students in the fourth year, "independence" means focusing on what makes them happy instead of just trying to please others.

Table 3.6 (continued). *Changes in Students' Beliefs, Plans, and Sense of Themselves over Time*

Change	2000	2001	2002	2003
Sense of Themselves Greater self-understanding/ self-acceptance	16%	24%	18% Mostly self-accepting	5%
Changes in self-confidence	15% About 75% more and 25% less self-confident	27% About 75% more and about 25% less self-confident	25% About 68% more and 32% less self-confident	24% 90% more and 10% less self-confident
Smarter, more knowledgeable, more accomplished	10%	9%	14%	
Greater desire to travel/study abroad		5%	7%	
More responsible, often in terms of world citizenship			7%	
More mature; wiser				10%
More committed to other people in their lives				10%
Experienced sense of loss				12% Including loss of confidence, of intelligence, of idealism, and of faith in the future

hard to see them age. They bought a condo nearby and were talking about how they were going to retire there. I could imagine myself coming to visit them there, and that was difficult—to think about them aging. I thought my mom was 39 for about 10 years. She just looked the same. Now she looks different.

In addition, several students discussed changes in how they evaluated their own educational experiences, noting that learning had become more important to them than grades. Our opening case study, Fiona O'Sullivan, serves as an example of this kind of change, and the many changes in beliefs that students discussed in interviews were also prominent in the focus groups.

Changes in Plans

More students reported changes in plans over the four years of the study than any other kind of change, as Table 3.6 shows. The steady increase in number of students who reported changes in plans is consistent with other evidence that students became more future oriented as they moved through college. Many but not all of the students who were focused on plans for their future in the first two years were transfer students. By the third year, nearly all the transfer students who were completing their educations and the freshmen entrants who had just completed their first year in their majors were concerned about some aspect of their majors or careers. That concern dissipated somewhat in the fourth year, but it is still the most frequently mentioned change of all categories. Comments from a second-year student illustrate this category:

> I like psych, but it is not a major I can find a very good job in without finding a post-graduate degree. I am kind of lost in that way. I am not sure what I want to do when I have to declare next year. I will see an adviser.

Changes in Sense of Self

As Table 3.6 shows, changes in students' sense of themselves varied the most of all the changes they discussed, and were hard to categorize across students. Furthermore, the themes that emerged seemed to fluctuate across time. Many students reported becoming more tolerant and open-minded in the first year, but that response tapered off over the next two years. This suggests that becoming open minded, a prominent change noted in research on student development (Pascarella & Terenzini, 1991) as well as in the UW SOUL focus groups, may occur primarily in students' first year in college. Changes in self-awareness and acceptance seemed to occur primarily in students' second and third years, while changes in independence and self-confidence, though felt by many students in all years of the study, appeared to fluctuate somewhat from year to year. Finally, in their fourth year at the university, many students pointed to changes in their sense of maturity and wisdom, increases in their commitment to others, and increases in their sense of loss. These changes seem consistent with that moment in the senior year when students often are looking both forward and backward, a time of "taking stock." The following students' quotations, one from the first year and one from the fourth, illustrate the range of changes in students' sense of themselves:

> *First year:* I've had to become a lot more independent. You have to do a lot more on your own, and you kind of believe in yourself more when you can take care of yourself. It makes it hard when I go home, though, because I am not used to waiting around for them when I want dinner or need to go somewhere.

> *Fourth year:* I think I have more self-confidence about me as a metals artist. I have gotten into a couple of shows, and I am going to Penland on a scholarship. I have realized that the grade doesn't matter. It's the work that matters—the things you make and how well they are made and how well you think they were done, if you were happy with the way they turned out.

What the Interview Question Told Us About Change

We can make a few general statements from our analysis of students' responses to whether their beliefs, plans, or senses of themselves changed over each of their four years in college. First, both transfer students and students who entered the university as freshmen experienced change in these areas. Second, change in one area often overlapped another. This student's comment, for example, focused on a change in "plans" for his approach to his major, but it also signaled a change in his sense of himself and perhaps even his beliefs about what his life should be about:

> Rather than focusing on one day being a great artist, I am focusing on learning how to make better art.

Third, students were concerned about working out their beliefs in college. They focused on spiritual beliefs, as well as on others. In general, they felt they became more broad-minded and open to others' ideas, even if they held onto their own beliefs, with the primary change in tolerance appearing to occur in their first year. This result—students reporting a broadening in their views—echoes focus group results about students' becoming more tolerant as they moved through college.

Another change apparent from this analysis was that students' responses became increasingly focused on plans as they moved through their time in college. We saw a similar movement in students' focus group responses. It is important to note that students were anxious to make plans right from their first days at the university, but this need to know what was ahead for them intensified over time. Some students experienced easy movement from plans to their realization. For others, planning was a bumpy road that took unanticipated turns. Some turns were satisfying. For example, one student who majored in business planned to use her background and interest in biochemistry in a business career. But her father was involved in an accident that left him comatose, and her experience with his illness and death led her to change her plans. Her comment about this change shows not only how students' plans for their lives can take new turns, but it also shows how students' plans, beliefs, and sense of themselves are connected to each other:

> I have changed my career path to medicine. And I think my sense of myself is much stronger, because I took that leap instead of doing business. I chose business because I didn't know myself well enough to want to commit to something more specific. The death of my father and being responsible for him while he was in a coma was the final trigger that helped me make this change. But it all came as part of the building process over the time I have been here. Taking business classes, doing an internship through the business department, and my dissatisfaction with those experiences, those also pushed me to do this.

Some turns were troubling, at least at first, as this student described:

> My plans have changed. I got rejected from the majority of the law schools I applied to, and that was a blow to my self-esteem. I was just angry, like "Who are you to not take me into your school?" I didn't get into the UW either, and I was especially angry at that. In retrospect, I think it has worked out for the best. It may be the best thing to go to Colorado, but no one likes rejection.

Above all, students' responses to this interview question about changes in their beliefs, plans, and sense of themselves demonstrate that the college experience changed students well beyond providing them with increased knowledge and bachelor's degrees in the areas of their majors.

Turning Points

In their fourth year at the UW, we asked the 63 students who remained in Group 1 if they had experienced anything that felt to them like a turning point in their time at the UW. About 85% of them said yes; 13% said no; and 2% of the responses were unclear. The turning points that students reported occurred at varying points in their college lives, with about 26% reporting such moments of change in their sophomore years and close to 30% of the students reporting them in their senior year—a year in which we might expect to see more stability than change.

The catalysts for change that students described were positive, negative, and neutral. No pattern emerged that would lead us to conclude that change more often followed loss than gain; rather, it appeared to follow both. Although Bok (2006), citing Light (2001), notes that defining moments in college often happen outside classes, the most frequently mentioned catalyst for change were classes, and at least four of the seven were connected with classroom learning. One of those, study abroad, was described as a turning point by nearly every student in the UW SOUL who had a study abroad experience. Clearly, study, travel, and living in a foreign country are powerful impetuses for change. The seven catalysts for change most frequently mentioned were:

- Classes (25%)

- Study/travel abroad (16%)

- Experiential learning, such as internships, undergraduate research, jobs (14%)

- Issues involving majors, such as not getting into one, getting tired of one (11%)

- Family issues, such as death in the family, parents' divorce (9%)

- Clubs and other groups affiliated with the UW (9%)

- Breaking up with a boy/girlfriend (4%)

In addition, the nature of the turning point varied from student to student, with only a few broad themes among them. First, for 19 students—or 35%— the turning point either led to, began with, or required a change in major. Students who described changing from one major to another were distributed fairly evenly across all four years of the study, with the fewest of them occurring in students' third year.

Second, most of the students identified learning as either the cause or the effect of the "turn" they had made in their lives, and the majority of those students—58%—spoke about what they had learned about themselves. Several of those students mentioned insights into their own interests and desired directions; others spoke of increased awareness of their own strength or limitations. Nearly all students turned toward something they valued, whether that was a different major, self-awareness, or a new understanding of the world. Only one student described a turning point that sent him into a downward spiral.

As might be expected, students' descriptions of the experiences that turned them in another direction revealed a great deal about the undergraduate experience, each one providing insight into the highly individualized paths students walk as they move through college. To illustrate the variety of changes students described, we have included six of their descriptions:

> *Business major:* My grandmother passed away in the winter. That schedule was so horrible for me. I was taking 18 credits, and I felt that I didn't see her as much as I should have. I didn't take my grandmother's illness as seriously as I should have. I wish I hadn't had as many classes, and I wish I would have told my group members that I had a family emergency. I was stressed, and plus I was working. I guess I didn't realize how serious it was. Or maybe I was just in doubt. I didn't want to confront it. I will remember this the rest of my life: that school is second to personal.

> *Computer science engineering major:* Chemistry 241—that was a turning point. I changed my major based on this class, I guess I learned something in here. I didn't like dealing with hazardous chemicals. I planned on majoring in biochemistry, but I switched based on this class. That changed my mental state. Up until that point, I believed I could do whatever I wanted to do—but that created a certain problem in that way of thinking. It created a little contradiction or a lapse of discipline. I wandered around aimlessly for a year.

History major: It started off with the first 200-level international studies class and then worked its way into study abroad. That international studies class made me realize that there was so much more than Seattle, that there was so much more going on in the world and I needed to try to learn about it. And then I went to Italy to study abroad. That was the same kind of learning experience, but I experienced it for myself. I grew up a bit, traveled on my own, which was scary. I feel a lot more grown up and independent.

Law, societies, and justice major. I was on the pre-med track and when I took that [sociology class on murder], I switched. I took it the second quarter I was here. When [the guest lecturer] came in and told us about his investigations on the Green River Killer and Ted Bundy—how they had to take the smallest bit of evidence and think so far outside the box to come up with suspects—it just struck me that that was something I could see myself doing as a career. It caught hold of me.

Sociology major: In the winter 2001, I found out some family information that completely shifted my whole perspective on life, and definitely I was less inclined to see my parents in the light of perfection. I saw them more as people who make mistakes, and that made me feel that maybe I could do the things I wanted to do and not worry so much about disappointing them, because they could disappoint me, too. I saw them as more human, and that impacted everything that happened after that. This gave me some freedom, but it was a bitter freedom.

Technical communication and philosophy major: I found out that there is a different door into the scientific realm; there's writing about it. And I am taught hands-on by example in the technical communication classrooms. If someone can give me an overview of the problem, I can get a grasp on it. And if I try to pursue something inventive later on, I will have the background.

Regrets

In the final UW SOUL interviews, we asked the 63 students who remained in Group 1 if they had any regrets about their experience at the UW. Close to one-third of them (32%) said they had no regrets. The majority—68%—expressed regret for something they had done or had not done. About 16% wished they had been more involved in academic and social activities, often as a means for meeting a wider variety of people. In addition, about 8% said that they wished they had started out with a different direction in mind, because they felt they had wasted time, and similarly, about 6% said that they wished they had been more academically motivated and self-disciplined about their schoolwork. All other regrets were highly individualistic.

Conclusions and Implications

In this section, we draw three conclusions from our findings and discuss their implications for assessment and for teaching and learning.

Students Enter and Exit College With Complex Ideas About Learning

We who work at the university define students' academic success as getting good grades and demonstrating in a variety of ways that they have mastered both the knowledge we are working to create and the academic skills we deem important. In contrast, undergraduates define academic success in multidimensional ways. Acquiring the disciplinary knowledge that is the province of the university is only one of them. Students want to learn about the world, about themselves, about their friends, about knitting and kayaking, about whether God exists, and which fork to use at a formal dinner party. They want to learn how to talk to people unlike themselves and what it feels like to grow up on a farm. They correctly see college as a place that offers them the chance to learn about all these things and more, and to a large extent, they measure their own academic success by how many of these aspects of learning they acquired and experienced while they were undergraduates.

Regarding teaching, colleges can and often do take advantage of students' multidimensional definitions of learning by providing them with opportunities inside the classroom to interact with peers, especially peers unlike themselves, and by asking them to work in groups. Eric Mazur's (1997) book on using peer groups in large-lecture classes, for example, offers a clear, easy-to-use process for fostering social and academic interaction in even the largest class. In addition, when colleges encourage students to participate in experiential learning opportunities connected with the classroom—service-learning, faculty research, and internship opportunities, for example—it helps students fulfill their own complex goals for learning.

Because of the complex and individualized paths students take as they move through college, assessing personal growth seems both tricky and value-laden.

We believe that it is clear from our own research, and the research of many others, that students will grow and change in positive ways as they move through college, at least in part because the culture of university life fosters the kind of exploration that Arnett (2000) says characterizes emerging adulthood. Indeed, colleges and universities foster exploration by engaging students in interactions with peers around intellectual topics, working to build a diverse student body, providing opportunities for experiential learning, and offering a wide range of affordable study-abroad experiences.

Even though evidence for college students' personal growth is abundant, we believe it is essential for institutions to know what students hope to achieve when they come to college and whether and how they believe they have achieved those goals. Further, we believe that asking students to consider and assess their own growth is essential to their learning in the ways that matter to them and to us. Such self-assessment helps them know what they know and what they do not yet know, see where they have come from, identify the significant markers along the way, and review where they hope they are headed. Self-assessment is a workplace skill, as well as a life skill, and we need to do a better job of building self-assessment opportunities—large and small—into our academic environments.

Academic Difficulty Can Be Productive, But It Does Not Always Foster Growth

In watching students' move through the hammering, we began to wonder if that experience was beneficial to students' growth. Students sometimes reported feeling grateful for the experience in hindsight. Often, though painful enough to cause students to doubt their abilities for a time, the hammering experiences seemed to recalibrate students' thinking in positive ways, calling on them to work harder, to rethink their ideas about their futures, to acknowledge that old ways of being successful in school might not be effective at the university, to figure out what it was they did not yet know, and to identify resources that might lend them a hand.

However, it is important to acknowledge that sometimes the hammering drove students out of school. Sometimes it caused them to stop advancing their learning in certain areas, such as quantitative reasoning or writing. Sometimes the hammering made them angry or cynical about the educational processes. Sometimes it washed people out of majors in which they may have made creative contributions *because* their approaches differed from those of others who conformed more easily to conventional ways of thinking in those disciplines.

Regarding teaching, faculty need to remember that students are experiencing hardship and doubt brought on by faltering or failure. This process can be generative for students, so faculty should not avoid it or soften it. Perhaps, however, faculty can help students manage its effects, stepping into its aftermath to identify it as a "natural" part of the learning process and helping students understand what it may signify for them by talking about what it signified to previous students. This step may be particularly important in 100- and 200-level courses. Of course, faculty at all academic institutions do this all the time. For example, it is a common practice for faculty to require students who received low scores on early exams or papers to meet with them in office hours, and, anticipating the hammering, many faculty members allow students to toss out one of their grades or write drafts of papers before they receive a grade.

In terms of assessment, we need to continue to track how students respond to academic failures, paying particular attention to how differing groups respond. Do women respond differently from men? Does a low grade on an exam mean something different to under-represented minority students than it does to students in the majority? How do students who are the first in their families to attend college interpret a low grade when their parents are not able to share stories about the low grades they received in college? Answers to these questions matter if we are working to identify ways to improve learning for all students.

Students Change Intellectually, Socially, and Personally While in College

Students experienced varying opportunities for personal growth within the structures of their majors, as subsequent chapters indicate. However, all of the students we studied exhibited personal growth. The teaching implications of the fact that college changes students are simply that those we instruct in our 400-level classes are different from those we taught at the 100-level. Often, the way we teach upper-level courses—allowing students greater intellectual freedom and requiring them to work independently of daily instruction—already acknowledges this reality. Our focus, then, needs to be on the earlier classes, when students are not yet acclimated to college and when they are juggling many goals. If we build opportunities for self-reflection, intellectual development, and social interaction into students' earliest learning opportunities, we will better prepare them to meet the demands ahead in their academic programs.

Endnotes

1) We did not include a control group of noncollege attendees in the study, although we would have liked to. Students' comments on challenges to and changes in their ideas, beliefs, and values appeared to be a natural consequence of the diversity found in the college environment. In contrast, it seems to us that young people who do not attend college need to seek out such diversity of thought and values. The types of challenge that students in college experienced daily without much effort may be more difficult for those not in college. Therefore, while students in and out of college may become more independent over these early adult years, we believe that the type of independence each group develops and the ease with which that occurs might differ.

2) The UW grades on a 4.0 system. Students can receive 0.0 or increments from 0.7 to 4.0. The latter is the highest grade possible.

3) Percentages here and elsewhere in this chapter may not add up to 100 because students often gave more than one response to open-ended questions.

Understanding and Appreciating Diversity

I think I realize now that you have to seek out your experiences, especially in regards to gaining anything from the diversity of students at UW. You won't learn anything just by being in proximity to diverse students. The learning comes with interaction and discoursing and attending functions, programs, or seminars related to diversity. I know that that might sound obvious, but it really requires you to be proactive about it. It would be very easy for the diversity of the students and faculty at the UW to not contribute anything to someone's learning here.

Like many postsecondary institutions across the nation, the University of Washington explicitly recognizes the importance of a diverse student body and of a curriculum reflective of the diverse society in which we live.[1] Research on diversity has shown that a diverse student population not only benefits democratic processes and historically underserved populations, but it benefits all students by improving the learning community (Appel, Cartright, Smith, & Wolf, 1996), improving students' academic and personal development (Astin, 1993b; Villalpando, 1994), and preparing students to become active members in a pluralistic society (Gurin, 1999). Diversity helps students develop their abilities to think and understand human behavior (Gurin, Dey, Hurtado, & Gurin, 2002)—goals that college students care very much about, as indicated in Chapter 3. In addition, Hurtado, Milem, Clayton-Pedersen, Walter, and Allen (2000) have shown that interaction with diverse peer groups positively affects students' decision-making abilities, lifestyle choices, and work performance in diverse environments. Hurtado et al. (2000) also point out that contact with diverse peers helps students challenge their views of the world. Additionally, strong arguments for the value of diversity arise from the nation's workplaces with predictions from many sources that by 2020 more than half of the working population will be of minority status.

The UW has benefited from the research on diversity from our own and other institutions of higher education, and we share much of the experience of other colleges and universities with regard to diversity. However, the racial composition of the UW undergraduate student body likely differs somewhat from that of colleges and universities across the country. As Table 4.1 shows, the UW includes a considerably higher proportion of Asian students than found in the national statistics. The percentage of African-Americans at UW is considerably lower than the national percentage; the percentage of Hispanics is also lower; and the percentage of Native Americans is a little higher at UW. One can also note that the national data include considerably fewer students in the Other/Unknown category. This discrepancy suggests a lack of consistency in use of this category. The data are self-reported and clearly not all institutions ask the question of students in the same manner. A study by the James Irvine Foundation (Smith, Moreno, Clayton-Pedersen, Parker, & Terguchi, 2005) found that many of the students who choose "unknown" or "other" for their ethnicity or leave the space empty are Caucasian students.

Table 4.1. *Racial Composition of American Colleges and Universities and the University of Washington[2]*

	Four-Year Public Colleges and Universities	NASULGC[3] Colleges and Universities	University of Washington
African-American	10.4%	9.8%	2.6%
American Indian/ Alaska Native	0.9%	0.8%	1.3%
Asian/Pacific Islander	6.1%	7.5%	23.2%
Hispanic	7.9%	7.3%	3.2%
White/non-Hispanic	70.4%	70.3%	56.8%
Other/Unknown	4.3%	4.3%	12.9%

In this chapter we explore what students told us in interviews, surveys, focus groups, and email responses about what diversity meant to them, what they valued, and what they learned about diversity in college. In broadest strokes, the diversity story our results tell is one of gains and losses. It begins with students arriving at the UW with high expectations for the contribution that diversity might make to their educations, moves through a time when those expectations diminish, and ends with a leveling off. We found that students tended to gain knowledge about diversity, while at the same time they became less active in seeking out diversity. To a great extent, our findings echo Tatum's (1997) description of diversity in the college experience in her illuminating book, *Why Are All the Black Kids Sitting Together in the Cafeteria?* In addition, our findings confirm the importance of structural diversity, defined by Hurtado et al. (2000) as the presence of significant numbers of students from various racial, ethnic, and gender groups on campuses. As Hurtado et al. (2000, citing Hurtado, Dey, & Trevino, 1994) note, when campuses have high percentages of Caucasian students (particularly "predominantly white institutions"—or those in which more than 50% of the students are Caucasian), there are typically few opportunities for students to interact across racial and ethnic lines; thus, students' learning experiences in and with diverse groups are also limited.

As with the other aspects of learning that we explored in the UW SOUL, the diversity story is a story of disciplines—for how much and what students said they learned about diversity was clearly influenced by their majors.

This chapter includes three main sections. First, to give the readers a view of differing diversity paths, we present case studies about academic learning and identity. Next, we move to our results, a discussion of students' gains and losses with regard to understanding and appreciating diversity. Finally, we draw conclusions and note their implications for teaching and assessment

Four Paths

We begin with four case studies. The first two focus on two Caucasian students whose learning paths primarily took them into an awareness of others' identities. The second two focus on multiracial students who are dealing with their own ethnic identities, a process which is described by Tatum (1997).

Carl Swenson and Jennifer Oswald

When they entered the university in 1999, Carl Swenson and Jennifer Oswald both assumed that they would not be deeply affected by diversity, but the origins of their assumptions appeared to differ. For Carl Swenson, this assumption was rooted in his belief that his upbringing had already taught him the value of tolerance. In contrast, it is likely that Jennifer Oswald's background, which included little exposure to diversity, caused her to have this assumption. Yet, in both cases the students experienced growth in their understanding of diversity.

Carl Swenson was a nontraditional transfer student from a local community college. In his mid-40s, Carl was certainly older than most students at the university. He arrived as a history major, and by the end of his first year, the history department had given him a scholarship for the next year. In his initial fall interview, Carl said, "I feel that [diversity] affected me a long time ago." To illustrate his point, Carl told a story about his father "taking issue" with his brother for making a negative comment about an African-American man. "His teachings were that you don't judge people by what they look like," Carl said about his father. Carl added that he, himself, lived that same philosophy, and that he felt that the diverse people or perspectives found on this campus would not, therefore, affect him.

But in that first quarter, Carl took a course on the history of women. He spoke about that class in a focus group held with UW SOUL participants during their second quarter, saying:

> One of the most enlightening and hardest courses I ever took was women's history. In high school, we never learned about women's history or African-American history, and it is amazing to learn about what has happened, and where this country is going. I want to teach history, so I can tell the truth about history—the story that was untold.

To this, a young woman—an African-American freshman—in the focus group responded: "I'd like you as my history teacher. I always hated history in high school because they always left things out, but here they really talk about all that stuff."

By the time he graduated with a double major in anthropology and history, Carl had taken classes that focused on Mexican Americans, Chinese dynasties, Javanese culture and aesthetics, and Native Americans. He had taken an ethnographic film class and linguistics. In each of these classes, Carl learned from his fellow students. In Carl's words over the years:

> I talked to a guy in the Javanese class who is Cambodian and who was there during the killing fields. I don't feel pity for him—that would be degrading after what he has gone through. But I feel a lot of sorrow for him.

> [A black guy in my poetry class] said I shouldn't be sad about a poem [by a black female poet], because the poem wasn't intended to be sad. He said it was just the normal social background of black people. I just think America should be better than that.

> In a history class I took, a Vietnamese woman said that college was fine but that she should prepare to get married. I would never say that to one of my daughters.

> I got to know a Native American reporter for the *Daily* [student newspaper]. He has a different perspective. He brings the perspective of someone who has lived on a reservation for years. I relate his perspective to my teen-aged daughter, who

thinks everything bad that America does was done years ago. I try to get her to think with his perspective. I may not agree with some of the stuff he writes, but he always makes you stop and think. If you can't question yourself, then you are not learning.

Not only did Carl learn about diversity from his classes and his fellow students, but he also observed diversity in his daily life. In his last interview, he said,

I ride the bus every day. I notice that different ethnic groups sit together on the bus. They will segregate on the bus. I sit next to anybody. I just noticed that one day when an Asian girl wouldn't sit next to me, but stood instead.

Carl felt so strongly about the importance of understanding and valuing diversity that by the time he left, he recommended that the UW require a class on the subject. However, Carl argued that such a class should not merely provide students with historical information on diversity but should connect with students at an emotional level as well. In Carl's words:

People from one side of the tracks need to realize what people from the other side have to go through to get where they are. I can't imagine growing up in an area where you are afraid to look out your front window. I think everyone should know how it feels to do that. They should teach a class that not only tells you what it is like to be a slave, but that makes you feel what it is like. There should be a mandatory class where you learn what it feels like to step off a boat in San Francisco and be forced to work in a mine where people hate you.

Carl came to the university, as nearly all the UW SOUL participants did, already valuing diversity. As he completed the undergraduate degree he had begun at a local community college, he sought out people whose experiences differed from his, learning as much as he could about the range of those experiences from people both inside and outside the U.S. In addition, he kept "testing" their experience against his own. We do not know if Carl was more tuned into white privilege as a result of this experience, but we do know that he thought about history differently when he left the UW than he had when he arrived.

Probably the keys to Carl's rich experience were that he actively sought it out and that he reflected deeply on it. Not all participants did that. Jennifer Oswald's story, for example, is different from Carl's in this regard. Jennifer came to the university at the same time that Carl did; however, she entered as a freshman straight from a private, religious high school in a nearby state. When she entered UW, she did not have a clear sense of how diversity might affect her. She said, "I'm sure it will affect me in some way—maybe broaden my views." By the end of her first year, when asked if she had any personal experiences that taught her anything about diversity, Jennifer said, "No, not really. People seem to be sort of different all around compared to home, but I can't really explain how."

An economics major, Jennifer took several courses that included content on diversity in her four years at the UW, including:

- One anthropology course that focused on race as a cultural construct

- A second anthropology course that focused on religion and culture

- A women studies course on race, gender, and law

- A speech and hearing sciences class that included a guest speaker who lectured about deaf culture

- A course in sociology that included discussion about culture and sexuality

Like most students at the UW, Jennifer liked learning about new ideas and new realities. About the anthropology course that focused on religion, Jennifer said, "It was interesting to see that there are so many different beliefs, so many different ways of worshipping." In her speech and hearing sciences class, Jennifer found a guest lecturer's talk on deaf culture interesting. She said, "I have never thought about the deaf as a culture in themselves."

Jennifer also took many economics courses that centered on supply and demand curves and the complex changes, events, and issues that affect them. She perceived a lack of diversity among students in her major, noting that there "aren't a lot of women who are econ majors," and because of that, other students "don't take you as seriously." She said that this was subtle in her courses—far more subtle than differences in gender treatment that she had experienced at work.

In her third year, when asked if her beliefs, plans, or sense of herself had changed in any way, Jennifer said that her beliefs had "changed a lot from when I first came to now, but it has kind of been gradual. I've just become more open to stuff. I've become more independent, too. Moving away from everything I knew helped me grow." And in her fourth year, as she was about to graduate, Jennifer talked further about that change, attributing it both to her one-on-one experiences with friends and roommates, as well as to her experience in college courses:

My roommates are kind of diverse. I have a roommate who is very, very liberal. He went to DC to protest the war with Iraq. I come from a family that is very conservative, and I associate with conservative people. I have had a lot of conversations with him, and it has been interesting to see a rational viewpoint from someone really intelligent with whom I disagree but whom I still respect. So it has been interesting having these discussions with him. I think the UW is pretty diverse, so I have been able to experience diversity first-hand, whereas before I was in a bubble—sort of. I guess I really didn't think too much about diversity before. Coming here has helped me to understand it more.

In their interviews, the focus of the changes that Carl and Jennifer described seemed to be in classes each took, and the classes affected change in two important ways. First, course content changed the way students thought about race, ethnicity, and gender, seen most fully in Carl's experience. Second, interactions with students within the classes offered insights into others' experiences and perspectives. Carl's description of these interactions spotlighted students of color. Jennifer's description spotlighted gender issues. Both students also mentioned being sensitized to experiences outside of class—for Carl, an Asian woman on a bus; for Jennifer, a liberal housemate.

Mickey Timmons and Shannon Wilson

Mickey Timmons and Shannon Wilson are examples of two young women whose racial identities came into focus at the university. Both Mickey and Shannon entered the UW as freshmen in 1999, and both women have one parent who is African-American and one who is Caucasian. Their journeys through college were distinctly different. One young woman's path was marked by a clear sense of direction early on and an academic focus and discipline that yielded a high GPA. The other young woman's path was marked by uncertainty about direction, an exhilarating sense of exploration, and a struggle during much of her university experience to make herself work harder in her classes while she felt pulled by her friends and the city to spend time getting to know them. Both students are self-reflective and articulate, and while each student's path was unique, both students experienced a similar challenge to their identities in their third year.

During that year, both Mickey and Shannon took several classes that taught content on diversity. Mickey's sociology courses in criminal justice and race relations focused on race in America. Shannon's courses in American ethnic studies and women studies brought up a range of issues—from those affecting Americans with mixed racial heritage to men and masculinity—"how young men supposedly become men," as Shannon put it.

Mickey's focus on her racial identity was connected with her participation in an organization called Mixed, a group for interracial, cross-cultural students. She said, "It is interesting to learn about other people who are biracial and their issues—how they deal with things and the struggle with having to fit into one category or another, and choosing not to." Mickey spoke at some length about her own experience of being biracial and of coming to terms with others' sometimes racist expectations of her, saying:

> I have been thinking about this lately. I think slowly I am coming to the realization that I am seen as black and my experiences are that of a black person, so I don't consider myself white. My roommate would tell me things like, "You are not a black person—black people are all like this . . . " To be black is to fit into this one category, according to other people, and if we are acting some other way, then we are said to be "acting white." I don't feel I have to act a certain way to be considered black. If I have interactions with people who have different backgrounds, they expect me to be a certain way—black people as well as white people. I know that I am initially seen as black, and that means people are going to come to me with certain expectations. With white people, I didn't care, but with black people—I'm afraid that they will look at me differently, as soon as they know me.

In contrast, Shannon's reflections on her own racial identity were elicited by a course she took that focused on African-American history. Shannon described that experience in an interview as a process in which she reconsidered the professor's comments about African-American identity in the light of her own experience, trying to identify what she found to be "important." As she described:

> What happened in that class, where my identity as a half-white, half-black person was challenged—I'm trying to understand if all the things [the professor] told us were important. He talked a lot about trying to get in touch with our African-American heritage. I'm trying to think about whether I've been neglected in that by my dad. Or is it enough to have had a strong, competent parent who has always been there for me and who happens to be white? In that class, it was very appar-

ent that to be black was something to be very proud of. I felt kind of weird in there, like I'm not sticking to my roots, like I've been missing out on something.

At the same time that Mickey and Shannon experienced challenges to their thinking about their racial identities, they also experienced other challenges to their identities from friends and family. For example, Mickey told us:

> My roommates confronted me—that I am an emotional robot. I think I didn't think they cared so much. I have the idea that people are interested in themselves, so I don't know how much they care about me. Now, I am being more open about myself and my experiences.

And Shannon said that she and her friends had:

> gone through some ups and downs. My best friend—we used to be really close—she has a different idea of what it is to be a friend than I do, and that makes us butt heads a lot. This is about mindsets.

These comments and others remind us that students' identities are being shaped and reshaped in large and small ways as they move through their time in college. Further, they suggest that questions about all aspects of students' identities are being raised at the same moment. However, students of color are often exploring a layer of questions that Caucasian students usually do not explore. At the same time that they are dealing with identity questions around class, gender, sexual orientation, and their roles as sons, daughters, siblings, lovers, and friends, students of color are also coming to terms with their racial and ethnic identities. Caucasian students are usually not exploring their identities as Caucasians (Tatum, 1997).

In their senior year, both Mickey and Shannon spoke about whether their perceptions about diversity had changed during their time in college. Changes in Mickey's perceptions seemed to place her in Cross's (1991) fourth or fifth stage of racial identity development—internalization and commitment, characterized by a sense of security about her own racial identity and a commitment to the identity needs of others like herself. Mickey's comment in her last interview illustrates this stage:

> I'm a lot more open. I have a different concept of the amount of diversity in the African-American population. I used to

think that I wasn't black enough or that I wasn't acting black enough. I realize now that I don't have to try to do things to be black enough. We can do a wide range of things and be black. I don't think that anything is not allowed for me because I am African-American. I realize now that there are no black or white things that people are supposed to do, and it's a stereotype to try to fit people into those roles. I told [a little boy in a program I was working for, who said he was not going to do something because it was for white people,] to imagine all the things he could do and that there weren't any white-people/black-people things to do.

In contrast to Mickey, Shannon felt that her perceptions of diversity had not changed much in her four years in college. When asked if her perspective on diversity had changed, Shannon said:

I've learned just that people are interesting. They never cease to amaze me. I would say that I am just learning more and more about other cultures and other kinds of people, but nothing that I wasn't open to before. So I haven't changed much.

Interestingly, while all four students—Carl Swenson, Jennifer Oswald, Mickey Timmons, and Shannon Wilson—experienced changes in their relationships to diversity, their experiences were likely hidden from each other. This is not only true of interaction between groups—Caucasians and multiracial students in this case—but it is also often true of interaction within groups. Mickey and Shannon may have known each other and shared their experiences through campus organizations such as Mixed or at the university's award-winning Instructional Center, which primarily serves underrepresented students, but their majors took them in different directions, as did their living circumstances. Because of differences in their ages, personalities, living situations, and majors, it would be unlikely for Carl and Jennifer to come into contact with one another. Even if they did, it would be even more unlikely that they would engage in a conversation about what they were learning about diversity. However, a meeting between Carl and Shannon—say, on a bus or in a focus group— might result in such a conversation. That possibility is not only wonderful to imagine but something that the UW and other institutions like ours might strive to produce.

Diversity Gains and Losses

This section provides results from the questions we asked students about diversity. These results broaden the perspective gained from the particular stories captured in our four case studies. As stated earlier, our results tell a story of academic gains at the same time students were feeling less confident that diversity could contribute to their learning. Furthermore, our results illuminate some of the difficulties in bringing diverse populations together at academic institutions. This section includes the following subsections:

- Definitions of diversity

- High expectations

- Changes in expectations

- Students' explanations for changes in expectations

- Changes in knowledge: diversity in course content

- Changes in students' attitudes and behavior

- Changes in perceptions over four years

Definitions of Diversity

Before we discuss specific results, it is important to note that although we asked students questions on diversity repeatedly throughout the four years, we rarely defined the term for them.[4] In one place on the diversity surveys, we told students that diversity was "defined as including people of different genders, races, nationalities, sexual orientations, ideas, and backgrounds." However, in interviews, when students asked for our definitions, we responded, "We mean whatever *you* mean by that word."

In letting the students' own definitions of diversity guide their responses, we hoped to learn what students included in the term. Changes over time in students' responses to questions about diversity appeared to reflect, at least in part, changes in how students defined diversity. Entering students, particularly the freshmen, tended to see even the smallest differences among themselves as constituting "diversity." A student might talk, for example, about discovering how "different" a roommate was because she had been raised a Roman Catholic, while the speaker had been raised with no religious background. Students noted differences between themselves and students from larger and smaller cities, with fewer or more siblings, from different city high schools, and with differing hobbies or interests. In speaking about diversity in their high schools, for example, students sometimes reported that their high school populations were diverse because they included "skaters," "jocks," and "preppies"—a definition of diversity based largely on people's clothes and where they tended to hang out between classes. Students were excited to explore those small gradations of differences. The attention and interest students gave to small differences among themselves was also reported in Richard Light's (2000) research on Harvard University students.

As the study progressed, students' definitions of diversity appeared to focus on two main categories: a "people" category and an "intellectual" category. The "people box" was social and usually included humans from different races, differing ethnic and experiential backgrounds, differing sexual orientations, and, for women, differing genders. The "intellectual box" included tolerance and respect for perspectives different from one's own, open-mindedness and willingness to change, and international and global perspectives, as well as historical and anthropological knowledge of the ways differing cultures might shape beliefs, values, and practices. Often it seemed as though these two boxes existed separately from each other, with students, for example, aware, sometimes passionately, of the effects of NAFTA on Mexico or the benefits of bilingual education, but unaware of the actual life experience of a single flesh-and-blood Latino student.

While we learned a great deal about how students thought about diversity, and specifically, about the ways in which their definitions of diversity differed from our own in academia, we also acknowledge that in not controlling the definition of diversity we missed gathering other kinds of information. We did not learn, for example, how students thought about power relationships in society. We learned little about racism on our campus, and we learned almost nothing about students' attitudes about sexual orientation. While it would be useful to know in greater depth how students think and what they know about diversity from the standpoint of race, class, gender, and sexual orientation, we felt that we could not understand how and what students thought they were learning about diversity and probe in those specific directions at the same time. Therefore, our results tell us a broad story, reflecting a range of ideas about what it means to be "diverse."

High Expectations

Students generally entered the university with the expectation that the diversity of the campus would be an important component of their education. We can see this from their responses to questions in the first interviews, conducted in fall 1999. We asked students how, if in any way, they expected the diversity at the university to affect their learning. About 62% said that they expected the diversity to have a positive effect on learning. Most of those students said that they felt that diversity would broaden their understanding and awareness of other people and other views. About 36% said that they expected diversity to have little or no impact on them. Like Carl Swenson, almost all of this group of students explained that they had already experienced a great deal of diversity in their high schools, community colleges, or through life experiences, and their attitudes were nearly all positive. For example:

> [Diversity] doesn't affect me at all. Before moving here, I traveled and worked overseas, in Asia and Africa. I have met people from different cultures, nationalities, traditions, and the more I talk to them the more I learn from them. I have a very broad-minded, a very open-minded approach to this.

Finally, a few students did not respond directly to the question, and only one student said he thought that diversity would have a negative effect on his learning. Therefore, as they entered the university, the majority of transfer students and freshmen in the UW SOUL believed that the diversity they would encounter would contribute in a positive way to their learning.

We administered a diversity survey three times in the four years of the study—at the beginning of the first year, the end of the second year, and the end of the fourth year. On the survey, students were asked to rate[5] how much they expected the diversity of students and faculty to contribute to their educations and how much they valued the contribution of diversity to their learning.

Students' survey responses for the first quarter were relatively consistant. On average, students rated the potential contribution of diversity to their learning as 3.07 out of 4. The average value they placed on that contribution was higher—3.21 out of 4.0. The differences between men and women were statistically significant, with the latter showing higher averages. Differences among ethnic groups and between students admitted as transfers and freshmen were not statistically significant.

Changes in Expectations

We asked students the same two questions in their second year and again at the end of their fourth year surveys. For a number of reasons, one might hope that students' sense of how much diversity might contribute to their learning, as well as their belief in the value of that contribution, would increase during their college experience. However, we found just the opposite—a statistically significant drop in average for both items.

Figure 4.1 shows the change in responses to both items. Students' average sense of diversity's contribution decreased between their first and second years (from 3.07 to 2.74), and increased negligibly between their second and fourth years (from 2.74 to 2.76). Similarly, students' average rating for the value of diversity to their learning dropped from 3.21 in their first year to 2.91 at the end of their second year. By the end of their fourth year at the UW, their average rating of the value of diversity had risen slightly to 2.99.[6] This decrease in the mean rating from the first to the sixth quarter was statistically significant[7] across all subgroups of students, except for Asian students. Asian student averages decreased, but not significantly.

Figure 4.1. Average Ratings on Each Diversity Survey for the Expectations of the Contribution of Diversity to Learning and the Value of the Contribution

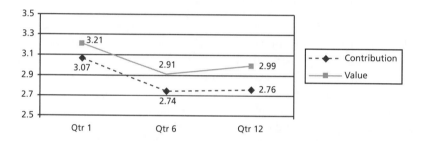

Viewing data from the 225 students who completed both of the first two surveys, we found that, regarding the first item—"How much do you expect the diversity of students and faculty at the UW to contribute to your learning?"— 34.5% of the students decreased their rating from the first to the sixth quarter; 49.8% stayed the same; and 15.7% increased their rating (Figure 4.2). For the item asking how much students valued the contribution of diversity to their learning, 34.5% of the students decreased their ratings; 51.6% stayed the same; and13.9% increased their ratings. From the second to the fourth year, the number of students who increased their ratings was essentially equivalent to the number who decreased their rating for both items.[8] Therefore, neither students' expectations for how much diversity could contribute to their learning nor the value they ascribed to that contribution returned to entry level expectations.

Figure 4.2. Percentage of Students Who Decreased, Increased, or Did Not Change Ratings From the First Quarter to the Sixth Quarter

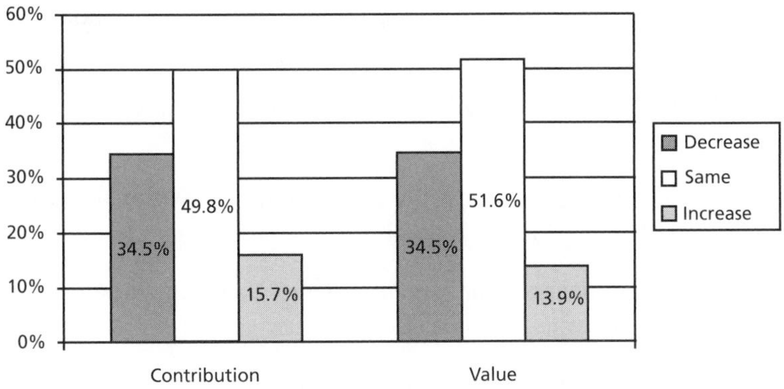

Students' Explanations for Changes in Expectations

We understood the role that structural diversity might play in these changes. Still, the decreases in students' sense of the contribution and value that diversity made to their learning puzzled and intrigued us. We decided to conduct a member check to ask students to help explain these changes. We sent an email question to UW SOUL participants in fall quarter, 2002, explaining the survey results and asking them to talk about what had happened to their own individual expectations and values around diversity. We sent the question to the 145 students who had not graduated or left the study (about 65% of the sample who had responded to both surveys). The drawback to this approach was that we were asking students to comment on results of two surveys that they had completed more than a year before. Students may have forgotten what they were experiencing at the time they answered the surveys.

Students' responses to this email question did not reveal negative attitudes toward diversity, nor did they identify ways that underrepresented students at the UW may be experiencing the kinds of pressures that Allen (1992) described as common in predominantly white universities and colleges (although both racism and such pressures likely exist). Instead, students' responses, which we summarize next, confirmed yet also raised questions about our survey findings, providing information about how and why diverse groups do and do not interact on campus.

Diversity's Contribution to Learning

In terms of whether/how their expectations for the contribution of diversity to their education had changed, students' email responses were as follows:

- 33% of the respondents expected *less* from diversity's contribution than they had previously expected.

- 32% said that they expected the *same* level of contribution from diversity.

- 15% said they expected diversity to contribute *more* to their learning than they had previously expected.

- 11% of the students did not specify whether their expectations had increased, decreased, or stayed the same.

- 9% said either that they could not remember what they expected as first-year students or that they had entered the UW with no expectations.

With the exception of the last two categories, these results roughly matched those of the surveys. Under both data collection methods, the percentage of those showing or describing a decrease was more than double those showing or describing an increase. In their explanations for why they now expected diversity to contribute less to their learning than they had when they arrived, students gave responses that fell into four major categories: the role of classes and majors, the level of diversity at the UW, self-segregation at the UW, and a shift in students' attention from social to academic learning after their first year.

Classes and majors. About 40% of those whose expectations had decreased said that their classes and majors limited the contribution that diversity could make to their learning. These students spoke of class size, content, and context as imposing limitations on their interactions with students who were different from themselves and on their learning about diversity. The following student's quotation illustrates this group of responses:

> I think people may reap greater benefits from diversity in classes that are more interactive, such as the social sciences, and in classes where opinion is valued. Since I am taking predominantly quantitative classes, where interaction among students is more academic than social, diversity does not play such a large role. There is, for the most part, one way to solve math problems, and it doesn't really matter that the person sit-

ting next to you is from a different background or has different circumstances than yours.

That students' sense that their classes and majors influenced how much they
learned about diversity was not surprising, because we were already learning
about the powerful connections between the shape of undergraduate learning
and students' majors. In their analysis of campus climate, Hurtado et al. (2000)
found that when faculty integrate issues about race and ethnicity into their
courses and use teaching strategies that include collaboration and group projects, they foster understanding about racial and ethnic diversity. While not surprising, UW SOUL students' email responses prompted us to go back to our
survey results and look at whether the disciplinary categories of students' majors
were related to survey responses. We classified majors into six broad categories:
the arts, business, engineering, the humanities, science/math, and social sciences.

Table 4.2 shows the averages within these six disciplinary categories across
students who took all three surveys for the item that asked how much students
valued the contribution of diversity to their learning. The results were similar.[9]
Because the sample of students we were able to track over all three surveys had
largely entered as freshmen, nearly all of those students completed the first survey before they had declared a major.[10] However, we see a statistically significant
difference by the category of students' eventual majors in the results of the first
survey, accounting for 19.3% of the variance.

Those disciplinary categories in which students' *eventually* chose a major
were significantly related to students' responses to questions about the contribution of diversity to their learning. This relationship of the disciplinary areas
in which students eventually majored to their attitudes about diversity's contribution to their learning in the first year was so strong that we wondered if we
could predict the former from the latter. The relationship certainly suggests that
students came to the university with attitudes about diversity already in place.

In tracking the relationship between area of major and attitudes toward
diversity, we noted that it weakened with the second survey, with differences
across disciplinary categories being noted but failing to reach statistical significance. Furthermore, students in all disciplinary categories except the humanities
mirrored the overall pattern of a decrease from the first survey to the second survey. More divergence was clear in the third survey, where the differences in students' opinions across disciplinary categories again reached significance and
accounted for 12.2% of the variance.

Table 4.2. *Average Ratings for "How Much Do You Value the Contribution of Diversity?" by Survey Year and Major Area*

Major Area	N[11]		First Survey	Second Survey	Third Survey
Arts	6	Mean	3.50	3.33	3.00
		St. Dev.	0.84	0.82	0.63
Business	9	Mean	3.22	2.89	3.56
		St. Dev.	0.83	1.05	0.73
Engineering	17	Mean	2.47	2.41	2.59
		St. Dev.	1.01	1.06	1.00
Humanities	8	Mean	2.75	3.00	3.13
		St. Dev.	0.89	0.93	0.83
Science/Math	23	Mean	3.13	2.91	2.61
		St. Dev.	0.81	1.02	0.99
Social Science	38	Mean	3.50	3.03	3.21
		St. Dev.	0.65	0.97	0.91
Total	101	Mean	3.16	2.90	2.98
		St. Dev.	0.87	1.00	0.95
F Value[12]			4.54	1.18	2.63
Significance			0.001	ns	0.05
Eta Squared[13]			19.3%	5.9%	12.2%

The small number of students in some of the disciplinary categories made it impossible to draw strong conclusions about disciplinary differences over the three surveys. However, the three areas with the largest numbers (social science, science/math, and engineering) show three very different patterns, as seen in Figure 4.3. As the figure shows, when they entered the university, future engineering majors believed that the value of the contribution of diversity to their learning would be relatively low, and that belief remained fairly constant across the four years. In contrast, the students who would eventually major in the social sciences believed that the value of the contribution of diversity to their learning would be high when they entered the university. Their beliefs dipped and then increased again—though not to their original level—over the three surveys. Students who would eventually major in the sciences or math initially believed that the value of the contribution of diversity to their learning would

Figure 4.3. *Average Ratings for "How Much Do You Value the Contribution of Diversity?" by Survey Year and Three Major Areas*

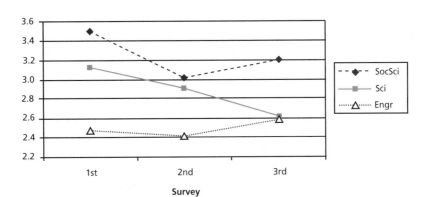

be fairly high, but their belief in that contribution steadily decreased until the third survey, where their average was essentially equivalent to that of the engineering majors.

These patterns suggest two things about the relationship between majors and the value students in those majors place on diversity. First, one's interest in and attitude about diversity as an area of study may influence students' choice of a major. Second, after a student chooses a particular major, the curriculum of that major affects one's attitude about the value of diversity's contribution to learning. As shown in Table 4.2, the averages of humanities majors, where aspects of diversity are regularly studied, began considerably below those of social science majors but rose steadily to near equivalence. In contrast, the averages of science/math majors, where aspects of diversity may be a less pronounced part of the curriculum,[14] steadily dropped to that of engineering majors. More research that focuses on larger numbers of students in specific major fields is needed to understand these results.

Less diversity at the UW than expected. Another theme in students' email explanations for survey results focused on the level of diversity at the UW; 27% of the respondents said that the UW was not as diverse as they had expected it to be. They indicated that the lack of diversity caused them to lower their previous expectations for how much diversity might contribute to their learning, as this student's response suggests:

> I don't think diversity has played a key role for me because I think our school lacks it. So I don't expect a lot of diversity in my classes. When it happens, it is always a good experience.

This category of students' email explanations was supported by students' survey responses to questions about the level of diversity in their environments. In their first-year at the UW, we asked students to indicate on the diversity survey how diverse five of their "environments" were, with diversity broadly defined as including "people of different genders, races, nationalities, sexual orientations, ideas, and backgrounds."[15] As Figure 4.4 shows, in their first year at the UW, most students, regardless of ethnic background, perceived the neighborhoods where they grew up as only a little diverse, and the UW student body as moderately to very diverse. As the figure clearly shows, when students entered the UW, they regarded the student body as the most diverse population that they had been a part of, with the exception of underrepresented minority students, who identified their group of friends as slightly more diverse than the student body.

There were interesting statistically significant differences in perceptions among the ethnic groups for four of the five items ($P < 0.05$). As Figure 4.4 shows, Caucasians perceived the campus as being the most diverse, followed by Asian and underrepresented minority (URM) students. Caucasians also reported coming from the least diverse neighborhoods of the three groups and having the least diverse circle of close friends and friends with whom they studied. Pairing these results, we speculate that because Caucasian students experienced less diversity prior to coming to the university, their "adaptation level," that is, what they were used to seeing, may have been lower than what they saw when they arrived, and thus the enhanced level of diversity may have seemed more significant to them.

In regard to students' close circles of friends and the students with whom they studied, relative numbers in the population may explain Caucasians' experience of less diversity than Asian and underrepresented minority students. Students of color—because they are in the minority—*have* to study, live, and spend time with members of other ethnic groups, while Caucasian students do not. Where the UW experience would seem to be the most similar—that is, in the classes taken by first year students—we found no significant differences in perceptions.

We also noted the discrepancy between perceptions of the diversity in the general student body and of the diversity in their classrooms, across all students. This gap gave us the first hint that students in their first year at the university may have perceived the university student population as more diverse than it actually was.

We asked students the same question about the level of diversity in their environments on each of the diversity surveys. Figure 4.5 displays the results comparing the three surveys. From their first quarter until the end of their

Figure 4.4. *How Diverse Are the Following?—By Ethnicity*

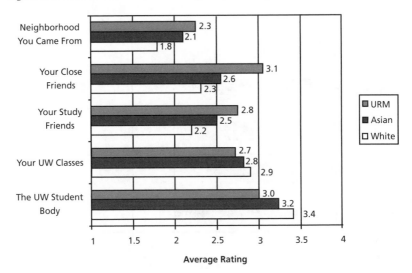

fourth year, students as a whole perceived no change in the diversity of the neighborhood in which they grew up. Since for most students there was, indeed, no change, this result is validating. Students also saw essentially no change in the diversity of their close friends. This result was quite illuminating, and anticipated students' comments, discussed later, that they stuck with the friends they first made at the university, friends who tended to be more like them than different from them. Over the course of the four years, students also perceived a statistically significant reduction in the diversity of the students with whom they studied. There was an even larger decrease in their sense of the level of diversity in the student body as a whole.[16] However, the composition of the student body changed little over the four years of the study.

The data from the survey questions on students' perceptions of the diversity in a variety of environments suggest two conclusions that are consistent with both of the two most prevalent email responses discussed above. First, students' classes and majors controlled the contribution of diversity to students' learning. As students moved through their undergraduate experience, even though they may have valued diversity, they experienced varying degrees of diversity—both in the content of their courses and in the demographics of the classroom. Second, the university was less diverse than students had initially thought, and over time as they became aware of this, students ratcheted their expectations down.

Figure 4.5. *How Diverse Are the Following?—Over Time*

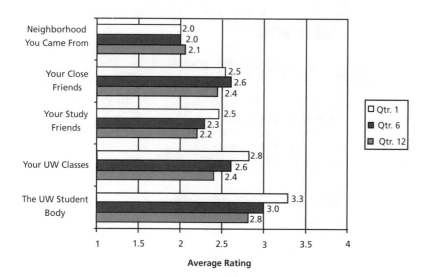

Average Rating

Self-segregation. In their email responses, students gave other reasons for why their expectations and values around diversity had changed. About 17% of participants' email responses said that the student body segregated itself along racial and ethnic lines, and, therefore, the contribution that diversity might make to learning was limited. The following responses from two students illustrate this perspective:

> I had assumed when I came here that simply having diversity of students meant interaction with those students, which I have found is hardly the case. It seems that the few African-American students on campus always seem to find each other and hang out exclusively; the Asian students have many exclusive clubs, fraternities, functions, etc; and the white kids are exclusive as always. It's sad to see that on such a big campus, people are only interacting for the 50 minutes they are forced to be together in class.

> Segregation, for instance. I've noticed that we segregate ourselves. The student body—the Asian community pretty much sticks together, the Abercrombie and Fitch team pretty much sticks together.

In addition to appearing in students' responses to our member check, the issue of self-segregation also came up in interviews, focus groups, and responses to other email questions. Occasionally, Asian and underrepresented minority students would talk about why they wanted to socialize with others like themselves, and their comments raised the question of whether Caucasian students came to college with differing "diversity needs" than those of Asian or underrepresented minority students. As their entry interviews indicated, most of the Caucasian students came to the university hungry for more diversity. They wanted to experience every gradation of difference, including the differences that race and ethnicity may make in other students' life experiences. In this desire, then, students of color become the "diversity education" for Caucasians. At the same time, survey results we discuss later in this chapter showed that Caucasian students were hesitant about seeking out friendships with students of color.

In contrast to the desire of Caucasian students to have contact with students unlike themselves, many of the students of color in the UW SOUL said that they felt fortunate to be at a place where they could meet and interact with a greater number of students like themselves than they had experienced in high school. A Cambodian immigrant, for example, suddenly found himself part of a large cohort of students who spoke his native language and whose experience of walking in two worlds—the world of his peers and the world of his parents—mirrored his own. An African-American student found a larger body of African-American students engaged in organizations interested, as she was, in social change. For these students, the number of other college students who were "like me" meant that they could explore a part of their identities that might not have been open to them in high school. Self-segregation, then, is likely the result of the differing identity needs of Caucasian, Asian, and underrepresented students, as Tatum (1997) and Cross (1991) have asserted, and a necessary step in the identity development of all students of color. In addition, self-segregation may be even more important for students of color in predominantly white institutions.

Whatever purposes self-segregation serves, it is obvious from students' responses to this email question, as well as to other questions, that reasons for self-segregation are not apparent to students. Also, it is clear that such segregation was a fact of students' social life at the UW, and we know that this is not unique to our institution (Rimer, 2002). This social reality, coupled with the learning benefits that diversity confers on all students (Hurtado et al., 2000), make what is done in the classroom doubly important.

Shift in attention. About 8% of the students in our study said that diversity, which was very important in the first year, became less important in the second and third years, because their attention over time became focused on academic success and direction. Furthermore, they said that after the first year, their social attention was narrowed to the communities they formed early in their college experience. The following student's comment illustrates this group of responses:

> Diversity was at first a great contributor because you could meet people from all walks of life and all areas and in that, still find a common ground. But later—sophomore, junior year— you tend to find yourself looking amongst the thousands of students for those more similar. I made good friends in my sophomore year and kept to them only. I found a major I was interested in, communicated with those profs or TAs that I would need to further my interest only. It's human habit to stick with what's comfortable.

These four reasons for the decrease in students' expectations of what diversity might contribute to their educations were essentially the same for males and females, students who entered as freshmen and transfer students, and Caucasian and underrepresented minority students. For Asian students, self-segregation and the change in focus from first to second year were more important reasons for the change in diversity expectations than were their classes or majors.

The Value of Diversity's Contribution to Education

In their email answers to our member check, students tended to respond more briefly, if at all, to the second question, which asked about changes in how much students *valued* the contribution diversity made to their learning. While their responses to the question about how much diversity might contribute to their learning validated and clarified survey results, students' responses to the question about the value of that contribution challenged survey results.

Across all respondents, 46% said that they valued diversity in the same way they had when they entered the UW, with nearly three-fourths of that group (73%) saying that they placed high value on diversity's contribution to their learning when they entered the UW, and that they still highly valued that contribution. Two students' responses illustrate this:

> The value of diversity on campus and in the classroom is huge, as it promotes better understanding of different peoples as well as facilitates more profound debate on the issues we are studying.

> I value the diverse student body and teaching staff very much. It's very comforting being a minority and seeing others who

> look like me. The diversity has also allowed me to get to know
> people who look nothing like me, as well.

In addition, 24% said that they valued the contribution diversity made to their learning more than they had when they entered the UW. About 21% of the students' responses did not clearly address the question or were missing, and 6% of the students merely asserted that they valued diversity's contribution to their learning. Only 3% said that they valued diversity's contribution to their learning less than they had when they entered the university.

While there were a few negative responses, the email responses about the value of diversity were generally more positive than the corresponding survey results. Three explanations for this difference present themselves. First, one might argue that because the two items (diversity's contribution to learning and its value) were similar and were located next to each other in the surveys, students tended to respond to them in the same way automatically. According to this argument, by requiring a written response, the email questions may have engendered a more differentiated result.

A second argument is also reasonable. According to this argument, students may have felt more anonymous when answering survey questions than they felt when sending an email response. If so, that sense of anonymity afforded by the surveys may have allowed students to express what they really felt, rather than something they believed they ought to feel.

A third explanation reverses the previous one, arguing for the validity of the email responses. This argument would assert that in open-ended responses, students take more time to think, are able to use their own words, and can provide clarifying examples to flesh out their ideas. Furthermore, this argument would point out that the email member check came late in the life of the study, and students had long been comfortable with the question askers, having already revealed a great deal about their personal opinions and lives, including volunteering information about their sexual orientations, their parents' marital problems, and their own fears.

Unfortunately, the arguments for the validity of one type of data over the other are all reasonable and grounded in methodological theory. We have no way of knowing which set of responses reflects the true value students place on diversity's contribution to their learning.

Changes in Knowledge: Diversity in Course Content

While students seemed to feel that the contribution diversity made to their learning decreased in their first two years at the UW, they also reported that they were learning about diversity in a wide range of classes during this time. With early and ongoing help of the Center for Curriculum Transformation (see http://depts.washington.edu/ctcenter/), many courses at the UW have integrated appropriate content on diversity into their curricula over the past 10 years. Students' responses to questions about what they had learned in their courses about diversity, both in interviews and surveys in the four years of the UW SOUL, demonstrated that the undergraduate curriculum is providing students with opportunities for learning about diversity.

Interviews

We asked UW SOUL participants in interviews each year whether their courses had deliberately integrated course content about diversity into their content. For each year of the study, more than 75% of the UW SOUL interviewees reported taking at least one course that intentionally taught them something about diversity. Over the four years of the study, the number of classes that integrated information relating to diversity increased from 1.4 to 2.0, per year, on average, for all students. In addition, between 36 and 44 departments were mentioned each year by students as offering courses with content on diversity. The departments mentioned most frequently over all four years were American ethnic studies, English, communication, psychology, women studies, international studies, history, and Spanish; however, nearly all social science disciplines were included in students' responses over time. Art, physics, and engineering majors reported experiencing less intentional content on diversity than did students in other majors.

Analysis of students' interview responses in their first year showed that students were primarily learning about cultural diversity (25%), inequality (20%), ethnic diversity and history (17%), and race and racism (14%) in their courses. Smaller numbers of students also mentioned learning about diverse perspectives, gaining understanding about differences in backgrounds and sexual orientations, and learning about biological diversity.

Surveys

As they had in the interviews, students in every major disciplinary area reported learning some content on diversity, and in some cases quite a bit of content, in their responses on the three diversity surveys and on the quarterly surveys. Survey results also confirmed differences in content and emphasis on diversity across majors, both in terms of the number of courses taken and the content learned. Regarding the number of courses that included content on ethnic groups different from one's own—a particular kind of diversity—the quarterly surveys results showed statistically significant variation by disciplinary category. For example, the typical humanities major took 15 courses over the four years at the university in which he "learned something about an ethnic group different from my own," whereas the typical engineering student took 4.5 courses in which she learned about ethnic groups that differed from her own. Both survey and interview results confirmed students' email responses about the role of classes and majors in the extent to which diversity contributed to their educations, discussed earlier in this chapter.

Gains in knowledge about diversity were addressed directly in questions on the diversity surveys and on the quarterly academic surveys. Table 4.3 shows questions asked on both kinds of surveys about gains in knowledge, and students' average responses over two years of diversity surveys[17] and for all quarterly surveys.[18] Also presented in this table are the results of one-way analyses of variance for each item, using area of major as the independent variable.

As Table 4.3 shows, across all areas of major, students on average felt they had learned the most about "working effectively with teams of people different from yourself" (2.98), followed by "listening to points of view that challenge your values" (2.93), and "identifying stereotypes, prejudices, and discrimination against others in oneself and in others" (2.86). The lowest rated item was "understanding and appreciating diverse philosophies, people, and cultures" (2.49). However, the mean for this item was not directly comparable to the others, because students were asked to rate their learning *each* quarter, not cumulatively for their entire time at UW. If the question were asked in the same way as the others, we would expect it to have a much higher average.

Table 4.3 shows that we found significant differences in the means among disciplinary categories for all items except one, which almost reached significance. Differences among the averages of the seven items also reached significance. If we assume that our seven items covered the universe of learning about diversity, which they certainly did not, then we would conclude that students broke into two groups with regard to how much they say they learned about diversity. The first group, which learned more about diversity, were students majoring in the humanities, business, the arts, and social sciences. The second group, which learned less than the first, were those majoring in engineering and the sciences.

The statistical analysis revealed a significant interaction between major and each item, indicating that what students perceived they learned about diversity depended upon their major area. For example, the table shows that for "working effectively with teams of people different from yourself," business, art, and engineering majors reported learning more than did students who majored in the humanities, social sciences, or science. In contrast, results for "understanding

Table 4.3. Results for Survey Items Relating to Student Learning About Diversity[19]

Item	N	Art 11	Bus 18	Engin 31	Hum 18	Sci 45	SocSc 83	Total[20] 238	F-Value	Signf. Level	Eta Sqrd
Listening to points of view that challenge your values	Mean	3.55	3.06	2.71	3.17	2.80	2.97	2.93	2.88	0.025	6.7%
	Std. Dev.	0.47	0.59	0.68	0.64	0.88	0.74	0.60			
Analyzing decisions and strategies for their impact on different groups	Mean	2.95	3.00	2.58	2.92	2.48	2.92	2.71	3.02	0.01	7.1%
	Std. Dev.	0.79	0.71	0.70	0.62	0.86	0.73	0.62			
Working effectively with teams of people different from yourself	Mean	3.27	3.42	3.02	2.75	2.81	2.75	2.98	2.82	0.025	6.6%
	Std Dev.	0.72	0.65	0.70	0.84	0.81	0.88	0.66			
Understanding the histories and experiences of other cultural groups (such as people with different racial/ethnic backgrounds, sexual orientations, and genders from your own)	Mean	2.73	3.00	2.16	3.14	2.59	2.99	2.77	5.92	0.0001	12.9%
	Std. Dev.	0.90	0.80	0.79	0.72	0.85	0.85	0.66			
Communicating effectively with people from other cultural groups	Mean	3.00	2.97	2.32	2.65	2.67	2.69	2.56	2.20	ns	5.2%
	Std. Dev.	0.77	0.67	0.78	0.84	0.77	0.79	0.61			
Identifying stereotypes, prejudices, and discrimination against others in oneself and in others	Mean	3.09	3.00	2.48	3.00	2.62	3.05	2.86	3.73	0.005	8.5%
	Std. Dev.	0.77	0.75	0.84	0.75	0.69	0.82	0.67			
How much did you learn this quarter about understanding and appreciating diverse philosophies, people, and cultures? (quarterly survey)	Mean	2.94	2.48	1.77	2.86	2.15	2.71	2.49	14.03	0.0001	26%
	Std. Dev.	0.65	0.56	0.47	0.66	0.64	0.71	0.74			
Total	*Mean*	*2.87*	*2.87*	*2.57*	*2.89*	*2.61*	*2.82*	*2.76*	*2.50*	*0.025*	*7.7%*
	Std. Dev.	*0.38*	*0.41*	*0.43*	*0.42*	*0.49*	*0.44*	*0.46*			

the histories and experiences of other cultural groups (such as people with different racial/ethnic backgrounds, sexual orientations, and genders from your own)" were considerably lower on average for engineering students than for students in any other major area, and the average for science/math students was the second lowest. These results, along with the statistically significant disciplinary differences among the remaining items, appeared to be a direct result of the curricula in these areas.

It is important to remember that our questions could not pick up subtle relationships that occurred in students' classrooms. For example, it is possible, and even likely, that students who worked in teams with diverse others in science and engineering courses were, in fact, learning about cultures, communication styles, experiences, and discriminatory practices that differed from their own experiences. However, sometimes when students are not asked to articulate learning, they are not fully aware of it. One would assume that effective team interaction with diverse others would depend on such learning, but we did not trace those connections. Similarly, the actual majors within these broader disciplinary categories probably vary quite a bit—for example, with students in some business and science concentrations learning a great deal about diverse others and students in other concentrations learning less. We were able to pick up only very coarse differences across these disciplinary areas.

As in their responses to questions on the diversity surveys, students' responses to how much they had learned about "understanding and appreciating diverse philosophies, people, and cultures" on the quarterly surveys showed large differences among the means for the various major areas, accounting for 26% of the total variance as indicated by the associated eta squared value (see Table 4.3). To illustrate these differences in a way that might be more meaningful than respective means, we divided the students within each disciplinary area into three categories based on their average rating for this item: those whose average was 2.0 or below (the scale point labeled "a little"), those whose average was 3.0 or above (the scale point labeled "a moderate amount"), and those who fell in between. Note that an average of 3.0 or above indicates that the student felt he learned an average of a moderate amount or more each quarter, not cumulatively over the four years of college. Thus, it is a rather high standard. These percentages for all students and within areas of major are presented in Figure 4.6. As the figure shows, there is a great deal of variability across all students, with about 40% percent in the middle category and about 30% in the upper and lower categories. Much of that variability comes from differences among areas of majors. No student majoring in the arts averaged 2.0 or lower in how much she had learned about understanding and appreciating diversity, but 58.1% of the engineering majors did. Other than the arts, all major areas had some students whose average rating fell at 2.0 or below. All major areas included students who felt they had learned a moderate amount or more about understanding and appreciating diversity, on average, each quarter. In both engineering and science, which were disciplinary categories in which majors reported the least learning about diversity, approximately 16% of the students felt that they had learned a moderate amount or more about understanding and appreciating diversity.

These survey findings confirm students' email responses to our member check, in which students stated that their courses and majors had profound influences on their learning about diversity. It is important to note that some students, even in the areas of lowest overall diversity learning, felt that they had learned a considerable amount about diversity. Figure 4.6 highlights one item, but we could illustrate this result equally well with the ratings for other items. We also saw this variability in the number of courses students said they took that included diversity as a topic. Therefore, even students whose majors do not naturally study diversity learned something about diversity from their courses over their four years in college, and some students apparently sought out greater exposure in their course work than did others.

Figure 4.6. *Average Ratings of "Understanding and Appreciating Diverse Philosophies, People, and Cultures" by Major Area*

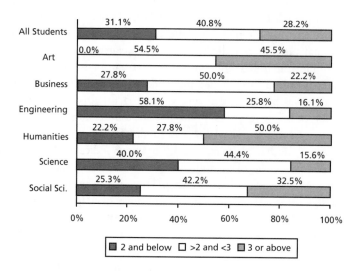

Changes in Students' Attitudes and Behaviors

In addition to the questions about diversity's contribution to education and how much students valued that contribution, our three administrations of the diversity survey asked students questions on various attitudes and behaviors related to diversity. Consistent with interview results, survey results of how much students learned showed significant increases over the three surveys for the following four items:

- Students' abilities to analyze decisions and strategies for their impact on different groups

- Students' abilities to understand the histories and experiences of cultural groups (such as people with different racial/ethnic backgrounds, sexual orientations, and genders from their own)

- Students' abilities to communicate effectively with people from other cultural groups

- Students' uncertainty that their beliefs and values would stay the same over the next few years

These survey results suggest that students perceived gains in what they knew and how they thought about diverse views, individuals, and cultures, at the same time that their general sense of what diversity might add to their learning decreased.

However, other survey items showed that while students' knowledge may have increased, their behavior and attitudes, on average, tended to decrease over time. Statistically significant downward trends were seen for the eight items that follow, which relate to the social or action-oriented aspects of diversity:

- I pay attention to laws and policies influencing diversity, such as I-200, and their consequences.

- [I value[21]] saying something such as "I think that's inappropriate" when I think something indicates prejudice.

- [I value] becoming active in a group or organization that challenges prejudice and discrimination.

- [I value] donating money to groups or organizations that challenge prejudice and discrimination.

- [I value] making friends with members from groups different from my own.

- [I have taken action in the past year to] make efforts to get to know individuals from diverse backgrounds.

- [I have taken action in the past year to] say something such as "I think that's inappropriate" when I think something indicates prejudice.

- [I have taken action in the past year to] become active in a group or organization that challenges prejudice and discrimination.

The downward trends for two of these items—the value students placed on making friends with members of groups different from their own and for taking action to get to know individuals from diverse backgrounds—seem especially important. They indicate that students' willingness to reach out to people unlike themselves decreased over their years in college. These results appear to confirm the students' email responses and take us back to two of the case studies that began this chapter. Carl Swenson was constantly reaching out to students who were different from himself, and, consequently, he learned a great deal about diversity. The diversity in his classes made that process easier for Carl. On the other hand, Jennifer Oswald's classes were not as diverse, as she noted herself, and she reported less learning about diversity than Carl did.

An interview question that we asked 112 students at the end of spring quarter 2001—students' second year at the UW—further confirms this finding that students' learning about diversity was more about knowledge acquisition than attitude or behavioral change. We asked students, "Have your attitudes about diversity changed since you entered the UW or not?" A little more than two-thirds said that their attitudes had changed in positive directions. Although we did not do a student-by-student comparison, it is safe to assume, based on the fall 1999 responses to the question about diversity, that when students reported no change in their attitudes about diversity, those attitudes remained positive.

However, more interesting to us was that although the question focused specifically on students' *attitudes,* when we prompted students to tell us what had changed, their descriptions focused on *knowledge gains.* The most frequently given categories of responses and the percentage of the students reporting each were as follows:

- Students realized that cultural experiences and norms vary (38%).

- Students became aware of the ways minorities are stereotyped and denied equal opportunities and treatment (18%).

- Students reflected on their own lives in order to better understand themselves and the struggles of others (13%).

- Students understood the relationship between economic disadvantage and other problems (10%).

It appears that class content seemed well designed to give students knowledge about diversity, admittedly more in some majors than others—from diverse perspectives to diverse cultural practices—but that this knowledge was not necessarily translated into students' attitudes and behavior. We recognize, of course, that changes in intellectual awareness often yield changes in behavior and attitudes that students cannot articulate. Perhaps more important, changes in knowledge often lay a foundation for attitude and behavior change that can follow years later.

In addition to tracking some attitude and behavior patterns for all students, we looked at whether the attitudes and behaviors students reported were influenced by their admission status, gender, and ethnicity. Each of these factors had some influence on students' responses.

Admission Status Differences

Students who transferred to the university tended to have nearly the same attitudes about diversity in their second year that they had in the first. In contrast, students who entered as freshmen tended to have less positive attitudes toward diversity in their second year than they did in the first.[22] Thus, most of the decreases found between the first and second surveys were attributable to freshman entrants. Because most of the students who had transferred to the UW had graduated by the study's fourth year, we did not have sufficient data to draw conclusions about the third survey and admission status.

We can speculate on why transfer students had more positive attitudes toward diversity than freshmen entrants after a roughly equivalent amount of college time. First, transfer students were usually older than incoming freshmen, so perhaps they brought a level of maturity to their experience that made them more open to diverse people, ideas, and experiences. Second, transfer students frequently majored in the humanities and social sciences, which may suggest a larger proportion with an inherent interest in diversity. Finally, certain transfer institutions may foster more open attitudes toward diversity and more diverse student populations than do four-year schools.

Gender Differences

Women generally began their college experience with more positive attitudes toward diversity than males, and that difference was maintained over time. Change tended to be parallel, with few significant interactions. Again, as with the difference between transfer students and those who entered as freshmen, we have no clear sense of why there might be such a difference, but we speculate that female socialization makes women more open than men to perspectives and people different from themselves. We know that women tend to major in areas that emphasize diversity, but that fact begs the question of cause and effect. Whether males and females are socialized differently around diversity does not clarify the role the university's classes, majors, and out-of-class experiences have played (or not played) in shaping male and female attitudes.

Ethnic Differences

The relationships among ethnic groups' responses were more variable than those among admissions groups or genders. Generally, underrepresented minority students exhibited the most positive attitudes, with Asian students occupying a middle position between underrepresented minority students and Caucasian students. There were exceptions, of course. One of the more interesting exceptions was that Asian students indicated significantly more learning about "working effectively with teams of people different from yourself" while at UW than did either underrepresented or Caucasian students. We suspect that this difference is explained by the tendency of Asian students to major in engineering, business, and science, where team projects are an integral part of those curricula. Half of the Asian students within our sample majored in one of these three areas, compared with 29% of the Caucasian students and 22% of the underrepresented minority students.

We also noted differences across ethnicities in the importance of gender, racial/ethnic background, socioeconomic status, religious group affiliation, and sexual orientation to students' identities. Underrepresented minority and Asian students gave significantly higher ratings than Caucasians to the importance of racial/ethnic identity across all surveys, as shown on Figure 4.7.[23] In fact, some students thought quite a bit about their ethnic identities, as Cross (1991) and Tatum (1997) would anticipate, and as Mickey Timmons and Shannon Wilson illustrated.

Figure 4.7. The Importance of Race/Ethnicity to Students' Identities

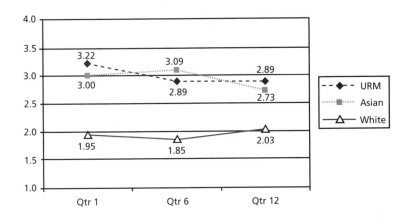

Changes in Perceptions Over Four Years

When asked if their viewpoints about diversity had changed in their four years at the UW, about 25% of the 63 UW SOUL students interviewed[24] said that they believed their viewpoints had not changed. The majority—about 70%—said that their viewpoints had changed, and the remaining few said that they did not know if their views had changed.

No Change in Perspective

Most of the students who felt that their viewpoints had not changed said that they had valued diversity when they entered the UW in 1999, and they still valued it in the same ways. The remaining students who believed that their viewpoints had not changed had wide-ranging explanations, several of which focused on limited exposure to diverse people and issues. The following student's comment is an example of these responses:

> I hate to say that I don't think it has. I don't think I'm a very diverse person. By looking at my group of friends, it is all white, middle-class people. I was in a sorority and that has something to do with it. How I feel about diversity is the same as when I entered.

Change in Perspectives

Students who felt that their perspectives had changed explained the changes in many ways. The most frequently given explanation—offered by about a third of the students interviewed—was that they had become more knowledgeable and aware of the issues and realities affecting diverse people, as well as of the value of diversity. This response was consistent with the picture created by survey, email, and interview responses to questions on diversity over time. It is a picture of acquisition of knowledge and understanding, rather than a picture of social interaction and friendship. About 15% of the students who said that their perspectives had changed reported that their definitions of diversity had broadened in their four years in college. About 11% reported that they had become more tolerant and open to other people and ideas, as this student's response illustrates:

> I have been more tolerant of differing opinions than I used to be. Living with my parents, who were pretty liberal, I used to have one-sided opinions before I came here. I accept diverse opinions now, because otherwise there is no comparison. Philosophy has taught me that there is always a counterargument, and college has taught me that there is a place for all of it, even on one strip of land. Despite how much people will argue with each other, they seem to coexist peacefully. The more informed, the less violent.

Sometimes students attributed their more open attitudes to life outside the university, as well as to their experiences inside. For example:

> I think over the years I have broadened my perspective on diversity. When I started, I thought diversity was only concerned with race or ethnicity and how that plays into politics and culture. Through a lot of my classes and being in a big city like Seattle, I've learned that diversity is not only about people from non-dominant races or ethnicities, but about people who are different ages, who have different perspectives, because of their ability levels, their sexuality, where they lived in the past, if their parents were in the military. [My thinking about diversity is] a lot more open now than it was when I started here.

Small numbers of students reported that they had become more self-aware because of their experiences with diverse people and ideas, that they spent more time thinking about diversity than they had when they were in high school, or that they had become aware of how segregated the UW's student population is.

These results on changes in students' perspectives lend some support to the argument that their email responses about the value they placed on diversity more accurately represented their views than survey results on the same question. The results also lend support to the argument that students made gains in knowledge that led them to tolerance and open-mindedness, while not necessarily making changes in their own behavior. However, while the results may suggest our work is not completed, these changes in knowledge and understanding are not small changes. They can lead to historical changes. As one of the students quoted above said, "The more informed, the less violent."

Conclusions and Implications

Our findings on diversity led us to the following three conclusions, and we note the assessment and teaching implications for them, as well.

Recruitment and Retention of Diverse Students Are Important to Learning

Efforts to attract, admit, and retain a diverse student body should continue, primarily because students from diverse experiences, ethnicities, and backgrounds are valuable in themselves and because these students need others like themselves to feel comfortable and to help them shape their own identities. Diversity in all its forms contributes to the learning of all students, and most students value that contribution. The more students of color, students from multicultural backgrounds, students with differing perspectives, and students with wide-ranging experience that universities admit, the richer the learning experience will be for all.[25] The same applies to faculty hires. It is also important to remember that when students think about diversity, they consider small differences important, as well as the broader categories such as race, class, and gender that we in academia usually regard as important.

Some of the implications for teaching a diverse student and faculty population are obvious. Such diversity will alter what is taught, as it has already done, and will require institutions to give diversity voice. If students are to learn from diverse others, they need to hear what those others have to say. This rather obvious requirement has profound and probably costly implications for class size and teaching methods.[26]

Regarding assessment, recruitment and retention of diverse students must be one of the ways that institutions review their own work. If interaction with students who are different from themselves helps students succeed in their chosen fields of study and in the workforce after they graduate, institutions must assess whether they are creating possibilities for such interaction. Increasing numbers of diverse students alone, of course, is not enough.

Student Learning Regarding Diversity Is Disciplinary

Student reports on the range and number of courses that included content on diversity show that efforts to integrate diverse content into appropriate courses at our university are paying off. However, clearly and perhaps predictably, the results are uneven across the disciplines. General education reasons for providing students with learning experiences around diversity are obvious. However, as research on learning about diversity makes apparent, departments also are likely to have reasons for fostering learning about and experience with diversity. Therefore, departments must determine what their majors should know and experience regarding diversity and assess whether their majors are learning those things.

Institutions Need to Build Structures for Interaction That Cross Disciplines and Ethnicity

It is clear that a *Field of Dreams* approach to diversity education—the idea that if we put students into a diverse environment, they will take full advantage of it—is not enough.[27] Our findings confirm the conclusions of Gurin et al. (2002), who suggest that institutions of higher education need to build structures—academic and social, formal and informal—in which students not only can interact but can hardly avoid interacting with those who are different from themselves. In general, entering students value and desire this type of interaction. However, at some point between their first quarter and the end of their second year, they become less willing to be proactive in seeking out interaction with diverse others. Their reasons for the decrease in willingness may differ. Underrepresented and Asian students, for example, may be developing stronger senses of their own racial and ethnic identities by interacting with groups like themselves. Caucasian students may find it easier to interact with others like themselves than to try to become socially engaged with students who are not. These practices are not only related to students' racial and ethnic identities. Religious students discover other religious students with whom to share housing, activists engage with other activists, and so on.

Regardless of students' reasons, this shift, along with the move of most students into majors, indicates that such structures are extremely important in students' first and second years in college, particularly for students who enter the university as freshmen. At the same time we consider what the nature of these structures might be, we must respect cohesion among members of minority groups and understand its function and importance. However, recognizing that students generally self-segregate into social groups based on race and ethnicity on campus, faculty can diversify small groups in classroom settings and in outside-of-class group assignments. Such small groups may be the only opportunities students have to interact with students from diverse backgrounds. Again, faculty should remember that small differences across students seem important to students.

Finally, regarding assessment, in addition to assessment of learning about diversity that is housed in the disciplines, institutional assessment should routinely include students' general attitudes toward diversity, retention and attrition rates among ethnic groups, and the campus climate for students of color, as well as for other students. We need to track institutional effects and students' perceptions of their own needs, expectations, and desires regarding diversity.

Endnotes

1) In January 1998, for example, the Board of Regents spoke of a "diverse student body" as an educational resource, stating publicly:

> Among the educational resources the University has to offer is a diverse student body. Students educate each other, in the classroom and in many informal educational settings; they challenge one another's assumptions, they broaden one another's range of experience and they teach one another to see the world from varied perspectives (University of Washington, 1998, ¶ 2).

In addition, the University of Washington Diversity Compact, signed by then-UW president Richard McCormick, other UW administrators, regents, and student leaders on October 21, 2000, stated that: "The university will work aggressively . . . to expand curricular offerings that enrich students' exposure to and understanding of human and cultural diversity" (University of Washington Office of the President, 2004, § II, ¶ 3).

2) See AASCU/NASULGC Enrollment Report (2002).

3) National Association of State Universities and Land-Grant Colleges, which represents more than 210 four-year public institutions.

4) We know the term *diversity* itself is contentious, with some people feeling that the term dilutes the focus on issues affecting students. We used the term because our institution uses it.

5) On a 4-point scale: 1 = *not at all*, 2 = *a little*, 3 = *somewhat*, 4 = *very much*

6) Using a repeated measures analysis of variance, the linear trend over the three years was statistically significant as was the quadratic trend for both items.

7)   Differences were analyzed using dependent *t*-tests.

8)   From the sixth to the 12th quarter, 25.6% of the students decreased their ratings, 51.2% stayed the same, and 23.1% increased their ratings for the contribution item. From the sixth to the 12th quarter, 23.7% of the students decreased their ratings, 47.5% stayed the same, and 28.7% increased ratings for the value item.

9)   Sixteen students were eliminated from these analyses because they had not yet declared a major (3) or their major was not classifiable into any of the six categories (13).

10) The first survey was administered early in the students' first quarter at UW. The third survey was administered toward the end of their 12th quarter (or fourth year). At UW, very few students enter a major before the end of their second year. Furthermore, by limiting this analysis to students who had completed all three surveys, only 10 of the 101 students whose data were included were transfers, since most transfer students had graduated by the twelfth quarter. The 10 who did not graduate were spread evenly among the six major areas and, given that they had been at UW for four years before graduating, they were unlikely to have entered UW with a major.

11) Numbers of students within areas of majors may differ somewhat among tables in chapters. See Chapter 2.

12) Significance of differences among major areas was tested using one-way analyses of variance.

13) Eta squared is a "strength of association" statistic that indexes the proportion of total variance that is attributable to group differences.

14) While social diversity was not mentioned by students as a prominent feature of the science curricula, biodiversity was frequently mentioned when we asked students if they had learned anything about diversity in their classes.

15) These five items, or environments, were rated on a 4-point scale: 1 = *not diverse*, 2 = *a little diverse*, 3 = *moderately diverse*, 4 = *very diverse*.

16) For statistical significance, a repeated measures analysis of variance was used.

17) In their first quarter at UW, we asked students how much they had learned about these items at the high schools and colleges they had attended prior to coming to the university. These results are not included in Table 4.3.

18) To make the analyses of the quarterly survey comparable to those for the diversity survey items, we included data for the latter from the same 238 students who were included in the analyses of the diversity surveys. On both the diversity and the quarterly survey questions, students were asked to respond on the following 4-point scale (scaling values in parentheses): 1 = *zero*, 2 = *a little*, 3 = *a moderate amount*, 4 = *a lot*.

19) The results of a two-way, repeated measures analysis of variance (items by major areas) showed significant main effects for items and majors, and a significant interaction between the two variables.

20) Thirty-two students were eliminated for the analyses by major area (11 students who had not yet declared a major, 5 students in miscellaneous professional programs, and 16 students double majoring in two distinct areas).

21) Note that our survey contained a series of items for which students rated how much they valued an action [Value], how confident they were in performing that action [Confidence], and whether they had performed the act in the last year [Action].

22) To illustrate, averages for transfer entrants were more positive than freshman entrants on 47 of the 55 items on the second survey ratings, whereas the two groups split 50-50 on the first survey.

23) The following 4-point scale was used: 1 = *not important to me,* 2 = *a little important to me,* 3 = *moderately important to me,* 4 = *very important to me.*

24) The students interviewed included Asian students (30%), Caucasian students (59%), and underrepresented minority students (11%). Nearly all of them entered the UW as freshmen in 1999, as almost all transfer participants had graduated by this time.

25) These finding mirror the findings of Gurin (1999) and Hurtado et al. (2000).

26) See Hurtado et al. (2000) for specific pedagogical approaches to diversity.

27) This concern is not only felt at the UW. See Rimer (2002) for a discussion of Dartmouth College.

Critical Thinking and Problem Solving

I think critical thinking often times we try to put into a box. We have become very academic about it and have tried to define it. We want to say that people are doing critical thinking when they do X, Y, and Z. But critical thinking is not about doing X, Y, and Z. It's about learning from others what others have done, learning from books what the writers of them think ought to be done, and then thinking for yourself what ought to be done. It is unique to each problem.

Critical thinking and problem solving are frequently used terms in academia and learning goals for most faculty in academic institutions (Bok, 2006), yet their definitions are highly contentious. Some scholars define critical thinking as a hierarchy of cognitive acts (Bloom, 1984; Perry, 1970). Others define critical thinking as a generic set of question-asking skills (Paul & Elder, 2002). In contrast to hierarchical and generic definitions, our findings suggest that critical thinking and problem solving are disciplinarily defined.

The student-supplied descriptions of challenging critical thinking and problem solving activities that we gathered convinced us that generic definitions, such as Paul and Elder's (2002), ignored the ways disciplines shade, shape, and bind what students do when they are thinking critically or solving problems. Interviews with faculty confirmed this perspective. As Sam Wineburg (now at Stanford University, but a former UW professor of education and an early advisor to the UW SOUL) asserts in an online interview conducted with Randy Bass of Georgetown University's *Visible Knowledge Project*:

> There is no looser term in the educspeak literature than critical thinking, which seems to embrace everything under the sun and the kitchen sink together. Some of the early formulators of the construct—Edward de Bono and Robert Ennis— depicted it as a general intellectual capacity to "problem solve," a kind of jack-of-all-trades intellectual capacity to solve questions on the Miller Analogy Test and change the oil in our car. Thirty years of subsequent research says it ain't so, big

time! Turns out that intellectual capacities are stubbornly domain specific: solving a physics problem and solving a historical one draw on different skills, dispositions, and most of all, deep familiarity with the ways of speaking within these respective communities of discourse. (cited in Fisher, Beyer, & Gillmore, 2001, p. 2)

The domain-specific nature of critical thinking colors all of the generic tasks often identified as critical thinking tasks, such as recognizing and defining problems, identifying stakeholders, gathering information that relates to the problem under consideration, choosing the best alternative after weighing related evidence, and testing the argument in a variety of ways (Bok, 2006). Our findings showed that what students do when they are thinking in these ways often varies profoundly from one discipline to another. Therefore, this chapter argues that college-level critical thinking and problem solving are context bound. In colleges and universities, that means that thinking is primarily bound by the academic disciplines.

Our findings align with Janet Donald's (2002) book, *Learning to Think*, which explores the different thinking demands that faculty in the disciplines place on students; Shulman's (1986, 1987, 2002) early work on teacher education; and the work of scholars, such as Wineburg (1991), Bransford, Brown, and Cocking (2000), and Bazerman (2000), who study how specific disciplines create and share knowledge.

Disciplinarity has two prominent effects: It specializes and, thus, it blinds. As we move through a discipline, we gain expertise in it. From music that moves us to medicines that cure us, we readily recognize the value of this expertise. It is much harder to recognize the blinding effect of disciplinarity. Learning to think and act within a disciplinary framework means thinking and acting according to the discipline's intellectual values and practices. It seems safe to say that when individuals live those values day after day through disciplinary practice they are reinforced as "standards" or "norms." Consequently, other sets of intellectual values and ways of thinking become increasingly difficult to recognize or appreciate. In other words, as we become experts in seeing one way, we adopt certain frames of reference that make it harder to see in other ways. And our expertise can sometimes compromise teaching effectiveness. Operating in what Nathan and Petrosino (2002) call the "expert blind spot," seasoned faculty sometimes have a hard time understanding what novices do not know about their fields.

Most of us can recount personal experiences with disciplinary thinking that demonstrate this effect—a social science major having difficulty writing papers about literature, for example. A psychology professor who heard a UW SOUL presentation that addressed the blinding effects of disciplinarity offered a perfect example from her experience. She had participated in a multiple-session workshop that included faculty from many departments. The first day focused on readings in the social sciences. The professor found those articles to be important, well organized, and clear. But when the workshop group discussed these readings, she was taken aback when a humanities professor complained that the articles were unclear, simplistic, and full of jargon. When she got home that night, however, she struggled to read the humanities essays that were assigned for discussion the next day. She wondered when they were ever going to make a point! The next day, she heard the same humanities professor praise those articles as insightful and clear. In that moment, she recognized the ways that expertise can blind us to others' ways of thinking and knowing, even when we are considering the same issues.

One of the roles that college plays in students' intellectual lives is to immerse them in the knowledge, methods, and practices—the thinking—of the disciplines of their majors. This chapter provides evidence that this process of enculturation occurs for undergraduates. The chapter is organized into three main sections. In the first, we track Trevor McClintock as he moves through several demanding critical thinking and problem solving experiences. Then we report what students told us through surveys and interviews about critical thinking and problem solving across the disciplines. We bring a few faculty voices into this section, as well. Next, we briefly discuss students' self-assessment of their progress. Finally, we present our conclusions and their teaching and assessment implications.

Trevor's Path

Trevor McClintock's story illustrates both the ways that critical thinking is shaped by a student's academic major and the critical thinking challenges that are raised by exploring opportunities typical in the stage of emerging adulthood (Arnett, 2000). Trevor, a 28-year-old transfer student from a state community college, had a circuitous journey to the university. "I blew it in high school and in my first year of college," he told us. "Then, I didn't do anything for eight years. It took a lot to say, 'Hey, I'm a smart person. There isn't any reason I shouldn't be able to accomplish this.'"

In his first year when asked how he defined critical thinking and problem solving, Trevor drew on an earlier acquired graphic arts certificate to distinguish between creative and critical thinking, concluding that "critical thinking uses known facts and creative thinking allows you to say 'what if.'" When asked where he had done his most challenging critical thinking that first year, Trevor described his math classes, saying, "The challenge was taking the tools that you learned and being able to decide when to use them, what to use them on, and how to use them all together."

By his second year, the most challenging critical thinking that Trevor described was an assignment in a class on restoration ecology in his major. A group of students was given a plot of land behind the intramural building. Their task was to assess the area and do what needed to be done to restore it. "We had a couple of graduate students in the group," Trevor said, "and everyone was motivated to be doing that work. We really tied into everyone's expertise." In describing what was challenging in the project for this course, Trevor said:

> The challenge was looking at the conditions we had and thinking about how to create a project where the plants will actually grow. We had soil that was completely waterlogged in the winter and completely dry in the summer. A lot of the stuff we put in we figured would never survive. We had sub-plots within our main plot where we did experimental treatments, using a cardboard mulch under a woodchip mulch, for example. We kept trying ways to figure out what we could do to make it a more viable habitat.

Trevor continued by talking about the critical thinking process itself:

> The classes that are the most challenging are not going to tell you how to do it. They basically tell you to fix something. You are scratching your head for awhile, trying to figure it out. Your first response is that you want to do it quickly, and it may not be to go through the critical thinking process. The one thing I've learned about critical thinking is that it may not lead you down the right road. It will lead you to some dead ends. But your job is to look at your options and to figure out which ones will work and which ones won't.

When asked if he felt his ability to think critically had improved or not in his second year, Trevor responded:

> Absolutely. My friends tell me I am very black-and-white. It either works or it doesn't. It is good or bad. To think critical-ly, you almost have to think on a different level. I think I've opened up to different ways of thinking. I'm able to look at a project and look at what won't work, think about why it does-n't work. Just because it doesn't work doesn't mean that it isn't

an option. There might be certain elements in that technique that are useful.

In his second year, Trevor also joined the UW's cycling team. He reveled in this experience, surprised to find himself a college athlete at 29 years old, noting:

> I felt it was something I missed out on and would never get to experience. I felt—and still feel—an amazing sense of pride every time I roll to the start line, wearing purple and gold with my teammates.

In addition to serving as a source of pride, Trevor's experience with the cycling team during his second, third, and fourth years at the university[1] also fostered critical thinking. This reminds us that while the kinds of critical thinking and problem solving required by academic disciplines may be the most interesting to academics, students were asked to use critical thinking and problem solving skills in a number of domains that we did not track.

Trevor's critical thinking journey took a different direction in his third year, when he went with 40 other students to Auroville, India on a design-build program cosponsored by the college of architecture and the program on the environment. Students were assigned small research groups to design and build a dormitory. Trevor's particular job was to work on a solar energy system for the structure—"rainwater harvest, wind, water-pumping. We researched all the technologies that were available in India, as well as all over the world. We went to the small libraries in Auroville, talked to people, did Internet research." Trevor described the experience in his 2002 interview:

> I never imagined doing any program like this when I enrolled here. I just stumbled on the program. It is a lot different learning to build an actual structure—implementing a real-world project—as opposed to doing more theoretical work or writing papers. We started almost from scratch when we got there. All the preliminary work we'd done, we had to scrap. It was more about learning how to work not only together as a group of students, but also how to work in a foreign country, using their methods and learning their work ethic, learning how you functioned in that environment. There was nothing to rely on—no familiarity, no comfort zones.

Trevor also described his experience, day by day, in a journal he turned in as part of his annual UW SOUL portfolio requirement. The journal is rich with details about Trevor's experience in India and includes fascinating accounts of learning to play cricket, mixing cement in intolerable heat, arriving at celebrations in the back of a dump truck, bicycle accidents, mini-monsoons, the joys of Indian food, birthday celebrations, physical exhaustion, pride, and loneliness:

> I'm feeling so unattached from what my life has been for the past several years. I miss my friends, my family, my bikes, my coffee, the Seattle rain, my soft feather bed—and it's only been a week. Only 67 days to go.

In terms of thinking critically, Trevor described his learning as focusing mostly on self-awareness, including his relationships with others:

> The biggest thing for me was just learning about myself, more than anything—how I relate to people, how I think about world issues and what not. The things I put importance on, I realized may not be the things that are really important to me. I spent a whole quarter with these students before we went to India, and I never really got to know any of them. I found myself developing relationships with them, making new friends, getting to know people, and sharing some really intimate things. Everyone was so eager, so open. I wondered why I had never talked to people about those things before, and all of a sudden I felt I had the freedom to talk with people and share with people. I am struggling now not to fall back into old paradigms.

The other critical thinking area Trevor described centered on changes in his understanding of how to solve a problem:

> With another student, I was designing the solar system for solar electricity. We decided that there needed to be some sort of separate storage for the batteries and electronics. The architects hadn't thought of that, so I was talking to one of the architecture instructors, telling him that we needed a structure for all this stuff, and he said, "Okay, do it." So I started sketching some stuff out, pulling from skills I hadn't exercised in a long time. I showed him some sketches, and he said, "Wow, you're an architect!" We settled on a design, and he said, "Okay, you need CAD drawings for this." The architecture students were really busy, and basically, I had to teach myself to use [it] to design the building. I stayed up all night,

fumbled through it, got it really really close, and then took it to an architecture student who cleaned it up and showed me some tricks. Then we started building it. I showed up one morning, and they were digging the foundation for it, and they told me I had to go do a layout for the building. So I had to figure out how to do that. That was really challenging because it was me and six Tamil workers who spoke little English doing a building layout. The whole time, I was thinking, "What the hell am I doing?"

Trevor's February 12 entry in his India journal captures more about that learning experience:

Critical thinking allowed me to open the box and look at the parts I had to build my project. Without looking at each part individually and evaluating its use and usefulness I would have ended up with a project that doesn't work.

In describing in an interview what he learned from this experience, Trevor added:

It is easy to look at a project and think—"Oh, I don't know how to do this. I need to find someone who does."—instead of asking, "What do I need to know to solve the problem?" I know that I can rationalize my way through a project now, solve it myself.

Critical thinking in Trevor's senior year contained all the themes of his previous interviews, as he linked his experience on the cycling team again with what he had learned in India:

I think that this year managing the cycling team has been a turning point. Doing that this year, I have learned an incredible amount of patience, and I didn't realize when I took on the role that I would be in a position where people on the team would actually look to me for leadership. I found myself in the role of being a coach, and I felt highly unqualified at first. It was a lot more than just taking care of the logistics of racing. I have always been in the other positions—looking to someone else for their advice, their confidence, and their leadership. A lot of the time I was really nervous about going to a road race, and they would be looking to me for the wise words before the race and to know what is happening. I think this is the same situation as in India—where you can't wait for the experts to come and tell you what to do. You have to seize the moment and do what needs to be done.

In addition to learning more about himself and his capacity for leadership, Trevor was asked to think critically in a new way in his senior year. Trevor described his three-course capstone experience as the most challenging critical thinking he did that year. The capstone experience focused on another restoration project and called on Trevor to learn some new skills:

The biggest problem in this project is political, dealing with the problem-solving issues and the politics. It took a lot of persuading to get the city to give us the freedom we needed, and finally they approved of a meeting between the community groups and us, and that actually improved the relationship between the city and the community group.

In talking about whether his own thinking about critical thinking had changed over time, Trevor once again talked about the differences between critical and creative thinking as he had in his first UW SOUL interview four years before:

I think getting the [graphic] arts degree, the train of thought I developed doing that—you would start a project without any end in mind, and you'd follow it to where it took you. I never had an image in my head of a painting; you just allow the painting to come out. And that really doesn't work all the time. In fact, it can get you into a dead end. I think I have learned to do projects with an adaptive process. I have an idea of what I want to end up with, and I know what my resources are that I start with, and the hardest part is staying on track so you end up with what you need to end up with. If something doesn't work, you need to be able to go back and still utilize the work you accomplished to take you in the right direction.

Later, he added that in his major, sustainable resource science:

A lot of the critical thinking is scientific and mathematical— knowing your data, knowing how to use it. But then, there is a pretty big creative thinking component to it. You are dealing with a lot of issues that need solutions. You are studying alternatives to the way you are doing things now. You know, for instance, that we are using a lot of fossil fuels, but what do we use instead? There's a moment in every project where you are asking what you can do that will possibly work and how are we going to test it. That's the creative side. But even with that creativity, at the end, you have to be damn sure you present your numbers correctly. Every single project I have done has required both scientific and creative thinking. I think a lot of artists don't realize how scientific their thinking is and a lot of scientists don't realize how creative their thinking has to be.

As Trevor McClintock's story illustrates, the terms critical thinking and problem solving can refer to a wide variety of thinking challenges. Sometimes one kind of critical thinking demand informs another, as Trevor's India experience informed his understanding of what he needed to do as captain of the cycling team. Sometimes critical thinking is only relevant to the very particular circumstance in which it finds itself, which Trevor's building project with Tamil workers suggests. Trevor's story models the critical thinking experience of all our undergraduates, showing that thinking challenges in college ranged from simple to complex, from obvious to subtle. They involved the personal and the academic, the intellectual and the experiential, the individual and the social, and, as Arnett (2000) suggests, they arrived on the backs of the many opportunities students have for exploration and development.

Thinking Across the Disciplines

Before we began gathering data on critical thinking and problem solving, we had to decide what we meant by those terms and whether to put them side by side in that manner. After input from our advisory committee, we decided that while we had generated a list of critical thinking and problem solving "moves" that we could use in our surveys, we would not define critical thinking or problem solving in interviews with students. Just as we had with diversity, we were hoping to learn how students defined those terms and whether those definitions changed over time. We also decided to use both terms instead of only one, because we did not want to privilege certain kinds of thinking over others.[2]

In all four years of the UW SOUL, students described a fascinating array of critical thinking and problem solving challenges, and their descriptions, as well as interviews with some faculty members, demonstrated the disciplinary nature of critical thinking and problem solving. This section addresses this argument in the following subsections:

- How much students learned about critical thinking and problem solving

- Most challenging critical thinking and problem solving

- Changes in how students defined critical thinking and problem solving

- Students' self-assessment

How Much Students Learned About Critical Thinking and Problem Solving

With help from our advisory committee, we generated eight items that related to critical thinking and problem solving and included them on our quarterly surveys. Students were asked to rate how much they had learned about each on a 4-point scale.[3] The eight items and results for each are found in Table 5.1. As the table shows, students' average ratings across all four years ranged from 2.86 for "thinking critically about issues" to 1.93 for "designing something." Thus, it is clear that students perceived themselves learning more about some kinds of challenges than about others. In particular, UW SOUL participants perceived that they learned less about the more creative kinds of critical thinking—or *creative thinking* as it was termed by Trevor McClintock in the previous case study—than they learned about analytical thinking.

As we had done with other data, we looked at general results through the lenses of students' majors, generalized into broad disciplinary areas—in this case six areas: the arts, business, engineering, the humanities, science/math, and social sciences. This analysis showed that for four of the eight items listed in Table 5.1, the students' areas of major made a statistically significant difference in the ratings. The means and standard deviations of the four items showing significant differences are presented for each disciplinary area in Table 5.2. As the table shows, art majors exhibited the highest mean on all four items by a fair margin. However, differences from item to item are apparent among the other majors, as well. Humanities and social science majors showed higher means for "critically examining my own thinking, arguments, or opinions," with the other majors clustered together with the lowest averages. The means of business, humanities, and social science majors were clustered together for "challenging a theory, conclusions, arguments, or results of an authority in a discipline," while the means of science and engineering majors were lower. In addition, both "creating something original" and "designing something" revealed large differences among majors, accounting for about half of the total variation. For both items, the averages of engineering majors were the second highest after averages for art

Table 5.1. *Comparisons Among Areas of Major for Critical Thinking Items on Quarterly Surveys*

Item	4 yr Mean	Std. Dev.	F-Value	Signif. Level	Eta Squared
Thinking critically about issues	2.86	0.58	1.44	NS	5.4%
Exploring questions such as "What does this mean?" "Why is this important?" "Why did this happen?" or "What are the implications, outcomes, of these results or choices?"	2.78	0.62	0.63	NS	2.4%
Critically examining my own thinking, arguments, or opinions	2.76	0.62	3.40	0.005	11.8%
Revising my attitudes and opinions in light of new information	2.59	0.54	0.98	NS	3.7%
Constructing arguments to support my own ideas	2.49	0.58	1.66	NS	6.1%
Challenging a theory, conclusions, arguments, or results of an authority in a discipline	2.19	0.64	2.86	0.025	10.1%
Creating something original	2.04	0.73	21.99	0.0001	46.4%
Designing something	1.93	0.78	25.73	0.0001	50.3%

majors. The other majors tended to show low averages on both of these items, with humanities and social sciences majors being especially low on "designing something," as we might expect.

It is easy to imagine how the goals and tools of the various disciplines led to these differences among items. For example, it is not surprising that humanities and social science majors felt that they learned more about challenging authority than did engineering and science majors, because humanities and social sciences majors are likely to be exposed to arguments and controversies earlier than majors in plant biology or electrical engineering. It is equally clear why engineering students would learn more about designing something, since competence in design is a primary goal for majors.

These differences in disciplines begin to lend a kind of shape to our argument that critical thinking varies from one academic field to the next. However, it is a loose shape. The survey questions and students' responses did not paint a

Table 5.2. *Means (Standard Deviations) Within Major Areas for Items Showing Significant Differences*

Item	Art (N=9)	Bsiness (N=14)	Engin (N=21)	Human (N=11)	Science (N=29)	Soc Sci (N=49)
Critically examining my own thinking, arguments, or opinions	3.32 (0.49)	2.58 (0.47)	2.52 (0.61)	2.97 (0.76)	2.59 (0.65)	2.82 (0.55)
Challenging a theory, conclusions, arguments, or results of an authority in a discipline	2.61 (0.59)	2.28 (0.44)	1.83 (0.55)	2.26 (0.73)	2.03 (0.68)	2.27 (0.63)
Creating something original	3.54 (0.52)	1.81 (0.37)	2.48 (0.58)	2.03 (0.60)	1.83 (0.51)	1.73 (0.54)
Designing something	3.19 (0.83)	1.72 (0.41)	2.77 (0.63)	1.53 (0.49)	1.83 (0.55)	1.53 (0.51)

clear picture of the thinking and practices that take place in those fields. For example, art and engineering majors both report the highest levels of learning in the category "designing something." But what they design, their purposes for designing it, the tools they use, the methods they must follow, the ways their materials constrain their choices, and the thinking and critique processes they go through to complete their designs differ radically. It is unlikely that a painter could easily transfer the critical thinking knowledge learned in that field to the thinking required to construct a bridge that could survive a hurricane.

This lack of specificity is also true for the four critical thinking items that showed no significant differences. It is possible that the reason there were no significant differences in the responses of students from various majors on these four items was because they were more general than the other four. The student descriptions of their most challenging critical thinking and problem solving, presented in the next section of this chapter, provide a second level of detail to our understanding of disciplinary differences.

Most Challenging Critical Thinking and Problem Solving

Each year we asked UW SOUL participants in Group 1 to describe their most challenging critical thinking and problem solving experiences. Their descriptions of those experiences provided evidence that critical thinking and problem solving are context-bound. As described in Chapter 2, we separated students' responses by the disciplinary categories assigning the challenging critical thinking tasks, and these included: architecture and urban planning, the arts, business, engineering, humanities, math, science, and social sciences.[4] Students' descriptions of their most complex critical thinking and problem solving challenges in these areas over the four years of the study, as well as descriptions provided by a few faculty members, are the focus of this section.

Challenges in Architecture and Urban Planning

In architecture and urban planning, students engaged in a wide range of critical thinking and problem solving challenges. Similar to students who spoke about challenges in the arts, students in this area described learning how to see and think differently about buildings and space, including visualizing something that is not there. One student described this change in thinking in these words:

> You are designing something that is not there, so you need to be able to visualize it. What does it mean if this wall ends at this point—what is its relationship to the sun. Most of the challenge is visualization, what would it look like, what would it feel like to be in there.

Students described using their new ways of seeing space and buildings when performing architectural critiques. For example, a student spoke about his architecture class in Rome:

> We were doing a lot more hands-on on the outside there, a lot more critiquing of the buildings on the spot, on-site, than we do here. Even if you weren't required to critique a building on the spot, you would do it for your own self. It was challenging to do that because we are still learning how. To tell if a building is good or not is such a complicated thing to do, I think.

Students in architecture and urban planning also learned to create design solutions to fit specific needs. In this process, they had to consider the many aspects of design, including material and cost constraints, engineering issues, building codes, and ideas to be represented. In addition, students had to consider the impact of the proposed solution, ranging from how it would feel from a human use perspective to how it would interact with its environment. The following student's quotation illustrates this complex challenge:

> This year, we are dealing with a building for bookmakers, and they gave us a list of specifications. It is called a program. We go look at the site because we will have to relate the building to the

> slope and what's around it. Then you have to follow code—how
> high can you go, how far back do you have to set it. Then you
> start putting it together, and it has to make sense for people who
> will use it—you don't want to have one bathroom for two mil-
> lion people. But you also have to design a good-looking, appeal-
> ing building. And you are thinking of the spaces inside—is it
> open or closed, cavernous, etc. There are different ways of cre-
> ating space depending on their use. You put that all together
> and then structurally, you have to think how well it holds up.
> We have to know how it is framed, if it is impossible for it to
> stay up. You talk with the other students about their designs,
> share ideas, and look at what people are doing.

Occasionally, students helped build the things they designed. A few of the students' project sites were abroad, and while there, they encountered a host of challenges not particular to the discipline, as the case study of Trevor McClintock illustrated—for example, learning to work with people from differ-ent cultures.

In addition to learning to rely on themselves in these processes, students mentioned having to learn how to work with others—peers, professors, and community members. The relationships with these other groups ranged from peer and teacher critiques to group collaboration to negotiating and meeting real-world client needs. For example:

> Our project throughout the quarter was to work with the
> client from the Parks Department on issues involving Golden
> Gardens Park. We were trying to establish beach usage and
> how people thought about the park, how policies could be
> better implemented, and what to do to solve the problems
> with bonfires and so on. It was challenging, first of all, to fig-
> ure out what the issue was, because we kept having contradic-
> tions about what the issues and problems were. That wasn't
> clear even after working on it for awhile. Also, it was chal-
> lenging to please the client. We had to give a community
> meeting presentation and report to the client. It was real-
> world problem solving.

Another challenge students in architecture and urban planning mentioned was unique to students in the college's community and environmental planning program (CEP). Several students described having to reflect on their own values and biases and discuss them with peers.

In addition to analyzing students' descriptions of critical thinking challenges, we interviewed Ellen Yi-Luen Do, a former UW professor of architecture
now at Carnegie Mellon University, about her definitions of critical thinking
and problem solving and about what architects are doing when they are engaged
in critical thinking behavior. According to Do, the phrase "critical thinking" is
not used in architecture, but the act of thinking critically is expected. Do's char-
acterization of "design thinking" seemed to overlap with much of what the students detailed above.

> In my past life, I used to design buildings. In that, the critical
> thinking part would be how do I find the opportunities to make
> the best form or to make the function efficient or communicate
> to the client to make things work. My [current] research is
> about finding out how people do design and what the design
> process is, what sequence of reasoning they do. I will always be
> questioning myself when I read or when I observe the videotape
> of what they are doing. I will be constantly trying to figure out
> their intention from what they draw. The other problem in my
> research is that I also teach graphic programming, so I am writ-
> ing software. So in my research, I am always getting questions
> and answers and feedback on the process. I can say that's think-
> ing or reasoning, and I believe that is always critical thinking. I
> did the same thing when I was with students. They would pre-
> sent a project and I would do the same thing I do with my
> design students. I would say "Why do you think that way and
> what do you mean by that?" So my students always have to
> define what they mean.
>
> I had a conversation with [a colleague] about whether he
> used the phrase "critical thinking" in his teaching. He said no.
> I don't use the word either, but we do expect students to use
> critical thinking. We probably use the words "design methods"
> or "design thinking" to embody doing question and answer to
> shape where students are going. So if they say they are going
> to put their bathroom in this area, we say "Why? What prob-
> lem does that solve?" They will come back and say maybe
> that's not a good idea, maybe we should move it there. Or they
> may explain the reasons why the location is better over there.
> This is a form of "reflection in action."

The critical thinking and problem solving challenges described by the students in architecture and urban planning and by Professor Do show some con-

nections with those described by students speaking about classes in the arts—primarily the representation of ideas and meeting the physical and intellectual challenges of the creative process. The difference between the two disciplinary areas, however, is architecture and urban planning's project focus—a specific goal of creating buildings or landscapes intended for human use—and the particular questions that arise with such a focus. Because the endpoint is human use, people in this field must balance structural issues—such as safety and material costs—with functional issues—"how can this space be used?"—as well as with aesthetic issues—"what will it feel like to use such a space?"

Challenges in the Arts

As with the architecture students, students who reported challenging critical thinking in the arts reported learning to see and understand the physical world differently. For example, a drawing class challenged one student to see physical objects in a new way, while a dance class made another student rethink space and movement:

> What is challenging is learning eye-hand coordination, foreshortening. Learning how to calculate scaling. Learning tonality values. These are hard because your brain wants to name things when we draw—"hand, foot" as opposed to thinking value, shade, curvature, line.

> The class was to teach you how to be a choreographer, and there are elements that have been laid down by other choreographers that they try to teach you. If you use music, for example, how do you move to the music and make it look okay? How do you fill the space? If you have two people on a big stage, how do you shrink the space with the two people? If you have a movement, then how does movement develop from a movement that you've made? We would have to make a phrase that used four people, and the four people had to be in unison at some point, so if you have movement where everybody is spread out everywhere, how do you get them all together?

Students describing challenges in the arts also brought up the need to investigate emotional, experiential, and intellectual issues. For example, one student spoke of the need to use various intellectual lenses when viewing a play:

> We looked through these different critical lenses [in Drama 302]—not just reading a play but looking at it through the view

of feminism, for instance. What is the play saying about women and society? What symbols were used? Also we looked at the purpose of the play—was it being used to incite someone or just for entertainment? It was challenging because you get used to looking at plays from one lens and then you want to use that lens forever. But then you have to switch gears completely. Once you got used to looking at plays through the lens of colonialism, for instance, you wanted to use that lens for the next play. But we'd switch. There was a lot of information there.

Students in the arts were asked to express/translate emotions, ideas, and ways of seeing into concrete objects or performances. This process was both intellectual—thinking about how to represent ideas/feelings physically—and physical—making the representations, as this example illustrates:

In the posters [for visual arts], we had to represent a country, and we were not given any ways to do it. We had to do whatever we thought would work. I had Mexico for my country. My first poster, I didn't know what to do. I had a guitar and some peppers on the page. My professor said that it wouldn't work. It was too iconic, not visually interesting. But at the same time he wouldn't suggest what to do, so you go and come back with something different. So I tried to use Mexican tiles to weave in some patterns. That didn't work. So in the end, I had the painter Frieda Kahlo's picture on the page with some of her work. It never worked very well. In these classes, we were given a problem to solve, and we had to expand our thinking so that we solved it.

In addition to creative constraints supplied externally, students learned to work with and use the physicality of the media, as this student's comment demonstrates:

Every week we would be using wire, but it was effectively a completely different medium. The major problem to be solved is that you have this piece with hundreds of little ends. How do you finish off the ends? A lot of the wiring types we used could not be soldered, so you had to come up with riveting techniques or something else. Gluing tends to be looked down on in my fine metals programs.

Not only did working within the constraints of their chosen media require students to find creative solutions to physical problems, it often caused reflective rethinking of the ideas, feelings, or meanings they were initially exploring and expressing. Through this reflective process, students often reported discovering the interplay between the various aspects of the creative process; developments in one area could trigger changes in another. The artistic process as characterized by the students was exploratory, dynamic, and unpredictable, as the following student described:

> [In my art classes] it is no longer painting still lifes; it is coming up with a creative thought process. It's no longer—here's a pear, let's paint this. That [new thought] process depends on what I want to express, how I wish to express it, and from there, it goes into once I do have the subject, then the creative thinking is focused on juxtaposition, composition, color theory, and perspective. The work is always metamorphosing into something else; there are not mistakes—it's just redoing, modifying. Nothing is ever planned out. You don't know when you start out where you are going to end up. That happens a lot.

Additionally, students in the arts learned how to critique their own and others' work, and how to incorporate critiques into their own creative processes. The following quotation illustrates this challenge:

> Just the critiques you have. It was my first art class, and it made a huge impression. Everyone walks around and talks about your work. At first everyone is really shy but then everyone talks about what they think, and it is not a critical matter. We just are talking about what we are seeing.

In addition to critiquing others' individual works, students worked together on projects, altering the critical thinking challenges in the creative process. For example:

> [In visual arts] we were asked as a group to develop a traveling exhibit on the theme of Seattle. What was challenging was that it was the first time we were working in a group to come up with the design. This was challenging because everyone had different ideas. Once we had agreed on a theme, then everyone had different ideas on how to make that happen. It was challenging to persuade others in the group to go with your own. It was interesting to see who was better at being

stubborn. It was also a great opportunity to work with others and appreciate how they think.

We interviewed a UW art professor, who is also a well known artist, on his views of critical thinking and problem solving in his discipline. His comments were consistent with much of what the UW SOUL students described when they spoke of critical thinking in the arts. He associated the phrase "problem solving" with learning to work with the medium. Interestingly, the art professor described the heart of the artistic process as "problem seeking"—rather than problem solving. Trevor made this same distinction in his discussion of the difference between working in graphic arts and working in the sciences. Below is a portion of the faculty member's description of critical thinking and problem solving:

> In art—and there's lots of different kinds of art, but again, in the most general way—artists tend not to be problem-solvers in the sense that they are given a problem and then they solve it. They tend to be more problem seekers. They don't know what they are after exactly. They have a rough idea based on what they've done before, what their desires are currently, and what the interface is. So as you start working on something, you do get results. To just take a simple example, you may decide you like portraits because you like people, and so you are going to make photographic portraits, let's say, and you start to do that, but as you do that, you start to find that the ones you feel the strongest about and the ones that are working the best really are more about the person in their environment and not just what they physically look like as a body. And so as you do more stuff, you learn more about both what your real questions are and what's actually working, and so it's a melding of those two. You wouldn't necessarily know except in the most general way what you were seeking, but you ended up there.
>
> In the discussion among artists and designers, the designers would tend to be oriented to problem solving. Now, that's not to say that there's not all kinds of problem solving that goes on in art that has to do with kinds of materiality stuff, you know—I want to put photos on plates, so you have to kind of research that, find out what emulsions are around and what's been done in the past. So you're solving that technical problem, but as a discipline, it tends to be more problem seeking.

In terms of critical thinking, there again, it's terminology, but within art in the last 20 years, there's what's called critical theory. It's not quite the same thing as critical thinking but in some ways it has relationships.

But if by critical thinking you mean the ability to think very exactly and broadly about what one is doing, trying to understand it from a lot of different perspectives, as opposed to just what it is considered to be on the surface, in a sense, all art does that. You're thinking critically about this thing that you're making. Sometimes you're working on something and you can't resolve it, and it might be something that if you just set aside, a year later, two years later, you're ready for it—like part of your mind can see this thing, but this other part is necessary to finish the job off. And that's why at least for some people, art studios seem kind of messy, because there are a lot of different things at different stages of completion, unlike science, which tends to be more rational in that sense. You are combining things, like how this image pulls people in, or how people respond to it, what it means in your life, what your experiences are, and then all the physical skills, like how do you physically create a picture, how do you get it to be more red or more green, brighter—all those factors together are part of what critically thinking about this endpoint, this final work of art, is. It's balancing all those things.

The window provided by the students' descriptions of critical thinking and problem solving challenges they engaged in the arts, and the excerpt from the interview with the art professor, show some of the intellectual and practical territory of the arts. While the details obviously differ across media and method, disciplines in the arts seem interested in a concurrent, reflective, and iterative process of exploring and expressing ideas, feelings, and understandings for the purpose of making them visible.

Challenges in Business

Students described a wide range of critical thinking and problem solving challenges in their business classes. One challenge they described involved learning how to think about financial data, including how to use data, how data related to each other, and what data meant in different contexts. Students applied this knowledge to individual businesses and global economies. The following quotation illustrates this group:

We had to do an assignment where we examined financial statements. We had to look at the numbers and try to understand what the company was doing—if they were inflating their income or what they were doing. When I initially look at statements, I don't see anything, so I had to look really really ly hard to see where everything was connected.

As well as learning how to think about and apply data to business settings, students learned how to use mathematical tools to generate data that would allow them to understand or solve business problems, as shown by the following quotation:

We had huge assignments using lots of math using some complicated computer programs. We used Excel, but we used it in ways that I'd never used it before. There were formulas I didn't know you could plug in. It was helpful. There were a lot of things I hadn't done before mathematically, like forecasting. Complicated business math formulas that were new to me— more what you do in the business world than what you do in a math class.

In addition, students learned about the ethical and legal issues that need to be considered in the business world. One student described this challenge as follows:

It was kind of a business ethics class, so you have to be able to look at issues from different views. When you are having group discussions, you discover that your view isn't the only view. There are a bunch of different opinions. You have to think differently in order to see others' views. A lot of times she would give us situations—say a discrimination problem in the company—and you would have to figure out a way to solve it. But you are constrained by different laws, how it might look PR-wise.

Students also reported learning how to perform market research and create good marketing strategies. This often involved learning to track and consider factors in international trade and markets. For example:

It was challenging because the product was challenging. We were supposed to give an export recommendation for a software product, so where do you export it, who is your distributor, and why. We had to talk about the logistics and laws about distributing it. The laws surrounding software export are brand new, and it is not as clear a roadmap as if you are shipping socks or something. Because of the level of specialization, finding the right distributor was harder. It was hard to find the information to do things correctly.

Another critical thinking challenge that students described in their business courses was the need to apply a wide range of business concepts and skills in analyzing real or imagined business situations. As the following example illustrates, students described these tasks for a range of businesses from small businesses to international markets:

> We had to figure out the break-even point of starting a business—how far along after you open the store will you be breaking even. It was challenging because you had to consider all the different costs of operations. We did a cafe, but the costs were really expensive. We had to consider everything, [such as] the projected number who would come into the store in the first month and how to increase that. And the costs of increasing that. So it was a lot guestimating, but it had to be based on numbers from other businesses. We had to do an analysis of costs—had to take into account how many people would buy our dessert.

Finally, students spoke of challenges in working independently, with little guidance, as well as challenges involved in group work.

In order to better understand critical thinking and problem solving from a business perspective, we interviewed Bill Wells, a faculty member in the accounting department, and Gary Sundem, associate dean, and Julius A. Roller, professor of accounting. We spoke with Wells and Sundem at the same time, asking them what critical thinking was in business. In responding to that question, both men quickly turned to how they tried to *teach* critical thinking and problem solving to students in accounting. Bill Wells began by sketching a graph similar to Figure 5.1 on a piece of scrap paper. He explained the graph, saying that in the earliest accounting classes, students learn the concepts and tools they will need to use in their later classes where they are asked to think critically and solve problems. Wells and Sundem agreed, however, that over time, more of the "using" side of the figure has become integrated into lower-level courses, so that their students in early-level accounting classes spend more time applying and using accounting principles, concepts, and methods than did previous students. Both professors said that they continue to look for ways

Figure 5.1. *Bill Wells's Teaching/Learning Graph*

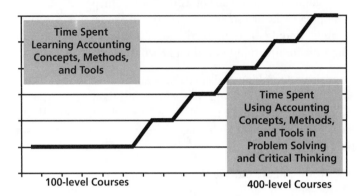

to integrate applications into students' accounting experiences at the earliest levels, because they understand that sometimes the best way for students to learn concepts and tools is to try using them.[5]

What follows is a portion of Wells's and Sundem's conversation about some of the challenges and processes for teaching critical thinking in the context of the study of accounting.

> *Wells:* I have to teach an awful lot of content about tools at the beginning [100- and 200-class levels], so I don't have time to do critical thinking stuff, but as time goes on, the critical thinking portion gets larger. If you were talking to someone at the 200 level, there's a lot of tool teaching and a little bit of critical thinking, but as you go up to the 400 and MBA levels, there's a lot more of the critical thinking.

> *Sundem:* For me, using the case method is what guarantees a lot of critical thinking. Even in the first MBA class, there's a lot of it going on. To me it's a process of gathering information, sorting and analyzing it, and coming to some kind of a judgment. I think that would apply in any discipline. But the context in which you do that makes it a little bit different in accounting than in math, philosophy, or economics. In a case discussion, more questions start with why than anything else. Hopefully those questions will help them see how they got to their answer and how someone else did. In most cases, there are no right answers, so what you want is for each of them to

understand why they did what they did, why someone else did what he did, and how they come together.

Wells: At my [teaching] level, there are more correct/incorrect answers than others, but there are always peripheral issues or questions. If somebody brings up an issue that is going [in the wrong direction], you are going to have to swing the conversation back, but you have to do that by explaining why it is not relevant or by asking the question of whether it is relevant or not.

Sundem: A case is even more that way. You start with a path, but there are different branches. You start down one and if that isn't going to be real helpful, at some point you need to cut that off and make an assumption, come back to the main line and see where else you want to go. Seeing what you want to cut down and where you want to go is part of the challenge of teaching these classes.

Professors Wells's and Sundem's comments about teaching critical thinking echo students' descriptions of needing to learn to apply learned strategies, concepts, and skills, as well as data, which they have sometimes had to generate in order to solve business questions.

Challenges in Engineering

Students' responses to interview questions provided a good window into some of the forms of critical thinking and problem solving required in engineering. The responses revealed dramatic differences in the critical thinking challenges posed by the various engineering departments. For example, the thinking challenges required in designing a bridge across a river were markedly different from those involved in designing a computer program that made a ball bounce across a screen. The comments of these two students illustrate these differences:

In the [material sciences and engineering] lab, we had to do a research project and come up with a conclusion about whichever material we chose. We ended up doing security glass. We had to come up with different tests for the glass, and based on those results, we had to come up with a recommendation for which glass would be the best one for a business. Coming up with the tests was challenging and also the comparison, in terms of which was the more effective, based on a mixture of test results. The glass performed differently for different tests, so the recommendation was challenging.

Programming is like learning a language. It is like translating. You have to figure out how to translate a ball bouncing across the screen into a language.

Even though the challenges presented by various engineering departments differed, we can describe some broad themes across engineering. For example, in many of their engineering classes, students described learning about the physical world and how to think about, understand, and account for the material constraints it imposes upon their designs, as this student's comment illustrates:

In Astronautical and Aeronautical Engineering, we are creating a satellite that can take mice up in space for 50 days. That is challenging because it has never been done before, and we are designing everything from scratch. During winter quarter we entered into a competition to get the project. We got part of the project and MIT and University of Queensland, Australia, got the other parts. We are all doing different parts of the spacecraft. The mice will be living for 50 days under Martian level gravity. Three will be giving birth up there. We are trying to find out what the effect of Martian level gravity is to mammals and to their offspring, to see if humans can successfully colonize Mars.

Students also described learning to use numbers, equations, and computer programs to perform a variety of engineering tasks, as this quotation illustrates:

It's a propulsion class. The class is not based on any kind of set equations. You have a really long equation and break it down. You have to know what you need to use and what you don't. It's a long process. I have learned to start in the middle, start at the end and work backwards, or start at the front and work back—depending on what they give you. It's crazy what you have to do with it.

In addition, students described learning engineering concepts and applying those to various problems, as these quotations exemplify:

I had to learn a whole new concept and do problem solving with that in the course of the quarter. This was the research mentioned earlier with the MEMS. MEMS were on a silicon wafer that had channels etched into it. We would put a chemical on there that would open or close those channels. It stretched my thinking at the time to figure out how it worked.

The challenging part was not the homework, but to understand the homework you had to understand the concepts. That was in the air for me; I just couldn't grab at it. It was a totally different way of thinking. It is not a math problem or a physics problem. It is not something that you can memorize. It is a kind of creative kind of thing.

Similar to challenges students described in architecture and urban planning, students speaking about engineering courses described having to create design solutions to engineering problems, which included anticipating potential problems in their solutions. As the engineering problems became more complex, students needed to draw on all their knowledge in the field, conduct research, and even learn new skills. For example:

We had to write code for these microprocessors that we didn't know about. They had certain ways of doing things that we didn't know. Instead of values, for instance they had signals from wires and stuff. So we had to problem solve to see how we could combine what we knew with what we were learning to make this embedded system work. We had to put together electronic components on a board and then interact with other boards—there were just a lot of things. You had to come up with the end result, but they never told us how to get there. I enjoy those problems—it's a challenge to figure out how to do something—where you are creating your own stuff to solve a problem rather than using a lot of other people's stuff.

In many cases, students created what they had designed. Examples of students' designs included computer programs, computer hardware, and objects such as bridges and spacecrafts. Often this design and/or build process was carried out independently, requiring a second set of critical thinking and problem solving skills from students. When asked to work independently, students had to rely on themselves, and often that meant that they consulted with faculty or other students to test their understanding. Students also worked in groups that were largely independent of faculty guidance. Both of these modes of operation forced students to collaborate. As one student said:

Basically [on our electrical engineering project] you were thrown into a group of three other teams, and you had to use your strengths to make up for their weaknesses. We had to figure out our strength and what would make us unique. There was a bridge in the middle of a field that would tilt one way or the other, and there was barrier on the other side of it, and our goal was to get our robots to the other side of the field. You could go over. We actually went under it.

Howard Chizek, a professor and chair of electrical engineering, discussed critical thinking in engineering, emphasizing the role of mathematics, the importance of understanding the problem at hand, and the value of asking how to solve the problem. Chizek said:

So you have probably encountered by now that engineers would prefer "problem solving" to be what's taught rather than "critical thinking." But there is an aspect where they're intertwined. In large part, we try to teach students how to think and analyze, which may mean building mathematical models. So this is analysis for understanding the workings and interactions of whatever it is they're studying, with then usually a step involved of using results and conclusions to predict outcomes under different conditions and designs.

Twenty years ago, it would have been design we were teaching. Now we probably say "problem solving." But I think both are really structured forms of critical thinking—very structured, but they are critical thinking. When the term was "design," the question would be "How do you know that your design will function well?" And so there's a process, which has some of the aspects of critical thinking. "How do you know that the model is valid?" And when it is problem solving, then there are two issues. One is understanding and defining the problem, which is very difficult and involves people in the outside world and environmental phenomena. And secondly, "How do you know that you are solving the problem?"

Based on the students' descriptions of critical thinking and problem solving challenges, and the design questions Professor Chizek mentioned in the interview, there was noticeable overlap between art, architecture, and engineering, if looked at abstractly. This connection was also captured by some of the survey questions. All three fields of study required students to learn technical knowledge about materials and how to use them, and to find creative design solutions to problems. However, the problems students tackled, the methods they used, and the materials they worked with were all quite different. And the wide range of project types, from propellers to spacecrafts, from building computer hardware to programming it, was unique to engineering. While the similarities across these disciplinary categories may be seductive, the particular contexts they represent made significantly different demands on students' thinking. Differences in departments inside each of these broad disciplinary categories complicate the matter even more.

Challenges in the Humanities

One task that many students found challenging in their humanities courses was learning to read and analyze texts—from literary works to philosophical arguments—individually or in the context of other texts. The following quotation serves as an example of this challenge:

> That would be because of the advanced analysis we were doing of particular authors' strategies and language [in English]. In order to really deconstruct those strategies, you have to think about the entire situation that the author was in, chronologically and politically, and also closely analyze the text. We looked at Ann Radcliff's *The Italian,* and we did close reading of particular passages, such as when the character is standing and listening and watching things that are going on around him, and he hears a funeral mass off in the distance. Every word choice, structure, and scenic detail is placed in order to move the reader towards this solemn meditative idea that Radcliff is trying to get across.

Another challenge related to textual analysis was thinking about authorship—who wrote the text and how that writer's experience may inform her writing.

A wide range of humanities courses—including linguistics, English, and foreign language study—asked students to think about the function and structure of language. For example:

> We had some theoretical problems to work out individually without a whole lot of background. It required individual problem solving and critical thinking. These were problems about syntax and how certain words are functioning in the language in general—in all potential uses.

Students were also challenged to think about issues—social, philosophic, and political—from multiple perspectives because of reading various textual perspectives and/or discussing the issues with others. Students in the humanities discussed being deeply challenged by these and other perspectives different from their own. Sometimes that challenge was part of a humanities-based, study-abroad experience; other times students spoke of course-based challenges. Whether those experiences were local or international, when students considered new perspectives, those views often elicited reflective thought about what the students believed, as these two students' comments illustrate:

> In South Africa just experiencing the culture and allowing myself to experience it instead of negating it was challenging. I had to say yes. I had to go out and talk to people, try to meet people, get around town on my own, figure out how to get places, talk to people, listen to people.

> The intro to ethics class challenged a lot of my personal beliefs, challenged my own ideas of morality. You think you are a pretty moral person, and then you think about what drives you to act. That makes you question how much of that is selfish and how much isn't. And then you start to doubt your own thinking on morality in general, and then you have to reshape your thinking on how you act and why you act.

In speaking of their most challenging critical thinking activities, students included the many thinking challenges involved in writing in the humanities. Challenges students described included incorporating their own ideas and analyses into a paper, sustaining a coherent argument throughout a paper, and determining what kinds of evidence were preferred and how best to use the evidence. Students in philosophy spoke of learning how to write good philosophical arguments. The following quotations provide examples of writing challenges:

> Just through readings and plays, figure out a strong argument, figure out something that is arguable and that you can get a paper out of. Something you are able to prove with evidence. And then finding the evidence that will support that argument. Those things are challenging.

> Philosophy—I'm taking it right now. There is no right or wrong answer as they say in the book, but there is a certain set of rules that you have to follow to interpret or analyze what you are doing. There is not a specific formula that works every

time, but there are still good and bad arguments. So you really have to understand how language works to make arguments
effective, and it seems like a practice-based thing, even though
you are following certain guidelines. It seems like a foreign
language. You don't understand it until you have gone over it
again and again. It is the whole way of thinking that is really
challenging in there so far. We haven't done anything but
some practice problems so far.

We interviewed Suzanne Petersen, a faculty member in the Spanish department,
about critical thinking in the humanities, particularly in language study.
Petersen drew a distinction between the first two years of language study and
subsequent years, saying that the first two years are primarily focused on acquiring and developing the four basic receptive and productive skills (listening com-
prehension and reading; speaking and writing), so the type of critical thinking
students do in those courses is less complex than the type they do later. Petersen
noted a difference as students' ability to use the language became more sophisticated. Her description of critical thinking in the study of Spanish abroad
echoes much of what students described as critical thinking and problem solving challenges in the humanities. Petersen said:

Obviously anyone teaching the study of literature and culture
would be interested in getting their students to think critically about what they are reading, about what the texts they are
reading mean. In my field there is all of Spanish-speaking
Latin America—19 countries—plus Spain (and Latinos in the
U.S.). The vast majority of students see Latin America as more
relevant because of its proximity to the U.S. and the relevance
of Mexico and trade. Students now tend to be less accepting
of the traditional canon that our department may have for-
warded some time ago, and so studying the literature or cultural phenomena of the 16th century doesn't seem so
immediately relevant to them. One of the challenges for the
faculty is to try to get students to reflect on that material, to
see how it is applicable, and what it has to say about human
beings in general and how that may or may not be different
from the issues that are relevant to contemporary culture. All
of that can involve asking students to think critically on these
kinds of matters.

I suppose any cultural differences, those reflected in literature or in the study of culture, will lead to the students learning

something about a culture that's different. And this will raise questions about why they do things differently than we do and whether their way might not be better than ours. Our students, for example, who go to Cadiz, go with an open mind, but they are struck by how different everything is. Many of them tend to go with the assumption that the U.S.—the way we do everything—is the right way, the best way, and that anything else is just that they haven't quite learned how to do it the way we do it. So one of the goals of foreign study programs like ours is to have them actually experience other ways of living, to get to know people who think differently, and to reflect about whether or not they want to continue to think that our way is the best way, that our way is the only way. This comes up all the time with issues like national medical care and university systems. So there's an awful lot of critical thinking that happens, but it is not a spelled out part of the curriculum. It's intrinsic, I would think, to the study of literature and culture of other nations.

Critical thinking and problem solving in the humanities appeared to focus on textual analysis and the construction of arguments to meet the standards of various disciplines. Through the lenses of these disciplines, students examine issues, are exposed to multiple perspectives, and often find their views challenged and changed by this experience.

Challenges in Mathematics

In discussions about disciplines, and, indeed, in most places in this book, math is often included with the natural sciences. However, while students described using math in other disciplinary areas, such as engineering, business, and both social and natural sciences, their descriptions of challenges in their math courses were unique and coherent, suggesting that we might profit by looking at math challenges separately from mathematical applications in other disciplines. In this category, several themes emerged. One challenge that many students mentioned was learning mathematical concepts, as this student described:

It was the calculus class, we did some problem solving, mostly general basic busy work equations. But some of the concepts, if they don't explain them to you right the first time, it is hard to get it yourself. The actual understanding of what was going on is the hardest part.

Students also spoke of the challenges in developing mathematical proofs. For example:

> We are asked in this class to give proofs of mathematical statements, and the problem with that, as our professor says, is that there is no hard and fast rule to doing it. The only way you can sort of learn how to do proofs is by doing them.

Students described learning how to identify what a problem was asking them to do and then figuring out how to work with it. Students often needed to translate story problems into mathematical problems, break problems into manageable components, and find ways to engage aspects of real world situations mathematically. The following quotation illustrates this challenge:

> That requires us to do a lot of word problem solving. Sometimes just the way the question is worded makes the problem more difficult than it actually is. The difficult part is having to break it into smaller steps, because a lot of the time, you want to maintain the bigger picture. You have to analyze the problem and first figure out what the outcome will be from the question. Then you have to break the problem down into steps to solve it. Then you go through the steps one by one until you get to the outcome.

Another thinking challenge that students described in their math classes was learning multiple ways to approach and/or solve problems. For example:

> It was the second of two [quantitative science courses], and we got into integrals and differential equations. It was more challenging than the previous course, but the math was starting to get into stuff for which there was more than one way of answering the question—some ways being easier. There was a lot of thinking about which way I wanted to go about solving the problem, how I wanted to deal with it.

Similarly, students described needing to extrapolate from what they had learned—formulas, theorems, and approaches—to solve new, more complex problems. For example, many students taking 100-level math courses said that exams often required them to complete problems that were more complex versions of homework, requiring them to take a "leap" in their thinking. As students moved deeper into the discipline, they described working with problems that forced them to draw on all their mathematical knowledge in new and imaginative ways. The following quotations illustrate these challenges:

> In math they always explain things to you, and then on the tests they expect you to take them to the next level. In this class, I could do it but it was more memorization, so on the final where I had to take it to the next level, it was kind of a shot in the dark. I kind of understood it, and I could play with it to see if it worked, to find the flaws in my hypothesis. What caused it to be so hard is that before, everything was really progressional; it wasn't a stretch of the imagination to see what was coming.

> Dynamical systems is one of the newest fields in mathematics, and we just have learned so much. We are pulling things together that we have learned in this class and pulling things together from previous math classes and then things I have yet to learn, at least rigorously. Things like topology and manifolds, we don't do too rigorously because we don't have time to get to the chaos part of it. In a way it is almost conceptual and intuitive, but we have this mass of resources at our disposal with which to talk about the problems, and those come from our whole math experience and stuff that we have learned recently.

In the students' descriptions of critical thinking and problem solving challenges in math, a clear process of thinking challenges emerge: recognizing and translating elements of a scenario into mathematical terms, working with those terms to get an answer, and translating the answer back into a meaningful form. In addition to this process, the students described the more creative, thought-expanding characteristics of learning to think mathematically.

Challenges in Science

Students who spoke of their most challenging critical thinking as coming from the natural sciences mentioned thinking tasks from a wide range of scientific disciplines—astronomy to zoology. One challenge that many students described in a variety of natural sciences courses was learning about the physical world, from genetics to the characteristics of space rocks. In learning about the physical world, students described the challenges of looking at physical phenomena up close, as well as understanding the relationships in a bigger system. For example:

In anatomy, learning all the bones. You have to look at it from a different point of view, not just a flat picture but as a 3-D. What the bone articulates with. You have to try to picture everything else besides the bone, see it from a cross-sectional point of view.

The issue of fisheries is enormous on how many people it affects. If you make a decision to stop fishing, there are a lot of people who suffer, and if you make a decision to keep fishing, then you eventually deplete the supply. It is impossible to please both the economy and the environment. So it is really challenging to be faced with hypothetical situations on what we would do and why in this class.

In addition, some students noted the challenge of seeing the world in ways that differed from their own perspectives. This student, for example, described the challenge of looking at the world through a biological lens:

I just don't walk around thinking in Darwinian logic. It is a mode you have to get into in class or when you are doing your work. It's the kind of thinking that says we are animals, and right in with them. We're a little more complex, but still pretty simple. Staying in that train of thought is challenging, and believing it. If you are thinking as a biologist or in a Darwinian-theory way, then that is able to explain it.

Students also reported learning to analyze, interpret, and work with scientific data. Another challenge students described was learning how to identify, set up, and solve problems. Often students were asked to do this work independently, with partial or no direction. In some cases, students described having to extrapolate from what they had learned to solve new problems and/or attempt to understand new situations. One student's quotation illustrates this challenge:

They give you a problem that looks simple on the surface, but unless you know what they are doing, you have to make assumptions about the problem. You have to be comfortable making assumptions and go off those. There are a lot of steps they leave out and expect you to figure out on your own. It's not just a matter of did you understand the formula and understand it conceptually, but can you think logically on your own and work though a problem that you haven't seen anything similar to before?

Students often mentioned learning to use math to solve problems within the discipline and according to its particular demands. For example:

> There was a lot of applied mathematics in biochemistry, as opposed to just being able to figure out different problems and solve them mathematically. The math itself wasn't hard, but figuring out when to use what and figuring out what the answer means—that part was hard.

Students also described the challenges in lab work, including setting up and conducting lab experiments, writing results in lab reports, and learning how to work with physical materials. These students discussed learning through trial and error to be precise, careful, and to analyze experiments from multiple perspectives. For example:

> We had to regurgitate results and do the math right, but that wasn't the thing they cared most about you doing. It was the conclusions you drew and your discussion afterwards, and that was up to your interpretation of what you did, what went wrong. And it was never anything clear like "I dropped my beaker on the floor." It was always a little bit off. You had to really understand what was going on.

In addition to these kinds of tasks, students described a broader challenge that required them to draw on all the knowledge and skills they learned to solve increasingly complex problems, develop and conduct research projects, and report their findings, as this student described:

> This is independent research, so the objective is to come up with your own experiment or one with the help of the professor, and then you have to set it up by yourself. You have to figure out how to keep a little ecosystem in a jar going as long as you can—algae and daphnia, and maybe some other things— to see how complex you can get the ecosystem and still keep it alive. These are sealed, too. You have to make an experiment that you think it is going to work and make a hypothesis about it. Taking something from thin air and making it work is challenging.

While most of the work students described took place in class or in lab, some students talked about applying what they had learned to real-world situations. One student described this challenge in the context of rehabilitation classes:

These are basically dealing with patients with lower extremity prosthetics and orthotics. Doing an evaluation of a patient and coming up with what kind of device they need with no help from the profs. We have to take muscle tests and other tests to figure out what is best for the patients. This is not just critical thinking where you look at a paper and figure out the problems. This is dealing with an actual person. What you do makes a big difference.

Physics professor Lillian C. McDermott and biology professor Barbara Wakimoto discussed critical thinking in ways that differed somewhat from students' descriptions. For both McDermott and Wakimoto, critical thinking in science—scientific thinking—was about asking questions to determine if the conclusions drawn from data were correct. While students described processes that necessarily incorporated a question/answer process, for the most part, they described concrete individual tasks, rather than the intellectual stance that McDermott and Wakimoto described. Lillian C. McDermott said this about critical thinking in science:

I have a separate name for the kinds of reasoning involved in scientific processes, the different kinds of reasoning that are used to build inferences. You could say that's part of critical thinking, but I'm putting it into something I'm calling "scientific thinking." And I would say another kind—and again, you could call it critical thinking—is "reflective thinking:" How do I know if I know? What kinds of questions do I have to ask myself to know if I really know something? And if I don't, what kind of questions do I have to ask myself in order to understand? So I guess what I'm trying to say is that I'm giving it a different name. I wouldn't argue if someone came in and said, "You know, everything you said is critical thinking." But I was using critical thinking in the narrower sense. Are these facts? What are the grounds for them? Are they data you can trust? And if so do your conclusions follow from that or are your conclusions coming from your opinions or your beliefs? And that applies to me outside physics. It applies to history, it applies to almost anything—history, English.

Similarly, Barbara Wakimoto said:

> I'm an experimental biologist, as opposed to what some peo-
> ple might call a strict observational or descriptive biologist. A
> descriptive biologist will analyze something by describing or
> observing it. This is an important scientific approach because
> it shows you what's out there in the world. However, an exper-
> imental biologist wants to know precisely how things work.
> For example, we want to understand the mechanisms under-
> lying how organisms exist, how they adapt, how they repro-
> duce, these sorts of things. So critically observing and thinking
> in experimentation are really key. Are you asking the right
> questions? Are you using the right tools to ask the questions?
> When you get an answer, are you interpreting the answer cor-
> rectly? When you make a conclusion, does it match the
> results? When you make a generalization, is it a fair general-
> ization? Asking and answering these questions require some
> critical thinking.
>
> I think all biologists will give you some form of these
> questions when asked to define critical thinking, but they
> might come up with variations depending on their approach.
> Science is like many human endeavors—there's a big compo-
> nent of creativity in it. Every scientist will bring in a different
> perspective in the way they look at a problem and in the way
> they do an experiment. I think the perception from the out-
> side world and from students when they first start to do sci-
> ence is that there is a right and there is a wrong way to do
> things. But as you become a scientist, you realize—and this is
> the creative part—that you bring all of your perspectives into
> your work. So if I would give five students the same project in
> my lab, they could each use a different way of approaching the
> project and would make different kinds of discoveries. That is
> actually the really fun part of doing science for many of us.

As with architecture, art, and engineering, students and the faculty with
whom we spoke described working with the physical world in the sciences. The
sciences seemed primarily concerned, however, with understanding the physical
world, rather than using that understanding for other purposes. Thus, the critical thinking and problem solving challenges in the sciences were quite distinct
from these other disciplinary categories.

Challenges in the Social Sciences

Perhaps because the social sciences encompass a wide range of disciplines, as well as interdisciplinary departments such as American ethnic studies, the critical thinking challenges described by students were remarkably varied. In speaking of challenging critical thinking in their social sciences courses, students mentioned learning new information, concepts, and ways of thinking, ranging from the relatively simple—learning bits of concrete data—to the very complex—learning how to conceive of complex systems. For example:

> [In my law, societies, and justice class] I learned a lot about the criminal justice system that I was not aware of—about the jails, for instance. That really solidified my interest in the major. It showed me how messed up our criminal justice system is and it made me think a lot about what is wrong with our society, when it comes to race, politics, and money.

> The [international studies] class is helping me better understand what it is to be a monotheist country and what monotheistic countries represent.

> [In African-American studies], we had to research court cases and present them to class. I'm not trained in legal analysis, so it was difficult for me to step into that kind of thinking.

Many students spoke of the challenges involved in learning to read and analyze social science texts, a process they often found difficult and which placed varied demands on the student. For example, students described imagining the historical context of a text, thinking about the perspectives of authors, staying aware of their own perspectives as they were reading texts, or reading a text multiple times. This student's quotation serves as an example of this challenge:

> [In history] I had to look at four or five different authors' versions of something that happened in Alexander the Great's time—like the fall of Thebes. I would have to trace back their sources, too. All of this to try to decipher what the truth of Alexander the Great was. Alexander's crossing the Bosphorus, for example. How significant was that? It was looking at things like that and trying to discern what had happened, trying to get all the authors' opinions and interpretations out of it. Olympus, for instance, his mother—historians would say

that she was an evil person. But there is no evidence. I tried to find out the bare facts.

Students also spoke of learning to work with various forms of data. This challenge included learning how to analyze, interpret, or generate graphs and charts, convert data into useable forms, and perform statistical analyses. The following quotation illustrates this challenge:

> It was a departure from my earlier economics class. It really specified something within microeconomics, looking at areas where you really don't have markets and you have to estimate valuations. The final was the most challenging exam I have taken here. The questions on there were nothing like we had seen before or had discussed. We had to apply previously learned concepts to those brand new problems. It was an intense test. A buddy of mine and I came out of there going, "What the hell was that?" But it was a great test. One question asked us how we would value gasoline during an energy crisis when the government tells you that we need to cut down consumption. You could see the argument for valuing it any of the three ways. Another thing about that class was we went through and looked at a bunch of cost/benefit analyses. To see the same kind of analysis applied in such different ways was really helpful.

Another challenge students described was learning how to think about issues, events, ideas, and/or texts from multiple perspectives. They did so because they were asked to read a single text that embodied a new perspective, because they read multiple texts offering a variety of perspectives about the same issue, or because they discussed the subject matter with others. The following example illustrates this challenge:

> In sociology, it had to do with writing a paper and taking the theory we learned about and applying it ourselves to the deviant behavior that we chose. We didn't talk about opium use [the behavior I chose] in class, but we did talk about the different theories. We were supposed to pick which theory best explained it, but we could offer up another one. I said that there was one that was the best—labeling theory—and I used the historic account in China, and I used other theories—consensus and conflict theory—as contrasts. The appli-

cation of the theories was the challenging part—thinking of all the different theories we had used. I think you could apply almost any theory to any deviant behavior, but it was picking the theory that best explained it and arguing why.

Students also described learning how to be reflective about their own thinking. This activity was sometimes assigned, and sometimes it simply followed from being asked to do other kinds of thinking. This student's quotation exemplifies this challenge:

> This class talks about racism and minority groups, and for me as a minority, it forces me to think about the other side of a lot of the issues, plus consider stuff I have never considered before. For me being an Asian American, I never considered the struggles of Native Americans. I became so absorbed with my personal story, I never thought of the macro level of how minority groups relate to the dominant groups in America. Now I am contemplating the other side of the issues.

Another challenge students mentioned in the social sciences was learning how to write thesis-driven papers. Students described writing assignments as challenging them to learn specific forms of writing, integrate sources into their own arguments, and sustain arguments in long papers. The following student spoke about the challenge of writing in an international studies course:

> This class was my first big paper, my thesis for a Latin American Studies degree. The thesis was about Guatemalan peasant mobilization in the 1970s. The topic was one I did not know anything about before writing about it, but I was directed to several good sources, and I felt that overall I gained a much clearer understanding about peasant mobilization and Guatemalan history. It was challenging for me to understand a new history, a new culture, and most of all it was challenging for me to connect all these themes into a big, thesis-driven paper.

Furthermore, students spoke of the challenge of learning to work independently, including relying on themselves to make intellectual decisions, as well as the challenge of learning to work on projects in groups that included both professors and peers. They also spoke of learning to think about real-world problems, often having to take into account many different factors, including the economic, historical, legal, ethical, cultural, and environmental elements of a problem. In some cases, students were asked to develop potential solutions to the problems. The following student's response serves as an example of this category of challenge:

> It was [my capstone] task force class and my topic was the US and Japan's relationship in the light of China's new leadership. The class was challenging because it required me to make foreign policy, something I had not previously done. All the variables that go into foreign policy-making forced me to take time in my opinions and develop my ideas wholly, which is something that seems easier in an essay format than it is when you are thinking about it.

Students discussed finding information and figuring out which information to use as part of other challenges, and as a challenge in and of itself. While other quotations in this section can illustrate this challenge, the following quotation serves as an additional example:

> Especially sifting through large amounts of information [in my communication courses], trying to organize it, eliminate the stuff that is not important and keep the important stuff, and then organize it according to what is most important and to begin there. And even before that process, you need to find the information, and that also requires an effort to think out where you are going to get it.

Finally, students spoke of meeting sets of challenges, where they needed to draw on everything they had learned to solve increasingly complex problems. Students met these challenges often as part of capstone or senior projects, as this student described:

> This was my senior thesis [in American ethnic studies]. I needed to come up with my own idea from what I have learned in the past three years. Just being able to formulate a thesis to go well with the information that I've gotten was challenging. I talked about language as being a powerful thing. I looked at a few cases that happened in Hawaii. A man applied for a job, and he scored the highest on the test, but they denied his application because he had a pronounced accent. He filed a lawsuit against the city and county. I was arguing that there is a subjectivity in understanding accents. If people hear a French accent, they think, "how cool, how

sophisticated," but if people hear other accents, like a Chinese accent or a Pidgin accent, they hear it differently. Language can go against or for you. The thinking was challenging because there were a lot of aspects of language I could have touched upon, and I just needed to focus on a particular part. Getting information was challenging and making it all concise. Also, making it all fit together was challenging.

The excerpt that follows is from an interview with Robert Stacey, a UW history professor who has served as chair of the department and as divisional dean of social sciences. Stacey describes the challenges involved in textual analysis and discusses the term *problem solving.*

I think about critical thinking as meaning that we're trying to get students to read texts critically. They need to understand that a historical source is not going to be a factual newspaper report—and furthermore, even newspaper reports are not immune from the need to ask when was it written? Who wrote it? What were their sources of information? What are the biases and purposes that shape what is being presented? And how do all of those questions affect your capacity as a researcher to draw useful information out of it? I think that these questions in a nutshell would be a good part of critical thinking. Also involved in it is the ability to frame a question that can then be researched and answered, the ability to break a large question down into several smaller questions and answer those, and then build an answer back up. All those would be aspects of critical thinking.

There are other challenges, but I wouldn't put them under the heading of critical thinking. They are more technical challenges—where do you go to find information? where might a set of records have ended up?—that kind of thing. But I don't see them as critical thinking in the same way.

I think problem solving is a very problematic term in history, because one of the things I will say to my first-year students is, "Look, what do historians do? Well, historians argue about the past and what it means." Problem solving carries with it a sense of "Right, got that one done. That problem is solved. I've solved for X." And of course, that's never what historians are doing. No historical question is ever closed, at least if it's of any interest. I can imagine questions being closed—for instance, on what day did the artillery barrage on Fort Sumter begin?— but historians, by and large, don't argue about those kinds of questions. That's just data. So we can certainly talk sensibly in history about how to frame a question, how to analyze a question, how to break a question down so you can think about it in chunks. But "problem solving"? It's a kind of instrumentalist vocabulary that doesn't mean very much to us.

Interestingly, in describing the critical thinking and problem solving challenges in archaeology, a social sciences area that leans far into the natural sciences, anthropology professor Donald Grayson's comments are quite different from Stacey's, highlighting the range of critical thinking and problem solving challenges in the social sciences.

There are two separate strains in archaeology, one more prominent than the other, I think. Most archaeologists see themselves as scientists, so they worry less about how they think than whether or not their work matches what they see as the requirements of scientific reasoning. If you ask them what critical thinking is, it's the kind of thinking that meets these requirements. It's thinking that meets the requirements of a scientific approach. Working within a theoretical framework, specify hypotheses concretely, specify implications of those hypotheses, test them objectively, and so on. Whether or not that's what archeologists do in any given setting, that's probably the kind of response you would get most often. We are teasing out hidden assumptions and things of that sort. Almost all my work occurs within a theoretical framework, usually derived from some version of evolutionary ecology, and where I try to think critically, what I do is to again specify a series of hypotheses that I can test with archaeological data. The hardest part—the most critical aspect of thinking in archaeology—is working in a conceptual framework in such a way that the statements that you make and the arguments that you make can be falsified.

There is a small branch of archaeology that is post-modernist in orientation. The belief there is that there is no way to test the true value of the data. They would have a different view of what critical thinking would be.

As students' and faculty descriptions show, more than any other disciplinary category, critical thinking and problem solving in the social sciences involved thinking challenges mentioned in other disciplinary categories. Various social science areas used mathematics, textual analysis, scientific reasoning, hypothesis-driven written arguments, and other elements found in sciences and humanities. Of course, as in other cases, the particular use the social sciences made of these elements was unique to the disciplines within this category.

Thinking in the Disciplines

Students' responses to questions about challenging critical thinking provide strong evidence for Sam Wineburg's assertion that "solving a physics problem and solving a historical one draw on different skills, dispositions, and most of all, deep familiarity with the ways of speaking within these respective communities of discourse" (cited in Fisher, Beyer, & Gillmore, 2001, p. 2) The academic disciplines create knowledge differently, as Table 5.3 demonstrates. They may all pose questions about realities, but the questions they ask differ, their methods for answering those questions differ, and the way they communicate their answers differ. Even the realities that get their attention differ. Furthermore, students' descriptions of critical thinking and problem solving challenges clearly showed that with our broad disciplinary categories, we could only just begin to identify differences.

Students enter this varied universe when they matriculate. In their first two years, they move from discipline to discipline, taking courses taught by faculty who have been experts in their fields for so long, they may have forgotten what it feels like to be a novice. The experience for students can be similar to being dropped into a society of people who speak a language and practice a culture that looks vaguely familiar but that the student does not understand. Time, focus, and intense interest help majors learn the language and culture of their disciplines. But students, especially freshmen, are often moving from culture to culture, taking classes in biology, English, and history at the same time, trying to navigate each one with few guiding stars to show them how to do so successfully. We know, as our next section in this chapter will demonstrate, that most successfully arrive at their majors, but the early journey can be bumpy.

Changes in How Students Defined Critical Thinking and Problem Solving

In addition to tracking students' descriptions of critical thinking and problem solving challenges, we examined students' definitions of critical thinking and problem solving over time. In the first, third, and fourth years, we asked students how they defined critical thinking and problem solving. In the fourth year,

Table 5.3. *Most Challenging Critical Thinking, 2000–2003*

Architecture and Urban Planning	• See and think differently about buildings and space, including learning to visualize something that is not there
	• Apply new ways of seeing in the critique of architectural drawings and plans
	• Create design solutions that fit specific needs and include consideration of material and cost constraints, engineering issues, building codes, ideas to be represented, and the human and environmental impacts of the proposed solutions
	• Build what they designed
	• Work independently, relying on themselves in the design and build processes
	• Collaborate with others—peers, professors, and community members
	• Think self-reflectively about their own values and biases, discuss them with peers
Arts	• See and understand the physical world differently
	• Investigate emotional, experiential, and/or intellectual issues using different lenses
	• Translate emotions, ideas, and ways of seeing into concrete objects or performances
	• Work with and use the physicality of the medium
	• Think reflectively: ideas, feelings, or the meanings explored and expressed
	• Work on projects together, which alters the critical thinking challenges
	• Critique their own and others' work; incorporate critiques into their creative processes
Business	• Think about financial data, including how to use data, how data relate to each other, and what they mean in different contexts—from small businesses to global economies
	• Use mathematical tools to understand or solve business problems
	• Understand the ethical and legal issues that need to be considered in business
	• Perform market research and create good marketing strategies
	• Track and consider factors in international trade and markets
	• Apply a wide range of business knowledge and skills to simulated or real business situations, involving small businesses and international organizations
	• Work independently
	• Work in collaboration with others as a member of a team

Table 5.3 (continued). *Most Challenging Critical Thinking, 2000–2003*

Engineering	• Think about, understand, and account for the material constraints the physical world imposes upon designs • Use numbers, equations, and computer programs to perform engineering tasks • Understand engineering concepts and apply them in solving engineering problems • Build what they designed • Rely on themselves • Create design solutions for engineering problems, including anticipating potential problems with their solutions, drawing on all their knowledge in the field and any other resources available, learning new skills; conducting research, and incorporating unfamiliar techniques in solving those problems
Humanities	• Work effectively in collaboration with others • Read and analyze texts from literary works to philosophy, either individually or in the context of other texts • Think about authorship—who wrote the text and how does that experience inform it • Consider the function and structure of language • Understand social, political, or philosophical issues from multiple perspectives, reflecting on their own beliefs in the context of others • Write papers that include analysis, critique, and their own ideas • Sustain coherent written arguments, paying attention to kinds of evidence preferred, how to use that evidence, and forms of argumentation allowed by various disciplines
Mathematics	• Understand mathematical concepts • Develop mathematical proofs • Understand multiple ways to approach and/or to solve problems • Extrapolate from learned formulas, theorems, and approaches to solve new, more complex problems
Science	• Understand the physical world, including being able to look at physical phenomena up close, as well as in relationship to larger systems • See the world in ways that differed from their own perspectives • Analyze, interpret, and work with scientific data • Identify, set up, and solve problems, often independently, with partial or no direction, and sometimes extrapolate from what was learned to solve new problems and/or attempt to understand new situations • Use math to solve problems in other disciplines and according to the particular demands of those disciplines

Table 5.3 (continued). *Most Challenging Critical Thinking, 2000–2003*

Science	• Set up and conduct lab experiments and write results in lab reports • Draw on all the knowledge and skills they learned to solve increasingly complex problems, including developing, conducting, and reporting their own research projects • Apply what they learned to real-world situations
Social Science	• Understand new information, concepts, and ways of thinking • Read and analyze social science texts, including imagining the historical context of a text, thinking about authors' perspectives, staying aware of their own perspectives, or reading a text multiple times • Work with various forms of data, including learning to analyze, interpret, or generate graphs and charts; convert data into useable form, perform statistical analyses • Reflect on their own thinking • Think about issues, events, ideas, and/or texts from multiple perspectives • Write thesis-driven papers in the social sciences: learn specific forms of writing, integrate sources into their own arguments, and sustain an argument in a long paper • Work independently, including relying on themselves to make academic decisions • Work on projects in groups that included both professors and peers • Find information and identify which to use • Think about real-world problems, including consideration of the economic, historical, legal, ethical, cultural, and/or environmental elements of a problem, sometimes developing potential solutions to real-world problems • Draw on everything learned to solve increasingly complex problems

we also asked them whether their definitions of critical thinking had changed since they entered the university. After they gave us their definitions, we asked them to describe how their majors defined critical thinking.

To assess how these definitions changed, if at all, we randomly selected a sample of 26 UW SOUL participants from the 63 who were still in the study in 2003. We then compared their 1999 definitions of critical thinking and problem solving with their 2003 definitions. Most likely as a consequence of a two-year immersion in disciplinary definitions of critical thinking, students' own definitions of critical thinking changed. Instead of the broad definitions students gave as freshmen, which often focused on general question asking, students' fourth-year definitions tended to line up with how they perceived their majors defined critical thinking.

Of the 26 students, we found change in 21 (about 81%). This included substantial change in 16 of them and some change in five. There was little to no change in five students' responses over time (about 19%). Furthermore, 17 of the 21 students (81%) whose definitions changed over time gave personal definitions that closely resembled those they supplied for their majors. Two of the five students whose definitions did not change over time gave definitions in their first year that closely resembled the definitions they gave for their majors in their fourth year. The definitions students provided for their majors echoed both differences we saw in students' descriptions of challenging critical thinking tasks and differences we noted across the faculty we interviewed. Table 5.4 provides students' definitions of critical thinking in their majors in seven disciplinary areas. The table demonstrates differences across these categories, but what it cannot capture are the impressive variations within them.

Our findings indicated that as the students moved deeper into the disciplines of their majors, they adopted the intellectual values and practices of those fields. Furthermore, interviews with faculty suggested that students learned how to operate in the discipline more by their immersion in it as majors than as a result of explicit teaching by faculty about the culture of their disciplines. Students repeatedly observed faculty, graduate students, and other majors modeling such thinking and methods, and these observations were reinforced by reading and work with peers. Without the benefit of repeated exposure, students outside those majors but taking courses in them—notably freshmen and most sophomore students—often never figured out how those cultures operated.

Table 5.4. *Sample of Students' Definitions of Critical Thinking in Their Majors*

Architecture & Urban Planning (Architecture)	It is to think of it as a useable building from a human point of view. How easy is it to use? How clear is it from "Where am I supposed to go and where are the stairs?" to "What is this building trying to say?" How clear is the message? What does it stand for? How does it reflect what is going on inside? Is it a church or a school? Do I design a circus in a cemetery? There are a plethora of questions, and you bring those to bear on anything you are looking at or doing yourself.
Arts (Drama)	I think that the biggest challenge is whether the project I'm doing right now is important. How is it important in the greater society or to the audience who is seeing it, and how can we better facilitate that? How can we facilitate what the author wants? Or, if I am writing it myself, why am I writing it? What do I want it to do? And then, how do the words do that? How does the way I perform it do it? The music? Everything that goes into that.
Business (Finance and Info Systems)	In finance, you have to have an understanding of what is going on in the environment you are in. Let's say I am looking at a case study. You look at the specific company, read about it, apply it to what you know that is going on in the environment, and then you have to put them together. What is going on in this little company will be totally affected by what is going on in the economy, so you have to put them together. In info systems, if you are consulting for a company that needs a new database, you just analyze the needs of the company and don't look at the external environment so much. You look at the company's needs and form a solution.
Engineering (Computer Science)	It means to be able to analyze a problem. Most of the time problems are somewhat poorly defined, and we need to make them well defined. Most people when they communicate something, there are unsaid specifications that we take for granted. But when you are writing a program, everything needs to be said explicitly. In Computer Science Engineering critical thinking is taking these real-world problems and determining what the parameters are, how to make the problems literal.
Humanities (Comp History of Ideas)	It means to be independent, to accept a lot of perspectives, and to be aware of the tradition of thinking that you are a part of. Being able to criticize. Self-reflection is part of this too.

Table 5.4 (continued). Sample of Students' Definitions of Critical Thinking in Their Majors

Sciences (Biochemistry)	In the sciences, thinking critically means putting everything up for scrutiny, as far as data and results. No theory can be proven. It can only be disproven. It only takes one negative result to disprove a theory and it takes a lot of positive results to get close to proving something. You have to be very critical about every step you take moving in that direction. A small mistake can lead you down the wrong path.
Social Sciences (Political Science)	It means thinking theoretically and applying theories. There is always a theory for everything. I'm taking a class on organizational policy and there is a theory on how bureaucracies operate, and there are theories about how you should look at things—as a realist or a liberal. When you are answering questions, you have to take a problem, learn what the levels of analysis are, then see a problem from the perspective of several theories—a realist would look at it like this, a liberal would look at it like this, the media would look at it like this.

Students' Self-Assessment

The majority of students said that they believed their ability to problem solve and to think critically improved every year—about 87% in the first year; 86% in the second year, 93% in the third year; and 84% in the fourth year of the study. The language students used in speaking about their improvement in the second year was more sophisticated—detailed and specific—than that used in first-year responses. Furthermore, this increase in sophistication and complexity continued over time through the third year. In the fourth year, students' descriptions of improvement were somewhat shorter than they had been previously, so it was difficult to see a steady increase in complexity.

In addition, as was true of students' descriptions of their most challenging critical thinking tasks, the role of the disciplines became more prominent in students' descriptions of improvement over time. For example, students in their second year identified the need to shift the kind of thinking they did when they moved from one discipline to another, while no students referred explicitly to the need to make such a shift in the first year. Finally, as students moved through their majors, their comments about why they had improved frequently took on the language of those disciplines. The descriptions of two students, the first a transfer student and the second a student who entered as a freshman, illustrate these changes. Included are each student's first- and fourth-year responses.

First year: Drawing daily, practice—these things have helped me improve. My teachers notice. I am getting less feedback on what is wrong and more on what I have done correctly.

Fourth year: I no longer had somebody with me throughout the steps of making a painting. I had to make a painting, come close to finishing it, and then present it to my instructor. I had to do the complete composition, color mixing, and perspective without guidance. I had to give myself that guidance. At this level of my education, I should be prepared to do that, and I actually did feel that way.

First year: The more you practice at something, the better you become, I guess.

Fourth year: It is sort of like my writing. It has improved in the fact that I can think more scientifically now than I could before. I have read more, and I know now how other people think, and that helps me focus the way I think about things.

Thus, students' assessments of their own improvement suggested that how students thought about critical thinking changed over time from broad to more disciplinary definitions of what it means to think critically and solve problems.

Conclusions and Implications

We end this chapter with three conclusions, noting the assessment and teaching implications for each.

Critical Thinking and Problem Solving Are Disciplinary

The most important finding in this chapter is that critical thinking and problem solving are defined by discipline. Generic explanations of critical thinking and problem solving, though perhaps accurate at some high level of abstraction, are fairly useless in helping students understand what they must actually do when they are asked to think critically or to solve problems in their academic work. It is possible, of course, to learn enough about the subtleties of thinking in the disciplines to abstract out a generic model. For example, all disciplines are likely to agree that they require students to "identify and describe a problem or an issue"—a task that many would include in a generic model of critical thinking. However, as we have seen by students' descriptions of the critical thinking and problem solving tasks they do, each discipline's operationalization of that phrase will differ. An art history major (or a professor of art history) who can identify and describe a problem or issue in her field is likely to be hard pressed to do the same in physics or psychology. The general task of "identify and describe a problem or an issue," therefore, is a kind of stick figure drawing that is misleading, to say the least. Such a picture cannot help students understand what they need to do when they are asked to identify signs of arthritis in the wrist bones, or argue why an individual might rob a convenience store, or determine how to move a disabled person through a landscape. In other words, the figure gives them little real information that they can use in their learning processes, and in fact, suggests that learning is simpler than it actually is.

Accepting that critical thinking and problem solving are defined according to the intellectual values, approaches, and goals of the disciplines has clear implications for assessment and teaching. Regarding assessment, we need to become skeptical of generic models and generic tests of critical thinking and problem solving. Even thoughtfully designed generic tests of critical thinking, such as the Collegiate Learning Assessment from the Rand Corporation,[6] often privilege one domain's approach to critical thinking over others—in this case, business majors over art majors. In addition, the context-bound nature of critical thinking and problem solving makes comparative assessment of achievement across disciplines on campus foolhardy. We recommend that institutions interested in assessing the presence or absence of critical thinking and problem solving in their programs focus on encouraging the disciplines, departments, and programs to identify their learning goals for students in these areas and assess them in ways that fit the cultures and practices of those departments. Institutions may even want to move away from the term "critical thinking" to a term such as "disciplinary thinking," which better reflects the realities on our campuses. Such a change might also help faculty become more explicit in their teaching about what it means to "think like an economist or a scientist."

Regarding teaching, our findings suggest that because critical thinking and problem solving are defined by discipline, faculty in the disciplines need to be explicit in teaching their students how to do the kinds of thinking they require. All too often, it is up to students to decipher the disciplinary demands in a particular setting and figure out how they differ from those in another setting. The problem lessens when students are immersed in the disciplines of their majors.

However, in their first two years, students typically move from discipline to discipline—often within the same academic term. During this time, students in the UW SOUL reported uncertainty, for example, about writing demands (see Chapter 6), often confusing disciplinary differences with professors' idiosyncratic preferences. By helping students become aware of disciplinary differences sooner, educators could make significant improvements in student learning.

Also, when the intellectual demands of the disciplines are more explicit, students will likely have an easier time figuring out where they want to focus their studies.[7] An increased awareness of how thinking and learning differ across the disciplines may have the added benefit of helping faculty better understand their own blind spots, as well as give them a clearer picture of the intellectual maze their students have entered and must feel their way through.

The disciplinary nature of critical thinking and problem solving also implies that effective pedagogy is relative to particular disciplines. How one effectively teaches students to think about improving an architectural design, for example, may be different from how one teaches students to identify bias in an editorial. There is a body of research on the relationship of pedagogy to disciplines, most notably that of Lee Shulman (1986, 1987, 2002), and Bransford et al. (2000), and many journals are devoted to teaching in particular disciplines. However, more work needs to be done in this area by faculty teaching in the disciplines.

Students' Abilities To Think Critically and Problem Solve Increase Over the Four Years of College

A second finding reported in this chapter is that students' critical thinking and problem solving showed movement toward increased complexity and specificity in their four years in college. This change was noticeable in the tasks they were describing, in the thinking they employed, and in the language of their responses, and it is consistent with many research studies that show that students make intellectual gains by going through college (Astin, 1993a; Pascarella & Terenzini, 1991).

This second finding has both assessment and teaching implications. The increase in student specificity and in task complexity is encouraging, even if unsurprising. However, an obvious question arises: Are these increases sufficient? To answer this question, disciplines and departments will need to define the critical thinking and problem solving for themselves. Then they will need to determine what path(s) they want their students to take. Finally, they will need to determine how best to measure success among their own students, using longitudinal as well as cross-sectional data collection procedures.

Students Gradually Adopted the Definitions of Critical Thinking and Problem Solving That They Perceived in Their Majors

A third conclusion is that students' personal definitions of critical thinking and problem solving converge with those they perceive are true for their major. This finding directly supports our speculation that gaining expertise in a discipline brings with it an unconscious blinding to the practices and values of other disciplines, and it suggests that this process begins early in the development of expertise.

As we train ourselves to think in a particular way, that way of thinking becomes more and more entrenched as *our* way of thinking (and unfortunately, sometimes as *the only right way* of thinking). For tenured faculty who have trained themselves to live and breathe their disciplines in ways they may not even recognize, the magnitude and subtlety of the long-term effects of this process are profound.

Again, implications of this finding point to assessment and teaching. Regarding assessment, the blinding effects of one's discipline make it imperative that people from inside the disciplines evaluate students' learning in those disciplines. Alverno College has used this process with great success and has shared it with others for more than 25 years. Researchers embarking on longitudinal assessment studies like ours should make better use of disciplinary faculty than we did to help them create definitions, determine expectations, identify research questions, and analyze findings.

The notion of disciplinarity as blinding also has implications for teaching. If we are unable to remember our own paths to expertise, it is difficult to help a newcomer become a participant in our fields of study, as Nathan and Petrosino (2002) demonstrated. There are many ways for faculty to overcome this obstacle in order to help students learn. In addition to the obvious need for faculty to become self-reflective about their own experience of falling in love with a discipline and learning how it goes about its work, faculty can easily call on the students to remind them of the major stumbling blocks along the way. Angelo and Cross's (1993) seminal work, *Classroom Assessment Techniques,* offers a wide range of methods for gathering such information, and Pace and Middendorf (2004) offer a model workshop design to help faculty identify those confusing places. But it is also very easy simply to ask students, formally or informally, what they are experiencing as they move through a course or a core sequence. This kind of direct approach is often the most illuminating.

Endnotes

1) Trevor said that he took longer to graduate than most transfer students for three reasons: His major required nearly four years of coursework, he completed an academic minor, and he chose to travel to India.

2) Our decision to link the two phrases may have added to the problem we were trying to avoid, because *problem solving* is a term explicitly used in science, engineering, and math. In the first year, students often mentioned classes that used problem solving explicitly more often than courses that did not. However, many students in the first year also were taking challenging math and science courses, so it is quite possible that linking the phrase "problem solving" with "critical thinking" had no effect. We cannot be sure if our terminology biased responses in the first year, but if it did, that problem disappeared after the first year.

3)   1 = *zero*, 2 = *a little*, 3 = *a moderate amount*, 4 = *a lot*

4)   Art, business, and architecture and urban planning did not appear in students' first year responses.

5)   We see evidence of this shift across the curriculum.

6)   *See* www.cae.org/content/pro_collegiate.htm; Matthews (2004).

7)   We gathered some information that suggested that the disciplinary areas premajors identified as presenting them with their earliest most challenging critical thinking experiences became the areas they eventually majored in.

Writing

The most difficult is probably the history papers I'm writing now, just because I don't know how to write a history paper. I know how to analyze books and novels, but I don't know how to include the historical context and other people's opinion. Doing the outside research was very hard, too.

—Leslie, first year

The most challenging paper was the second paper for Biology 401. It was a group paper, and it was hard to work with four other people and have five different writing styles. Also, the material wasn't the easiest to write about. We had to describe biochemically and molecularly what happened when someone has malignant hypothermia—all the proteins involved, all the chemicals involved. It was ten pages long, and we had to do research. Six drafts later we had the final paper.

—Leslie, fourth year

Student writing ability is often the centerpiece of the assessment of learning. Institutions of higher education want to know if students' skill in writing improves over time, and often they use writing to assess other skills, such as critical thinking and information literacy. Yet, assessment of writing is challenging for a number of reasons. While students in every major write, the purposes for that writing and the conventions and practices that guide it vary from one discipline to the next. This variation raises questions about who can credibly assess the writing of undergraduates and what it means to graduate from college with good writing skills.

Another challenge in assessing writing is that college writing is usually a response to something specific—an assignment, a context, a prompt—and it is often hard to tell from students' responses whether one is assessing the quality of the student's response or the quality of the assignment that prompted it. As anyone who has looked at portfolios of students' work has seen, good writers can falter when asked to respond to an unclear, confusing, or simplistic assignment. Still another problem with assessing writing is that often it is unclear whether one is assessing the students' writing or the amount of support and instruction students received to produce their papers. Papers written in two different history courses, for example, may vary dramatically in quality, because students were required to draft papers, received feedback on those drafts, and revised them in one of the classes, but not in the other.

Other challenges involve how to gather information about writing from students. In earlier studies on writing (Beyer, 1997; Beyer & Graham, 1992, 1994a), we learned that students' definitions of what constitutes a "paper" or what counts as "a writing assignment" varied. When we provided definitions to avoid this variation, students did not always follow them. Even a question as apparently simple as the number of pages required by an assignment could be (and was) interpreted in several ways by students, with some students counting the tables and graphs included at the end of the paper in the page count and others not, or with some counting the title page and the bibliography and others not—to give two examples. In addition, definitional problems make it challenging to trust students' identification of the purposes for the writing they were assigned. If asked to identify whether an assignment asked them to produce an argument or an informative piece, for example, they often selected "both," because argument always involved some kind of information. These definitional problems make the validity of data on writing collected by surveys questionable, including carefully constructed surveys such as the National Survey of Student Engagement.

In the UW SOUL, our purpose regarding writing was primarily to understand students' perceptions of their writing experience; however, we also wanted to report more quantifiable information, such as how many papers undergraduates wrote, the length of the papers, what percent required research, and so on. We relied heavily on students' interviews, where we had the possibility of asking and answering clarifying questions. We also built in some possibilities for comparing interview results with survey results. In addition, we provided students with consistent definitions in both interviews and surveys over the four years of the study. We gathered portfolios of student work as a way to check our findings and to use in future assessment work with faculty.

Consistent with the argument that runs throughout this book, this chapter asserts that what students learned about writing was largely mediated by their majors. An accounting major may be praised by a business professor for a paper that the student's sociology professor would consider inadequate; an English major may write an analysis so powerful that it lifts his English professor off his feet, while faculty in anthropology would assert that the argument lacks evidence. As was true in critical thinking and problem solving, what counts as good writing varies from discipline to discipline. This reality makes a generic assessment of the writing skills of college graduates invalid. Perhaps worse, a generic assessment produces results that departments cannot use to think about or improve their work.

The argument that writing is discipline-specific and that writing practices, conventions, and purposes vary from one academic community to another is not new. The manifestation of that argument, the writing-across-the-curriculum movement, began with Janet Emig's (1977) important essay asserting that writing is a mode of learning. David Russell's (2002) rich history of the movement details the earlier strands that led to Emig, as well as those that came after. Since 1977, writing-across-the-curriculum programs have been created at many universities and colleges, including the UW Interdisciplinary Writing Program,[1] and research on writing and thinking in the academic disciplines has been extensive. Bazerman and Russell's (1994) book, *Landmark Essays on Writing Across the Curriculum* includes much of the earliest scholarship, as well as extensive bibliographies. Bazerman's (1981, 2000) own early essay comparing three pieces of writing from the disciplines of sociology, English, and biology has been particularly influential in the current movement. In addition, recent research that clarifies how thinking in particular disciplines drives the writing that expresses that thinking (Bransford, Brown, & Cocking, 2000; Donald, 2002) adds support to the argument that writing norms are created by the academic communities in which they are situated. Findings from the UW SOUL provide strong support for the disciplinary nature of academic writing.

Furthermore, our results reveal a gap between the writing students did in their high schools and community colleges and the writing they were required to do at the university. Recently, *The Chronicle of Higher Education* conducted a survey of high school and college faculty members (Sanoff, 2006) that revealed a gap between high school and college instructors' perceptions of students' writing ability. The survey found that 44% of college faculty and only 10% of high school teachers felt that students were unprepared for college writing. In contrast to differences in length and frequency identified by the *Chronicle* study, the UW SOUL focused on differences in the kinds of writing required at students' previous institutions and those required at the university.

In addition to providing evidence for the arguments about the disciplinary nature of writing and the gap between high school and college writing, this chapter illustrates the power of a longitudinal study to provide an institution with detailed information about undergraduates' writing experience. This chapter begins with a case study that tracks a student, Julianne Guest, through her four years of writing. We move from Julianne to a presentation of our findings and conclude with teaching and assessment implications that result from those findings.

Julianne's Path

Julianne Guest's writing path looked like the paths of many students at the UW. She came to college with little experience in writing the kinds of papers we required. She learned how to write those papers successfully—in her case, by taking a writing course designed to teach her what it meant to write in a discipline; by working closely with TAs in her two main areas of study, women studies and political science; and by being required to write frequently for a wide range of purposes. The challenges Julianne described in her writing—difficulty understanding and integrating complex reading into arguments, moving her argument through the paper (which she described as a "tying together" process), navigating and using disciplinary approaches, coming up with her own arguments, conducting research, and others—were the same challenges many students spoke of experiencing but filtered through the lenses of their majors.

Julianne's path differed somewhat from the paths of other students, because for Julianne, writing was the yardstick she used the most often to measure her own learning. When asked about critical thinking, Julianne talked about writing. When asked about classes that taught her the most and the least, Julianne talked about writing. When asked about personal growth and development, often Julianne talked about writing.

A ballet student for 15 years, Julianne Guest entered college thinking she might major in dance. Like many college students, Julianne had taken honors and Advanced Placement English classes in high school, where writing instruction focused on "the thesis." Not a fan of math courses, Julianne "took the least amount [of math] possible to graduate." Her favorite class in high school was psychology, because the teacher in that class "was an awesome human being and teacher" who "cared about you and about how you were learning, what you were learning."

Julianne's high school writing experience was like that of many other college students. Writing mostly occurred in English courses and mostly focused on literary analysis or argument. When writing was assigned elsewhere, it was primarily informative writing. A college student for only a few months, Julianne said about these high school papers, "I wasn't proving anything, and I think that is the big difference between here and there."

In her first months of college, Julianne felt that she had learned more about writing than she had learned in all of high school:

> It has actually been in the past couple of months here that I've learned the most about writing papers. Here, I've been learning more about tying things together, and in my women studies class, we've been given more exercises on tying ideas

together and writing conclusions. Maybe I feel like I'm learning more here since I'm writing so much.

At the end of her first year, Julianne decided to put dance on hold for awhile when she became intrigued by women studies. She noted that writing had been the most challenging aspect of her first year in college. In that year, she wrote nine papers[2] for political science, history, and two writing courses, as well as short pieces of writing[3] for women studies and Spanish classes. She said that her political science and women studies courses were "big challenges for me—the concepts and papers," and she spoke of what she had learned about writing from her English 198 course, a writing course linked to her history class:

> My writing link this quarter was a lot of cramming my brain for ideas and really working to come up with ideas. We had to really think about what we were writing and work with peers. In my other composition class, we have to do peer reviews, but he doesn't check them. They aren't as important, and we don't spend as much time on them.
>
> The final paper for the history/English link was a history paper where you had to go to the library and find a primary and secondary document, and that was definitely the hardest [paper I wrote this year]. I had tried to avoid the library system like the plague, and I was really forced to go in there and use microfiche. The research was hard, and trying to think like a historian was hard, but I really liked having the linked comp class because we really worked up to it. For the paper, we had to come up with a thesis [based on the primary document]. I did mine on Rosie the Riveter, so my thesis was that women were called up to work through propaganda like Rosie, and then they accepted the fact that they had to go back home after the war. I had to prove that by looking at secondary sources, and I found lots of web sites and articles that supported that. There was a drafting process in the writing link, and I also turned in a draft to my history TA. We had peer reviews in our English class and a conference with the teacher of the link. By the last paper, we knew what we needed to do for each other.

In discussing how writing in college differed from writing in high school, Julianne said that there was more help in college than there had been in high school, more "step-by-step guiding you through the process." Julianne also said that college writing was more difficult, noting that she had difficulty writing a paper for a political science class—"I pretty much had no clue what I was doing and my grade on the paper reflected that"—as well as difficulty writing for history—"They were asking me to think like a historian, and I'd never tried to do that before."

By the end of her second year, Julianne had been admitted to political science and women studies majors, but she was planning to drop the women studies major for several reasons, including that she was "becoming more interested in political science." She also noted that she thought she might want to go to law school. In her second year, Julianne wrote 13 papers, averaging about four pages each. As will be clear later in the chapter, that number of papers is about 50% higher than the average, but the lengths of Julianne's papers were much shorter than average. When asked in her interview which of those papers was the most challenging, Julianne pointed to a paper she wrote for a political science class, saying that the reading on which it was based—Socrates—was difficult.

When asked how her writing assignments changed over her time at the UW, Julianne said that she felt they had become more demanding. She explained:

> I had some demanding papers last year, but I think that was because I wasn't used to the library system or I wasn't as disciplined. I just wasn't as focused, so that made the writing of the paper a lot harder. Now I think the papers are harder, the concepts are harder, but I am also spending more time doing the critical thinking and writing analytical papers. I am really having to think hard about the concepts. I think that becoming a lot more disciplined is helping a lot. Having some really good TAs and writing teachers has helped me, too. They have given me really good feedback on papers, been there for email questions, been willing to read rough drafts of papers. Things like that have helped me improve.

At the end of her second year, Julianne connected her growing confidence in her own intellectual ability with her developing writing skills. She said:

> I learned I am intelligent—getting high grades on papers that I wasn't sure about showed me that I do know what I am talking about sometimes. Last year, I thought I would like to go to law school, but I heard all those things about how hard it is to get in. But this year, I started thinking I can do it.

In her third year at the university, Julianne wrote 10 papers and 19 short pieces of writing for seven courses, five of them in political science. The papers ranged from three to nine pages long, averaging about six pages each. Julianne felt that the writing was continuing to be more demanding as she advanced through her major, but, she noted, "I'm more comfortable with it and more confident. The first political science paper I wrote in freshman year, I totally tanked it. Now, writing that paper would be a piece of cake." She also noted that the most common type of college paper she had to write was "the weekly reading paper" and described how she had learned to write these kinds of papers:

> I learned from a lot of classes, but my women studies class in fall quarter freshman year taught me a lot. I really think the writing assignments in high school were really different. I'm sure that in my AP class, there were some hard writing assignments, but [not like] the weekly reading paper. You have to pick something in the reading and be really specific and not just give a summary of the whole chapter [but] getting down and arguing about a few passages. I spent time with my TA in her office hours, and she really helped me work out issues. My women studies TA helped me figure out how to do that. I needed someone to kind of pull me in and show me what was going on, and that gave me a foundation that first quarter.

The hardest paper Julianne had to write in her third year was a paper for a 400-level political science course. Her description of that paper shows her understanding of the way theory guides argument.

> It was a theory of multiculturalism class. You had to write about a particular issue, like a rights issue. I wrote about female circumcision. From a theoretical standpoint, I had to step back and write about what was the right thing to do, rather than just my opinion. The reading was really dense, so it was hard finding the right material to work with. The professor expected a lot of us. I had to write a strong argument for the opposite of what I really felt, and that was what was the most challenging. I believed that women should be able to have control over their bodies, so on that premise, I had to support that women who want to be circumcised should be able to do that. We were looking at the clash of Eastern and Western culture, too: Do we have the right to tell her that she can't do what her own culture practices? Does her culture have

the right to do that, even though mainstream U.S. culture doesn't agree with it? Politically, I agree that women should have the right to do that, but personally, I find the practice repulsive. If I'd written the paper a few months earlier, I'd have written a completely different paper. But after going through the course, I had to write the paper I wrote.

In her senior year, Julianne had a ten-week internship with the Department of Defense in Washington, DC that, among other things, taught her a great deal about the Israeli/Palestinian conflict, as well as about other conflicts around the world. That year Julianne wrote ten papers, averaging seven pages each, and no short pieces. Among those papers was a particularly challenging one in which she argued that the politics of the budget, the domestication of foreign policy, and the role of the U.S. in the global economy were the issues that became politically important in the 1990s. When asked at the end of the year if she felt prepared to take the next step in her life, Julianne again pointed to gains she had made as a writer:

> I'm going to law school. I feel moderate to very well prepared [to take this step]. I think that my writing has improved a lot. I feel I've become a much better writer in four years. Thinking analytically is something I've had to do a lot for my major, and, hopefully, I've become decent at it. Reading comprehension has prepared me for the next step, too.

In her final year in college, Julianne continued to feel that her writing had improved.

> I think that this year, I was willing to take more risks in my writing, through this one poli sci class. I had that professor before, and she is a really, really hard grader. It was challenging for me the first time, so when I had her again, I really pushed myself to do well on my papers. I got a 4.0 on one of them and a 3.9 in the class. I really pushed my writing for her.

While Julianne's college writing experience may have been more intense than that of other students, some aspects of it are similar to most students' paths. She arrived at the UW with little experience writing the kinds of papers assigned in classes across the university curriculum. She began learning how to write papers required in her social science classes by taking a writing course linked to history that deliberately focused on writing in that discipline. She also took the initiative to meet with teaching assistants in the social sciences to discuss writing. As early as her second year, much of the writing she did was concentrated in her major field—political science. This immersion in the cultural practices and norms regarding writing and thinking in the discipline shaped Julianne's understanding of how to write well in her major—as it does for the writing of most students.

Undergraduate Writing Across the College Curriculum

Two strong findings emerged from our study of students' writing experience. First, we learned that students' writing experience varied widely by area of major. This finding—sometimes muted by the fact that students appeared to have a shared language about writing that was not apparent when they spoke about critical thinking—was clear in both interview and survey responses to questions about writing. Second, we learned that, in part because of the disciplinary nature of writing at the college level, there was a gap between students' previous writing experience and the writing they were required to do at the UW. We have divided this section into the following subsections:

- How much students wrote and where they wrote

- Students' most challenging papers and what they required

- Differences between first-year writing and writing before the UW

- Students' self-assessment

How Much Students Wrote and Where They Wrote

Colleges and universities of every size and type are often so decentralized that it can be extremely difficult to gather even basic information on student writing, such as how *much* writing undergraduates do. But for many people, basic questions such as these are connected with perceived strengths or weaknesses in academic programs. As this chapter illustrates, a longitudinal study *can* give institutions some sense of the scope of the broad "writing program" across and within majors. Furthermore, information about even basic activities, such as we describe in this section, reveals some differences across the disciplines.

How Much Writing Did Students Do?

Each year during interviews we handed students copies of their transcripts and asked them to tell us how many of their courses had assigned papers[4] that year, how many papers they had written for those courses, and how long those papers were. Table 6.1 shows the results for all four years of the study. As the table shows, students wrote an average of eight papers per year, or about 33 over the course of their four years at the UW. On average, students wrote these papers in four of their classes each year (about 40% of their courses).[5] Papers averaged seven pages in length. In addition to the papers, students wrote about six short pieces annually. Transfer students, on average, wrote one more paper per year than did students who entered as freshmen, and those papers were one to two pages longer. In spite of changes to the writing requirements at our institution over the years, the number of papers students wrote between 1999–2003 was similar to that noted in studies of the writing conducted in the 1990s, which found that students wrote seven or eight papers a year (Beyer, 1997; Beyer & Graham, 1992, 1994a).[6]

Table 6.1. *Average Number of Classes in Which Papers Were Written, Number of Papers, and Average Length*

Year	N	Avg. # of classes	Avg. # of papers	Avg. # of pages	Most frequently mentioned disciplines (15% or more of respondents)	# of short papers
1	134	3	8.5	6	English, sociology, chemistry, history, political science	5
2	112	4	7	7	English, chemistry, communication, engineering, history, business, architecture and urban planning, sociology	7
3	88	4	8.6	7	No department reached 15%	9
4	63	4	8.5	7	No department reached 15%	4
Total		**15**	**32.6 (8/yr)**	**7**	---	**25 (6/yr)**

As one might expect, the amount of writing students did in their four years in college depended largely upon their majors. We divided students into the following broad categories that represent their majors and/or eventual majors: the arts (including architecture because there were so few architecture majors), business, engineering, the humanities, math (until the fourth year, when we combined our few math majors with science majors), science, and social sciences. Table 6.2 shows the number of papers students in each category wrote in their second, third, and fourth years. We did not include the first year of the study, because at that time students were not yet in majors. As the table shows, the amount of writing students did varied quite a bit by major, with social science majors doing the most writing. Students majoring in the arts and engineering wrote the fewest short pieces.

Table 6.2. Disciplines and Amount of Writing

Area	# of classes requiring papers			# of papers			# of short pieces		
	2001	2002	2003	2001	2002	2003	2001	2002	2003
Arts	1.2	1.8	1.1	1.6	3.3	2	5	11.8	13[7]
Business	4.6	4.4	6	7.3	7.4	10	3.3	8.3	14
Engineering	2.9	3.4	2	7.9	10.7	5	2.4	6.4	1
Humanities	4.8	3.9	3	10	8.8	6	16	7.2	10
Math	2	2.3	See Sci	2.5	3	See Sci	5	16	See Sci
Science	3	2	2.5	5.8	4.3	5	2.1	2.8	8[8]
Social Sciences	4	4.4	5	7.6	9.5	10	7.2	9.3	5

How Many Classes Students Wrote in

Although our focus in the surveys was on *how many classes* students wrote papers for each quarter, rather than on *how many papers* they wrote, survey results support the argument that college writing is a disciplinary act. As Table 6.3 shows, students in social science, business, and humanities wrote argumentative essays for the greatest number of classes. Those majoring in engineering wrote the arguments for the fewest classes. These differences accounted for 42% of the total variance.[9] Differences in informative writing were also significant, but not as large as for argumentative writing.[10] Business majors reported writing informative papers in the most courses, while science and art majors wrote the fewest informative papers.[11] These results on writing in disciplinary areas are consistent with findings from our interviews, which showed that students in the social sciences,

Table 6.3. *Classes Requiring Argumentative and Informative Writing by Disciplinary Category*

Disciplinary area	N	Average # of classes requiring arguments	Average # of classes requiring informative papers
Art	8	10.1	8.8
Business	13	15.6	14.2
Engineering	19	5.9	9.9
Humanities	11	14.5	10.4
Science	26	9.2	8.3
Social Science	44	15.9	11.1

engineering, business, and humanities wrote more papers than students in science or the arts.

Finally, as in the interviews, we asked students how many of their courses had required short pieces—or writing that was two pages long or fewer. The survey results showed that students turned in short pieces of writing in an average of 12.1 classes, or about one class per term. In interviews, students described about six short pieces each year, on average. These combined results suggest that assignment of short pieces of writing might be concentrated in a few of the courses students took each year. As was the case with longer papers, survey results showed large differences in the average number of short pieces of writing across disciplinary areas, ranging from 15.9 classes for humanities majors to 7.6 classes for engineering majors.[12]

Does it matter how much students wrote? Astin (1993a) found that seniors who felt their writing had improved had done a great deal of writing and received a great deal of feedback from their instructors. Light (2001) found that students were more engaged in courses that required writing. How much a student writes does matter, if we assume that learning to write well is a process, that grappling with assignments in a discipline helps students understand not only what they think or have discovered but also how that discipline thinks and creates knowledge, and, further, that feedback on writing helps students improve both their writing and thinking in a given area. However, there is no agreement in the literature or elsewhere on how much writing is "enough." One might well argue that the amount of feedback students receive on their writing and how clearly that feedback directs writing improvement is more important than how much they write.

Although these results suggest that students majoring in the arts wrote significantly fewer papers than did other majors, and that science majors tended to write fewer papers than students who majored in the social sciences, business, or the humanities, we cannot conclude from that result that arts and science majors are not writing "enough" to become skilled at writing. That decision must be made by their faculty, who best understand the purposes for the writing they assign and who assess the writing their majors produce.

Students' Most Challenging Papers and What They Required

In entry and annual interviews, we asked students to describe the most challenging paper they had written that year and to tell us why that paper was particularly challenging. The challenges students noted shared some features in common across broad disciplinary areas (such as the challenge posed by research), but for the most part, they made differences across the curriculum apparent (such as what it meant to conduct research for particular assignments). As this section shows, students' descriptions of challenging writing also show change over time, as students became immersed in the practices, conventions, and purposes of writing in their majors.

No Challenging Writing and No Writing

Each year a small number of students in the study said that they had either done no writing that year or that they had done no writing that they felt was challenging. Interestingly, the number of students in this category increased over the four years of the study (from 4% in 2000, to 14%, 15%, and 22%). For each year, the majority of these students said that the writing they had done was not challenging, rather than that they had done no writing. In the early years, business and engineering majors were overrepresented in the population of students who said they had either done no writing or no challenging writing. In the second two years, these students came from all majors.

It seems counterintuitive that the number of students who experienced no writing or no challenging writing would *increase* over time, because descriptions of challenging papers became more complex, and students were expected to work more independently over time. It is possible that, as Julianne Guest described, students learned how to write the papers they had to write, particularly in their second and third years when they were becoming immersed in their majors, so that by their fourth year, the papers seemed less challenging. Increases in students' confidence levels and self-discipline may have also made fourth year challenges less significant. However, this area needs further investigation.

Type and Lengths of the Most Challenging Papers

We analyzed students' descriptions of their most challenging pieces of writing to identify, among other things, the types of papers they described. We sorted papers according to their purposes into the following categories:[13]

- Arguments about issues, events, and ideas: supporting an assertion about a subject with plausible evidence (Arg)

- Literary analyses/arguments:[14] giving the writer's interpretation of aspects of a literary text or texts (Lit Arg)

- Informative papers: presenting information about a subject (Inform)

- Personal essays: connecting the reader with the life/perspectives of the writer through description and narration (Personal)

- Creative writing: poems, short stories, plays, or novels that students produced (Create)

- Miscellaneous: purposes varied, such as a student's application for admittance to a particular UW program (Misc)

Students' most challenging writing before entering the university was fairly evenly spread across four paper types—arguments about issues, events, and ideas; literary arguments/ analyses; informative essays; and personal essays,[15] as Figure 6.1 shows. However, as soon as students entered the UW, more than half of the papers they described as their most challenging were arguments about issues, events, and ideas, and this type of writing increasingly was their most challenging over their four years in college. This difference in the type of writing students considered their most challenging foreshadows the gap between high school and college writing that we address later in this chapter, and echoes results of previous UW assessment studies on writing (Beyer, 1997; Beyer & Graham, 1990, 1992, 1994a, 1994b). These studies identified arguments about issues, ideas, or events as the most common UW writing assignment.

Regarding paper lengths, many faculty members believe students find longer papers to be more challenging than short papers. In general, students reported that very short papers—two pages or fewer—were easy for them, requiring little time or thought. However, the lengths of the papers that students described as their most challenging ranged from 2.5 pages to more than 50 pages.[16] When speaking about length, students occasionally identified length requirements that were perceived as too long and those that were too short as factors that made papers challenging. However, we should note that length is also a feature of disciplinary practice.

Figure 6.1. *Types of Papers That Students Identified as Their Most Challenging Writing*

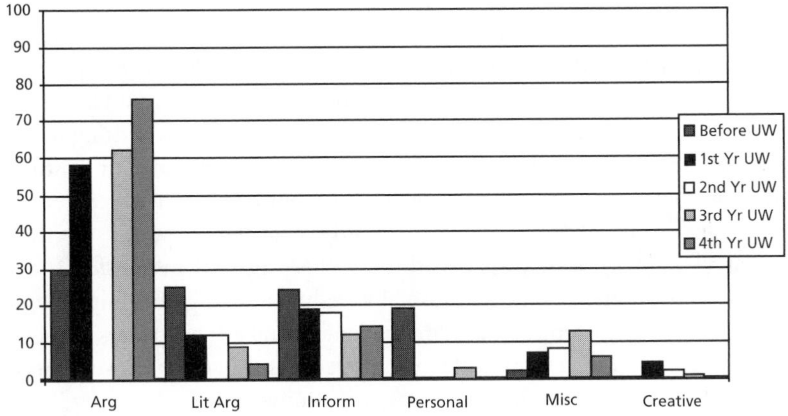

Research

Many of the papers that students identified as their most challenging required research, and, again, this challenge has disciplinary implications. About 60% of the papers that students described as the most challenging papers they had written before coming to the university required research. In contrast, in their first year at the university, only 40% of students' most challenging papers required research, and most of the research required was minimal—locating some information on the web, for example. This percentage was likely the result of students taking 100-level classes that typically require students to use course texts rather than research as resources for writing.

This picture changed by students' second and third years, when 63% and 62% of the papers they described as their most challenging required research. By the third year, however, students' descriptions of research varied widely, including papers requiring students to develop hypotheses and do the research necessary to test them, to conduct interviews with other students and analyze the data, and to conduct traditional library/Internet research. In the fourth year, about 74% percent of the papers students identified as their most challenging required research, and, as was the case in the third year, the kinds of research students completed varied widely.

Differences in how research translated across the disciplines are illustrated in Table 6.4, which provides students' descriptions of challenging writing in several disciplinary areas. The examples illustrate how misleading it can be to note research as a generic writing challenge.

Draft, Feedback, and Revision Opportunities

We can get an idea of how much support was provided to students writing challenging papers by understanding how many of them included a requirement that students submit drafts to faculty, TAs, or peers; get and give feedback on those drafts; and revise the drafts before turning them in. Many writing instructors believe that the latter process leads to the greatest improvement in student writing. In their first year at the UW, students reported that they were required to draft and revise about 32% of their most challenging papers. Freshmen reported taking twice as many papers through this process than transfer students reported. This difference may be caused by freshman taking beginning composition courses, which typically require students to take their papers through a drafting process. However, this difference also suggests that transfer students did not get help in revision in their first year at the university.

In their second year, students reported that about 41% of their most challenging papers were required to go through a draft/revision process. That number decreased to 27% by students' third year, and 30% in students' fourth year. Some of the papers students wrote, particularly in their fourth year, were extremely complex, so it is surprising that so few included draft stages.

The infrequency of revising opportunities is supported by survey data on revision. Survey results on drafting and revising opportunities suggest that over their four years at the university, students wrote drafts of papers and submitted them to professors or TAs for feedback in an average of six classes, or about 16% of the classes they might be expected to take in four years. Therefore, it is perhaps not surprising that most students did not have opportunities to take their most challenging papers through such a process in their four years at the UW. Survey results also show that students, on average, asked other students, friends, or family members for feedback for papers written in seven of their courses. However, correlating average responses over all four years, we found that use of faculty and use of friends for feedback correlated positively. It appears that students who used one source tended also to use the other sources; comments on drafts from students' friends and family were not substitutes for faculty comments.

Table 6.4. *Research Across the Disciplinary Categories*

Architecture & Urban Planning	The class is Roman Architecture—an advanced special topic. The paper was any research we could come up with that he'd approve. I am talking about the relationship between two sites—a Roman bath built above a previous structure. I am researching what elements in the Roman bath probably belonged to the previous structure based on the orientation differences. But there is not much left of these two structures—a couple of bricks here and there, a couple of walls, and some old, old drawings from the Renaissance period. I have to try to figure out the answer from this and the few walls here and there.
Arts	In drama, the final paper for lighting was an entire project. I had to analyze a Beckett piece, and he is a very difficult writer to crack open. We had to read the play and write about the theme of the play and how lighting would be used from the point of view of the scene and what role lighting would play. It required research because we had to pick a picture [from the art library] that represented the style of the piece to inform our paper.
Business	We had to discuss an issue that is controversial today in the news. We had to make arguments for both sides and come up with a conclusion, with how you think you should solve the issue. Mine was cell phone cancer risk. I concluded that the manufacturers are already taking enough steps to give the public enough information to know if it is safe or not, and the government has already done their tests, so I said it is "let the buyer beware." The paper was hard because you can't be biased toward one side. You have to research both sides and then figure out your opinion and argue in favor of it.
Engineering	Aeronautics and Astronautics—all five papers for that class. These were lab reports. Trying to make sense of the data and answer the professors questions are challenging, trying to find theories to explain the data. For one[project] we [built] a damping system for the vibrations of a rod being excited by an outside source. The writing is challenging because of the experiments. Research is required.
Humanities	It was challenging to find a topic [for the Russian research paper] because we could write on anything. I wrote on the Russian primary chronicles and how that influenced later literature and the evolving literature of Russia. We were required to use a lot of library resources, periodicals, books, international databases from Russia. Also we had to use the Internet. It was good to become acquainted with the library.

Table 6.4 (continued). *Research Across the Disciplinary Categories*

Science	I think the oceans paper was the most challenging. I guess the physics, understanding what the paper was about. The subject of my paper was glacio-isostatic rebound of the earth's crust. On the papers that I read for that paper, most of them said that over the entire globe sea level on average is lowering. We always hear about sea level rising, but it is rising just along the European coasts and in N. America. Trying to understand the process, how loading ice onto the continent here in America could actually change the shape of Australia was hard to understand.
Social Science	In psychology, we were assigned to observe an animal and write a scientific paper on one behavior that animal did. I decided to write on pigeons and their pecking behavior. We had to observe them for five hours. I was arguing a hypothesis about why the pigeons pecked. We had to use our field data as evidence for our hypothesis. My first hypothesis was that they were pecking at the ground because of some fixed action pattern. They didn't need to forage since they were just given food. But as I observed them more and more, I began to see field data that would go against my hypothesis. So my hypothesis turned out to be wrong, but that was okay. We were also required to look at scientific journals on pigeons. I didn't get much out of those journals. It was like a foreign language. It was also hard to find specific information on my topic—foraging.

Longitudinal analysis of survey results showed that students received more faculty feedback in classes they took in their first year than in those they took in subsequent years. Again, this might be because of freshman composition courses taken early in students' academic programs. Differences among disciplinary categories for faculty feedback were not statistically significant.

We can conclude from these results that very little of students' writing received feedback from faculty or teaching assistants at the draft stage, except in their first two years. In addition, transfer students received less draft/revision/ feedback support than did students who entered as freshmen.

What Was Challenging About Challenging Papers?

As we did when we examined students' responses to questions about critical thinking and problem solving, we analyzed students' responses to writing challenges by first grouping papers in the seven broad disciplinary categories in which they originated (see Chapter 2 for discussion of this approach). We also paid attention to how many of the students identified papers in the disciplinary categories of their majors as their most challenging writing. This varied somewhat across years and disciplinary categories, as one might expect. Generally, however, when students wrote their most challenging papers outside their majors, they wrote them in the social sciences or humanities, with most occurring in the humanities. This tendency was strongest in students' third year at the UW, when those who identified humanities papers as their most challenging were largely majoring in disciplines outside the humanities.

Results on writing challenges in each of our seven broad disciplinary categories across the four years of the study reveal interesting similarities and differences. Table 6.5 summarizes the challenges we identified in each disciplinary area and is included at the end of this section.

Challenging papers in architecture and urban planning. Few students mentioned papers in architecture and urban planning as their most challenging in any of the four years of the study. Those who provided examples from architecture and urban planning said that the level of thinking required was challenging, the assigned topics were unfamiliar, and the incorporation of written information and images into a single document was challenging. This student's comment serves as an example of these papers:

> The Urban Design and Planning 481 paper was challenging. We had to prepare a presentation about a topic we were given. Then we had to write a paper about that topic. It was challenging because I didn't know anything about the topic, which was housing and basic services in developing countries. I presented the basic problems that developing countries in general had in housing. Those problems relate to quality. The policies don't take the poor people into account, so that was a big issue.

Challenging papers in the arts. As was the case with architecture and urban planning, few students identified papers in the arts as their most challenging over the course of their time in college. In the first year, nine students identified papers in the arts as their most challenging, and eight of these were papers for art history classes. Two students said the art history papers were challenging because they did not understand the art pieces they were writing about or how to look at them. As one student said:

> The ones that are difficult are the ones where I don't fully understand the piece, and when I turn the paper in, I don't necessarily believe the conclusions I come to.

Another student said that the paper was "beyond my writing abilities" because it required research and a critical eye. In addition, three students spoke explicitly of challenges involved in navigating and using disciplinary practices, as this student's comment illustrates:

> The paper for Art History 201 was the most difficult because with the lab reports you just write down the numbers and what you are doing, and there is no learning process involved in doing those. The art history paper was difficult because I have never taken a class like that before. We had to compare three pieces of artwork—three paintings of Odysseus. They gave us the passage those paintings were based on, and we had to compare the artists' work and relate it back to the passage. It was pretty difficult.

In the second, third, and fourth years of the study, only a handful of students identified papers in the arts as their most challenging, and there was no agreement among them about what made those papers challenging.

Challenging papers in business. In the first two years, students who identified challenging business papers described the difficulty of understanding and using disciplinary writing practices for business. They also noted having trouble with aspects of argumentation, such as use of evidence. One student's quotation illustrates these challenges:

> It was investigative accounting and it was kind of fun, but it was hard to know if I was doing it correctly. It was lots of interpretation—an argument. We had to use the methods that they use in industry—charts and ratios and compare that to the general industry and try to see if there was something funny going on.

Another challenge students identified in writing papers for business was the difficulty of being self-reflective, as this student noted:

> One of the Human Resource Management and Organizational Behavior papers. It was a self-assessment paper on what kind of employee you'll be, what kind of things motivate you, what kind of leadership style you have. It is hard to sit down and think about those things, what motivates you. But it is very rewarding, too. So it was very helpful. That paper was ten pages long. You had to take all these tests from the CD that came from the book, and then you had to self-assess yourself in these different areas that he gave us, using the test scores from the CD as evidence for what we said about ourselves. We had to agree

> or disagree with those results. It was challenging to find the correct words to phrase what you were thinking, and in general, it is hard to write about yourself. It was hard to figure out what motivates you and sometimes you are surprised by the things that do—and sometimes you don't want to admit those things. I hadn't ever written anything like this before.

Students in their first two years also said that some of the assignments in their business courses were unclear, and that made fulfilling the requirements challenging. Students mentioned the challenge in working with groups of students on a shared writing project. One student said that it was challenging to "keep the integrity of what [others] wrote" in the paper even when he did not agree with all group members' interpretations of things.

Working in groups was a challenge noted by students who cited business papers as their most challenging in the third and fourth years of the study. Another challenge students noted in the third and fourth years of the study was research, as this examples indicates:

> In International Business, we are to take a company that operates within the EU and a current event that has happened in that country and apply it to European policy within the scope of the class we are in. I'm doing a bank called BBVA. It's a Spanish bank involved in quite a few scandals over the last few years. I am looking at how that will affect the EU's banking policy and different finance houses throughout the EU. Finding a lot of resources that reference this case in particular is challenging. I am finding some, but they are all saying the same things. I would prefer to find a gamut of different opinions on the issue. Sifting through EU documents is both an acronym generator and a paper generator. They love bureaucracy.

Third- and fourth-year study participants who described papers written for business as their most challenging spoke of the difficulty of using disciplinary practices, including following a format and being creative at the same time, using correct methods for analysis of financial data, and understanding and using numerical results in support of recommendations. Students also spoke of topics that were challenging, either because of the level of thinking they demanded or because students were unfamiliar with them, and this kind of challenge often blended in with the challenge of correctly using disciplinary practices in writing.

Challenging papers in engineering. In their first two years, participants in the UW SOUL who said that their most challenging papers were written for engineering classes noted several specific areas of challenge. One area mentioned frequently was the challenge posed by the readings about which students were writing. Another challenge for students was the research that was necessary to write the papers, as well as the difficulty of the experiments upon which the writing was based. Students also spoke of challenges in understanding and using disciplinary writing practices, as this student said:

> The paper focused us to make sentences and words concise, and explain things clearly but without dragging on. It was kind of the opposite of what English would tell you to do, so it was like learning to write a paper again.

In the first two years, a few of the students who identified engineering papers as their most challenging suggested that having to figure things out on their own made the writing challenging. By "figuring things out," students usually meant that they had to identify the tools they needed to solve a problem, use them to attempt a solution, identify what worked and what did not, attempt to solve the problem again, and so on. The writing process intentionally required a process of "doing" and analysis, with minimal guidance and often with explanation of failed attempts included in the writing.

In their third and fourth years at the UW, many students who said that engineering papers were their most challenging noted that the level of the material they needed to understand in order to do the writing and/or conduct experiments upon which the writing was based made the writing challenging. Others indicated that research was the most challenging aspect of their writing, and often the two challenges came together. For all of these students, "research" meant conducting experiments—usually of their own design—to answer questions. One student's description illustrates these challenges:

> The chemical engineering lab reports were the most difficult. They were all difficult. The hard part was trying to understand what I was writing about. About half the time I didn't know what I was talking about. The format of the reports was familiar. But we had to develop our own procedures for the last two experiments, and that was really hard. And understanding the results you obtained was hard too. Research was required to write these.

In addition, students sometimes describeded challenges in engaging in other kinds of research, for example, reading technical papers to help guide their thinking.

Students spoke about difficulty in determining what they had to figure out in order to write the paper they were assigned. One student's description, again of a chemical engineering assignment, illustrates this challenge quite well:

> I've only done one so far for this [chemical engineering] class, but it is challenging. This is different from the papers we had to write for general chem labs as freshmen. This is different because we are given the project, and we have to find a way to solve the problem. So each experiment is a new research design that we have to come up with. They just tell us what equipment we can use, and we have to design the equipment. Every one gets a different lab. We have to look up stuff on-line, because if we have questions about who made the gas pump that we are working with, we need to find out the maximum and minimum values we can work under, for example, or some of the pressures we need to work at that will give us the best results with the equipment we are working with. Sometimes we have to call vendors and ask what the capacity is for the model. We also ask questions to the professors, and they do require a meeting prior to your experiment with a TA. You have to sit down and think through what you are going to do and how you are going to do it, and then go over that with the TA. What is challenging is that before this, we were always given how to do something, and now they are trying to teach us to come up with our own procedures. They are trying to teach us how our bosses might approach us with problems when we get out in the workforce. What is difficult is that most of us have been told, "This is the formula. Use it." There was always an answer, but now there isn't. You have to go out and find that answer or figure out what to do to find that answer.

Interestingly, many of the challenges students found in writing for engineering happened both before the act of writing began and during the process. Indeed, students speaking of challenging writing in engineering often did not distinguish between doing the work that enabled the writing and doing the writing itself, which captures something of the nature of writing in engineering fields.

Challenging papers in the humanities. In their first year at the UW, more than a third of the students in the study identified papers written for the humanities as their most challenging, and close to half of those papers were written for freshmen composition courses.[17] Papers written for other English courses and for philosophy classes were also frequently mentioned. Students most frequently mentioned three challenges in their descriptions of what made freshman composition papers their most challenging. The first were challenges related to argumentation—most often creating a thesis about a given topic, finding and using evidence to support that thesis, moving that thesis through the paper, and organizing the argument effectively. This student's description serves as an example of the challenges inherent in argumentation in composition classes:

> The topic was a definition of academic success, based on what we had read. We couldn't just define it, but we had to take what we had read, extrapolate it from that, and then support it with evidence. Identifying a claim was fairly straightforward, but what gave me a lot of problems was the structuring of the paper, the identifying of suitable quotes, and the analysis of those quotes, and the transitions—that gave me a lot of problems. I had not been used to such a narrow perspective, and I felt confined, limited. I learned a lot from it.

Another frequently mentioned challenge posed by the composition papers was trying to respond to assignments that the student found unclear or confusing. First-year students also discussed the challenge in writing about reading that was difficult for them to understand, as this student described:

> Probably the one where we had to analyze an essay about something as a commodity for English composition. It was on tourism as a commodity, and I didn't understand the whole essay we had to analyze. We had to read that essay and write another essay that went off from that essay.

Finally, students who spoke of composition courses in their first year talked about the challenge of moving from the kinds of papers demanded in high school writing to those required in college.

In addition to papers assigned in freshman composition courses, many of the papers that students described as their most challenging in their first year were assigned in philosophy. Nearly all students who reported philosophy papers as their most challenging said that understanding and using the writing practices in philosophy were the most challenging aspects of those papers. For example:

> The paper, itself, was difficult, too, because in philosophy you write in a completely different way than we were taught in English. It is what's your claim? what's your evidence? what's your opposition? It is a different kind of writing—proving your point.

In their second year, third, and fourth years at the UW, significantly fewer students mentioned challenging papers written for the humanities than had identified papers in the humanities in the first year. Most of the students who identified humanities papers as their most challenging in these years noted aspects of argumentation as their most significant challenges, and many of these students identified having to come up with their own arguments as particularly challenging. Students also found working with difficult reading to be challenging. This student's example illustrates several of those challenges:

> All of them for my English class were difficult. But the most challenging was on the *Structure of Scientific Revolutions,* by Kuhn. This was the longest paper, 9–10 pages. The assignment was to read that or *Absalom! Absalom!* He gave us a list of questions we could answer. I chose to answer something about the paradigms and how they affected the scientific community. I was making an argument in this paper, but I can't remember what argument I was making. The paper was hard because understanding the book was hard. It was difficult to get a firm enough grasp of the material so you could make a claim on it. In the class I didn't want to dispute anything because I felt I didn't have enough knowledge. So it was difficult to go into the paper thinking I could make any kind of claim at all.

In addition, many of the students who reported completing their most challenging piece of writing for humanities courses said that writing in a foreign language made the paper especially challenging. For example:

> My Spanish one-page essays. That doesn't sound like a lot of work, but it took a long time for me. The teacher wanted perfect final drafts with several drafts before that. It was very arduous. And it was frustrating because it was in Spanish, and the language is difficult for me to be perfectly correct in.

Another challenge in writing in the humanities that students frequently mentioned in their later years was the research required to complete assigned papers, as this student reported:

> The class is on contemporary France, and the paper is supposed to pull from something that we have talked about in class. We are supposed to find articles from the period we've looked at in class—the most current articles—and write on that subject, for example, unemployment or Islam in France. I wrote on women's health in France. I was arguing that women's health in France is affected by some of the topics we discussed about French culture, such as the role of fate, defiant protest, the agricultural tradition, subsistence agriculture, and the mythical vs. the practical vision of the body. I did library research online through Lexus Nexus. What was difficult was finding coherent proof that I could use to support my argument. I used what I could—laws that get passed or things like that, but I wasn't sure how much to focus in on one thing or how broad to be.

Among other things that these descriptions of writing challenges in the humanities revealed was the inability of a disciplinary category as broad as "the humanities" to provide clear information about writing challenges. Writing challenges in composition courses seemed unique to those courses, as did writing challenges in philosophy and in foreign languages. These differences suggest that the assessment of writing belongs in the hands of departments, rather than centralized or even—in the case of disciplinary categories—conducted by "regional" efforts.

Challenging papers in science. Students' descriptions of writing challenges in science (including math) were similar to those for humanities in that the first year was quite different from subsequent years, particularly the fourth year, when the students who identified their most significant writing challenges in science writing were all science majors.

In their first year, more than 10% of the students in the study identified papers written for science as their most challenging, and half of those students mentioned lab reports written for the three-course, introductory chemistry sequence offered at the UW. Similar to the comments of engineering students, for most of the chemistry lab reports, it was the experiments that students had to conduct and then report on that made writing challenging. Regarding these lab reports, students spoke of the difficulty of understanding and using the writing practices of the disciplines in science. One student's description illustrates this point:

> My chemistry lab report was probably the hardest because I had never written a formal lab report before. I spent a lot of time trying to figure out how to convey a scientific idea through words. We had a bit of instruction—"here is the format you follow, this is what I want to see, basically."

Several students mentioned the difficulties posed by having to do research, as this student described:

> It was supposed to be a peer review journal type article; I guess you could call it informational. We had to review at least six articles, and the paper had to be at least six pages. I used the Medline in the health science library. I think I made it harder than it needed to be. I chose a pretty difficult topic, and finding specific articles on it was a little harder. I found a lot of brand new data that was unfounded or the data was really old. There weren't a lot of long-term studies on things.

Students in the first year noted that the difficulty of the concepts they were working with made the writing challenging, and a few students said that it was challenging to create tables and figures in Excel.

After the first year, students noted several challenges, most frequently mentioning research as the aspect of writing papers for science that made them challenging. Two students' descriptions illustrate second- and fourth-year research challenges:

> The assignment was to answer the question: Can we save endangered Chinook salmon—why or why not? I argued that we could, and the most challenging part of it was to find the information to support my opinion. I utilized the libraries a lot; I bought several books. I chose to find a lot of outside information, and it was certainly beneficial. It is so much easier to argue something when you have scientific documentation to back up what you are arguing.

> It was challenging because the research we did showed absolutely nothing. We had a hypothesis, did our research, and we had to include a summary that said our research showed nothing. It was challenging and frustrating because

you get into a pattern of thinking: get an idea, write a paper, and everything turns out great. But what if you have a hypothesis, do your research, and nothing turns out? In reality, that happens all the time, but not in your classes. It was challenging looking at this as something other than a failure. We spent all this time, did all this work, and we ended up learning absolutely nothing. When you look at it, you did learn a lot, but maybe not what you planned on learning.

In addition, students discussed the challenge in understanding and using disciplinary writing practices, as well as challenges created by unclear assignments or expectations, by problems in the context surrounding the assignment, and by working with groups.

Students who cited science papers as their most challenging in their fourth year spoke of challenges that were similar to second and third year science challenges, with one difference: They were more focused on specific disciplines. Disciplinary demands challenged students, such as determining what to include and leave out, knowing how to compare two procedures that were dissimilar, and being able to identify what was missing from an experiment. Students also described the challenges in doing research—both finding information from sources, figuring out what to use, and determining how to gather information in a field in which few experiments had been conducted, because it was so new. Some topics were challenging for students because of the level of thought they demanded or because they were unfamiliar. Many of the papers these students described were extremely complex, demanding a wide range of scientific knowledge, independence, and careful processes from students. One student's description illustrates this group of papers:

> This was a class in forest soil microbiology. I wrote a paper about designing and developing a Soils Health Assessment Card to be used by restoration ecologists for urban soils. I got the idea from the USDA. They have a card for agriculture. Farmers use these cards to help them judge how healthy their soils are. Urban soils are different. They are almost always disturbed. I used the USDA's model and adapted it to urban ecology as opposed to agriculture and to disturbed urban soils as opposed to agricultural soils. And all of this was in the context of soil microbiology. This was an introduction to the problems found in urban soils—and I was offering the solution: the Soils Health Card for the USDA. The guidelines are on the USDA website and they tell you step-by-step how to

develop an agricultural soils health card. I gave the criteria and a proposed layout. It was big. A big paper. Each criterion had almost a page of explanation. I had to explain each one in the context of urban soil, and that was a big challenge. Choosing things that were important was a challenge too—choosing aspects of what was originally intended for agricultural soils. I had to know what to ignore. Then I had to look at urban soils and add things that wouldn't be on any other list of criteria. It was a lot of fun. I took what I wrote in my paper and actually developed the card. I haven't tested it out yet.

Challenging papers in the social sciences. Consistent with the general UW population, more students in the UW SOUL majored in the social sciences than in any of the other disciplinary areas. Therefore, it is not surprising that many students identified social science papers consistently across all four years of the study as their most challenging.

In their first year at the UW, about one third of the students we interviewed mentioned papers in the social sciences as their most challenging papers. Challenges included a range of aspects of argumentation, particularly in finding and using evidence to support a thesis, in identifying a thesis, and in providing an effective organization for the argument. For example:

> For each of the papers we wrote in history, you had a book that corresponded to it. The book I read, there wasn't much information in, so it was difficult to pull examples out. The assignment was whether we thought McCarthyism helped promote the red scare, and if so, to support it with examples from the textbook we were reading. I said that I thought it did. We were just supposed to use that one book.

Writing about difficult reading, and understanding and using the practices of specific disciplines, were also challenges that students described. Also, some first-year students noted the challenges of doing research.

In the second year, about 40% of the UW SOUL students interviewed identified papers in the social sciences as their most challenging. The most significant challenges noted by most of these students were the research the papers required and the challenge in identifying and supporting one's own arguments. Unclear faculty expectations, a challenging level of reading, and navigating the demands of the discipline were also mentioned frequently. The example that follows illustrates two of these challenges—research and using disciplinary practices:

Either of the two papers from my sociology class. It was a research methods class, and the first one had to do with designing a study—how would we go about researching it. The second one expanded on that—the results we expected to obtain if we were to do a study. I think I wrote about the effects of a broken home on children's education. We had to think up a hypothesis in the first paper and then talk about our methodology for developing a research project to test that. The second one was about the results. We were making an argument through our hypothesis. We had to do both library and online research for the papers—especially using academic journals. I think just the fact that these papers were different from my normal classes made them challenging. You couldn't just BS them. It was science based. In other classes, you can just talk about your own opinion and not use research. This one was based in facts and the format was challenging. It was an essay but it was written with more scientific terms. You had to understand all the scientific methodology and apply that to the paper.

As was the case for papers students identified in the second year, the challenge most frequently mentioned in the third year was research. Two students' descriptions serve as examples:

For a communication course, we had to pick an organization or group that is anti-corporate and examine how they use logo campaigns to spread their message. I picked Starbucks and the group that campaigned against them was Global Exchange. It was challenging because you had to do a lot of Internet research and find examples of what the group was doing to challenge what Starbucks was doing. Also, you had to incorporate material and concepts from class about what made logo campaigns successful, and you had to apply that to what the group was actually doing. To put all that together into a coherent paper that shows that you know what you are talking about was challenging.

The one I am writing now for international studies. It is the most lengthy one, and it is more traditional: you have a thesis and you have to essentially prove your thesis. Also, because I have to do the research and find the information I need from all that is out there, it is harder. I chose a topic about the World Trade Organization. I am arguing that any international agreement by its nature will limit the sovereignty of all nations, but that the WTO is different in that it limits the sovereignty of developing countries more than it limits the sovereignty of developed countries.

Another frequently mentioned challenge in the third year was argumentation, particularly coming up with one's own argument. In addition, several students brought up the challenges of being self-reflective in their writing. As one student said of an anthropology assignment:

> It was hard because we had to look at how we perceive ourselves in the culture and how other people perceive us—how that categorizes us, the factors that categorize us. I hate talking about myself, so that was hard. We had to look at the things that happened in our lives through a book called *Venus on Wheels*. It's about a quadriplegic and how she deals with the world. A lot of people look at her and think she can't do much, yet she has done many things that were completely normal. I wrote that society had labeled her as disabled, and that as an African-American woman, I have that same disability, because sometimes my color will prevent me from doing things that normal—and I had to define normal—people do. I had to go through some experiences that demonstrate that.

Finally, students who identified social science papers as their most challenging third-year writing also spoke of length as a factor that made those papers challenging—mostly page restrictions that were too short for the assignment.

In their fourth year, about a third of the students in the study—all of them social science majors—identified papers in the social sciences as their most challenging that year. As they had in the previous two years, students most frequently mentioned research as the aspect of those papers that made them challenging. Students' descriptions of the research they had done were more complex in this year than in previous descriptions. For example:

> All of the papers for my history course were difficult. I've never done more research in my life. The class was about the Victorian era. We'd find a topic within the reading for that time that interested us. I learned so much about the library. We had to use primary and secondary sources. One [paper]

was about D.W. Holmes, and one was about the contagious diseases act. One was about vivisection, and I can't remember what the other one was about. These were all about the social history of that period, the culture and the diseases of that period. We were making arguments in these papers. The research was really challenging.

Many students mentioned aspects of argumentation that presented challenges, most frequently the challenge of having to come up with one's own argument and then support it. Several students noted problems in understanding and using the disciplinary demands posed by the paper. Sometimes these were unfamiliar demands imposed by disciplines in which they had been immersed for two years, as the following example illustrates:

> [For my thesis in women studies], my topic is gender relations in the world of skateboarding. My hypothesis is in the works still, but I am hoping that there will be some sort of correlation with the sex of an individual and how their parents socialized them growing up in relation to skateboarding. I am trying to find out why fewer women are skateboarding than men and why people give such strange looks to girls when they are. This paper is challenging because I have to write in a different style. All the other papers I've done in my classes have been kind of—present these ideas the author is giving and interpret them in your way. This is very structured and I'm not used to doing that. There isn't a lot of room for me to run my mouth. The structure comes from the major—you want a paper that is academic in caliber.

And sometimes the unfamiliar disciplinary demands came from disciplines outside the major in which the student had been immersed, as the following example shows:

> The research paper for African studies. We were only allowed to use the text, a big fat law book, and one of the challenging things was writing in a new style. She wanted us to write as lawyers. It was difficult trying not to write as a women studies major or from the comparative history of ideas classes or even philosophy. Its focus was on education, about Brown v Board of Education, 1954-55—its social effects. You weren't allowed to go into historical texts. You had to figure out the

effects by looking at the law cases in front of you. The fact that
I had to pull out the social effects of something from case history and law is what made it challenging.

Finally, in the fourth year, a few students reported that the reading upon
which the papers were based was difficult and that the topics were challenging
because they were new or they required a high level of thought.

What Can We Say About Students' Most Challenging Writing in College?

Students' responses to the question about challenging writing over the four years
of the study gave us information about what made writing challenging in general, as well as what made writing in the disciplines challenging. In terms of general challenges, we learned that students' most challenging papers were
arguments about issues, events, and ideas, written mostly for disciplines other
than English. Students did not find papers that asked them to respond to something or summarize something very challenging. Challenging papers varied
quite a bit in length, but length was not a significant contributor to challenge
level, and students more often said that length requirements were too short than
that they were too long.

Another general feature of the papers that students found the most challenging was that most of them required research. Furthermore, while students
often described complex research and complex assignments, most of the faculty
assigning those challenging papers did not require students to go through a
process of drafting the paper, getting feedback from faculty, TAs, or peers, and
revising the draft.

Sometimes the challenges students described in one disciplinary category
seemed quite similar to those described frequently in another. Challenges students noted in writing in the social sciences were similar to those noted in the
humanities, for example. In addition, students seemed to have a shared language
for speaking of writing challenges. However, when viewing the summaries of the
most frequently mentioned challenges for the seven disciplinary categories in
Table 6.5, it is important to remember that the same words often indicate different cognitive moves. The reading upon which writing was based, for example, often posed a challenge for college writers. However, for students in the
social sciences, that reading might be research studies about juvenile delinquency; for students in the humanities, it might be literature; and for engineering
majors, it might be specifications on the shear strength of steel.

Not only does the content of the reading differ, but the way students would
be expected to do the reading may differ as well, with literature students doing

Table 6.5. *Most Challenging Writing, 2000–2003*

Years	2000 & 2001	2002 & 2003
Architecture & Urban Planning	• The level of thinking required by the papers • Unfamiliar/new topics • Incorporation of written information and images into a single document	*See* 2000–2001.
The Arts	• The art pieces on which papers were based were difficult to understand, and students were not sure how to look at them	*See* 2000–2001.
Business	• Understanding and using disciplinary writing practices • Research and a critical eye • Aspects of argumentation, such as use of evidence • Self-reflection • Unclear assignments • Working with groups on shared writing assignments	• Research—finding and using business information, including financial data • Using disciplinary writing practices • The level of thinking required by the papers • Unfamiliar/new topics • Working with groups on shared writing assignments
Engineering	• Reading upon which writing is based • Experimental demands upon which the writing was based • Understanding and using disciplinary writing practices • Having to figure out things on one's own	• Level of material that they needed to understand to do the experiments on which the writing was based or to do the writing • Research—conducting experiments • Determining what they had to figure out to write the paper

Table 6.5 (continued). *Most Challenging Writing, 2000–2003*

Years	2000 & 2001	2002 & 2003
Humanities	*Freshman Composition (other than linked)* • Aspects of argumentation—creating a thesis about a given topic, finding and using evidence to support that thesis, moving that thesis through the paper, and organization • Unclear/confusing assignments • Reading upon which writing was based • Moving from the kinds of papers required in high school to the kinds required in college *Other Humanities* • Understanding/using disciplinary writing practices (particularly in philosophy, first year) • Aspects of argumentation—coming up with one's own argument • Research—finding information on the Internet and in the library • Unclear assignments/ expectations • Reading upon which writing was based • Writing in a foreign language • Length (too short) • Having to start over at the last minute	• Aspects of argumentation—coming up with one's own argument • Research—finding information on the Internet and in the library • Understanding and using disciplinary writing practices • Unclear assignments/ expectations • Reading upon which writing was based • Writing in a foreign language • Length (too short) • Having to start over at the last minute, because the research/evidence does not support one's original thesis • Personal challenges (e.g., illness)

Table 6.5 (continued). Most Challenging Writing, 2000–2003

Years	2000 & 2001	2002 & 2003
Science	• Chemistry experiments upon which writing was based • Understanding and using scientific writing practices • Research—especially finding and understanding scientific articles • Concepts upon which writing was based • Creation of tables and figures in Excel to be included in the written product • Unclear assignments	• Research—particularly issues discovered as one moves through the experimental research process, challenges in finding information, and the difficulty in figuring out what to use, what to leave out, and what is missing • Understanding and using scientific writing practices • Difficult or unclear material upon which writing was based • Unclear assignments • Unfamiliar/new topics • The level of thinking required by the papers
Social Science	• Argumentation, particularly in finding and using evidence to support a thesis, in identifying a thesis, and in providing an effective organization for the argument • Understanding and using the practices of particular disciplines • Research—mostly Internet and library • Unclear faculty expectations • Reading upon which writing was based	• Research—particularly finding information and integrating it into one's own argument • Aspects of argumentation, particularly having to come up with one's own argument and support it • Understanding and using writing practices in disciplines with which students were familiar, and in disciplines that were new to them • Reading on which writing was based • Unfamiliar/new topics • Level of thinking required by the assignment

close reading and political science students skimming the text to identify the argument and key points of evidence.

The disciplinary meanings attached to the shared language of writing challenges are illustrated in Table 6.4, which includes descriptions of papers that students said presented research challenges in each of the seven broad disciplinary categories we examined. As the table shows, there were overlaps across the types of research described. For example, students often used information acquired online or in libraries. Differences in what it meant to do research are also clear in the table. The student doing research for the architecture and urban planning paper, for example, had to extrapolate a reality from incomplete physical evidence. In contrast, research in both engineering and science required hands-on experimentation and the ability to understand the written results of experiments. The research required in the social science paper included observational data and library research in support of hypothesis-driven arguments about animal behavior, unlike the humanities paper, which made use of the library and Internet sources for a literary analysis.

In addition to differences that become clear only when we unpack students' shared language about writing, many of the disciplinary differences in the writing challenges were starkly apparent in students' descriptions of those challenges. A comparison of challenges students frequently mentioned concerning science papers with those frequently mentioned about papers in the humanities serves as an example. Argumentation was not much of an issue for students writing difficult papers in science. Similarly, the complexity of the material on which writing was focused, the challenges posed by having to create one's own evidence in the experiments one conducts—these factors were not mentioned in the humanities papers. Although students in both the sciences and the humanities mentioned difficulty in understanding and using disciplinary practices, the practices students needed to use differed depending on the disciplinary context. For humanities students, the challenge was often knowing how to argue. For science writers, the challenge was fitting information into a prescribed format and explaining what was missing in ways the science disciplines understood.

Finally, it was clear from students' descriptions that the broad disciplinary categories we used to help us understand the writing challenges students described were inadequate to capture real differences inside those categories— the differences between difficult reading for anthropology and psychology, for example, or between challenging research in accounting and marketing. Future research would benefit from a closer filter, such as the lenses of majors inside each disciplinary area.

Differences Between First-Year Writing and Writing Before the UW

There was a gap between the kinds of papers students wrote in high school and those they wrote in college, just as previous studies on writing at the UW had found (Beyer, 1997; Beyer & Graham, 1990, 1992). This gap was particularly a problem for students in their first year in college. In interviews conducted at the end of participants' first year, we asked students if they noticed differences between the kinds of writing they had to do that year and the writing they did before they entered the university. Overall, 68% of the students said that writing at the UW was different from the writing they had done previously. Close to one in five students said the writing was the same as the writing they were required to do in their high schools and transfer institutions. Eight percent said that university writing was both different from and similar to the writing they had done previously. About 5% said that they had not written previously or in their first year at the UW, so they could not answer the question.

While there was much agreement among students that the writing they were required to do at the UW differed from that required at their previous institutions, there were differences between transfer students' responses and those of freshmen. About 74% of the freshmen in the study said that writing at the UW differed from writing at their previous schools, compared with 58% of the students who transferred to the UW from other institutions.[18] About one in four of the transfer students felt that their writing experience at their previous institutions was the same as that at the UW, compared with only 16% of the freshmen. About the same percent of both groups mentioned that there were both differences and similarities.

How Writing Differed at the UW

What was it about writing at the UW that students felt differed from writing they had done previously? While students' descriptions of differences varied quite a bit, five themes emerged.

Structure demands differed. Only freshmen identified changes in structure as a significant difference between the writing required in high school and the writing required in college, yet so many freshmen cited changes in structure that it was one of the two most frequently mentioned differences. In many cases, when referring to changes in structure, students said that at their previous institutions they were required to write the "five-paragraph essay," but at the UW this format was neither used nor valued. They said that as university students, they instead had to develop and use a variety of organizational structures to complete the writing tasks they were assigned. One student's quotation illustrates this category of response:

> High school was a lot easier. My high school teachers always wanted five-paragraph essays, or some really rigid structure. Here you can do so many things. I think it is different what each teacher wants, but still there is a bigger range even in one class compared to what we could do in high school.

Higher expectations/standards. A second dominant theme was higher expectations, and in contrast to comments about structure, more transfer students than freshmen mentioned higher expectations. Transfer students' responses, however, do not necessarily mean that standards at transfer institutions are lower than they are at four-year institutions. These responses could just as well mean that writing expectations increase for *all* students as they move into their majors. The following quotation represents these responses:

> When I was at [my community college], I was just taking my entry-level English courses. They were primarily just teaching me how to write, the rules of the game and things like that. But now my writing has a different focus. They are asking me to look at things analytically, asking me to do projects that are creative, asking me to do projects in different languages. So I am much more challenged and stimulated as a writer now than I was when I was taking those intro courses.

More argumentative assignments. A third theme, introduced by many freshmen and a few transfer students, was that the UW required them to write more arguments than were required by their previous institutions. Quotations from a transfer student and a freshman illustrate this point:

> It seems like here I have done a lot more interpretive or argumentative writing, where at [my community college], it was more factual writing.

> In high school they give you a topic that you had to research and you would write a paper based on the research. Here they integrate the readings into their lectures. You have to go out and read the books, formulate a theory, and support it. You aren't just writing about what you learned from your research. The writing before was more informative, and here it is more theory based. There is a lot more thought processes that have

to go on. You have to eliminate things from your reading to make your argument.

The disciplinary nature of writing. This theme and the themes of structure and argument overlapped somewhat. Both freshmen and transfer students noted changes in writing demands as they moved from discipline to discipline. The following student's quotation represents this theme:

> In high school, I either wrote papers for history or English. It was the same writing style. The proper way to write a paper— you don't use first person. All of a sudden in philosophy, here are a whole new set of rules that pertain only to philosophy papers. Writing in the history class here was harder than in high school, but I didn't feel stressed out about it like I did in political science or philosophy.

Higher expectations/standards at previous institution. The fifth theme to emerge from students' responses to how writing at the UW differed from writing at previous institutions was that students' writing experience prior to the UW had been better or more demanding than that demanded by their first-year UW courses. One student's quotation along these lines follows:

> The writing assignments at [my community college] were more demanding. They were longer. They required more research out of class. They seemed to be harder in order to prepare you for the university, and then when I got down here, it seemed like overkill.

Other areas of difference. In addition to these responses, students identified other areas of difference, including an emphasis on the use of support/evidence (mentioned only by freshmen); more specific and complex topics; better guidance and feedback in college and a greater focus on the writing process (also mentioned only by freshmen); more required writing at the UW than at previous institutions; and a focus on content rather than on the mechanics of writing.

Similarities Between Previous Writing and Writing at the UW

In response to the interview question about whether writing at the UW was the same or different from writing at their previous institutions, many transfer students—about one in four—felt that their writing experience at the UW was comparable to the writing experience they had at their transfer institutions. In contrast, few freshmen reported such an overlap. There were few discernible themes in the similarities students mentioned.

Other Elements of the Gap Between High School, Community College, and UW Writing

Two comparisons of students' descriptions of their most challenging writing yielded interesting information on the nature of the gap between writing at the various institutions. First, we compared 20 randomly selected students' descriptions of the most challenging writing they had done in high school with their descriptions of the most challenging writing they had done in their first year at the UW. Then we focused on a comparison of similar disciplines, matching eight descriptions of students' most challenging high school/community college papers with descriptions of eight UW papers from the same or similar disciplines. These two views of student writing showed us that the most apparent difference between writing at the UW and the writing students did before they came to the UW was how deeply embedded the UW papers were in the course and disciplinary contexts from which they came. In contrast, contextual connections in students' earlier "challenging" papers seemed loose or general.

Both views of student writing—by student and by discipline—also suggested subtle differences between the arguments students were asked to write before they entered the university and those they wrote in their first year. The arguments written for previous institutions tended not to be deeply connected to reading, and they often asked students questions such as "What do you think about X?" In these papers, the intellectual conversation seemed to be between the student and the topic or the instructor. In contrast, the university papers tended to require critical analysis and understanding of difficult reading material, and arguments were focused on "What do you think about these other ideas about X?" The university papers suggested that the student was being asked to join a conversation around a topic, an idea, or an event and to take other participants' views into account. This student's quotation captures that difference:

> I took English comp courses at [my community college]. There it was more like the purpose was to write a paper and now the purpose is more like to study something in depth. When you actually write a paper, that is when I am learning something about a subject. I have my own opinion on it, and I know the research.

The papers that transfer students wrote were closer to those written at the university than were papers written by high school students. This similarity was confirmed by many transfer students' own perceptions of their writing, as reported in the previous section. However, more than half of the transfer students noted differences between their community college and UW writing, which suggests that helping students become effective writers cannot be limited to 100- or 200-level courses in college, and that all courses might bridge this gap by providing explicit instruction about the ways that disciplines mediate what good writing is and does.

Students' Self-Assessment

We asked students to assess their own learning about writing in two ways. First, we asked them in their annual interviews whether they thought their writing had improved or not and to explain those responses. Second, we asked students via the quarterly surveys how much they had learned about writing argumentative and informative papers. Students' self-assessments in both interviews and surveys provide further evidence for the disciplinary nature of writing in college.

Interview Results

Changes in students' interview responses to questions about their writing improvement show that students began to think of "good writing" in the contexts of their majors over time. Most students said that their writing had improved in each of the four years of the study. About two-thirds of the students in the first two years and about three out of five in the second two years believed that their writing had improved.

Students' statements about *how* their writing improved changed from year to year. In their first year, the strongest themes in students' responses were improvements in constructing a thesis or focusing their arguments, as well as improvement in structuring an argument. These responses make sense, in that many of the entering freshmen in the study took required composition courses, which focus on general argumentation. In the second and third years, students' responses about how their writing improved became highly individualized. The only general theme that emerged was improvement in their ability to revise their own writing. This student's description serves as an example of comments about self-improvement:

> Yes. I think that going through the writing of the international studies paper was very informative. I can definitely see a slight change in the way I look at writing. I used to write a lot more based on argumentation, using limited evidence and building big long arguments with those, whereas in the inter-

national studies paper, through the revision process, I was able to incorporate a substantial body of evidence from a variety of sources and come out with a coherent paper that made sense.

In the fourth year, students' responses again showed no strong themes about how writing had improved. However, about half of the time when students identified areas of improvement in their writing, they focused on writing in specific contexts. For example, several students said that they had become better at scientific writing, learned to use specific formats in technical writing, learned American Psychological Association (APA) style, or improved their close reading and code-commenting skills. These two students' comments serve as examples of writing in specific contexts:

Yes. It has improved scientifically. I have an easier time articulating what I want to say in a more scientific way than I did before. I think the practice of writing scientific papers and reading so many in the past year has brought this about.

In some ways yes, because I have written in new ways—like the sales proposal format and different formats. But grammatically probably not. If you keep writing and you aren't getting a lot of feedback about your grammar, you aren't getting any better.

This shift to a more context-based focus in students' later years shows that, just as they did in thinking about critical thinking and problem solving, students' thinking about their own writing became more defined by the disciplines of their majors as they moved through college.

In contrast, students' comments on *why* their writing had improved did not seem bound by the contexts in which students found themselves. In all four years, students attributed improvement to the same three causes:

- Frequent opportunities to write

- Courses that provided them with instruction in writing

- Feedback from faculty, teaching assistants, or peers on *how* to revise their written work

These three causes of improvement often came together for students. For example, in their second year, about half of the students who mentioned that feedback from others had helped them improve their writing also mentioned practice. A fourth theme, less pronounced than instruction, feedback, and practice, was the role that reading played in helping students improve their own writing. The following quotations illustrate some of these causes students noted for improvement:

> In science, you have to go back to remembering how to do it on your own. In the English class I am taking right now, she will shred our papers and then allow us to do rewrites. I think some people think that's for earlier writers, but it is good to do rewrites at this stage too.

> I think it has. I would hope it has, because the more practice you get, the better your writing is. I've learned to be more precise in what I say, not ramble on quite as much. In business writing, more is not necessarily better. You need to be to the point. And I've actually started to work more with people on my writing. I've gotten together with groups for my accounting papers. That's one good thing the major does—gets you getting together in groups. When I do that with my papers, it helps to have someone else read it to see if it makes sense. I always have my dad read my papers too, because he has a financial background.

The students who said that they believed their writing had not improved came from every major. In every year, those students attributed that failure to the same causes, some that were completely opposite of why some students felt they had improved. Most frequently mentioned causes of failure to improve were:

- Few opportunities to write

- Little writing instruction

- Little or no feedback on how to improve their writing from faculty or TAs

- Assignments that were not challenging or required too little thinking to help them improve their skills

- Not needing to improve because writing skills were already good

Students' responses to interview questions on writing improvement over the four years of the study suggest three things about students' development as writers. First, their responses identify the conditions under which writing improvement occurs. Interestingly, students' ideas about what helped their writing improve are not controversial. They included:

- Having many opportunities to write

- Receiving instruction in their classes about how to understand writing requirements

- Receiving feedback on written work that allowed them to revise (and, perhaps more important, to learn how to revise)

When these things were not present, students said that their writing did not improve. In addition, they noted that writing did not improve when assignments were not challenging.

In a trend that was similar to one we noted in Chapter 5 about critical thinking, students increasingly identified improvement in writing with improvement in mastering disciplinary writing practices. This trend was also noted in earlier studies on writing, in which students increasingly described good writing as writing in their majors (Beyer & Graham, 1994a), and it suggests that writing instruction should focus on demands of the discipline in which writing occurs.

Finally, students' comments on improvement suggest that their ability to reflect upon their own work may have increased over time. This finding was similar to a result discussed in Chapter 5. In that chapter, we noted that when students spoke about their improvement in critical thinking and problem solving, the number of improvements students identified increased over time. This trend was also true about the number of improvements students noted in writing.

Survey Results

In addition to the assessment students provided in annual interviews, they indicated in the quarterly surveys how much they had learned about argumentative and informative writing. Survey results over the study's four years showed that students rated their learning about writing arguments as 2.29, on average, on a 4-point scale.[19] For writing papers that presented information but not arguments, the average rating students gave to their learning was 2.09. This difference was significant.[20] Thus, we can say that students perceived that they learned more about writing arguments than about writing informative papers, which is consistent with earlier evidence that showed that they wrote more arguments than informative papers and that argumentative writing was their most challenging.

An examination of survey responses by disciplinary category shows that students perceived most learning about argumentative writing in the humanities (2.62), followed by social science (2.55) and business majors (2.45). Students perceived the least learning about argumentative writing in art (2.08), science

(2.04), and engineering (1.76). This result is consistent with those discussed earlier in this chapter, which showed that students in the first three disciplinary areas wrote argumentative papers in more classes than students in the latter three areas. For informative writing, the differences in how much students learned across major areas were not statistically significant.

Students' self-assessments, whether through interviews or survey responses, provide further evidence of disciplinary differences. These assessments give us an interesting insight into how students evaluate their own growth as writers and provide support for the argument that writing is a disciplinary, rather than a generic, set of skills.

Conclusions and Implications

Our analysis leads us to the following conclusions and their teaching and assessment implications.

There Is a Gap Between High School and College Writing, and Students Falter in That Gap

Differences between high school and college writing may be inevitable and even desirable. However, as noted by the students themselves, these differences are more complex than can be explained by colleges ratcheting up the amount of writing students must do or the degree of difficulty in assignments, and they present special problems for freshmen and sophomores. A hypothetical freshman who finds herself in a 200-level sociology class, an introductory chemistry course, and a literature-based composition class in her first quarter will have to navigate three differing sets of writing demands if she is to write successfully in all three classes. What will change from discipline to discipline? A partial list might include the purposes for writing, what counts as a thesis and where it belongs in a paper, what is arguable in the discipline and what is not, the preferred organizational patterns or formats in each field, what counts as evidence and whether and how it is graphically displayed, and the preferred citation practices in each discipline.

Our hypothetical student's attempts to figure these things out on her own may be made even more challenging by the fact that university manifestations of subjects can be quite different from their high school forms. For example, in contrast to the often quiet, orderly, narrative world of high school history, the world of college history is loud and discordant; students are expected to enter the fray with their own ideas about which scholar presents the best argument and what they believe the primary documents suggest about why an event occurred.

The implications of the gap between high school and college writing are clear for college instructors: Faculty who assign papers in the disciplines should provide students with writing instruction that makes the writing practices of the discipline explicit to students. They should also provide examples of good writing in the field. Such instruction is crucial in students' first two years in college, the years when they are navigating a wide variety of disciplinary demands and experiencing the most confusion about how to find their way. However, faculty should remember that transfer students also are sometimes confused about disciplinary practices and conventions, so instruction should be provided at gateway courses into the major, as well as earlier.

In offering more and better instruction in how to complete writing assignments, faculty should remember that turning in drafts of papers,[21] getting feedback from instructors and peers on those drafts, and revising drafts with that feedback in mind provide students with the best chances for improving their writing. In addition, at the class level, discussing an example of a successful student response to the assignment, talking about why an assigned article or book is well written, and making the bones of one's own arguments explicit to students are all very helpful to students learning to navigate the writing demands of a new discipline.

Regarding assessment, the difference between high school and college writing raises questions about the ways we currently evaluate students' writing. A high score on the SAT essay, high grades in high school English, even AP English, and an eloquent personal statement on a college application form say little about a student's ability to write a lab report for chemistry or an argument about the three-strikes-and-you're-out law for sociology. Therefore, we need to help students understand the limitations of these traditional assessments, and perhaps we need to familiarize high school faculty with some of the differences students find here.

Challenging Writing Is Argumentative and Research Based

Students write arguments in every discipline, and they find those arguments challenging, particularly if they must formulate their own central theses/hypotheses, provide strong evidence in support of their arguments, and conduct research—whatever "research" means in the discipline—to assist them with that support. Furthermore, with the exception of lab reports, students do not believe that short papers of three pages or fewer merit much of their time or energy, even if the assignments are challenging. They also report that papers that require them to summarize or give their personal responses to events, ideas, or books are easy to write.

Regarding teaching, these results do not mean that faculty should stop asking students to write short summaries or response essays. Short pieces of writing can serve many learning purposes. However, they are limited in what they can teach. They cannot teach students to sustain an argument over time, to structure a complex argument with many sections effectively, or to bring to bear a wide array of sources in support of their opinions. Furthermore, in students' minds, short papers do not count as serious writing challenges, unless they can see that brevity is a function of the discipline in which they are writing.

Regarding assessment, the implications of this finding are that departments should be sure to examine the kinds of writing students consider their most challenging when they seek to know how well their majors have learned to write. Furthermore, it is often useful for departments to review a series of assignments from the freshman to the senior level to understand their majors' experience of the writing program in their disciplines, to get ideas from each other, and to see where assignments connect and where they do not.

Writing Is a Disciplinary Act From Students' First Classes to Their Last

All college writing that students do is mediated by the disciplines. In their first and second years, students must figure out and implement the writing practices and conventions of several disciplines, usually simultaneously. As Chapter 5 discussed, sometimes faculty do not make these requirements transparent because their expertise in their own fields shields them from awareness of how the novices in their classes think (Nathan & Petrosino, 2002). For example, faculty and teaching assistants may tell students to "write clearly" or to "support arguments with evidence from the text," but often they provide no examples of what "clearly" means in the context of their courses and rarely do they specify what constitutes "evidence from the text." As noted previously, in an English course, evidence from the text usually means quotations; in political science, it might mean a summary of a case; in international studies, evidence from the text might mean statistics about economic health; and in physics, it might mean data from an experiment.

Institutions often bury distinctions in the writing practices and conventions of the disciplines under talk about general education. The phrase itself, "general education," implies that a paper assigned in a freshman-level history course would have different standards for argumentation and evidence from a paper for a junior-level history course, but it would have the same "general" standards as those of a freshman-level ecology course. This is, of course, untrue.

While it is clear that writing, like critical thinking, is domain specific, we do not suggest that students get no writing benefits from introductory composition courses. When not focused exclusively on writing about literature—a model that primarily serves the purposes of English and other language departments—freshmen composition courses often function as a gateway into college, announcing to students that they have entered a world where thinking about ideas and forming one's own ideas are not only invited, they are required. These first writing courses often give students a safe place to read difficult texts, try out arguments they never would have made in high school, connect opinions to resources outside themselves, and learn how to go about revision. However, generic composition courses sometimes could do more to help students navigate the college writing demands ahead of them. For example, if composition faculty and teaching assistants simply announced to students that what it means to construct a thesis, to locate and use evidence, and to organize an argument will change when students enter new disciplines, students might be better able to apply information from introductory writing courses to subsequent contexts. In addition, inclusion of reading and explicit discussion about writing from varying disciplines—for example, readings from biology, sociology, and literature about alcoholism—can be very instructive for new students and can signal what they might look for in their next courses.

These issues tend to be resolved by the time students graduate. As students become immersed in the disciplines of their majors, they begin to learn the writing approaches that will serve them in those fields. The more practice and feedback they receive, the more students master those approaches.

We believe that there are ways to teach writing that are more appropriate for one discipline than for another. Shulman (1986, 1987) has argued that some pedagogies are more effectively used in some disciplines than in others, and Pace and Middendorf's (2004) approach to working with faculty in the disciplines can encompass writing instruction. If we look around our campuses, we can see evidence that faculty teach students disciplinary content and practices in varying ways. Therefore, it makes sense to suggest that effective writing pedagogy might shift from discipline to discipline. However, the role of disciplinarity in writing pedagogy is one that has not been fully explored by the literature or by our study. Furthermore, one aspect of writing instruction seems to apply to all disciplines: Helping a student improve his writing requires instruction in revision, and instruction in revision demands a required draft/feedback/revision cycle.

Because writing is a disciplinary act, it cannot be centrally assessed. Generic, value-added writing assessments imposed on all students at the point of graduation cannot tell us what students have learned about writing in college. Neither can faculty, administrators, or "trained essay guides" brought in from one discipline to judge writing assigned in another. Assessing writing is the necessary work of the faculty in academic departments who teach their majors what it means to write effectively in their disciplines.

Endnotes

1) http://depts.washington.edu/engl/iwp/

2) Papers were defined as longer than two pages, written outside class, and graded.

3) Short pieces of writing were defined as one to two pages, written inside or outside class, graded or ungraded.

4) We counted every paper students reported, but at the point of analysis, we divided the papers into two groups: papers and short pieces of writing. We defined *papers* as more than two pages of graded writing, at least some of which was written outside class. *Short pieces* of writing included all required writing, two pages long or fewer. The interviewer recorded students' descriptions of the writing they had done and categorized that writing when she analyzed it. Thus, she was able to make consistent decisions about any writing that fell somewhere between the two definitions—a three-page paper written in class, for example.

5) According to an in-house study on how students use their time conducted by Norman J. Rose, dean and professor emeritus, for the UW Teaching Academy

6) As far as we know, the only other research institution that has published data on the number of papers its undergraduates wrote is Harvard University. According to Richard Light's (2001) interview study of seniors, Harvard's undergraduates wrote about ten papers per year, averaging around six pages each, during the years of his study.

7) Two students accounted for nearly all the short pieces of writing (50 and 20), and those short pieces were done for courses other than classes in the arts.

8) One person wrote 50 for a math class, so the real average is closer to four for science majors.

9) One-way analysis of variance (f = 16.7, p < 0.0001), eta sq = 41.9%)

10) One-way analysis of variance (f = 3.69, p < 0.005), eta sq = 13.8%)

11) Because students may have defined "argument" and "informative paper" differently from each other and over time, survey results on the kinds of papers students reported writing in their majors are somewhat suspect.

12) One-way analysis of variance yielded the following: f = 6.08, p < 0.0001, eta sq. = 20.9%

13) These categories were the same as those used in earlier UW assessment studies on writing (Beyer, 1997; Beyer & Graham, 1990, 1992, 1994a, 1994b), so it made sense to use them again, even if only for purposes of comparison.

14) We separated this category from "arguments about issues, events, and ideas," because we knew from earlier studies that students' high school writing tended to focus primarily on literary argumentation/analysis. We wanted to be able to track how much of that type of writing was required of students in college. The "arguments about issues, events, and ideas" category included papers written for English courses when the purpose of those papers was not literary analysis or when those papers did not use literary pieces as their only sources of evidence.

15) Two of these categories are larger than they might be. The "arguments about issues, events, and ideas" category for writing before the UW is larger than it might be if we had focused only on freshmen. Many transfer students reported that their most challenging pre-UW paper was a researched argument they wrote for a composition course that community colleges require transfer students to complete. In addition, the "personal" category is larger than it might be, because many freshmen identified the "personal statement" required for college application, as the most challenging paper they had written before coming to the university.

16) The average length of challenging papers in high school and at transfer institutions was about 9 pages.

17) Papers written for writing courses linked to courses in the disciplines were counted among those for the linked discipline. Freshman composition courses were free-standing writing courses offered by the English department.

18) Most of the transfer students in the UW SOUL came from community colleges; however, several transferred from other four-year schools, including Eastern Washington University, University of California–Berkeley, Seattle University, and University of Southern California.

19) 1 = *zero*, 2 = *a little*, 3 = *a moderate amount*, 4 = *a lot*

20) Using a paired *t*-test, $t = 4.85$, $p < .0001$, eta sq. = 13.4%

21) Students will turn in drafts for feedback when they are required to do so; we found that most students did not take advantage of the opportunity when it was optional. In addition, review of an outline of students' papers is usually less effective than looking at a draft or even a partial draft, because an outline often fails to show connections between the pieces of an argument—a feature that is frequently missing from undergraduate writing.

Quantitative Reasoning

I enjoy calculus. I think it is beautiful. You have this one function that expands into a big origami-like structure. Remember those ring things that would fold and unfold and come back together into a simple structure? Math is like that. I enjoy how it unfolds into a complex structure and then comes into a simple answer like 2.

The assessment of quantitative reasoning (QR) presents an interesting paradox. In comparison with other areas of learning, such as writing and critical thinking, many people consider QR relatively easy to assess. This perception is likely caused by the assumption that quantitative thinking is only about getting correct numerical answers to problems and, thus, its assessment can be objective. Yet in our experience, assessing QR on a campus-wide basis has been consistently intractable in spite of repeated efforts to design effective methods for doing so. One such attempt involving a state-wide study of the effectiveness of standardized tests in computation concluded that what was valued by faculty and staff in Washington could not be measured by such tests (Washington Council of Presidents and State Board for Community College Education, 1989).

Our inability to measure quantitative reasoning effectively is shared by others; indeed, we know of few universities of any size that assess quantitative reasoning on anything close to a campus-wide basis with any measure of success. One reason for the difficulty of assessing QR is definitional. There are two ways to conceive of quantitative reasoning. Both approaches view QR as something other than mathematics, consistent with the Educational Testing Service's (ETS) definition (Dwyer, Gallagher, Levin, & Morley, 2003): "Quantitative reasoning is, however, fundamentally different, both conceptually and practically, from mathematical content knowledge" (p. 2). However, each conception suggests a different approach to assessment. First, one can view quantitative reasoning as a general education outcome that ought to be shared by all students. This conception is most commonly designated *numeracy* or *mathematical literacy*. It is defended in a report, published by the National Research Council (1989) as follows:

> To function in today's society, mathematical literacy—what the British call "numeracy"—is as essential as verbal literacy. . . . Numeracy requires more than just familiarity with numbers. To cope confidently with the demands of today's society, one must be able to grasp the implications of many mathematical concepts—for example, change, logic, and graphs—that permeate daily news and routine decisions—mathematical, scientific, and cultural—provide a common fabric of communication indispensable for modern civilized society. (p. 7)

Nine years later, a Mathematical Association of America (1998) report identified what the quantitatively literate college graduate should be able to do, asserting:

> In short, every college graduate should be able to apply simple mathematical methods to the solution of real-world problems. A quantitatively literate college graduate should be able to:
>
> 1. Interpret mathematical models such as formulas, graphs, tables, and schematics, and draw inferences from them.
>
> 2. Represent mathematical information symbolically, visually, numerically, and verbally.
>
> 3. Use arithmetical, algebraic, geometric and statistical methods to solve problems.
>
> 4. Estimate and check answers to mathematical problems in order to determine reasonableness, identify alternatives, and select optimal results.
>
> 5. Recognize that mathematical and statistical methods have limits. (¶ 6)

Similar standards have been adopted by the National Council of Teachers of Mathematics, and there is essential agreement among the mathematical organizations that QR is an ability that all high school and college students can and should develop.

The other major approach to quantitative reasoning is rooted in the belief that students need to know the QR that is most closely related to their majors. Using this conception, each major or program is responsible for defining and measuring the unique QR demands it requires as an end-of-program outcome. This conception aligns itself most comfortably with the movement toward mathematics (or quantitative methods) across the disciplines. It focuses on making the quantitative dimensions of any discipline more explicit, usually in the form of learning goals. Also, it takes the teaching and learning of mathematics and other QR skills out of mathematics departments and into a position of shared responsibility across all disciplines.

The University of Washington has a distributive model for completion of its QR requirement that appears to fall into the "QR in the majors" approach. Undergraduates must fulfill a quantitative and symbolic reasoning requirement by passing a course selected from a list of 52 courses spanning 17 academic departments, one of which is mathematics. Many majors require specific QR courses for entry into the major or for graduation.

Given this model, what do undergraduates experience? This chapter focuses on answering that question. We begin with brief case studies of four students' QR experience in college. Next, we examine students' perceptions of their preparation for quantitative reasoning and their descriptions of the quantitative reasoning that they actually did at UW, where they did it, and what they learned from it. We also present a faculty perspective obtained through interviews with chairs of 15 academic departments. Finally, we draw conclusions and discuss their teaching and assessment implications.

Consistent with the major theme of this book, we make the case that quantitative reasoning is discipline-specific. Compared with our discussion of writing and critical thinking in the disciplines, the QR argument is easier to make, because the disciplines of students' majors had an even more profound influence on their QR experience.

Four Paths

We begin our exploration of quantitative reasoning with four case studies based on students' responses to interview questions about their quantitative reasoning experience. The cases illustrate the role the major plays, not in only the content of QR but in its emphasis.

Laura Habb: Computer Science Engineering Major

Laura Habb came to college with relatively strong quantitative reasoning skills from her high school education. She had taken chemistry and physics courses in high school that she felt had prepared her well for college-level work. Furthermore, she took second-quarter calculus in her first quarter, because she felt she also had excellent math preparation in high school. About her most challenging QR experience in high school, Laura said:

> I would say the chemistry lab write ups have always been challenging. They expected us to come up with certain conclusions from our data, and then they will teach that section after that. It was hard to make the transition from classes where they tell you exactly what you are looking for and make sure your data supports that. In my sophomore year, they kind of held your hands. The change in how to do those labs happened my junior year. That's why I feel well prepared in college now. My teacher opened my eyes—showed me that you have to learn to teach yourself certain things.

In her first year, Laura reported having to do QR in a general engineering course, a computer science course, two chemistry courses, and two math courses. She found courses in college to be different from her high school QR courses, saying:

> It is definitely more in depth and, of course, at a quicker pace. It is more mentally demanding, because the answers won't be just handed to you at the end. Most of the time, you have to understand the concepts because the tests take it to that next level. If all you know is formulas, then you won't do well. But in high school, it was okay to just know the formulas. That is all they were asking.

During the first year, Laura believed that she had improved her QR ability by learning to look below the surface to understand concepts and by no longer relying on memorization of formulas.

Laura's second year presented a contrast to her first in that she felt that she had done no quantitative reasoning, even though she was enrolled in math, computer science, and astronomy courses. She felt that the 300-level math course she took did not require quantitative reasoning, with emphasis on the *reasoning* part of the phrase:

> Even though I got a 4.0 out of that class, I didn't understand a thing of what was going on. It was just going through the motions, just plug and chug. It wasn't like having a lab, where you have to look at your data and see what the numbers mean.

She also said that she used more logic than quantitative reasoning in her computer science courses. Laura concluded that she had not improved her QR ability during this year because she had not done anything challenging.

In her third year, Laura felt that she had done QR in three courses within her computer science major, as well as in two physics courses and a math course. She found doing the formal proofs of why division works to be particularly challenging in one of her computer science courses, even though the math itself was no harder than division and multiplication. About her work in that class, she said, "It is really hard to do formal proofs of things you take for granted." In her third year, Laura felt that her ability to do QR had improved because she learned new techniques.

In her fourth year, Laura listed six computer science courses, two statistics courses, and a philosophy course as those in which she had done QR. However, she did not find the QR she had done to be challenging in any of these courses.

In her four years in college, Laura took about 20 QR-intensive courses—courses that many faculty and students would describe as very challenging in terms of QR. Yet she did not feel challenged by her second- and-fourth year QR requirements, and her sense of her own improvement dropped in her second year. Unlike many engineering majors, Laura took many detours off the engineering track. She studied art history, for example, learned Italian, studied abroad in Rome, took on several internships, and questioned her commitment to the engineering major off and on over the four years of the UW SOUL. Not too long after she graduated, Laura resolved this issue by beginning a Ph.D. program in computer science at a prestigious university.

Cyndy Schwartz: Accounting Major

Cyndy Schwartz entered college confident in her math abilities, feeling that she had been well taught in high school. She had taken a math-oriented physics course in high school that made extensive use of QR. A high school course she described as challenging signaled her early interest in accounting.

> I had an accounting class. We did lots of projects in that class. We had a packet representing a business, and we had to track their finances. We had to calculate all their tax stuff, and put it in and if it didn't work out, you had to spend hours and hours tracking back to figure out what happened to the five dollars you lost along the line. I liked tracking that back. Some people just hated it, and I got really into it.

In her first year, when asked about courses in which she had to do QR, Cyndy said that she had taken two calculus courses for business majors, a statistics class, and two economics courses. At the beginning of fall quarter, soon after she had started the class, Cyndy found the calculus course difficult. She said:

> In the class I am in now, there are a lot of graphs. I haven't
> quite caught on to that yet—marginal revenue, for instance.
> Sometimes the math problems are five sentences long, and I
> don't know quite what they are asking for. If you don't know
> what they want in the end, then you won't get the answer. You
> need to figure out what they are asking for.

By the end of the year, however, when asked what her most challenging QR experience had been, Cyndy focused on her economics courses, rather than calculus:

> Econ 200 was the most challenging, but Econ 201 had more
> quantitative reasoning type stuff. The quantitative part of
> those classes was challenging because I had so much trouble
> understanding the concepts. For Econ 201, depreciation of
> products was hard.

While Cyndy felt that she had been challenged, she did not feel that she had
learned very much that was new in her first year QR courses, except that the
constant application of concepts "really made you understand what you were
doing." When asked if she had noticed any differences between QR in college
and the QR she had been required to do in high school, Cyndy focused on
applications of math, saying:

> In high school, we never had to use numbers in any class
> besides math, and even then it was just 35 problems solving
> for the answer. Here, you have to apply everything, and that
> was really different for me. In high school it was really a big
> deal when the teacher applied some math concept to a real-
> world problem. But here, everything is like that. There may be
> ten answers to one problem. Here it is all applied numbers. I
> like that. It is easier to understand and to do.

Cyndy reported that her confidence in her QR ability had increased by the end
of the year, mainly because she had anticipated college math to be harder than
it turned out to be.

In her second year, Cyndy took two accounting courses, a quantitative
methods course, and a finance course, and she found them all challenging,
because, as she said:

> There are so many ways you can mess them up—picking the
> wrong data or the wrong figure. Any time you use numbers,
> you are doomed to mess them up somewhere along the line.

In that year, Cyndy saw improvement in her ability to be patient and to go back and carefully check her numbers.

In her third year, Cyndy's exposure to QR was through four accounting courses, a business economics course, and an operations management course. Of these, she found business economics to require the most challenging QR, primarily because she believed that the economists' perspective was too one-sided. She said:

> I don't understand economics, so anything that has to do with econ is extremely hard. It just doesn't click. It's its own way of thinking. Our professor would say, "Economists would say this," so I guess they are all grouped into one category and no one disagrees. I don't like the right-or-wrong answer approach.

However, throughout the year, Cyndy felt her QR abilities had improved by "Just doing stuff—trying new things."

Cyndy's heavy QR load continued into her fourth year, when she was exposed to QR in four accounting courses and one operations management course. That year, she felt her abilities further improved, and she found two accounting courses challenging. Her description of what made these courses hard provides insight into the nature of the QR expected of an accounting major:

> Accounting 450 was hard just because you are doing corporation tax returns and figuring out their bases and stocks. You have to know how to calculate to the final number. There's a procedure you have to do, and if you don't know it, you get nothing. Accounting 311 was like that, too. It was managerial accounting. You had to know the right formulas to use and if you didn't you were out of luck. The number was your ultimate goal at the end of each of these classes, but you had to know the right procedures. They would give you a list of 20 items, and you had to figure out which ones to use. If you could figure out the right approach to use, finding the number wasn't hard.

Throughout her four years in college, Cyndy identified classes outside business as presenting the most significant QR challenges. She became annoyed in her third year about a QR-focused course—economics—that appeared to her to be an extended argument for one way of thinking. In contrast, she believed that her accounting major taught that there were "no right answers" but approaches that worked better in some situations than in others. And she valued that about her major. Cyndy's love of accounting took her through her CPA and to a job with an accounting firm.

Nicole Ramsey: English Major

When Nicole Ramsey arrived at the UW, she felt comfortable with math up to algebra, but she did not find it interesting. She was frustrated with QR, because her need for it beyond the classroom was limited:

> Just applying it to everyday life. I have never understood why we have to learn so many formulas and so many difficult ways to do math, and I have never had to use three-fourths of the math I've learned outside the classroom.

She stated that she did QR in physics and chemistry classes in high school, but never had any QR-related projects to do in any of her classes, "just everyday problem assignments."

During her first and second years in college, Nicole said that she had done no coursework that related to QR. During her third year, probably to fulfill her UW QR requirement, Nicole took a course in sociological methods, described by the sociology department as a course focused on "the logic of analysis in social sciences. Students learn to recognize good research design, understand and interpret main arguments employing different methods, and evaluate whether research findings support stated conclusions" (University of Washington, 2006). Nicole said the course required her to "solve some problems and make a few graphs. But I hated it. [It] made me realize why I'm an English major. Math is sooo boring." She found the course challenging only because she was not motivated to do it. Nicole did no QR in courses in her fourth year and assessed her improvement in quantitative reasoning as follows:

> No. It hasn't improved since about my junior year in high school. It just keeps getting worse. That's my own fault, because it is nothing I've been particularly interested in or worried about.

Nicole took the one QR course required by the UW for graduation and pursued QR no further. Interestingly, she chose a course required for sociology majors and, therefore, heavy on the interpretation of "mathematical models such as formulas, graphs, tables, and schematics" that the Mathematical Association of America (1998) report identified as one of the things that defined a quantitatively literate college graduate. Nicole got a writing-intensive job in public relations when she graduated.

Antonio Zambrini: Math and International Studies Major

Antonio Zambrini grew up and went to high school in Italy where he received extensive exposure to QR. He described this experience in these words:

> We had physics for five years and used quantitative analysis there. And not as much in other classes. In chemistry we had to use math for chart analyzing. In philosophy, to some extent—a very little extent—when we were studying Marx— he had a very mathematical approach in his analysis of certain problems. And statistical analysis of populations in history classes. And in art history, and especially the first couple of years when we were studying Greek art, we were relating archi- tecture and so on to mathematical figures—ratio and height and so on.

Antonio's example of a challenging QR task in high school was as follows:

> During a final exam that all students have to take in Italy to graduate from high school, we had to solve two out of three problems that involved some pretty tough calculus. At the very end of the third problem, we were required to find when a certain line was of minimum length. I found it challenging because as far as that point, that exercise had primed you to use mathematical analysis to solve it. But it was impossible to solve with mathematical analysis. It required you to shift your analysis and look at it in a much simpler way—to see that some geometrical analyses applied.

At the UW, Antonio took the three-course calculus sequence and the three- course calculus-based physics sequence in his first year. The main difference he found between these courses in college and those in his high school was that the college courses stressed applications much more, and the focus of the problems was converting the words into mathematical formulas. In high school, he was accustomed to just the mathematical form of the problem—a comment we heard from many students, including Fiona O'Sullivan (see Chapter 3) and Cyndy Schwartz (earlier in this chapter). Antonio found one of the physics courses especially challenging because the content itself was very abstract and also required calculus for solutions. He said that his QR abilities increased dur- ing the first year, but mainly because he felt he was making fewer algebraic errors than he had made previously.

In his second year at the UW, Antonio listed four math courses and one geography course as requiring QR and felt his QR ability had improved as a result of taking these courses. When asked about any QR he had done that was especially challenging, he highlighted the geography course:

> Looking at the geography class, we will have to do a research project on some industry concerned with consumption. I figured we'd look at the advertising industry, because we got a really cool article on it that inspired me. The challenge is quantifying the data we collect from TV—Saturday morning cartoons, Nick at Night—and figuring out exactly how we put one commercial into one slot and another into another slot, and then having to derive some statistics from that. I have never really [done anything like this]. This is kind of our methodology. I was thinking of looking at what message advertising uses to sell their stuff. It seems like there's the message "buy this product to show your creativity." I am wondering what industries use that message. We are going to watch an hour of TV a day and quantify what we see.

Antonio saw the improvement in his QR skills that year coming from the geography course as well as from his math courses.

In the third year, Antonio was required to do QR in five math courses and two economics courses. He listed three 400-level math courses as being the most challenging, noting the difficulty of dealing with abstract material:

> The main challenge that I had was that the material we are covering is very abstract. In other math classes I have taken, if you sit down with the book and do a lot of problems, eventually you will notice a pattern. Once that pattern is clear, then you just have to pay attention to the detail. With these problems, in modern algebra, there is no pattern. There just aren't several problems that deal with the same issue. So every problem presents itself anew, and then you have to go back to your bag of tricks and see if you have anything that applies.

Even though it appeared that he had been asked to do a great deal of QR in his third year, at the end of that year Antonio did not feel his QR abilities had increased. As he put it, "When I had to figure out to divide complex numbers, for example, I had to research it and practice it, but I don't think my quantitative skill has improved."

In his fourth year, Antonio listed six math courses as demanding QR. He found one of these courses as particularly challenging.

> It was challenging from a different perspective, because we were analyzing physical situations, and the method that we had I found fairly complex. To apply that method to a specific situation was pretty tough. We started out, for example, looking at the distribution of heat on a one-dimensional line and how that changed over time. Then with a set of understandings, concepts about the differential equations that we used to describe that, we moved to more dimensions. Going from one to the next dimension always involved a certain degree of "Whoa, what just happened here?"

Unlike the third year, Antonio felt his QR abilities had improved during the fourth year.

> Absolutely. I think just all around, if I am confronted with a problem, I think that not only do I have a greater variety of perspectives, but my basic confidence would allow me to figure out a way to approach the problem. That has increased.

In his analyses of the QR in his curriculum, Antonio heavily emphasized his math major over his social science major, particularly in his later years. While it seems clear that the shape and quantity of QR was driven by the math side of his curriculum, in some of his responses to interview questions not related to QR, Antonio appeared to be applying math to the social sciences and vice versa. Such a synthesis of these seemingly unrelated fields would not be surprising, for Antonio demonstrated impressive relational thinking skills over the years. This quotation about critical thinking serves as an example:

> Inevitably your perception of something will depend on the values you begin with. I have really thought of what value system I am applying when I interpret the world. And when interacting with other people, it is important to identify what value system they are coming from. If those two systems are opposed, there is no way you can argue for one over the other empirically. This is true in math obviously. Your conclusions, if you are logical, have to follow from your premises. That's one way I feel that I am more critical now than I was before. I am always trying to look for the underlying value that is being expressed by a particular phrase. Also, especially when

thinking about the world, I don't rely on one source of information. I don't assume that because someone says something, it is correct. Once you start leaving the world of math and science behind, things get less objective. I think inevitably, whenever you tell a story of the fact, you embed your viewpoint in it.

In addition to his academic work, Antonio was deeply committed to social justice issues. He taught high school math in the Teach for America program after he graduated.

Students' Quantitative Reasoning Experiences

Our findings about students' quantitative reasoning experiences support the argument that learning in this area, as in other areas of learning, was discipline-specific. However, in the case of quantitative reasoning, the argument is fairly simple to make. Although some people see QR as part of critical thinking (Bok, 2006), few people in academia argue that quantitative reasoning is a generic skill. Everyone understands that biochemistry majors learn a different kind of QR than the QR students who major in art history learn. And indeed, we found that students' majors accounted for more variation in their QR responses than they did for other aspects of students' learning that we tracked. This section focuses on what students said they learned about QR and is divided into the following subsections:

- University QR and students' previous QR experience

- How much QR students did and where they did it

- Most challenging quantitative reasoning

- Students' self-assessment

- Interviews with department chairs

University QR and Students' Previous QR Experience

We hoped to understand whether and how students experienced quantitative reasoning at the university in relation to their high school and community college math experiences. A report on a survey conducted for the *Chronicle of Higher Education* (Sanoff, 2006) stated that 37% of high school teachers and only 4% of college faculty felt students were well prepared to do college math, but our surveys of entering students suggested that the students, themselves, were more positive about their abilities. Because there is so much talk about math anxiety and its debilitating effect on students' performance, we asked students in entering and end-of-first-year interviews about their comfort levels with math. We also asked them at the end of their first year about differences between QR at the university and the QR they had done earlier.

Comfort Levels

When asked in entry interviews about their level of comfort with their abilities to do math, only 13% of students said that they were uncomfortable with their ability to do math, and most of those were freshmen; about one-third of them were underrepresented minority students. The majority of students—about 72%—said that they felt comfortable with their math abilities, as Table 7.1 shows, but many of them added a ceiling to that comfort level. About 38% of those who said they were comfortable with their math abilities indicated no limitations to their levels of comfort; close to 40% of this group were transfer students. Many of this group of students cited their past and current math successes as reasons for their complete comfort in math. One student, for example, got a 5 on the AP calculus test; another received a perfect score on the SAT math exam; and another read math books for pleasure. Of this group, about a third were planning to major in engineering, math, or the sciences. Table 7.1 shows, however, that many who expressed comfort with their math abilities specified a level at which they were no longer comfortable.

We asked students the same question about their math comfort levels at the end of their first year. In comparison with their earlier responses, about 64% of the students reported that their comfort levels had stayed the same, 22% reported increased comfort, and 8% experienced decreased comfort with math. About 6% of the students we interviewed gave unclear responses to the question. About 76% of the transfer students reported feeling the same comfort levels they had experienced on entry, compared with about 57% of the students who entered as freshmen. There were no strong themes in students' explanations for why they felt more comfortable with their math abilities at the end of their first year than they had felt as they entered the university.

Finally, we looked at changes in students' descriptions of their comfort levels with math by the disciplinary category of their eventual majors. Because of the small numbers in most of these disciplinary areas, these results were more suggestive than definitive. They suggest that science, math, and engineering majors experienced the least change in comfort levels over time. Students in the arts and humanities—who took the fewest math courses—felt their comfort levels had decreased on average more often than students in science, math, and engineering. Social sciences majors fell between the two groups.

Table 7.1. *Entering Students—Are You Comfortable With Your Ability To Do Math?*

Response (N = 140)	Percent of Total
Unclear Response to Question	5
Yes and No	10
No	13
Yes	72
• Completely comfortable	38
• Comfortable up to Algebra	4
• Comfortable up to Geometry/Trigonometry	4
• Comfortable up to Pre-calculus	9
• Comfortable to Calculus or to a Point in Calculus	15
• Comfortable through Calculus	2

Differences Between UW QR and QR at Students' Previous Institutions

As well as focusing on students' comfort levels in math at the end of their first year at the UW, we asked 134 interviewees whether they had noticed differences between the type of quantitative reasoning they had done in their first year at the UW and the QR they had done before they came. The majority of students—69% of those we interviewed—believed that there were differences. About 15% of the UW SOUL interviewees said they had done no QR that year, so they could not say, and another 13% said that they noted no differences. About 3% of the responses did not clearly address the question. If we compare students who were enrolled in a QR course, about the same percentage of transfer students (80%) experienced a difference in QR as the percentage of freshmen who did (85%).

Three strong themes and several minor themes emerged from differences students described. Table 7.2 lists these themes and the percentage of students who identified them. As the table shows, the themes that dominated students' responses included the integration of QR into non-math courses, the level of thinking demanded by university QR, and the focus on word problems.

Integration of QR into non-math courses. Students were surprised to find QR integrated into courses such as biology, astronomy, economics, sociology, psychology, and architecture. Quotations from a freshman and a transfer student illustrate this theme:

> In high school, I didn't use quantitative reasoning for anything but math. It was just number based. By the time you get up into

Table 7.2. *Differences Between UW QR and QR at Students' Previous Institutions (Percentage[1] of Total "Yes" Responses)*

Theme	% freshmen	% transfer	% total
QR is integrated into many courses other than math at UW	35	36	35
QR at UW is harder, demanding a higher level of thought	25	21	24
QR at UW is more focused on word problems and applications to real-world questions than on numbers	25	18	23
At UW, there is a "leap" between the QR required to solve problems for homework and that required for tests	5	7	5
QR at UW is faster paced	5	4	4
QR at the UW requires more depth	6		4
QR at the UW requires more independence, self-discipline	5		3

calculus, they abandon the story problems. But [here], I was using actual numbers about an actual inlet to figure out what was going to happen to it. It was a lot harder, but it is a lot more satisfying. With math, you get a number and you figure you could throw it away and no one would care. But here, you get a number and you figure out someone might really care about it.

The classes here seek us to apply memorized information as opposed to simply regurgitate formulas and facts. It is more an information-processing based learning as opposed to information collecting. I am still figuring this out. No one ever said that to me. If anything, I was led to believe that science classes here would be more fill in the blank and less think for yourself.

Level of thinking required by university QR. Another difference that many students identified was that quantitative reasoning was harder at the university, requiring a higher level of thought than had been required at their previous institutions. There was a great deal of overlap with this theme and others. Two students' quotations illustrate this response:

> I'd say it is different here because the level that I am thinking about math here is far more than in high school. In high school, you never really get out beyond that three-dimensional space where you can still visualize it.

> I have noticed that what I learned here, they were trying to teach you how to think in order to solve a problem. But in high school, they were just trying to teach you to solve the problem. A lot of professors specifically say that, especially in Computer Science Engineering. They tell you that it is not about this specific problem but about the concept behind it.

Focus on word problems in university QR. A third major difference noted by interviewees was the shift to word problems and real-world applications, particularly in their math courses. One student described this move as "blending abstract concepts with numerical evidence." Another student had this to say about the change:

> The main difference that I noticed, especially in the math courses but in physics as well is that this is much more applications-based math. I was used to doing—here is a circle with two tangents. I was used to dealing with mathematical objects, not "you have a fence and you want to build a pig sty." So it was much more application based here and the main part of the problem was converting the word problem into mathematical terms.

Other differences. As Table 7.2 shows, in addition to these major themes, both freshmen and transfer students noted the need to make a "leap" between the problems done as homework and those required on exams, and adjust to the faster pace of QR at the UW compared to previous institutions. Freshmen also identified the greater depth of their QR work, and the greater level of independence and self-discipline required to do QR relative to QR work at their high schools.

How Much QR Students Did and Where They Did It

Each quarter, we asked students to respond to survey questions about how many courses they had taken that required them to do quantitative reasoning. In addition, each year we asked students in interviews if they had done any QR in the courses they had taken that year. Both the quantitative and qualitative measures provided evidence for the dominant role of students' majors in determining how much QR students did. What students meant by quantitative reasoning also varied by area of major as we discuss later in this chapter.

Survey Data on How Much QR Students Did

On quarterly surveys, students from Group 1 and Group 2 were asked to indicate the number of courses they had taken that quarter in which they had done the following:

- Used quantitative reasoning to solve mathematical problems

- Used quantitative reasoning/analysis (e.g., use of statistics, charts, or graphs) in thinking about solving problems other than math problems

- Used quantitative reasoning/analysis to support an argument made in a paper or in a presentation

Table 7.3 presents averages and measures of variability for all three items. It should be noted that the content of the three items was not mutually exclusive; therefore, a single course could cover more than one kind of QR. As Table 7.3 shows, the average number of courses over the study's four years in which students used QR to solve mathematical problems was 12.2, or about one course per quarter. The average number of courses asking students to use QR in problems other than math was 11.6. And finally, the average number of courses for which students used QR to support an argument in a paper or presentation was 6.6. The data included a large range of numerical values for each question, especially for the item that focused on using quantitative reasoning to solve math problems.

The factors largely responsible for the variation were students' area of major. Table 7.4 shows that differences among areas of majors were significant for all three items, but especially for using QR to solve math problems, where these differences accounted for close to 60% of the total variance and the number of courses students reported ranged from an average of 27.5 courses for engineering majors to 3.7 courses for humanities majors. There was also considerable variability evident for "used quantitative reasoning to solve problems other than math." As the table shows, the least variability across majors was for the item asking students in how many courses they "used quantitative reasoning to make arguments in papers." However, even for this item, the differences were significant and accounted for 16.4% of the total variation. Engineering and business majors took the most courses requiring arguments with quantitative reasoning, while humanities and art majors took the least.

Table 7.3. *Averages and Variability Across All Students for Number of Classes*

	Math Problems	Non-Math Problems	QR in Papers
Range	0–38	0–32	0–23
Mean	12.2	11.6	6.6
Standard Deviation	9.2	6.9	5.1

Table 7.4. *Differences in Survey Responses About QR by Areas of Major*

Area of Major		Math Problems	Non-Math Problems	QR in Papers
Art	Mean	4.88	5.75	4.38
(N = 8)	*Std. Dev.*	4.29	7.38	7.31
Business	Mean	15.15	15.23	10.23
(N = 13)	*Std. Dev.*	5.30	4.04	4.13
Engineering	Mean	27.53	17.53	9.16
(N = 19)	*Std. Dev.*	7.76	8.60	6.18
Humanities	Mean	3.73	5.36	3.45
(N = 11)	*Std. Dev.*	1.85	3.26	2.73
Science	Mean	15.00	14.50	6.96
(N = 26)	*Std. Dev.*	7.03	4.76	4.49
Social Science	Mean	6.80	8.86	5.32
(N = 44)	*Std. Dev.*	5.60	5.41	4.52
	F-Value	34.15	12.51	3.83
	Signif.	0.0001	0.0001	0.001
	Eta Sq[3]	59.8%	35.2%	16.0%

The interaction between year and major area was statistically significant[4] for the average number of courses requiring students to do math each year within each major area. Figure 7.1 shows that the number of courses for which quantitative reasoning was used to solve math problems increased for engineering and business majors and decreased for the other majors. The steady downward trends for humanities and social science majors were especially marked, with humanities majors' averages declining from about 1.5 in the first year to almost none in the fourth.

The interaction of "used quantitative reasoning to solve non-math problems" with year was not significant. However the interaction between year and the third item, which focused on using quantitative reasoning to make arguments in papers or presentations, was strongly significant.[5] Figure 7.2 shows this interaction. The simple effects across majors for the first and second years of the study were not significant, as shown by the closeness of the lines in the figure. The effects of the third and fourth years, however, were significant, accounting for 13.8% and 38.7% of the total variance, respectively. As the figure shows, the averages for business majors rose across the first three years. The averages for engineering majors rose steadily after the second year. Averages for science majors increased between the second and third years. The averages for the remaining majors were steady across the four years or decreased slightly.

Figure 7.1. *Interaction Between Year and Major Area for Math Problems*

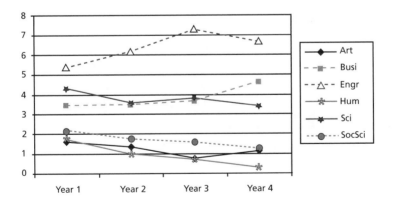

Figure 7.2. *Interaction Between Year and Major Area for QR in Papers*

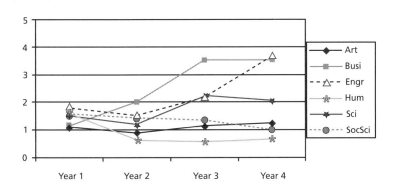

Interview Results on How Much QR Students Did

Quantitative reasoning questions on annual interviews confirmed what the survey data showed. In conducting these interviews, we defined *quantitative reasoning* for students as "the use of numbers and symbols to solve problems, make arguments, design or create something new, find answers, or analyze something." Students had their transcripts in front of them during the interviews to remind them of the courses they had taken that year. Table 7.5 shows the number of students who said they took no courses that required QR each year and gives the percent of that group who were transfer students and who were freshmen. As the table shows, each year the majority of students in the study reported doing quantitative reasoning in at least one of their courses, but across all students, the percentage of students reporting doing QR decreased each year. Our results showed that 10%, 14%, 18%, and 29% of the interviewees said they took no courses that required QR over the four years of the study. Transfer students were less likely than freshman entrants to take a QR course during their first two years, which is consistent with other data, since most transfers entered the university as juniors.

The majors of the students who reported doing no QR each year were predictable. Students in the arts and humanities were the students who most frequently reported doing no QR. Students majoring in business, engineering, science, and math rarely reported doing no QR. Students who were social science majors were split, with a few reporting having done no QR each year, but many reporting having been required to use QR in at least one of their courses.

Table 7.5. Students Reporting Doing No Quantitative Reasoning

Year	% No QR	% of No QR Entering as Fresh	% of No QR Entering as Transfers
1999–2000 (N = 134)	10	43	57
2000–2001 (N = 112)	14	37	63
2001–2002 (N = 88)	18	75	25
2002–2003 (N = 63)	29	89	11

The students who reported doing quantitative reasoning each year described QR for courses in every discipline across the curriculum—from math to drama. We did not ask students to describe all the QR they had done, but occasionally students provided brief descriptions. As one might predict, the kinds of QR that students reported doing varied quite a bit from course to course. Below is a sample of seven students' brief descriptions of the QR they did in courses that we might *not* expect to include QR:

> *Architecture:* I had to use numbers that related to measurements, ergonomics, and human-scale.

> *Spanish:* I had to analyze economic figures for Spain and analyze economic factors that indicate growth—like the consumption of cement from one quarter to another.

> *Art:* [In] a "Topics in Metals" course that I am taking this spring, we have to use this stuff, a cement-like substance called investment, and you have to figure out the ratio—how much investment you need and how much water you need in a ratio with the investment.

> *African-American Studies:* We had to use a study of the number of African-American males who have been disproportionately sent to prison for killing white males.

Drama: You had to figure out how many volts or wattage the circuit could hold. You had to make a model to scale and do a cost estimate for a set design.

Comparative History of Ideas: I have used questionnaires and surveys for my senior thesis.

Community and Environmental Planning: I looked at a lot of census data on poor women and children and compared the numbers.

Most Challenging Quantitative Reasoning

In all five interviews, we asked students to identify their most challenging quantitative reasoning. Students' responses add further evidence to the argument that QR is a disciplinary act.

Where Students Reported Doing Challenging QR

Students' responses to the question of where they had done their most challenging QR shifted over time from a focus on QR done for math and science courses to a greater distribution of QR across the curriculum. Prior to coming to the UW, about 63% of the students said their challenging QR was in math or science. This percentage decreased to 45%, 35%, 29%, and 17%, over the four years of the study. While to some extent this change shows students experiencing the integration of quantitative reasoning into the disciplines of their majors, such as business and social science, it also shows the front-loaded nature of most students' QR experience. The percentage of students indicating that they had done no QR or no challenging QR each year rose from 17% of the students before they entered the UW to 36%, 34%, 43%, and 52% of the students in their first, second, third, and fourth years at the university. It is interesting that students in every disciplinary category, including science and engineering, sometimes indicated that they had done no *challenging* QR in a given year. Laura Habb, one of our opening case studies, is an example.

We noted some differences in responses of entering freshmen and transfer students to questions about where students did their most challenging QR. In responses about their experience prior to coming to the UW, a larger proportion of transfer students (21%) than entering freshmen (15%) said that they had done no challenging QR. In addition, more transfer students said that they had done challenging QR in the social sciences before coming to the UW than did entering freshmen (14% for transfers vs. 5% for freshmen).

Differences between entering freshmen and transfer student responses about first-year QR experience at the university were as follows:

- A greater percentage of transfer students than freshmen reported doing no QR in their first year at the university, presumably because they had completed QR requirements at their transfer institutions.

- More freshmen than transfer students mentioned doing challenging QR in the social sciences in their first year (all in economics).

- Transfer students were more likely to be doing challenging QR in disciplinary categories across the curriculum, while for freshmen entrants, QR was more concentrated in math and science, most likely because transfer students had begun their majors in that first year.

In their second year, which was the last year at the UW for many transfer students, a higher percentage of transfer students reported that they either did no quantitative reasoning or did no QR that they found challenging than freshmen reported. QR for transfer students in the second year again appeared to be concentrated in students' majors more than it was for students who entered the UW as freshmen.

In addition to looking more closely at freshman and transfer students' QR experience, we examined the number and kinds of courses in which students considered the QR that they had done *not* challenging. We noticed only one theme in this group: Very few students who were required to do QR as part of their arts and humanities courses reported that it was challenging, even though the work they described sometimes resembled QR work in the social sciences or elsewhere across the curriculum. Though we could not identify trends, we found students' descriptions of their unchallenging QR work—when they provided them—fascinating. We have included a sample of students' "no challenging QR" responses in Table 7.6.

Quantitative Reasoning Challenges

A few broad themes emerged from students' descriptions of the challenging QR they had done in business, engineering, math, science, and social sciences courses. A summary of these challenges can be found in Table 7.7 at the end of this section.

Challenges in business courses. In the second year of the study, students began to identify QR challenges in business courses, and many of these students spoke about the challenges in accounting. Notable themes in students' descriptions of QR in accounting included understanding accounting concepts; selecting correct methods to answer questions and solve problems; tracking where many numbers came from and where they needed to go; and being able to understand and explain what the numbers meant. The following quotation illustrates some of these challenges:

> I found the 200-level accounting classes to be very challenging. Having to make the numbers make sense to other people was challenging. It is hard because you have to apply the different methods. There are a whole bunch of different ways you can make an income statement. You have to know how to do that. You have to know what goes on the balance sheet, the order and so on. You also have to know when one way of making a balance sheet is more beneficial than another way.

Students—nearly all business majors—continued to speak of QR challenges in their business courses in the third year of the study, focusing on classes in finance and business economics. Three themes emerged in the third year. The first was understanding the effects of one transaction, institution, or process on another. The second, echoing challenges other students spoke of in math and science, was the challenge in translating problem situations described by words into numbers and back. A third theme, less pronounced than the others, was the challenge of dealing with the snowball effect of a simple error. A third-year student described the QR challenges in her course:

> The business economics class is challenging because you have to think about what the effects of government spending are, for example. How will that affect the curve, demand, supply, or inflation? You have to think what the ripple effects will be, and you have to figure out that if it went up by a certain amount of dollars, how many dollars will be affected somewhere else? It's challenging because you have to be able to visualize the different graphs in your head. You have to be able to visualize the effects of something on all the other elements.

Fourth-year QR challenges that students described in their business classes included a deep understanding of business concepts, the ability to figure out the right processes or formulas to use in a given situation, and an understanding of survey construction and analysis.

Challenges in engineering courses. Understandably, students did not mention QR challenges in engineering before coming to the UW. However, in their first year, several students identified engineering as the location of their challenging QR, but there were no traceable themes across these students' descriptions.

Table 7.6. Quantitative Reasoning That Students Did Not Find Challenging

Architecture	We have to redesign the outdoor space next to the Henry Art Gallery across the street from Gould. You have to use measurements—how big the space is, grading, drainage, how big the trees will get. It's more spatial analysis than math.
Arts	Does music count? For our test, she gave us a jumble of notes in a line, a rhythm, and we had to figure out how many went into this line or that one to make music out of it. Music is based on numbers. It is based on a rhythm, counting. Each measure has to be equal so the rhythm inside it has to coincide across measures. I learned a whole bunch about music and how it all fits together, but I don't know how challenging it was.
Business	[I did QR in 300- and 400-level accounting, business economics, management, marketing, and business politics.] They were all kind of equal in their level of difficulty, and the level isn't that high. The numbers part isn't that difficult. There is a right answer somewhere, and that makes the level of difficulty not that high.
Engineering	[I did QR in 100-level engineering.] Math is not quantitative reasoning. It is just getting one set of numbers to equal another set of numbers. It is just pushing things around, so it is more like problem solving, a puzzle skill, not quantitative reasoning. My dad used to make me do all that stuff. My dad has been abusing the backyards of every house we have lived in since we were little. We would do all sorts of stuff like figuring out the drainage of our yard. Our backyard would flood in Everett, so we did all this restructuring to manage the drainage. We had to figure out the slope of the ground between two points in the yard. We had to use math to figure things out, like the stress points in building a shed. So again, the natural learning process triumphs over all.
Humanities	[In philosophy]we had to use a matrix to examine the idea of genital mutilation and whether it should be right or wrong for society. We assigned numbers to specific things.
Math	[300-level math] was rather on the easy side.
Science	Chemistry 142, 152, and 162 required you to input numbers to record values, so it made more sense and was more conceptual. The answer was always quantitative—how much heat was produced. The chemistry has a conceptual element to it. I was liable to make mistakes doing math, but in chemistry if I made a mistake I could tell because it gives me a value that I was not expecting, whereas in math, I can end up with an answer that I have no idea if it is anywhere close to what I want. I can count on my expectations in chemistry, but in math, I wouldn't necessarily know I had the wrong answer.

Table 7.6 (continued). *Quantitative Reasoning That Students Did Not Find Challenging*

Social Science	I did QR in sociology methods. In all three papers we used datasheets of statistics to support our arguments. Our teacher did teach us how to interpret and use the statistics. It was pretty straightforward. The teacher explained really well how to analyze the statistics so that made it easy.

Challenges in engineering ranged from learning the vocabulary of engineering disciplines to determining how research design would affect the end result of a study.

Students' comments about QR challenges in engineering in the second year included two themes. First, because so many of their comments focused on quantitative reasoning in computer science, students spoke of the challenges in writing code, and specifically in translating input into binary or base-10 language. Another theme, less pronounced than the first, was that the QR in engineering was becoming more theoretical and abstract. This echoes students' comments in math, where they noted the increasing complexity of the concepts they were learning and using. The following student's comment captures this move into greater abstraction.

> [My third year computer science course] is especially challenging because it is pure theory. You have to do proofs there. I haven't done completely abstract proofs before, not that often anyway. These are formal proofs as opposed to just conceptual proofs. You have to write a proof using certain rules; you have to be careful of the assumptions you make, and the steps you take have to be very precise.

Three themes emerged from the third year in engineering majors' descriptions of their most challenging QR, all of which occurred in their engineering courses. As did students who described challenges in math and science, students who spoke of engineering challenges described an ascent to increasingly abstract problems, requiring them to have mastered complex concepts and a wide range of tools. A less pronounced theme was the challenge in having to deal with the long effects of a single error. Engineering majors also spoke about specific challenges such as having to derive complex equations or do vector analyses. Two comments illustrate these challenges:

> [The 400-level computer science engineering course] was the toughest theoretical course I have taken here. It was all algorithms and it required very abstract thinking, very disciplined

thinking. It was pure abstraction. It was the core of the field. I was definitely challenged.

[In the aeronautical and astronautical course] these were huge ugly triple integral equations with five or six terms and vectors.

Fourth-year engineering challenges largely mirrored those of previous years. In addition, students mentioned specific challenges related to individual courses, such as using a new development system to produce computer code and creating algorithms from a complex idea. The following student's comment illustrates some of these themes:

In chemical engineering, we were put in a group of two and asked to solve this problem that none of us really knew about. Each group gets a separate problem. We had to go into the lab and find the best solution. The challenging math comes when you are analyzing the data. There are so many different variables you have to take into consideration. Sometimes you aren't sure which variables are most important, so you have to understand the math to figure out how the variables are affecting your problem. For instance, if you are changing the temperature of a certain experiment, you are going to see how it is affecting your process. Sometimes that temperature matters a lot at the beginning but not at the end. But by doing the calculations and quantitative thinking, you would find out how much the temperature change affected your actual results. You would have to run another experiment to find out how much this mattered. Then you'd have to go back to your original experiment with that data.

Challenges in math courses. Three main themes emerged in students' descriptions of the QR challenges they faced in their math courses during their first year at the UW. Students, particularly freshmen, noted that the application of numbers to words was a challenge—understanding what to do and then doing it in a word problem. This theme was also prominent in first-year students' comments about QR challenges in science. A second theme was the need to understand new math concepts fully so that they could be linked appropriately to calculations. Finally, students, especially the transfer students, noted that the level of complexity of the math at the university was greater than they were used to. Two students' comments that illustrate these themes follow:

> Third-quarter calculus is a lot of new concepts. It isn't some-
> thing you can put a formula on and use it over and over. You
> have to know the background, why a question is structured
> the way it is, and what the tools are that are going to help you
> find the answer you are looking for.

> Just those anti-derivatives in Math 145. When you got into
> the really big, ugly ones is when it got hard. You kind of lose
> track of where you are when you are going through all the
> steps to go backwards through the functions.

We could track only two themes in the responses of students in their second UW year regarding challenges in math. The first theme was the broad challenge of thoroughly understanding the concepts at each stage of instruction
when those concepts were becoming more complex—keeping up with increases
in conceptual complexity. In addition, just as in students' responses about science, we noted a more particular focus on specific challenges related to individual courses in math, such as the challenge of finding derivatives, of figuring out
numbers in space, and of understanding vector analysis. This course-related
specificity is captured in this student's quotation about a 300-level math course:

> [The course is] especially challenging, because the matrices are
> used to represent other systems—other sets of equations,
> other parameters. It is not something just on its own but
> something that represents some other thing. That's what made
> it hard.

Students' descriptions of challenging third- and fourth-year math included
themes that were similar to earlier ones. Students mentioned that the challenging QR work they had done in math was becoming more abstract and conceptually complex, and that it was challenging to apply numbers and mathematical
concepts to word problems. Also, a few students mentioned a challenge that
came up in science, as well—the "leap" between what they were asked to do in
their homework and what they were asked to do on exams. As they had the previous year, students also mentioned specialized tasks as being challenging, as this
student's quotation illustrates:

> The material requires the continuous building of theorems. So
> it really requires that you have a mastery of all of the subject,
> the totality of the subject.

Students' fourth-year comments brought out no new themes. Again, students spoke of the challenge in applying math to science and again, students mentioned specific tasks assigned to individual courses as challenging.

Challenges in science courses. In speaking of QR challenges in the sciences, students in all five interviews most frequently mentioned physics and chemistry courses. Four themes, shared by both freshmen and transfer students, emerged from students' descriptions of the challenging QR work they had done in science in their first year at the university. First, students mentioned the "leaps" they were required to take between what they were studying in class and what they were asked to do on exams or in the labs. In addition, students noted the challenge in learning the unfamiliar and complex concepts of the sciences they were taking. Third, students talked about the challenge of applying math concepts to science. Finally, students noted that a deep understanding of the concepts they were applying and the relationships between them was necessary to complete the QR work for their science courses. The following quotations illustrate these themes:

> Third quarter chemistry, but also the other two [quarters in the series]. We are moving fast. We are asked to ingest a lot of information in a short period of time, and then there are jumps between the level you have learned and what you are asked to perform. There is quite a difference there. There is more math than in the chemistry we did in the second quarter, but it is not that difficult. It's just one of those things that if you mess up a step, you've messed it all up. There are a lot of variables and you have to set them all up correctly. You have to know a lot about those variables—you have to know it inside and out.

> The first-year physics series. I guess the most difficult part that I found is the amount of material covered is large, and it introduces topics that are new to me. I haven't had them before. Then, applying math principles to figure out these concepts—where sometimes the relationship isn't always crystal clear for me—that is difficult. And sometimes the lecture is good and sometimes not. This quarter the lectures have been excellent, but the topic has still been difficult enough to grasp that it is not just applying quantitative reasoning to the problem but also understanding why you are applying that reasoning to the problem. That's where I run into trouble—when I don't understand why I am using the process or principle.

In the second year, four themes were noticeable in student descriptions of challenging QR work in science. Again, UW SOUL students mentioned the challenge of using equations appropriately in science. They also mentioned the challenge of having to think and analyze at a higher level than they were used to. A third challenge students mentioned was correctness, one mistake having a snowball effect on complex problems. Also in the second year, students' discussion of the challenges in the sciences appeared to "spread out"—focusing very specifically on individual challenges in particular courses. For example, students spoke about the challenge of making graphs in environmental science, using numbers and dates to determine origin of rocks in geology, and the difficulty in visualizing magnetic materials in physics. The following student's quotation illustrates some of these themes:

> In chemistry, maybe just the amount was challenging—having to use so many formulas in one situation. The information you collected and the point you wanted to get to made you incorporate lots of theorems and formulas—lots of mathematical things to get to where you wanted. Figuring out what you wanted to use from your mathematical toolbox and when.

In the third year of the study, once again students talked about the challenges of applying math to scientific problems, the need for thorough understanding of increasingly complex concepts, and the ability to interpret results correctly. As one student said:

> In biochemistry what made it difficult was understanding the data that the computers spit out after a sample was inserted. Making sense of the data. I cried at times. We were tested on the material too, so we really had to know it.

Students also identified specific problems that they found challenging, such as turning the Mirror Equation into a quadratic equation. Physics courses accounted for close to half the science courses students mentioned, but the range of courses broadened to include courses in botany, astronomy, fishery sciences, and other disciplines. Courses ranged from the 100- to the 400-level.

In the fourth year, students identified QR challenges in collecting data and in the need to understand the meaning behind the numbers they collected—interpreting results. Two repeated themes emerged from students' responses—the challenge in using numbers to understand scientific phenomena and specific challenges in problems assigned in individual science courses. The following student's comment about data collection in a forest ecology courses illustrates the fourth-year themes:

> The work I have done for [my 300-level forest ecology cours-es] has been challenging. The basis for the QR has been data I have gathered in the field. So there are a lot more variables, a lot more potential for error than when you are given data. You really have to understand things at a higher level when you have to go out and get it. It's a lot harder than when some-one just hands you a data table.

Challenges in social science courses. In students' first year at the UW, there was a difference in how freshmen and transfer students described QR challenges in the social sciences. Freshmen who identified QR challenges in the social sciences all referred to economics. Two themes emerged from their responses. First, they noted the challenge in understanding the concepts in economics, and second, they mentioned that using math and graphs to understand and explain the rela-tionships between the concepts was challenging, as the following student's quo-tation illustrates:

> In economics, making the relationships between all the differ-ent things on the charts—supply, demand etc. Organizing the data and understanding how each of those variables are sup-posed to relate to one another.

In contrast, transfer students' responses to challenges in social science QR focused specifically on particular challenges presented in a range of individual social science disciplines. The following quotations serve as examples of the comments of transfer students on QR in the social sciences.

> The last assignment I had in geography, where I had to take the history of the place and apply it to the population graphs was difficult. It was easy to look at the history and see what made the population change for major events. But I had trouble tying it to the minor events. And that made it difficult to prove the theories and models of the city and how the city has grown.

> This one example I am doing [in sociology] is not easy, but I am not interested in it. I am really into crime theory, but I just am not a numbers guy. I am not awed by one group having a large percentage and another group having a lower percentage. It doesn't do anything for me. I see the significance that may

have to the theory, but I don't get excited about loading up the SPSS. I don't like looking at Excel spreadsheets of numbers and numbers and numbers.

Two themes emerged in students' second year. The first theme focused on quantifying human behavior recorded by observation. The second theme was identical to that which we observed in science and math in the second year—the move to specialized responses related to QR questions or issues in specific disciplines. For example, one student spoke of the challenge of deriving supply and demand curves in economics; another spoke of timing "distractions" to match treatment times for burn patients in psychology; and a third spoke of learning statistical techniques in sociology that made him a better critical thinker in the discipline.

In the third year, we could identify few themes in students' descriptions of QR challenges in the social sciences. Again, students mentioned the use of statistics to understand places, social issues, and relationships between countries and institutions. A minor theme that emerged was the need to think critically about statistics. Quotations about QR in the social sciences from students in two different disciplines illustrate some of these themes:

> [In geography], it was challenging, because I don't think numbers tell the whole story. You can't just look at the statistics and tell what the country is like. What has been hard is the significance that the numbers carry, how just seeing the number will lead people to all these conclusions. I don't think the number has a direct causal relationship to X, Y, Z, so just the reliance on numbers is weighted more than other things. Numbers just give you black and white relationships—are you literate or not literate, for example.

> In economics, I had to research some macroeconomic data from Mexico. It was challenging to go on line and find the information. It was challenging to use that data and find a suitable answer that made sense with that data. I was looking at the gross national product, per capita income, the consumer price index—major economic indicators—and I had to write a report on the Mexican economy based on this information. It was a rewarding project but it was hard because some of the data didn't turn out the way I wanted it to. The information was a little conflicting on some of the data—and I wondered if it was just me not calculating it right, which I think it was.

Themes in the fourth year focused on the use of data to understand social issues or test hypotheses. Students also spoke of having to interpret data on their own. Students again mentioned specific tasks for individual social science courses. The following student describes a QR challenge in a 300-level psychology course:

> Psych was more challenging, because we had to test hypotheses using data and come up with a number that allowed us to reach a conclusion. It was challenging because there were so many different tests for differing hypotheses, and how you carried out your research would determine which test you would use. Choosing the method was the hardest, and we did a lot of computer work.

Challenging QR Summary

Table 7.7 presents a summary of the most frequently mentioned QR challenges in the five disciplinary areas in which significant numbers of students discussed these challenges. UW SOUL findings on challenging QR illustrate the role of the academic disciplines in how much and what kinds of QR students learn and practice in college. Our findings suggest a significant difference between QR and the other skill areas we investigated. In each year, only a few students said that they had done no challenging critical thinking or writing, but many said that they had done no challenging QR, and many, particularly in the third and fourth years, said they had done no QR at all. This difference suggests that the institutional value placed on quantitative reasoning may be less than the value it places on other skill-based learning, such as critical thinking and writing.

Students' Self-Assessment

At the end of each year during interviews, we asked students if they felt they had improved in quantitative reasoning or not. We also asked questions on quarterly surveys about how much students felt they had learned about QR. Finally, we sent students two open-ended email questions about QR in the winter quarter of their senior year, 2003. This section provides results from all three methods.

Interviews

Most students felt that their QR abilities had improved in the first and second years of the study, but in the third year, the percent of those who felt they had improved declined to about half of the students. Perceptions about improvement varied by entry status in the second year of the study, with about 63% of the freshman entrants saying they had improved that year compared with 54%

of the transfer entrants. This difference makes sense if we consider that in the second year of the study, many of the transfer students were in their fourth year of college, and their responses were similar to those of freshman entrants in their fourth year. Other than the second year, freshmen and transfer responses were similar. Differences in perceptions by gender and ethnicity were not significant.

Regarding reasons for nonimprovement, students consistently attributed their failure to improve to not being asked to use or learn QR skills in any of their classes. A second frequently given response—this one from the population of students who reported doing some QR that year—was that they had not had to do any new or challenging QR.

Reasons for improvement were opposite those for lack of improvement and were also consistent across the four years of the study. Students said that their QR abilities had improved because they had been asked to use them repeatedly and because their individual classes had provided particular challenges. As a social science major reported:

> I think once I got into economics, it was strictly math—but it was word problem type math. It was a lot of manipulating numbers, making charts, and figuring things out. The obvious answer wasn't always the correct answer. And computer science brought back a lot of the basics I had forgotten.

In terms of *what* had improved in their QR abilities, freshmen entrants spoke about developing general QR skills, such as having a better understanding of QR concepts, being better able to approach a problem, and becoming more independent in their problem solving than they had been in their first year in college. Freshmen also spoke about being able to apply QR to a wide range of areas, including science, economics, and their lives. In contrast, first-year transfer students focused almost entirely on improvements in understanding the disciplines of their majors—for example, improvement in "engineering intuition;" better understanding of quantitative reasoning in oceanography; better understanding of ratios, proportions, and scaling in art; improvements in incorporating QR into writing in the social sciences; better at writing code for computer science; deeper understanding of the relationship between calculus and physics; and improvements in applications in geography.

In the second year, students' descriptions of the ways they improved primarily mirrored those in the first, with freshmen entrants again speaking more in terms of general improvement in their QR abilities. A few minor themes in those responses were improvement in analyzing and using charts and graphs and improvement in applying mathematical tools and concepts to new kinds of problems. As one science major described:

Table 7.7. *Most Challenging Quantitative Reasoning, 2000–2003*

Business	• Understanding accounting concepts
	• Selecting the correct accounting methods to solve problems
	• Tracking where large quantities of numbers came from and where they went
	• Understanding and explaining what numbers mean
	• Understanding the effects of one transaction, institution, or process on another
	• Translating word problems into numbers and back to words
	• Dealing with the snowball effects of a single error
	• Deep understanding of the increasingly complex business concepts
	• Figuring out the right process/formulas to use in a given situation
	• Understanding survey construction and analysis
Engineering	• Writing code—translating input into binary or base-10 language
	• Understanding increasingly abstract and theoretical problems
	• Mastering a wide range of increasingly complex concepts and tools
	• Knowing when to employ concepts and tools
	• Being able to consider a wide range of variables in a single problem
	• Dealing with the snowball effects of a single error
	• Specific challenges related to particular engineering disciplines
	• Applying numbers to words—understanding what to do and then being able to do it
	• Complete understanding of new concepts so that they can be linked to calculations
	• Making the "leap" between homework problems and problems on the exams
Math	• Successfully understanding and dealing with greater complexity than previously experienced in math
	• Understanding and figuring out how to solve more abstract, conceptually complex problems
	• Specific tasks in individual math classes

Table 7.7 (continued). Most Challenging Quantitative Reasoning, 2000–2003

Science	• Applying math concepts; using equations to solve problems in science
	• Making the "leaps" between material presented in class and exam or lab questions
	• Deep understanding of the scientific concepts to be applied
	• Understanding relationships between concepts
	• Performing at high level of thinking/analysis demanded
	• Dealing with the snowball effects of a single error
	• Understanding increasingly complex concepts
	• Collecting own data
	• Understanding the meaning behind the numbers; interpreting results
	• Specific tasks in individual science classes
Social Science	• Understanding concepts (in economics)
	• Using math and graphs to understand and explain the relationships between the concepts (in economics)
	• Using statistics to understand social and political phenomena and relationships
	• Using data to test hypotheses
	• Analyzing and interpreting data on one's own
	• Thinking critically about statistics and sources of statistics
	• Quantifying human behavior via observations
	• Specific tasks involving statistics in individual social science classes

> Even sitting in class, I remember days when I realized that I would never have been able to make the connection I made before that. I feel that I have more tricks in my bag now. I think I have become better at using pieces that I know and combining them to solve new problems now.

Transfer students, again, spoke of change related to specific courses, usually associated with their majors, as this art student responded:

> In the art-related ones, yes. Estimating is a very good skill to learn. It is also basically visual memory. Things look about right.

In the third and fourth years, students' responses to what had improved became more difficult to track, with only a few themes recurring in those two years. Students said they had learned more skills with statistics; that they had become better at looking at a problem, figuring out what was needed, and doing it; and that they had made specific gains in QR required by their majors.

Surveys

In addition to asking students questions about improvement during interviews, each quarter, we asked students to rate how much they had learned about QR in two areas:[6]

- Understanding and solving mathematical problems

- Using quantitative analysis or reasoning to understand issues, make arguments, or solve problems in courses other than math

The mean over all four years for the first item was 2.17 (on a 4-point scale; standard deviation = .76). The mean for the second item was 2.21 (a standard deviation = .65). The averages over all four years of the two items correlated at .68. Figure 7.3 presents averages for each year for each of the two items. For both items, the linear trend was strongly significant and negative.[7] Thus, students perceived they learned less about understanding math and solving mathematical problems, as well as about using QR in areas other than math as time went on. The drop was considerably steeper for using QR for solving math problems than it was for using QR for dealing with issues outside math.

Consistent with students' interview answers, students' responses to these two questions varied considerably by area of major. Table 7.8 shows the averages for six disciplinary areas across all four years of responses. As the table indicates, there were large and significant differences across the disciplinary categories, especially for "understanding and solving mathematical problems," for which the differences among departments accounted for 55% of the total variance. There were no surprises in these results; they confirm interview findings. Students majoring in business, engineering, and science reported learning more math and non-math related QR than did others.

Figure 7.3. *QR Learning Averages Over All Four Years*

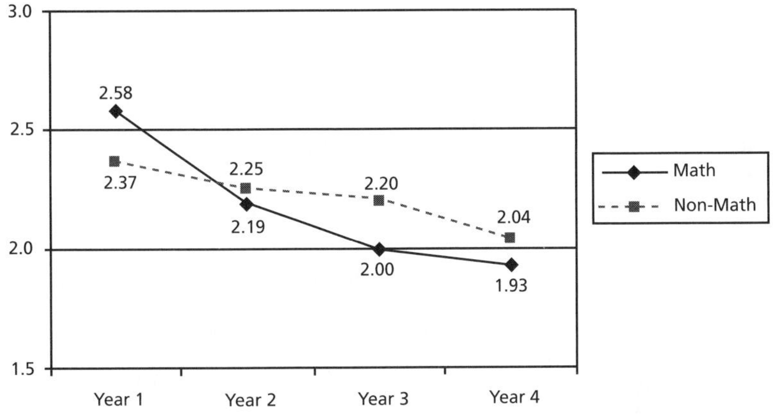

Email Questions

In winter quarter, 2003, just before the study's end, we sent two open-ended email questions to all UW SOUL participants about QR in their majors. The first question asked students to describe and give an example of the kinds of QR required in their majors, defining the term once again for participants. The second asked them how comfortable they were with their ability to do the QR necessary to be successful in their majors. All students said that they felt comfortable with their ability to do the QR necessary for their majors. Students in engineering, math, and science, however, pointed out areas where they had difficulty ("knowing how to apply the equations is where the struggle lies; it's not so much in how to use or manipulate the equations") or noted that they were not as strong in QR as others in their program. Students in other areas did not offer these qualifications. The ways the engineering, math, and science majors qualified their responses to the question about their comfort levels suggested that they may have understood their own QR abilities and limitations in deeper ways than students did in other majors. As would be expected, students' descriptions of the kinds of QR required by their majors varied by disciplinary area of their major and echoed students' descriptions of challenging QR reported earlier in this chapter and summarized in Table 7.8.

Table 7.8. *Averages Over All Years for Major Areas*

Major Area	N	Solving Math Problems		QR in Non-Math Courses	
		Mean	Std. Dev.	Mean	Std. Dev.
Art	9	1.34	0.46	1.59	0.71
Business	14	2.66	0.39	2.69	0.46
Engineering	22	2.97	0.52	2.65	0.58
Humanities	11	1.51	0.29	1.67	0.40
Science	29	2.52	0.59	2.49	0.41
Social Science	52	1.71	0.53	1.94	0.53
F-Value		32.2 ($p < 0.0001$)		15.4 ($p < 0.0001$)	
Eta Sq.		55.1%		37.1%	

What the Interviews, Surveys, and Email Responses Say About Students' Perceptions

In speaking about QR improvements during their interviews, students seemed to have a shared language, as they did in writing. In QR, this was the language of application. Again and again, students mentioned having improved their abilities to apply mathematical concepts and approaches to disciplines other than math, even when they were speaking about their math courses. Furthermore, the amount of practice students got at performing such applications determined to a great extent how much they felt they had improved in these areas. Similarly, survey responses showed that the disciplinary areas where students reported getting the most practice were the areas where they felt they learned the most.

However, we need to keep in mind that what students in business majors meant by such application was entirely different from what engineering or psychology majors meant by the same term. Students' email responses, as well as other responses noted in this chapter, shed some light on these differences across disciplinary areas. Regarding the finer differences of QR required within those broad disciplinary categories, we were unable to identify most of them, although we believe that they are critical to understanding and credibly assessing students' growth in QR. Regardless of these differences, at the end of their college experience, nearly all students felt competent in the QR required in their majors, regardless of what those majors were or whether they felt that they had improved in their QR ability over time.

Interviews With Department Chairs

In order to better understand how disciplines define and require quantitative reasoning, we interviewed chairs from 15 academic departments,[8] 13 of which were selected because they represented the most popular majors at the university, and the remaining two because they represented smaller, interdisciplinary majors.[9] These interviews were conducted and analyzed by Rebecca Hartzler, a physics instructor at a local community college who graced our office during a sabbatical. In this section, we have liberally used the results she presented in a report to our office (Hartzler, 2002). The interviews Hartzler conducted lasted about an hour and consisted of ten questions. Eight themes could be identified in interview responses, and all themes reiterate other findings in this chapter. These themes are detailed in the following subsections.

Quantitative Reasoning Versus Quantitative Literacy

While department chairs understood that a consensus on the quantitative reasoning needs for undergraduates would be impossible, quantitative *literacy* (or numeracy) was an issue of concern for a majority of the 15 chairs (Hartzler, 2002). Generally, chairs described quantitatively literate people as capable of critically analyzing and using quantitative data to draw conclusions about issues affecting their health, political, and financial decisions. Chairs felt that it was possible that undergraduates capable of abstract levels of mathematical (or quantitative) reasoning might still be uncertain how to interpret a newspaper article that discusses false positive testing for HIV. Even though there was agreement among many department chairs that a certain level of quantitative literacy was desirable, there was no consensus on how it might be defined across the disciplines or how it might be required.

Undergraduates' QR Skills Vary Greatly Across and Within the Disciplines

While it was clear to the department chairs we interviewed that the QR experience of undergraduates varied across majors, they also noted that undergraduates' experiences could vary quite a bit within majors.

Quantitative Reasoning Requirements Change Over Time as the Disciplines Change

Chairs told us that changes in QR requirements, when they occur, are largely responses to changes occurring in the disciplines themselves. For example, chairs noted that questions about the usefulness of quantitative research in anthropology, communication, history, geography, and political science have been raised by participants in these disciplines, and currently, scholars can do sophisticated and well regarded research without being well versed in quantitative methods. Some see an ascendance of qualitative methods in these social sciences and have added courses in this area, in addition to offering quantitative methods courses. In contrast, chairs in biology, electrical engineering, psychology, and zoology reported that they felt the need to increase quantitative coursework because these fields have become more mathematically based over the last 30 years.

Faculty Perceive Students as Resistant to Using Quantitative Reasoning in Their Classes

Another theme in the interviews was that nearly all chairs reported that students resisted doing quantitative work. The perception that students were uncomfortable with QR conflicted with students' self-reports about comfort levels, reported earlier in this chapter.

Students Have Difficulty Applying the Mathematics They Have Been Taught

Some department chairs reported that many students seemed unprepared to apply quantitative work to problems in other areas. Consistent with this view by chairs, students noted in their discussions of their most challenging QR that the application of mathematical concepts and principles to problems was especially challenging. Furthermore, it is one of the gaps students described between high school and college work in quantitative reasoning.

Department Chairs Are Not Sure What Types of QR Are Taught in High Schools

When the chairs were asked whether quantitative literacy should be taught in postsecondary education, many remarked that they did not know what was being taught in the high schools, and their answers would depend on what was happening there. Our findings in the UW SOUL suggest that the QR taught in high schools and at the university are very different. Specifically, the application aspect of QR that chairs and students speak of as challenging to students in college is the area that students reported was weakest in their high school experience.

Higher Education Has a Role To Play in Quantitative Literacy

Chairs believed that much of the mathematics supporting quantitative literacy should be taught in high school. However, they also felt that the QR analysis of complex problems, including social problems, should be taught at the college level. Chairs' comments centered on a need for undergraduates to understand how to use statistics, and they suggested a range of ways to address this need, from infusing statistics within the major to adding new general education courses.

Postgraduation QR Needs Differ Across and Within Departments

The interviews with chairs suggested that departments could be divided into three categories with regard to their QR needs. In the first category were those with no gap in QR knowledge among undergraduates, practitioners, and the skills needed for graduate education, because those QR skills were minimal. Most of these were disciplines in the humanities. The second category included disciplines in which the QR needs varied greatly depending upon specialty. Many of the social sciences, for example, include areas of concentration in their undergraduate curricula that require students to master QR at various levels. The chairs of some of the social sciences were concerned that students in their programs who graduated with limited QR skills might not be well served by those skills after college, particularly if they sought advanced degrees. Third, some fields required QR as integral to all aspects of the discipline. Chairs in departments such as biology, psychology, and electrical engineering felt that their students were well prepared but might need additional QR courses as a natural consequence of pursuing more complex issues.

Conclusions and Implications

In this section we draw three conclusions based on our UW SOUL research on quantitative reasoning and identify the implications of those conclusions for teaching and assessment.

There Is a Gap Between High School and College QR, and Students Falter in That Gap

College level quantitative reasoning differed from high school QR. Students felt that QR was harder, more complex, and more broadly applied across the curriculum at the university. A substantial number of students described the key difference in terms of greater emphasis on application to real-world problems or word problems in many courses across the curriculum, including math courses. Memorizing formulas and then plugging them in, which students said worked in high school, often no longer yielded success in college. Furthermore, with the exception of a few departments and faculty whose curricula were intentionally closely linked with the high school curriculum (most notably math), department chairs indicated they did not have a clear sense of what and how QR was taught in high school; therefore, bridging this particular gap seems challenging.

The teaching implications for this result are similar to those discussed in the previous chapter about writing. College faculty who require students to do QR need to be aware that they are asking students to do something with which they have had little experience. They need to provide instruction that helps students cross the gap between high school and college. This instruction should occur in social science courses as well as in math, and in urban planning as well as engineering. The more explicit disciplines can be about the kinds of QR they value and why, the more motivated students in those disciplines will be to learn them.

Closer conversations between university faculty and high school teachers on subjects such as QR and writing would also be useful. However, it is difficult to imagine a university structure that could regularly foster such conversations across the curriculum. It is also difficult to imagine how high school faculty, needing to focus their attention on helping students meet "no-child-left-behind" test requirements, would be able to respond. In spite of these limitations, some departments, notably math, regularly work with high school instructors.

Regarding assessment, our findings suggest that student success in high school math courses may not predict an easy time with QR at the college level. Students need to be told explicitly that there is a difference between their high school math courses and college QR and what those differences imply.

Most Students Are Comfortable With Their QR Abilities, But . . .

UW SOUL students' attitudes about quantitative reasoning spanned the space from something approaching rapture to something akin to Dante's seventh circle of hell. However, for the most part, students entered the university feeling comfortable with their ability to do math, at least to certain levels. By the end of the first year, when instruction in QR was most widespread, the general level of comfort stayed about the same. However, results showed that students identified serious differences between the math they were doing at the UW and the math they had done previously. Students reported that the QR required at the university was harder and required more thought. Many students adjusted to the new QR demands experienced in college, though some apparently remained comfortable with their QR abilities without having to increase them. By the time they graduated, UW SOUL students in every disciplinary area felt that they had mastered the quantitative reasoning required by their majors.

With such a positive view from the students, how can we explain the perception of our chairs—as well as our personal experience when talking to faculty about students' QR skills and attitudes—that students are not well prepared to use the QR they need to use in college? This view is not only true on our own campus, but the *Chronicle of Higher Education* survey (Sanoff, 2006) suggests that it is widely held across the country. Further, faculty not only agree with chairs that students are not well prepared to use QR, they agree that students are often resistant to instruction that involves QR. At the same time, many students do not feel challenged by the QR they are asked to do.

We can identify this gap between student and faculty/chair perceptions, but we are uncertain how teaching and assessment might address it. It seems clear that more instruction in QR is needed, so that students understand better how to apply mathematical concepts to complex problems in a wide range of disciplines. Both classroom-based and departmental assessment of students' QR abilities would give us (and our students) better information about whether they are learning what we need them to learn. Increased instruction and assessment could take advantage of students' perceived comfort with QR (or disabuse them of it when appropriate), while, at the same time, help them move forward in their abilities.

Our results show little QR learning in the arts or the humanities, and it is possible that our focus was too broad to capture it. Nevertheless, we believe that one assessment implication of this finding is that arts and humanities departments may want to discuss the kinds of QR necessary to meet departmental learning goals, articulate the results of those conversations clearly to students, and then make sure that instruction in attaining QR goals is offered throughout the departmental curricula.

Students' Learning Paths in QR Depend Upon Their Majors

Very generally speaking, math and QR instruction appear to be front-loaded in the curriculum, and as students become more immersed in their majors, the emphasis on QR and the acquisition of new QR tools decrease for many. This front-loading seemed evident from decreases in students' survey ratings of how much they learned about QR, in the number of courses students said required QR in their interviews, in the number of courses students described as requiring *challenging* QR, and in the number of students who stated that their QR abilities had improved over the four years of the study.

The front-loaded nature of QR learning is the only general statement we can make about learning in QR, and even that is not true in all disciplines. The paths students took were highly variable across and within disciplines, and the real student development story must be seen through the lenses of students' majors, as the case studies, surveys, interview responses, and interviews with department chairs made clear. As students entered their majors, the focus on QR applications to those fields increased. Different applications required knowledge of different QR principles and techniques and distinct uses of these underlying principles and techniques.

This discovery leads us to advise departments to be explicit in their teaching about QR, particularly in students' early courses. It would help students to know what quantitative reasoning in a marketing class can show them that other resources cannot show them, and what quantitative reasoning in a sociology course can tell them about racism and capital punishment that case studies and theories cannot reveal. We suspect faculty are making these values explicit in many courses already, particularly those that include a discussion of methodology.

Regarding assessment, our conclusions are the same as those for critical thinking and writing—namely, that quantitative reasoning varies so much from discipline to discipline, only the disciplines can assess the QR learning of students in the majors. But there is a crucial difference between QR and other areas of learning that we studied that has significant implications for assessment. While we found differences across disciplines in the emphases as well as the content around the learning areas we studied, none of the disciplinary areas excluded consideration of writing, critical thinking, and information literacy. However, when asked about the QR they did, many students majoring in the arts, humanities, and even some social sciences reported they did little or no QR in their majors and that which they did was not challenging. Our second case study, Nicole Ramsey, is an example of this group.

If an institution made assessment of QR a requirement for all disciplines, some would find such an assignment artificial or impossible. One option is to excuse some departments, or tracks within departments, from the chore. However, an alternative is the quantitative literacy approach, which suggests developing campus-wide QR goals and building corresponding assessment devices either to stand alone or supplement departmental efforts. Such an effort would strongly imply that the elements of quantitative literacy can be agreed upon and are valued at an institutional level. Our own interviews with chairs suggest that quantitative literacy is valued. However, to achieve agreement on the elements of quantitative literacy, administrators must take disciplinary perspectives into account. Centralized efforts to assess the learning of graduates without taking these perspectives into account generally fail to capture what departments and faculty care about. As a consequence, the results of such assessments seldom change teaching or improve learning.

Endnotes

1) Students sometimes identified more than one difference, so numbers do not always add to 100.

2) We were able to track 121 majors for this analysis.

3) Eta Squared is a statistic that indexes the proportion of total variance attributable to differences among levels of the independent variable; in this case, the differences among major areas.

4) $p < 0.005$

5) $p < 0.0001$

6) Students used a 4-point scale in their responses: 1 = *zero*, 2 = *a little*, 3 = *a moderate amount*, 4 = *a lot.*

7) For "Understanding and solving mathematical problems," $F = 66.23$, $p < 0.0001$, Eta sq = 31.5%. For "Using quantitative analysis or reasoning to understand issues, make arguments, or solve problems in courses other than math," $F = 16.52$, $p < 0.0001$, Eta Sq = 10.3%. In addition, the quadratic trend for "understanding and solving mathematical problems" was significant ($F = 11.11$, $p < 0.001$, Eta Sq = 7.2%).

8) This number represented about 18% of departments offering undergraduate majors.

9) The departments represented were: anthropology, art, biology, chemistry, comparative history of ideas, communication, economics, electrical engineering, English, geography, history, international studies, political science, psychology, and zoology.

Information Technology and Literacy

Like one thing that happened was that I was reading my psychology book and they mentioned this lady named Frances Farmer. I noticed there was a Nirvana song about her too. So I looked her up on the net and found out about her life. She was a fascinating lady.

The Information Literacy Competency Standards for Higher Education developed by the Association of College and Research Libraries (ACRL; 2000) define information literacy as: "a set of abilities requiring individuals to 'recognize when information is needed and have the ability to locate, evaluate, and use effectively the needed information'" (p. 2). In its standards, the ACRL distinguishes between three aspects of competency: information literacy, fluency with information technology, and computer literacy. If the three areas were arrayed in a hierarchy, computer literacy, which the ACRL defines as an understanding of hardware and software applications, would be at the bottom. The next rung in the hierarchy is fluency with information technology, which the ACRL describes as "understanding the underlying concepts of technology and applying problem-solving and critical thinking to using technology" (p. 3). In contrast to the focus on the technology side of finding and using information, the ACRL defines information literacy—the top of the hierarchy—as:

> an intellectual framework for understanding, finding, evaluating, and using information—activities which may be accomplished in part by fluency with information technology, in part by sound investigative methods, but most important, through critical discernment and reasoning. Information literacy initiates, sustains, and extends lifelong learning through abilities which may use technologies but are ultimately independent of them. (p. 3)

For the ACRL, information literacy is a process. For students to be considered information literate, they must have the ability to take the following steps:

> Determine the extent of information needed
>
> Access the needed information effectively and efficiently
>
> Evaluate information and its sources critically
>
> Incorporate selected information into one's knowledge base
>
> Use information effectively to accomplish a specific purpose
>
> Understand the economic, legal, and social issues surrounding the use of information, and access and use information ethically and legally (pp. 2–3)

The ACRL (2000) asserts that students will need to use this information-literate process in investigations that they will need to direct themselves—on the job, during internships, or related to coursework. In addition, the ACRL points out that the methods used for such investigation are likely to differ from one discipline to another:

> To obtain the information they seek for their investigations, individuals have many options. One is to utilize an information retrieval system, such as may be found in a library or in databases accessible by computer from any location. Another option is to select an appropriate investigative method for observing phenomena directly. For example, physicians, archaeologists, and astronomers frequently depend upon physical examination to detect the presence of particular phenomena. In addition, mathematicians, chemists, and physicists often utilize technologies such as statistical software or simulators to create artificial conditions in which to observe and analyze the interaction of phenomena. As students progress through their undergraduate years and graduate programs, they need to have repeated opportunities for seeking, evaluating, and managing information gathered from multiple sources and discipline-specific research methods. (p. 5)

The ACRL report goes on to supply performance indicators and outcomes for each of the six steps in the information literacy process.

We hoped to be able to determine if students in the UW SOUL followed the six steps in the information literacy process as they went about finding and using information. In other words, did students take steps to determine the extent of information needed? Did they then access the information effectively and efficiently? Did they evaluate that information critically, looking at its sources with care? And so on. However, as this chapter makes clear, we were unable to make this determination for three reasons.

The first reason is that, as our data showed, information technology and literacy (ITL) are discipline-specific. If we compress the ACRL (2000) definitions somewhat and define ITL as "finding and using" information, we can say that processes for "finding" and for "using" information are related to students' purposes for doing both. Those purposes, when academic, were related directly to disciplinary methodologies and practices. While there was some common ground across disciplines—the use of literature reviews, for example—there was also a great deal of activity and thinking unique to disciplines. These distinctions were clear when we considered what disciplines meant by "research" and how they asked students to practice it (see Table 6.4). While the ACRL statement on disciplinarity appears to predict UW SOUL findings in this area, the six steps in the ACRL intellectual framework are generic. As such, they need to be translated into specific disciplinary contexts before we can know how accurately they reflect an information literacy process that all students should undertake.

A second reason that we could not match student processes to the six-step framework concerns who is in control of the finding-and-using-information process. Our results suggest that faculty and administrators are no longer in complete control of those processes. Prior to 1990, information flow was fairly unidirectional, with faculty members channeling information to students either directly or by assigning accepted books and articles in the field, available through the library doors. In contrast, students in the UW SOUL reported information-gathering processes that were motivated by a variety of interests and needs that they, themselves, controlled and that took them in many directions. Our students have multiple ways to access major daily newspapers, radio stations, sports events, music, video clips, lyrics to the songs they listen to and to the songs their grandparents loved, speeches, old photographs, literary magazines, and class lectures. The whole world of information is in dorm rooms and coffee shops, as well as in the classroom and library. And it gets passed around. Students can email information to their friends, who email it on to others.

Not only do faculty and administrators have less control than they once had over the information that reaches students, they may have less control over *how* it gets to them. Sometimes faculty are less knowledgeable than their students about computer technology and fluency with technology. This gap means that not only might our undergraduates be better able to locate the demographic breakdown for the population of The Gambia more quickly than many of us could, but students are also likely to be highly adept at skills that faculty and staff might not think to require. For example, many students learn computer skills by accessing tutorials online, but many faculty might not think to count this ability among computer literacy skills. In terms of lifelong learning, it might be more important, given the whiplash pace of technological change, to know how to download information onto one's portable music player than it is to be able to find the demographics of The Gambia online. However, if faculty do not have 30GB of music (i.e., 15,000 songs) they are aching to store on portable players, they may not think about where MP3 technology could lead in terms of information literacy. Therefore, because those of us involved in assessment may have less knowledge about some methods for finding and using information than the people we want to evaluate, assessment of information technology and literacy is highly problematic.

A third difficulty we had in determining whether students followed the ACRL's (2000) six-step process for finding and using information was that many of the decisions that are critical to evaluating and understanding information are hidden from view. When we view the products of student work, for example, it is difficult to infer the information literacy-related processes that went into them.

With these three issues in mind, we begin this chapter, as we have others, with a case study. After a look at Anya Bellmont's UW experience in finding and using information, we present findings on information technology and literacy from the UW SOUL, results of an interview study with faculty, and our conclusions and their implications for teaching and assessment.

Anya's Path

Anya Bellmont came to Seattle from Yakima, Washington, a small town on the eastern side of the Cascade mountains. When she arrived, she was unsure what her major would be. Thinking she "might major in psychology, biology, chemistry," Anya said that she was "leaning toward the science classes." This interest in science was, perhaps, predictable, because in describing her challenging academic work in high school, Anya spoke frequently about assignments in her AP biology classes that involved challenging research, some of which was experimental and some of which was library research. For example:

> In my AP biology class, we went down to a stream near my school and we ran some tests on the water—pH and percent carbon dioxide. We had to find places on the bank of the river, pick up our little samples of water, and run the tests right

there. We were supposed to figure out how fast the current was moving, and we debated how to do that. My idea was to put an orange ball on a string so that we could time how fast it went in 10 feet, and then, from those readings, we could get the speed of the stream.

In AP biology, right after the whole cloning thing with Dolly, the sheep, we were supposed to gather information from a variety of sources—news articles, medical journal articles, and so on—and write a statement for or against cloning. It was supposed to include the moral or ethical reasons for our positions. To look for information on cloning was hard, because when we were all looking together, there were articles that some group members didn't like, so they wanted to say that they weren't really there. The whole class was supposed to come to an agreement on the issue—20 people.

Anya conducted experimental research in her high school physics and chemistry classes and was required to design an original experiment in physics. When asked to describe the research process she usually used in high school, however, Anya focused only on library research. She described her process as follows:

I usually begin my research on the Internet to see if there are any books or magazine articles they refer to. Then, I will go to the school library and the regional library and look in the card catalogue, based on my topic or subject or ideas related to that. I also looked in the encyclopedias. I usually do my research all at once. I procrastinate first, do all the research, then write my paper. It isn't really hard for me to distinguish between good and bad sources on the Internet. Usually, I know what I am looking for. I can think of related ideas fast and look them up quickly and decide if they are what I need.

After high school, Anya's college experience was marked by changing ideas about what she wanted her major to be. These changes meant that she was asked to find and use information for a number of different purposes, as well as with a number of different methods.

At the end of her first year, Anya felt that she would major in "one of the sciences, like biology or chemistry" but she was still unsure. Her research that year included gathering information to complete lab reports for chemistry, as well as looking up information on her own about a discovery mentioned in her chemistry course that she found interesting. Anya worked at a library on campus that year, and through that job, Anya learned more about how to do library research:

> I learned about a lot of the resources and how to do web searches for general articles or books in the libraries. I help other people with their research at work, so I see what good search engines are and what kinds of words you can find information under and that kind of stuff.

In her second year, Anya thought she would like to double major in sustainable resource sciences (a program in the College of Forest Resources) and in biology. However, when asked for the best class she had taken in her first two years, she named a 400-level women studies class that she had taken in spring. Anya's research experience in her second year was quite similar to her first-year experience. She did experimental, Internet, and library research in connection with chemistry labs, as well as simple web-based work for an environmental science class. On her own, she went to the library to gather background information on an author whose article she was presenting to her women studies class, saying:

> I wanted to see other things she had written, see how she structures her arguments, see what else I might bring in to help the class understand what we were reading.

In addition, because she was interested in these things, Anya also looked up information online about renewable energy in Europe and Asia, about mining in Idaho, and about the world on the *New York Times*'s web site.

At the end of her second year, Anya thought she might go to the UW's lab at Friday Harbor in the San Juan Islands to do some research the next year. However, instead of going to the San Juans, Anya went to India. In fact, she went to the same program in Oroville, India, that a fellow sustainable resources major, Trevor McClintock, attended (see Chapter 5). While Trevor's job in Oroville was to work on solar energy for the dormitory the group was building, Anya's job was to work on the composting toilets. This work involved an impressive amount of information gathering and use, as her description illustrates:

> We were trying to make bathrooms that people would use but that they would also learn how their waste can be incorporated into the soil and be beneficial. We also wanted to make it easy enough so that they would use the bathrooms. We had to find all these materials in India that we were used to using in the U.S., and we couldn't do that, so we were constantly modifying our designs. Meanwhile, the people living in the community

weren't really sold on composting toilets. We had to justify it to them, but we weren't really sure they actually would work. The climate is radically different than the climate here. We were trying to apply all these radical new ideas to this new climate, and we had to get a lot of advice from people, get their ideas, and decide if we wanted to use them or not.

Building the toilets, I learned how socially people are afraid of handling their own waste. I wasn't aware of how big a taboo it is, and the people in India were concerned that people who do a lot of cleanup work are from India. There are a lot of cultural influences in India—colonialism, imperialism. There was a total hierarchy in that place, where many of the people living there were not Indian. It was interesting to see how they treated Indians and how the Indians responded. I could kind of see their resistance. It expanded my understanding of my space and the world around me. It was right there in my face.

By the time Anya went to Oroville, she had given up on the idea of majoring in biology and was double majoring in women studies and sustainable resource management. In addition to the wide ranging research she did in India that year, Anya did library and web-based research for courses in environmental science, women studies, anthropology, and geography. The anthropology paper required Anya to gather and use information from interviews. One of the technologies Anya learned in her third year was digital technology and video recording—"how to edit it and so on. We learned how to document everything we were doing [in Oroville] so you could train someone else."

In her fourth year, Anya dropped her sustainable resources major and was planning to graduate with a double major in women studies and geography. She explained the switch by noting that she felt more drawn to the questions asked in geography than those asked in her sustainable resources courses:

Last spring, I took two environmental classes and a geography class. What struck me is that in the geography class, we looked at the same problems we were looking at in the environmental classes—soil degradation, for instance. In environmental science, we looked at how to fix it—add lime to raise the pH or whatever. In geography, we would look at the same thing and ask why it was degraded. Why is our intervention necessary?

During that year, Anya conducted library and Internet research for papers and presentations assigned in five geography and three women studies courses, as well as in one English composition course linked with tutoring in Seattle elementary schools. She also did some observational research at her tutoring site, describing that work as follows:

> We did tutoring in the elementary schools. I'm still doing that on my own. This made a lot of connections with other classes, especially women studies where we talk about the whole socialization process. In an elementary school, you can see that happening on a moment-to-moment basis. It helped to solidify the connections between the theoretical things I'm learning in school and how they are playing out in the world. It made me aware that there are spaces where you can disrupt and interrupt the process.

At the end of her fourth year, facing seven more geography classes before she could complete that major, Anya said that she regretted having spent so much time in science courses. She spoke about the draw of greater student-to-student and student-to-faculty interaction, more possible in the smaller majors she eventually chose than in the larger science majors she considered when she entered the university.

But because Anya walked several paths before finding the paths to her majors, her experience in finding and using information in college was extremely varied. She conducted experimental, library, Internet, interview, and observational research for courses in science, social science, and humanities, as well as the on-the-ground research required by her composting toilet experience in India. It is likely that the ways Anya located and used information in one arena assisted in others; it is also likely that Anya's research processes had to shift in essential ways when the contexts in which they occurred shifted. Unfortunately, Anya's descriptions of her research processes were never detailed enough for us to learn if she followed ACRL guidelines, perhaps because so many of the decisions that constituted those processes were primarily internal for Anya, as well as for others.

The internality of decisions in finding and using information is more difficult to penetrate than the disciplinarity of those processes. Decisions about what sources to investigate, how to gather information from those sources, and how to use it were not only controlled by disciplinary practice and preference that Anya may know but be unable to articulate. They also might involve large and small decisions that are even harder to track—such as decisions about where not to look for information and why. We saw this problem in interviews with students like Anya and when looking at a small sample of students' portfolio descriptions of ITL processes. Students had great difficulty speaking about these processes. They tended to speak very generally, covering a wide expanse of decision-making and behaviors with simple words such as "looked up" or "searched," and rarely or never talked about what brought them to that activity in the first place. In addition, when asked about their processes for finding and using information, students nearly always spoke of the difficulties they had and the advances they had made in *finding* information. They rarely acknowledged any challenges or any growth in *using* it. Decisions about the "using" part of the process, therefore, were even more invisible to us.[1]

Learning About Information Technology and Literacy

Finding and evaluating information were difficult to define, because nearly every aspect of student learning in college can be defined as a finding or evaluating moment. A student sitting in his first animal communication course listening to a lecture on crows, for example, can be said to be *finding* information, and if he is listening critically, he can also be said to be *evaluating* it. In addition, we had trouble deciding what constituted *information technology* compared with "just plain old technology." For example it seemed unlikely that a student would learn to use Microsoft's PowerPoint to *find* information, but it clearly is a way to *use* information. Therefore, could we consider this program to be information technology? Students could use web browsers and online library databases to find information, but they also could use their feet—walking to an art gallery, for example, to look at an exhibit of Tiffany glass or jogging through a park to pick up ideas for a landscape architecture class. Which of these methods count as information gathering technology?

National studies suggest that we already have information on students' general uses of traditional information technology. For example, an EDUCAUSE Center for Applied Research study reported by Kvavik and Caruso (2005) found that students estimated their skill levels for most technical activities, including using word processing, using spreadsheets, accessing online library resources, and computer maintenance, at between a 2.5 and 3.5 on a 4-point scale. Furthermore, Kvavik and Caruso found that 98% of the students responding to the national survey used the Internet to support coursework, about 95% used the Internet for pleasure, 88% used library resources to complete course assignments, 75% used technology to access music or DVDs, and 65% had used technology to create presentations. These findings, as well as our own institution's survey research on students' uses of technology, suggest that there is much we already know about general uses of technology in information literacy.

In the face of these challenges, we decided, rather arbitrarily, to ask students questions about finding, evaluating, and using information that were focused on research. We also asked them questions about technology that they used to find or use information. Our results from both surveys and interviews showed that finding and using information were disciplinary acts. When and how a student gathered information and how that information was evaluated and used depended on the student's major. In addition, our results, which are similar to Wineburg's (1991), show that ITL processes can differ by level of expertise. This section includes:

- Survey results on how much research students engaged in and how much they learned in doing it

- Interview results on research that was required as a part of coursework and research that students did on their own

- Results from an interview study of faculty on research

Survey Data: How Much Research Did Students Do and What Did They Learn?

We gathered two kinds of survey data on information literacy and technology. First, each quarter we asked students to note the number of courses in which they had done the following:

- Used printed materials in the library to do research for a class project

- Used resources in the library, other than printed materials, to do research for a class project

- Used the Internet to do research for a class project

We then asked students to report how much they had learned each quarter about finding and using information and about evaluating information.

Table 8.1 tracks the average numbers of classes that required the use of printed materials, use of other library resources, and use of Internet research for each of the four years. As the table shows, the relative ordering is the same for each year; thus, in every year, students took more classes that required research on the Internet than classes that required use of printed resources from the library, which in turn was greater than use of nonprint resources.

While the number of classes that required these types of research, when combined, may suggest that students were doing a great deal of research, it is possible and even likely that students were doing all types of research for the same class. In fact, the three research types correlated positively as follows: library print with library nonprint = 0.72; library print with Internet = 0.62; and library nonprint with Internet = 0.65. These relationships suggest that some curricula required more of all three types of information collection.

Table 8.1. *Number of Classes in Which Research Sources Were Used*

Used printed materials in the library to do research for a class project				
	Mean	**Std. Dev.**	**F Value**	**Significance**
Year 1	1.56	1.21	21.56	0.0001
Year 2	1.81	1.43		
Year 3	2.24	1.74		
Year 4	2.33	1.94		

Used resources in the library, other than printed materials, to do research for a class project				
	Mean	**Std. Dev.**	**F Value**	**Significance**
Year 1	1.31	1.24	34.88	0.0001
Year 2	1.70	1.41		
Year 3	2.15	1.89		
Year 4	2.26	2.00		

Used the Internet to do research for a class project				
	Mean	**Std. Dev.**	**F Value**	**Significance**
Year 1	2.48	1.62	76.76	0.0001
Year 2	3.17	1.92		
Year 3	3.87	2.14		
Year 4	4.30	2.33		

The linear trend for all three categories was strongly significant and positive, as shown in Figure 8.1. More classes required research as students progressed. The upward trend for use of the Internet was stronger than that for the others, increasing from an average of 2.48 courses to 4.30 courses annually. The curves for use of the library for print materials and for nonprint materials did not increase as rapidly and were close together and nearly parallel.

In addition to tracking general library and Internet use, we looked at use across majors. Table 8.2 presents averages for the three items across disciplinary areas and shows that differences among disciplinary areas were significant for all three items. They accounted for 14.9% of the total variance for library print materials and the Internet, and for 20.1% of the variance for other library resources. These averages are graphed in Figure 8.2. As the figure shows, majors in art and business were required to use these three sources of information in the greatest number of classes, and engineering majors in the fewest. The other three areas were fairly comparable. For all major areas, the Internet was required for

Figure 8.1. *Use of Research Resources Over Time*

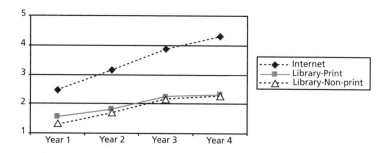

research information in more classes than either library source, on average. Within major areas, business and engineering showed the greatest proportionate emphases on use of the Internet over library sources. Humanities and engineering majors showed the largest preference for library print materials over library nonprint materials. The other major areas were comparable on these two sources. We note here, however, that additional types of research, such as experimental, creation and administration of surveys, and on-site observations, were used in specific disciplines, and we have not accounted for these methods in our survey questions.

Table 8.2. *Average Number of Courses (and Standard Deviation) Across Areas of Majors*

Major Area	Print	Nonprint	Internet
Art (N = 8)	11.6 (5.4)	11.8 (5.1)	15.1 (6.3)
Business (N = 13)	9.0 (3.6)	10.0 (3.9)	19.0 (4.2)
Engineering (N = 18)	5.2 (3.6)	3.6 (3.7)	11.2 (4.2)
Humanities (N = 11)	9.1 (3.1)	6.1 (3.3)	13.2 (6.0)
Science (N = 26)	6.5 (4.6)	6.3 (5.5)	11.7 (6.4)
Social Science (N = 42)	8.4 (4.1)	8.4 (4.6)	14.5 (5.8)
F-Value	3.93	5.62	3.91
Significance	0.005	0.0001	0.005
Eta Squared	14.9%	20.1%	14.9%

Figure 8.2. *Using Library and Internet Resources by Major Area*

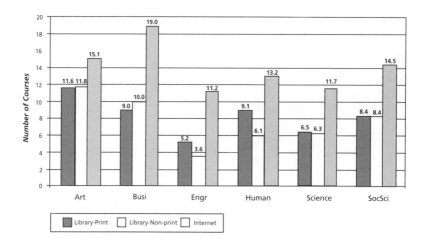

Figures 8.3, 8.4, and 8.5 show use of library print sources, other library resources, and Internet resources across the study's four years. For use of library print materials, the interaction between year and major area barely failed to reach significance. Except for art majors, the use of library print materials was fairly constant across all four years for all disciplinary areas, as Figure 8.3 shows. However, for both use of other library resources and use of Internet sources (Figures 8.4 and 8.5), the interactions were significant at the .005 level.

All three items showed fairly consistent patterns across majors. The number of courses requiring art majors to use library and Internet sources over the first three years appeared to increase steadily, followed by a precipitous drop in the fourth year. Engineering majors' use of library sources tended to be rather flat across the four years, except for Internet use, which increased. The averages of the remaining majors tended to increase over the four years, with business majors showing a particularly large increase between the first and second year in courses requiring Internet use.

We asked students to report how much they had learned each quarter about finding and using information and about evaluating the validity and accuracy of information.[2] The yearly averages for students, as well as the overall averages for all four years of the study, are included on Table 8.3. As the table shows, the mean for finding information (2.55) is higher than the mean for evaluating information (2.43),[3] suggesting that on average students felt that they learned more about finding and using information than they learned about evaluating it. In addition, the two items correlate (.71), suggesting that students who perceived they learned more about one aspect tended to feel they learned more about the other.

Figure 8.3. *Use of Printed Material in Library by Major Area, 1999–2003*

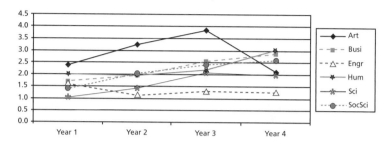

Figure 8.4. *Use of Other Library Resources by Major Area, 1999–2003*

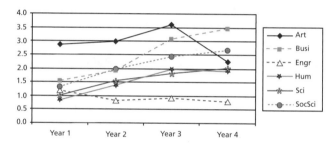

Figure 8.5. *Internet Use by Major Area, 1999–2003*

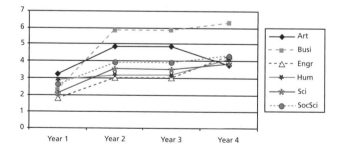

Table 8.3. *Averages for Finding and Evaluating Information*

Year	Finding Information		Evaluating Information	
	Mean	Std. Dev.	Mean	Std. Dev.
Year 1	2.45	0.68	2.44	0.68
Year 2	2.48	0.66	2.34	0.70
Year 3	2.60	0.71	2.44	0.75
Year 4	2.65	0.74	2.51	0.77
Total	2.55	0.53	2.43	0.55

The trends over four years for the two items are found in Figure 8.6. The trend for evaluating information is not statistically significant, but the linear trend for finding and using information is significant and positive. For both finding/using information and evaluating its accuracy and validity, learning continued over all four years, with the former increasing significantly. This result may reflect the fact that students were asked to do more independent research as they progressed through the four years, as indicated by students' descriptions of challenging critical thinking (see Chapter 5).

Figure 8.6. *Yearly Average Ratings for Learning: Finding and Evaluating Information*

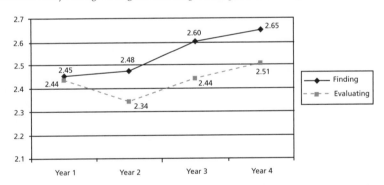

As we had with data on frequency, we looked at learning by major, and the differences among averages were not significant for learning about either finding/ using information or evaluating it. It appears that students perceived their learning about these important aspects of information literacy to be roughly equivalent across majors.

Finally, we looked at the interaction of year and major area. Even though differences among majors for finding and evaluating information were not statistically significant, the interactions in both cases were significant.[4] Figure 8.7 displays results regarding finding and using information. As the figure indicates, in terms of how much students learned, business and engineering majors, on average, showed a strong and significant upward trend over time, while social science majors showed a weaker, but significant, upward trend. As noted previously, when tracking the number of courses requiring research in art, averages for how much art majors learned about finding and using information increased through the first three years and then decreased. This consistent pattern for both sets of questions suggests that the art curriculum changes in the fourth year, perhaps away from integrating other sources into one's own work. Humanities students perceived the greatest learning about finding and using information in their first year, after which a drop is shown until the last year. This may be in response to the requirement of a major thesis or capstone course.

Figure 8.8 shows the interaction of year and major area for evaluating information. The curves in this figure are somewhat more jumbled than those for finding information. Perhaps most interesting is the rapid rise for engineering majors after the first year and the steady decline for humanities majors from years one to four. Positive linear trends for business and engineering are significant, as is the negative linear trend for humanities.

These survey findings suggest that students in all majors were involved in research and learning about information literacy and that students' learning generally increased over time. As we found in other areas of learning, there were differences in the patterns across disciplinary areas.

Figure 8.7. *Finding and Using Information by Major Area*

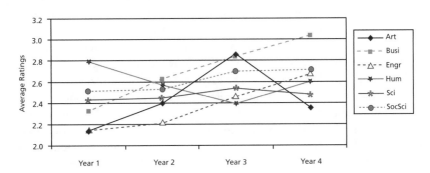

Figure 8.8. *Evaluating Information by Major Area*

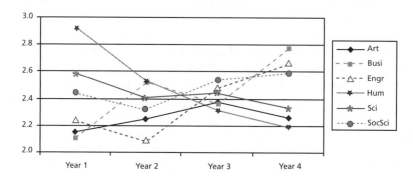

One additional finding in the survey data provided insight into what students learned regarding finding and using information. In the series of items concerning how helpful each item was to student learning, we compared the total average for "Using the Internet to do required research" with that of two other items:

- Using the library to do research

- Using the Internet to find additional information on a topic, even though I was not required to do research

The means for all three items were essentially identical. Thus, on average students equated the helpfulness of the library with the helpfulness of the Internet. Since many of the library resources are becoming accessible through the Internet, this distinction between the library and the Internet as a source for information is increasingly unclear. However, it *is* clear that students spent a disproportionate amount of time in front of their own computer screens relative to pacing through the library stacks. The easy availability of journal articles online makes questions about validation of referenced Internet information less critical, and the question of what makes a good source remains a disciplinary question. In summary, the Internet is changing the way students do research and is altering who has control over information on the college campus—results confirmed by our interviews.

More surprising, students indicated that they were helped to learn by using the Internet to do elective research as much as by doing required research! These results were confirmed in interviews. In other words, students were often interested enough by something said in class or brought up in assigned reading to chase it down on the Internet on their own time. This potential individualizing of the educational experience may not connect very well with ways we assess student learning. Content-based examinations, for example, may reveal less learning than has actually taken place.

Interview Results

As stated earlier, interview questions about information literacy and technology over the four years of the study focused on research and technology use. We asked students to review their transcripts and tell us how much research and what kinds they were required to do for their courses and how much, if any, they were doing on their own. Confirming the survey results, findings from students' interviews showed that students were doing research for their classes, and more interesting, a good deal of class-related research that was not assigned. In addition to questions about required and elective research, we asked students in their second and third years, if they had learned to use any new technology while at the UW.

Required Research

When asked if they had done any required research, the vast majority of the UW SOUL students we interviewed each year reported doing some kind of required research every year.[5] Furthermore, the amount of research they were required to do increased somewhat over time. Table 8.4 shows the number of freshmen and transfer students who reported doing required research and the average number of courses that required it for each of the four years of the study. Because there were so few transfer students still enrolled in the study's fourth year, we did not divide that year's responses by entry status.

As Table 8.4 shows, the great majority of students did some required research every year. In addition, the table shows that students in the first year reported doing research in the fewest courses, on average, and students in the fourth year reported the greatest number of courses that required research. Differences between freshmen and transfer students' numbers show that, on average, students who entered as freshmen reported doing required research for about 11 of the courses they took at the UW, which is a little less than a third of the courses they could be expected to take in four years. Transfer students reported doing research in about nine courses, or about 40% of courses they might be expected to take (assuming that transfer students spend approximately 2.5 years at the UW). These results are consistent with our survey findings.

Most of the research that students reported doing took place on the Internet, as Table 8.5 shows, and the amount of Internet research increased over time, from 70% of the students reporting doing research in the first year of the

Table 8.4. *Percentage of Students Who Did Required Research and Number of Courses Requiring Research*

	1999–2000		2000–2001		2001–2002		2002–2003
	Freshmen	Transfer Students	Freshmen	Transfer Students	Freshmen	Transfer Students	All
% Did research	77.0	80.4	94.3	80.4	86.1	91.3	87.4
Average # Courses	1.9	2.4	2.2	3.1	3.3	3.2	3.8

study to more than 90% in the third and fourth years of the study. Students spent a good deal of time using the university library for research, as well, with 63% reporting doing library research in their first year and 85% or more reporting using the UW libraries for research in their third and fourth years of college. These results are somewhat inconsistent with survey results, which showed that students did more research on the Internet than they did in the library. However, we must note that all results are confounded by confusion over what "library research" is these days. If students were accessing journal articles via the UW library in their dorm rooms, were they doing Internet or library research? Most students assumed that library research meant going to the library, but perhaps not all of them did. In addition, during the life of the study, materials that students had previously accessed at the library became available online, which complicates the question further. Besides library and Internet research, as Table 8.5 shows, the increasing numbers of students engaged in observation-based and interview research over time is an interesting development, perhaps reflecting a trend toward qualitative methods in some of the disciplines.

Table 8.5. *Percentage of Students Reporting Specific Kinds of Research*

What Kinds	1999–2000	2000–2001	2001–2002	2002–2003
Internet	70	88	96	91
UW Library	63	71	87	85
Observations/on site	16	7	14	25
Interviews	7	18	26	40

In addition to these four major kinds of research, students reported a wide variety of other types of research. This included conducting laboratory experiments, media research (TV, film, music), survey research (creating, administering, and analyzing questionnaires), and research in newspapers and other popular media. In the first two years, a few students mentioned public library research, but no students mentioned researching in public libraries in the third and fourth years. Furthermore, students reported that research was most frequently conducted in order to write papers. However, many students conducted research in order to give presentations and to do other kinds of projects, as well. Several students mentioned doing research as background or for homework assignments.

Consistent with the survey data, the increases in the number of students who reported engaging in required research, the number of courses requiring it, and the kinds of research students conducted suggest that research demands increased for most students over time.

Research That Was Not Required

In the first three years of the study, we asked students in their end-of-year interviews if they had done any research that was *not* required by their courses. We did not ask this question in students' fourth year, because by then, we already knew the answer. The majority of students—75% in the first year, 78% in the second, and 89% in the third year—reported doing research on their own. Over the three years, 70%–80% of the research that students reported doing on their own was conducted online. In addition, about one in five students each year reported using books to do independent research. Often students who conducted research online were also reading books and using the library to find information. In addition to gathering information from the Internet and books, students mentioned documentaries, magazines, maps, old textbooks, newspapers, site visits, and interviews, both face-to-face and conducted via email, as information sources.

Interestingly, most of the research that students reported doing on their own in each of the three years was course-related. About 70% of the first-year students, 56% of the second-year students, and 63% of the third-year students who reported doing independent research said that it was motivated or inspired by the classes they were taking. Three students' quotations illustrate this group of responses:

> For the murder class my professor gave us a list of all the books we could read, and instead of getting one, I got six of them just so I could read them later on.

> Difficult concepts like in the philosophy course that I didn't feel I had a good grasp on from lecture or texts, I would look up on the web to get others' ideas on aspects of a particular theory or issue. Some for physics—and calculus as well—looking up formulas or to see if I could get a better explanation from the net than I was getting in lecture.

> The instructor put links on the web site that she thought were interesting, and I checked those out. Most of my surfing was connected with links professors had put on their web sites.

Sometimes information gathered for one class led to other investigations, as these students described:

> Since the American ethnic studies course was a 300-level class, we were expected to have read material in other ethnic studies courses, and since I hadn't done that, I had to do some research. I looked up information about Richard Rodriguez on the web. I looked up information on religion on the web—and I looked that up because I was interested in the different religions and because of Richard Rodriquez—how he changed [his] religious beliefs.

> I looked up different disorders on the Internet because that stuff really interested me from psychology. I think I'll do that for stuff from my sociology class too because it interests me.

Whereas the research that students did on their own was primarily connected to their courses, their own needs and interests controlled when they sought additional information, where they sought it, and how they used it, much in the same way that they conducted research that was motivated by their own personal interests. About 23% of UW SOUL interviewees in their first year, 20% in their second, and 35% in their third year reported doing research—mostly Internet—on some area of personal interest. As might be expected, interests ranged quite a bit and included looking up medical information on specific conditions, such as Lou Gehrig's disease; information on health and fitness; statistics on professional sports or information on sports that students regularly participated in, such as biking, white water kayaking, and sailing; information on jobs and/or internships; travel information; and web-based instruction in how to do a task, such as create a web page. Three students' responses illustrate this wide range of exploration:

> I am into biking, so I always try to find books and online resources to see how I can make my own bike. My dad welds, and if I can buy my own materials, my dad can help me. I am taking an ME class now, in CAD, and I can program the specs and design it on that.

> I've done a lot of baby and pregnancy research because my fiancée is pregnant. So I need to find out things because I don't have a clue. I went online to figure out how to crochet again.

> September 11th—I've done a lot of research since then regarding issues about Afghanistan and the racial relationship between Muslims and Americans. I personally felt responsible to be informed because these are issues that affect me.

Other reasons given by more than one student for doing Internet or other kinds of research on their own were to find jobs or internships, to find housing, to prepare for study abroad, to investigate a serious purchase, and to identify potential graduate schools.

These interview results confirm the survey results. Students were required to do research in a third or more of their courses, but they continuously conducted research that was course-related. This research was sometimes prompted by faculty members' inclusion of web sites in their course syllabi and in their lectures. More often, it was prompted by students' own desires to further investigate an area of study. Furthermore, the line was blurred between "surfing the net" for information about one's personal hobbies or curiosities and going online to gather information about Elizabeth Barrett Browning or the latest information about mapping the genome.

Conclusions From Survey and Interview Results

Interview and survey results seem to argue that undergraduates are information literate, according to the ACRL (2002) definition. They appear to possess: "a set of abilities requiring individuals to 'recognize when information is needed and have the ability to locate, evaluate, and use effectively the needed information'" (p. 2). Furthermore, the ACRL identified literacy as the most important of the three information technology and literacy skills, connecting facility with this process to lifelong learning and self-directed investigations that students may need to conduct for jobs, during internships, or related to coursework. UW SOUL results suggest that students came to the university with some facility in conducting these investigations. Their use of information technology increased over time for research that was required and research that was not, for research that was related to coursework, and for research that was related to their own job, travel, and consumer needs.

However, the ACRL (2000) asserted that while information literacy included fluency with information technology and sound methods of investigation, "critical discernment and reasoning" (ACRL, p. 3) was most important to literacy. This was an area of students' information literacy that we could not discern for two reasons. First, as Chapter 5 demonstrates, critical discernment and reasoning are rooted in the disciplinary cultures and practices, and we are not experts in the cultures of all disciplines.

Second, as we noted earlier, tracking students' information literacy is often a matter of looking for the footprints of a ghost. The process of critical discernment and reasoning is often an internal process, invisible to the practitioner, as well as to the observer. Often, we can only assume the process is in place because of the results. If the student produces an excellent research paper, we assume she used critical discernment and reasoning. However, results that do not immediately reveal discernment and reasoning are not evidence that students are incapable of employing them. Such results may only demonstrate that students did not understand how to discern and reason in that particular discipline.

Therefore, while we believe that we saw evidence of what the ACRL defined as *information literacy* in students' responses, we were not able to find evidence of steps in the ACRL process. It might be instructive for faculty in their disciplines to use those steps to think about what information literacy means in their particular contexts and how they might teach and assess their students.

Technology: Student and Faculty Viewpoints

The data we gathered from students about the technology they learned to use for finding and using information were consistent with data from a second study, which gathered information from faculty. For both sets of data, the meaning of "information technology" was unclear, and for both sets, definitions appeared to be highly contextual.

Students' Perspective

In the second and third years of the study, we asked students if they had learned any new technologies at the UW, and, if so, what they had learned, where they had learned it, and what it was for. Out of the 85 students whose responses we could track for both years, 77 (91%) said they had learned new technologies. Only 9% said that they had learned nothing new. We had a difficult time sorting their responses into "information technology" and "just plain old technology" categories. We ended up letting the students define information technology, and we simply recorded what they told us.

Table 8.6 shows students' most frequently given responses. Approximately one-fourth of those who said they had learned new technology said they had learned Excel. Although Excel in not a tool for *finding* information, it can be used to process and display information that one has found. The same can be said for web page editors, PowerPoint, and Access—all of which students noted learning. In contrast, about 17% of the students identified the library databases as new technology they had learned, which is technology designed to help them find information. Missing from this list is any mention of the Internet, probably because students already knew how to use it when they arrived at the UW.

Table 8.6. *Most Frequently Mentioned Technology Learned*

Software	# Students	% of those who said they had learned a new technology
Excel	18	23
Web page editors (Dreamweaver, FrontPage)	16	21
PowerPoint	13	17
Library databases	13	17
Access	11	14

Disciplinary areas had some effect on the technology students learned at the UW, as Table 8.7 shows—again, particularly technology used to present information—but a great deal of technology was shared across disciplines. Microsoft's Excel and PowerPoint, for example, were used in a wide range of disciplines. Some students responded to this question with the generic "computers," and others described technology for specific purposes, such as MatLab, Illustrator, and SPSS. The range in this list suggests that an assessment of information technology and literacy that focuses only on traditional or general technologies (Table 8.6) would not fairly assess student learning. Such an assessment would miss the technology learning necessary for students to successfully complete their academic majors.

And for most students, learning the technology they mentioned was connected with their majors. When they were asked why they had learned the technology they reported, the majority—62%—said that they had learned the technology for reasons related to coursework, and the majority of those students said that the coursework was in their majors. Other reasons noted were that students learned the technology for fun, their own interest, a UW job or internship,

Table 8.7. Technology Learned in Major Areas

Disciplinary Area	Technology
Architecture and Urban Planning	PowerPoint, GIS, AutoCAD, Form Z, Photoshop, Illustrator, PageMaker, web page editors, video production/editing software, library databases and search engines, SolidWorks, animation programs, woodshop equipment, Word, Excel, photography/darkroom equipment, FTP, computers
Art	Scanners, printers, woodshop equipment, computers, Photoshop, video production/editing software, Illustrator, Visual Basic, Web page editors, sewing equipment, lightboards, architect's 3-scale ruler, sound equipment, dance software, computers
Business	Web page editors, Visual Basic, Access, SQL Server, ASP, Peachtree, Zip/Unzip software, Excel, Word, Powerpoint, Publisher
Engineering	Engineering/Aerospace lab equipment, MATLAB, LabVIEW, Visual Basic, web page editors, animation programs (Flash, etc.), networking, Access, Photoshop, Visual C/C++, Unix OS, engineering software (DesignWorks, Smock, SPIM, Tickle), Java, email, computer programming/language software, Linux, Satellite Toolkit (STK), Mathematica, PowerPoint, Prolab, Unigraphics, ANSYS, library databases, Windows NT, computers
Humanities	Microfilm, computers, electronic bulletin boards, PowerPoint, Excel
Science	Scientific laboratory equipment, scientific software, Circuitmaker, Excel, Unix OS, MATLAB, GIS, ArcView, construction equipment (rammed earth construction), Excel, web page editors, Catalyst, video equipment, Breathalizer, data-entry programs, PowerPoint
Social Sciences	Excel, PowerPoint, microfilm, library databases, E-views, MATLAB, SPSS, OUGL Media Center equipment, scientific laboratory equipment, ArcView, Archaeology software, Access, computers
Nonacademic	Antivirus scan, networking, video equipment, Internet, email, web page editors, Access, Photoshop, PowerPoint

research projects, or organizations or clubs. In addition, the majority of students described technologies that were computer related. Only 6% described technologies that were not computer-based. The following student responses illustrate the relationship between students' majors and the information technology they learn:

> *American ethnic studies major:* Yeah. I've gotten really good at computers since I came to the UW. I bought a new computer and set it all up for myself. I can help people with their computers now. When I go home and watch my parents fumble around with their computers, I just laugh. I use PowerPoint every quarter. I know Excel, Access, Outlook. I didn't know this when I came here.

> *Aerospace engineering major:* Yes, I learned how to use a plasma deposition chamber. I have learned to use a lot of technology for the research that I have been doing. I have learned to make optical fibers. I learned computer programming in CSE 142—C programming. An oscilloscope and other things for research.

> *Art major:* I learned to use a torch. I learned to use a kiln. I learned to use solder—and that takes a lot of practice. I learned to use lots of machinery—casting with a centrifugal casting machine. I learned to use a rolling mill, lots of different hammers. No computer stuff.

> *Spanish major; dance minor:* In dance composition class, they are working with a new software that allows you to record your classes, review them on the computer, and raise commentary on the computer too. You can note, for example, where the spacing is a little off. As a dancer, you never get to see the piece that you are in. We had to tape and review our pieces with the new technology.

Faculty Perspective

These responses from students were consistent with faculty comments about the kinds of technology they required their students to learn to use, as a separate 2002 interview study showed. In this study, Jessica L. Beyer, then acting coordinator of the UW's Undergraduate Research Program, interviewed 46 faculty members from 24 UW departments.[6] Faculty members were selected from the

15 largest majors at the UW, as well as from some of the smaller departments.[7] The purpose of the study was to provide information to the Undergraduate Research Program to assist it in its goals. However, some of the results Beyer (2003) noted in her report provide faculty perspective's on finding and using information that is relevant to our purposes, and the information we include on those perspectives comes from Beyer's report. Beyer's study included the following questions about information literacy and technology:

- What technology do you use in your research?

- Do you require undergraduates to use the same technology you use?

Faculty responses to the first question were highly individualized, with the only recurring response being "computers." Most faculty reported using some kind of technology to gather or to process information, but the kinds of technology they reported differed. For example, regarding gathering information, a faculty member in the community and environmental planning program reported using a tape recorder; a faculty member in history reported using historical archives; and a professor in electrical engineering said he used a "machine shovel."

Nearly all reported use of some kind of software to process data that they had gathered. However, the software varied quite a bit from one discipline to another. Economics faculty reported using the same software packages to process the information that they had used in gathering it, as did the mathematics professors, although the software used by economics and mathematics faculty differed. In addition, the mathematics professors reported writing their own programs to help process information.

Faculty reported requiring students to use the same technology they used to find and use information, *if* the students needed that same technology to conduct their research. When faculty did not believe that students needed the technology they used, they taught students something else. Three faculty responses from Beyer's (2003) report illustrate this point:

> *Anthropology:* All students who do original research use computers, spreadsheets, statistical software. In the field, you use the typical tools, trowels, and shovels. Students in the field school use computerized survey instruments. Some other old fashioned things. In some ways, you can't escape technology. Some [kinds of technology] are primitive; some are more sophisticated. What we use depends on the skill level, the problem that needs to be addressed.

> *Psychology:* In my courses, psych pushes students to use Excel, though people who do research don't use Excel. What we use is too esoteric for them.

> *Art:* The technology that is available are the kilns. Most of them are computer programmed now, and most students learn to use them. On another level, they also need to know how to document their work with photography or video to be taken seriously in the field. . . . A lot of students are light years beyond us.

Beyer reported that several faculty mentioned that students sometimes contributed to the choice of technology they used, as this psychology professor said:

> The students have to do the same thing, but I encourage them to think of new applications, and if it would benefit the study, we'll look into it.

Beyer (2003) concluded that *technology* was a concept defined by the disciplines; therefore, the information technology used within a discipline could also vary. Furthermore, her findings showed that while faculty trained and expected undergraduates to use information technology, *what* they trained them to use depended upon what undergraduates needed to conduct their research. Training was, therefore, as much a practical matter as a disciplinary one. Beyer noted that faculty were somewhat "wary of blanket definitions of ITL."

These findings on information technology are consistent with students' reports about technology they learned to use. Together, they demonstrate that even aspects of learning that appear to be universal—such as information technology—are subject to disciplinary needs, practices, and purposes. Given that reality, it would be difficult to centrally assess student learning of information technology or literacy.

Conclusions and Implications

In this section, we conclude with our findings regarding information literacy and technology and discuss their implications for teaching, learning, and assessment.

Information Technology and Literacy Are Disciplinary in Nature

While there was universal use of computers "to Google" topics and use of the UW libraries' interface to access titles and the locations of books and journal articles, the technology that students used to locate information, the way they sorted through and evaluated it, and the purposes for its use varied quite a bit across disciplines. Even definitions of research varied by discipline, and we found differing patterns of learning about and doing research across the four years of college. Furthermore, departments often taught their majors which websites, library databases, and resources were the best to use in their fields.

The process for evaluating and using such information, however, may not always be as clear to students as where to look for information. Therefore, faculty need to be explicit in their teaching about how one goes about finding information that is credible in their fields, how one can tell if the information is credible, and how to incorporate the information within their own work. As with other areas of learning, the use of student examples and faculty annotation is very helpful for students' learning.

In addition, because of variances from one discipline to another in how research is defined, how it is conducted, and how information is evaluated and used, it is impossible to develop a universal method for assessing learning in this area that would provide departments with information helpful in improving student learning. Therefore, in the area of information technology and literacy as in other areas of learning, assessment of student learning must be conducted by departments. Departments can begin with the ACRL process to see if and how that process applies to their understanding of what it means to find and use information in their fields. However, departments should feel comfortable straying from the process if it does not reflect their actual practices.

An issue that remains for both teaching and assessment, however, is whether faculty and administrators are knowledgeable enough about the most recent technologies to teach students how to use them and to assess that use. There is a great deal of conversation about the ways that today's millennial students approach technology use. Because it appears that young people's approaches to technology differ from the approaches of previous generations, it might be wise for faculty to form undergraduate committees to help them in their teaching and assessment work in this area.

Nearly All Students Are Adding to the Knowledge That Assignments, Lectures, and Research Impart

Students are constantly gathering information, both academic and personal. This is a new phenomenon, made possible by the Internet and the easy access that search engines give us, as well as by the access to experts and their knowledge that email provides. The methods for gathering both personal and academic information were quite similar, and calling one kind of information "research"—information on the genome project—and another "personal"—information on how to build a faster bicycle—seemed more and more arbitrary to us. Universities and colleges and their faculties have little control over the information that students obtain; instructors may not even be aware of the ways that students are adding to the information that faculty present during class by surfing the net outside class. Furthermore, students are using their laptops to add to their knowledge of how to use their laptops, their search skills, their presentation skills, and a multitude of other areas of knowledge. In other words, accessing information online is not simply a way to gather information; it is also a way to learn. It seems likely that this new reality, in which students are researching all the time, could create amazing new teaching opportunities for faculty, but we do not know what those opportunities are or how one might assess them.

Endnotes

1) An interesting study conducted with a small number of students in 2003 at Evergreen State College in Olympia, Washington sought to get around this problem. A report on that study can be found at: www.evergreen.edu/library/archwww/1989 Accessions/Accession89-30/The%20Activity%20of%20Information%20Literacy %20(paper%20for%20JGE%20Sep%202003).htm

2) Students used a 4-point scale: 1 = *zero,* 2 = *a little,* 3 = *a moderate amount,* 4 = *a lot.*

3) Dependent *t*-test, *t* = 3.56, p < 0.0001

4) P < 0.025 for finding information; p < 0.0005 for evaluating information.

5) What the term *research* meant, however, varied quite a bit. Table 6.4 shows some of that variety.

6) Beyer conducted structured, 30–60 minute interviews with faculty members in 2002. She did not define terms, such as *research,* for faculty because she wanted to learn how they defined those terms. In addition, she cited a study (Beecher & Trowler, 2001) that found that in interviews with graduate students and faculty, definitions of research were consistent inside disciplines. Beyer took notes on faculty responses, transcribed the notes immediately after the interviews, and analyzed results, using an inductive process similar to that used for UW SOUL responses, grouping all answers to the same question together and arriving at categories of response with a constant comparison approach. All interviewees reviewed and approved a draft of Beyer's 2003 report before it was finalized.

7) According to the UW's Office of Institutional Studies' "Summary of Degrees Awarded by Level and Time to Degree, 2000–01" and "Average Annual Majors Count, 2000–01," the 15 most populated majors on campus were as follows: art, business, political science, psychology, English, biology, electrical engineering, economics, communication, sociology, history, anthropology, zoology (later merged with biology), chemistry, and international studies. The ten additional departments from which faculty members were drawn included: drama, philosophy, comparative history of ideas, social welfare, women studies, community and environmental planning, mathematics, computer science and engineering, astronomy, and Spanish and Portuguese studies.

General Learning

9

What helps your learning? "A really good professor—someone who can communicate and knows his subject well, and when you are in the presence of that, you can't NOT learn. You go to class."

What hinders your learning? "The first day you realize the world is not going to fall apart because you do not attend a class is a very dangerous day."

At its beginning, the UW SOUL focused on six areas of learning: personal growth, understanding and appreciating diversity, critical thinking and problem solving, writing, quantitative reasoning, and information literacy. However, we also gathered information on areas of students' learning that fell outside these six areas. This more general information is the subject of this chapter. In addition, this chapter presents comparisons of learning across the six areas.

The chapter makes two major arguments, both of which seem ridiculously obvious. First, we argue that students learn and develop skills in their four years in college—that is to say, they leave knowing more and being able to do more than when they arrived. To those who know the research on learning, this assertion may seem to be an already well-established fact that requires little further support. However some groups continue to raise questions about whether students actually learn anything in college. Others, most recently and eloquently Derek Bok (2006), acknowledge that research shows that students do make learning gains in college (Astin, 1993a; Pascarelli & Terenzini, 1991) but argue that students should be learning more. Bok (2006) argues that faculty need to focus on what students learn, integrating active learning strategies into their classroom teaching, assessing their goals for student learning, and engaging in a continuous improvement process that can foster key institutional purposes (or outcomes) for learning. While these arguments are not entirely new (see Barr & Tagg, 1995), Bok's call for reform, with its emphasis on each institution assessing the learning of its own undergraduates, is welcomed. Indeed, that was our purpose in the UW SOUL. However, as results in this chapter and elsewhere in this book demonstrate, we can show that students are learning, but we cannot determine if they are learning all they could be or whether they had learned "enough." That judgment must be guided by standards and practices in the disciplines.

While all students knew more when they graduated than they had when they entered the university, students' knowledge gains were uneven. Some students improved their abilities to write computer programs but learned little about who they were and what they valued. Some students learned a great deal about power and oppression but little about how to see the empty spaces in a landscape and imagine what might fill them. Still others learned how to talk with ease with people different from themselves at the same time they learned a great deal about globalization and life on the ground in Argentina.

This chapter demonstrates the unevenness that we believe characterizes undergraduate learning. The chapter shows that learning comes from many directions, and that learning in one arena often inspires learning in others in ways that are hard to predict and track. This complexity lends support to Arnett's (2000) theory of the role of exploration in emerging adulthood.

A second argument in this chapter is that faculty are the key to how much students learn. Again, this point seems obvious on its surface; however, many projects and programs in higher education are dedicated to reducing faculty time with undergraduates in the classroom as both a cost and energy saving approach to learning. Many of these efforts are laudable as approaches to actively engaging students in the learning process, but when they remove faculty from students, institutions also remove possibilities. While we also note the importance of peers to learning, as well as the significance of the mindset and motivation of the students themselves, students told us again and again that, more than any other source, faculty inspired and delivered learning. This learning was not only academic. Sometimes faculty inspired self-awareness. Sometimes they showed students how to understand their neighbors. Perhaps because of the transformations faculty can inspire, students want more interaction with faculty, not less (see also Kvavik & Caruso, 2005).

In contrast, when asked about what hindered learning, students told us that hindrances most often come at their own hands.

Rather than beginning with case studies, as we have in other chapters, we move from this introduction to nine students' comments near the end of their college careers about their learning. The kinds of learning these students describe were nonlinear and messy, demonstrating processes that are difficult to track. Next, we focus on findings related to general learning and on what helped and what hindered students' learning. Finally, we draw conclusions and discuss their implications for teaching and assessment.

Nine Paths

American ethnic studies major: I am more confident in myself and my abilities to talk to people and in my ability to communicate my ideas. I have learned a lot about myself and what I must do to be heard in this society and how as a minority I am often overlooked, so I must make myself unforgettable.

Art major: Every class and every professor has given me something new and valuable, but if I had to pick out one class, it would be the Global Classroom project that I was fortunate to participate in during the 2002 school year. It was unlike any other project. The concept was to create learning opportunities for faculty and students across international boundaries by collaborating with the School of Arts and Design at Tsinghua University on creating posters on a central theme, water awareness. From this project, I really learned what learning through exploration meant. The students had to make a lot of the decisions along the way. From that point on, I began to learn to see many things within context rather than just accepting them on a surface understanding. The global project was also the first time that I really worked in groups. I learned to appreciate others' thoughts and working together. Overall, it was a project that really changed my perception of learning and school.

Business major: There was an astronomy professor who really inspired me with his enthusiasm and his desire to make his students feel the same way he did about astronomy. As a result of his opening lecture, where he posted a chart of the dates and viewing locations of the next full solar eclipses, I decided to go to Madagascar for two weeks this summer to view a full solar eclipse. I told him about this and my plans for the trip, and he was very excited for me. He asked me to let him know of my progress and to send him photographs. This has made me feel like I can contribute to his classroom and to his teaching, because he has not yet been able to see a solar eclipse himself, and I know that he will be excited enough by [my experience] that he will show his future classes some of my photographs. In some small way, I feel like a pioneer for the astronomy department on his behalf, as much as this trip is also a personal journey.

Biology major: Academically speaking, I have learned how to manage my time better, how to hold down classes, homework, a job, and social aspects without having to sacrifice one or the other. I think I have become better prepared for work loads, am better at approaching staff for questions, and am more focused (finally) on what I want to do in the future. Personal growth has also occurred in the form of maturing, being more open minded and accepting of other views and people. The classes I have taken have been especially helpful in giving me a more diversified outlook, and granted me the ability to be more accepting and open to others' ideas. With some 40,000 students on campus, I have met many with entirely opposite views and backgrounds than my own. The opportunities that are available through the UW and the surrounding area have also participated in my growth and change.

Dance major: I had a mystical experience in my ballet class. I felt comfortable with the movement enough to play with the music. I let go of all my fears of falling, messing up a step, and being watched. Then, I just felt the music of the cello through my entire body.

Engineering major: [In my senior year] I learned that I couldn't take my classes as I had done the past three years. I learned that I wasn't studying to the best of my ability. In the past, I thought studying meant staying up really late and doing a lot of homework problems. But last quarter I learned that going in and having a one-on-one conversation with the professor really helps you learn. I don't know what changed me. I think it was the people I was doing my homework with. It was that we felt really comfortable with the way the professors were teaching the class, and that inspired us to go in and ask questions. And they really encouraged us to go to office hours.

Geography major: I just watched the 2003 commencement two days ago at Husky Stadium. It was the third consecutive time I had seen it, but this one had a profound effect on me. Unlike the previous commencements, I was supposed to be a part of this one. The class of 2003 would have been my graduating class. Constant changes in my major [i.e., I applied to and was turned down by majors four times before I ended up in geography], the specific classes I have chosen to take, and other reasons contributed to the fact that I will be graduating in five years instead of four. . . . Surprisingly enough, I don't regret it. Honestly, graduation is a small objective to strive for while you are at college. As discussed in the UW SOUL focus group this year, going to college dramatically changes one's life. For some, the UW may be the first and only diverse place they have seen or will see. Learning about other cultures makes you grow as a human being. By living and experiencing college life, you are learning about the differences and similarities that each of us possesses—not only culture and ethnicity, but personality as well. In contrast, lingering in a small town is almost like limiting the amount of air you were allowed to breathe. Going to a university and living the experience helps you breathe easier by offering an infinite amount of opportunity. It seldom happens, but sometimes these opportunities beg you to jump at them. Most other times, however, the opportunities are there and one just has to search for them. This is probably the most important thing to learn while at the university.

Scandinavian studies and Norwegian major: After the events of September 11, I am no longer secure in my own ignorance. I knew that Americans weren't liked by some, but had no idea that some people actually hate our very being. The United States is not as safe as I thought it was. Now I know that we are just as susceptible to attacks as other countries. I had to fly two weeks after the attacks happened, and I don't think that I've ever thought about my own mortality as much as I did on that flight. [Also,] two weeks ago my host sister and friend were aboard a plane that crashed outside Milan, Italy. My host sister was just two months younger than me, and now she is dead. I have heard it said many times that the death of young people is meaningless. I have never come to grips with that saying until now. I didn't know about the immense hole loved ones leave behind when they die unexpectedly. I know now.

Women studies major: At the beginning of this year, I realized I needed to get my butt in shape and start being self-motivated in regards to school. It hit me at the beginning of the quarter that I am going to be the first person to graduate from college in my family. I feel that a lot of weight is on my shoulders for me to do good. I think I have taken my classes or my time here for granted, and that is recognizing that I have put in some time but not as much effort as I could have. This year, I manage my time better. I actually manage it; I don't let it go to the wind, even though that is how my personality is. I guess I realized that this really does matter to me. I've realized how much my mom has sacrificed for me to be in this place.

General Findings About Students' Learning

This section of the chapter reports our findings on the following:

- Students' perceptions about how much they learned

- What students said helped their learning

- What students said hindered their learning

Students' Perceptions About How Much They Learned

Each quarter, we asked students to indicate on the quarterly surveys how much they had learned in 26 areas, using a 4-point scale.[1] As stated in Chapter 2, in analyzing their responses, we averaged quarterly ratings to arrive at a yearly average and averaged over years to arrive at a total average. This approach allowed us to view change over four years. In the few cases where a student did not take all three surveys in a given year, because she took a quarter off or was studying abroad, we averaged across those she did take.

Learned the Most/Learned the Least

Previously, we presented the results of the learning items that were relevant to each chapter. However, we have included those items again in Table 9.1 to provide a comparative view. The table presents responses to each item averaged over the four years, as well as the ranking of these average ratings. It is important to keep in mind that the means for these items do not represent the cumulative amount that students learned in that area; rather, they represent the average amount students reported learning *each quarter*. For example, the mean for "learning about writing papers that make and support an argument" indicates that each quarter, on average, students learned 2.29 out of 4 in this area.

Table 9.1. *How Much Did You Learn This Quarter About . . . ?*

Mean	Rank	Item
		Writing
2.29	15	Writing papers that make and support an argument
2.11	21	Writing answers to essay questions on exams
2.09	22	Writing papers whose main purpose is to present information
2.04	23	Writing drafts of papers and using feedback to revise them effectively
		Critical Thinking
2.86	3	Thinking critically about issues
2.78	5	Exploring questions such as "What does this mean?", "Why is this important?", "Why did this happen?", or "What are the implications and outcomes of these results or choices?"
2.76	6	Critically examining my own thinking, arguments, or opinions.
2.59	8	Revising my attitudes and opinions in light of new information
2.49	10	Constructing arguments to support my own ideas
2.19	18	Challenging a theory, conclusions, arguments, or results of an authority in a discipline
		Information Literacy
2.55	9	Finding and using information
2.43	12	Evaluating the validity and accuracy of information
2.29	16	Using a variety of sources to define and solve problems
		Quantitative Reasoning
2.21	17	Using quantitative analysis or reasoning to understand issues, make arguments, or solve problems in courses other than math
2.16	19	Understanding and solving mathematical problems
		Diversity
2.46	11	Understanding and appreciating diverse philosophies, people, and cultures.
		Personal Growth
2.92	2	Understanding more about who I am and what I value
2.81	4	Working and/or learning independently
2.67	7	Making new friends; being more socially confident
2.34	14	How to work/study with others
		Other
3.24	1	Information, theories, and perspectives from your classes
2.42	13	Understanding the interaction of society and the environment
2.13	20	Speaking effectively
2.04	24	Creating something original
1.94	25	Doing well on multiple-choice exams
1.93	26	Designing something

As Table 9.1 shows, the five areas where students indicated that they learned most, on average, were:

- Information, theories, and perspectives from their classes

- Understanding more about who they were and what they valued

- Thinking critically about issues

- Working and/or learning independently

- Exploring questions such as "What does this mean?", "Why is this important?", "Why did this happen?", or "What are the implications and outcomes of these results or choices?"

These five items represent a wide range of learning, from course content ("information, theories, and perspectives") to self-knowledge ("who they were and what they valued"), and they reflect goals students had for their own learning when they arrived, as described in Chapter 3. Furthermore, they echo students' definitions of what it means to be educated.

The five areas where students reported that they learned the least, on average, were:

- Designing something

- Doing well on multiple-choice exams

- Creating something original

- Writing drafts of papers and using feedback to revise them effectively

- Writing papers whose main purpose was to present information

Again, these results were not surprising when seen in the context of results reported elsewhere in this book. The acts of designing and creating, as we reported earlier, occurred primarily in engineering and arts disciplines and seldom elsewhere. Also, students reported that most of their challenging writing focused on argumentation rather than informative writing. As stated in Chapter 6, students' opportunities to draft papers and receive feedback from faculty or TAs on those drafts decreased dramatically after their first year in college, so it is little wonder that they did not learn as much about revision as they did about other aspects of learning.

Finally, the item ranks within our six categories of learning show that the areas with the greatest learning were critical thinking and personal growth, while the areas of least learning were writing and quantitative reasoning (QR). As we will see, the former categories tended to be present in all disciplinary areas, while the least learned categories tended to be more unevenly distributed across the disciplines (e.g., writing in humanities, QR in engineering). Furthermore, writing and QR are more easily defined, tangible activities than are personal growth and critical thinking, which are broader and more fuzzy.

The Effect of the Major on Learning

To better understand the results shown in Table 9.1, we compared students' responses to all 26 items by the disciplinary area of students' majors, looking at averages for each year and for all four years.[2] In broad-brush terms, we obtained two results: first, that students' assessment of their learning on various items tended to be influenced by their major, which was expected, and second, that this differentiation by major began in the freshmen year, which we did not expect.

The influence of major. There was a significant effect for disciplinary areas for more than one of the years and total across years for 14 of the 26 items.[3] The 12 items for which area of students' major appeared to make little or no significant difference, ordered from the smallest overall eta-squared value (1.6%) to the largest (7.9%), were:

- Evaluating the validity and accuracy of information

- Information, theories, and perspectives from their classes

- Exploring questions such as "What does this mean?", "Why is this important?", "Why did this happen?", or "What are the implications of these results, outcomes, or choices?"

- How to work/study with others

- Revising one's attitudes and opinions in light of new information

- Finding and using information

- Understanding more about who they were and what they valued

- Thinking critically about issues

- Writing papers whose main purpose was to present information

- Working and/or learning independently

- Constructing arguments to support their own ideas

- Making new friends; being more socially confident

It is tempting to suggest that these items, especially those toward the top of the list, may be true goals of a general education, because students perceived that they learned these things at a certain level regardless of discipline. However, it is important to remember that students can place very different meanings on these terms, and those meanings often depend upon their majors, as we noted in previous chapters. For example, we see that students from various disciplines were reasonably equivalent, on average, in their perception of what they learned about "thinking critically about issues." But as shown in Chapter 5, how students thought critically about issues, what those issues were, and how they expressed that thinking varied greatly as a function of their chosen discipline.

In contrast with these 12 items, 14 of the 26 items showed consistent significant differences by disciplinary area. These items, ordered from highest eta-squared value (55.1%) to lowest (10.4%) were as follows:

- Understanding and solving mathematical problems

- Designing something

- Creating something original

- Using quantitative analysis or reasoning to understand issues, make arguments, or solve problems in courses other than math

- Writing papers that make and support an argument

- Writing answers to essay questions on exams

- Understanding and appreciating diverse philosophies, people, and cultures.

- Writing drafts of papers and using feedback to revise them effectively

- Doing well on multiple-choice exams

- Understanding the interaction of society and the environment

- Using a variety of sources to define and solve problems

- Speaking effectively

- Critically examining one's own thinking, arguments, or opinions

- Challenging a theory, conclusions, arguments, or results of an authority in a discipline

Table 9.2 shows the seven items for which the disciplinary area was the most influential (23.6% or more of the variance explained). The two highest rated areas and the two lowest showed large differences among means for majors. These results largely confirm those reported in previous chapters. Majors in the arts and humanities, for example, reported learning less about solving mathematical problems than did business and engineering majors (Chapter 7); art and engineering majors learned more about design than majors in the humanities and social sciences reported (Chapter 5).

Early differentiation. The result that surprised us was that differences in learning by major began in the freshmen year, before many UW SOUL students were in majors. At the UW, essentially all students enter as premajors. Freshman entrants are expected to declare a major at the end of the second year. Thus, during the first and second years of college, few entering freshmen have been admitted to a major. In spite of this, analysis of the first-year surveys showed that 14 of 25[4] items exhibited statistically significant differences among students' *eventual* majors. This proportion of statistically significant items actually decreased slightly for the successive years of data—13 of 26 items for the second and third years and 10 of 26 items for the fourth year. We can also see the near equivalence in average of the eta-squared values across all items for each year, which were 11.4%, 13.1%, 12.3%, and 11.2% for the four years, respectively. If these results were retrospective ratings taken at the end of four years, there would be room for skepticism, but they were not. These were questions students answered at the end of each quarter.

We believe that these results show that students began specializing in their majors early. In the years when faculty and administrators may think that students are engaged in "general education"—broad-based learning about a variety of disciplinary content and methods—students have already oriented themselves toward a specific area, such as humanities or science, if not toward a specific major or department within that area. The distributive model of general education makes this practice particularly easy, and we know that much of this specialization comes about through course selection. For example, students hoping to major in engineering must lock into the engineering curriculum early in order to graduate in a reasonable amount of time. However, our results suggest that early specialization occurs in other disciplines, as well. We also speculate that even students who take the same classes may emphasize different learning outcomes, given their ways of thinking and nascent disciplinary orientation. An

Table 9.2. *Survey Items Exhibiting the Greatest Effect of the Major*

Item	Eta Squared	Areas With Highest Means	Areas With Lowest Means
Understanding and solving mathematical problems	55.1%	Engineering (2.97) Business (2.66)	Art (1.34) Humanities (1.51)
Designing something	46.9%	Art (3.19) Engineering (2.67)	Humanities (1.53) Social Sci. (1.55)
Creating something original	44.2%	Art (3.54) Engineering (2.42)	Social Sci. (1.74) Business (1.81)
Using quantitative analysis or reasoning to understand issues, make arguments, or solve problems in courses other than math	37.1%	Business (2.69) Engineering (2.65)	Art (1.59) Humanities (1.67)
Writing papers that make and support an argument	31.9%	Humanities (2.62) Social Sci. (2.55)	Engineering (1.76) Science (2.04)
Writing answers to essay questions on exams	24.1%	Social Sci. (2.34) Business (2.35)	Engineering (1.59) Art (1.93)
Understanding and appreciating diverse philosophies, people, and cultures	23.6%	Humanities (2.88) Art (2.74)	Engineering (1.87) Science (2.25)

eventual psychology major may have learned different things in a sociology class than an eventual English major, for example.

Fall and spring interview responses conducted in students' first year support the survey results that suggest early specialization. In these interviews, we asked 84 freshmen and 47 transfer students what they thought they would major in. Then we compared those responses to their actual majors. By the end of their first year at the UW, 50% of the freshman population and 98% of the transfer students had correctly identified their eventual majors, even though they had not necessarily been admitted to them.

While the university's distributive model of general education makes it easier for students to specialize early than a set of core requirements might, Smart, Feldman, and Ethington (2000) suggest that students come to college *predisposed* by their temperaments to major in certain areas. This is an interesting field of study that needs further investigation. However, whether predisposed by temperament or influenced by classes that captured them, our results show that students specialize early.

What Helped Learning

Information on what helped learning came from a variety of sources—quarterly survey, annual focus groups, interviews, and email questions. The picture drawn by these separate sources of information is coherent: Faculty play the most important role in advancing student learning. It is important that we note here that we are not saying that faculty are solely responsible for learning. Students as early as their second quarter in college note that they are responsible for their academic choices and behaviors. However, faculty have profound influence even on this awareness.

Survey Results on What Helped Learning

The web-based surveys asked students to identify the extent to which 36 items helped them learn. Students were asked to respond on a 4-point scale,[5] or they could indicate that they "did not do" that which was described by the item. Overall, students' responses demonstrated that they believed that faculty, their own efforts, and their peers played key roles in helping them learn.

Table 9.3 shows the average ratings for all the survey items over all years on what helped students learn. As before, we averaged quarterly responses for the four years of the study, so the mean is the average amount students felt they learned *each quarter.* The table is organized by the average percentage of students who said they had done or experienced the item during each year. Therefore, the first section of the table reports how much the 90%–100% of the participants who reported doing that item said they had learned from it; the second section reports how much the 66-89% of the students who reported doing those items said that the items had helped their learning; and so on.

As Table 9.3 shows, students found faculty expertise nearly as helpful as they found faculty concern about their learning. This result is interesting because students and the public often emphasize faculty teaching ability over their level of expertise about a subject, but these results suggest that the two may go hand-in-hand for students, or that at least one is as important as the other. In addition, students got a good deal of help by speaking with faculty one on one, and it is interesting to note that about 90% of them reported they had done so, regardless of the size of classes or of the institution. In addition to help that faculty gave students, survey respondents reported that peers' opinions of their intellect were about as helpful to learning as faculty opinions. In addition, as the table shows, students found that thinking for themselves and being presented with multiple perspectives in class helped their learning, as did email interactions with faculty. Writing papers, learning about multiple ways of looking at ideas, and doing challenging reading were the least helpful, on average, in this group of items.

Table 9.3 also shows what 66%–89% of the students reported had helped their learning. This group found having course materials on websites very helpful. In fact, overall, the average rating for "having course readings, assignments, lecture notes, or other content materials on the web" was the highest of all the items that students said were helpful to their learning. The table shows that most students found using the Internet on their own to find information was helpful, which is consistent with findings reported in Chapter 8.

Students reported that asking questions in class was helpful. Asking questions and speaking in class were aspects of learning that came up elsewhere in the study. While students knew that asking questions was important to learning, students, particularly in science, math, and engineering reported in interviews and email responses that they were often afraid to speak even in classes of 40 students or fewer. This fear was related to students' concerns about what their peers and faculty members might think of them. Two students' comments on this concern illustrate this issue:

> My greatest challenge was learning to communicate with professors, especially in settings of 30 or more students. This is an obstacle which I have to try to overcome with each new professor, each new personality.

> In really big lecture halls, sometimes the professor almost doesn't seem like a real person, and they seem unapproachable. It is like the feeling you get when you meet a celebrity—like you shouldn't be talking to them because they are in one space and you are in another.

In addition to identifying question asking as helpful to learning, this 66%–89% identified two items related to peers as helpful—learning that came from discussions with students in class and learning that came from working in groups on projects. These are aspects of class that faculty can orchestrate, but whether or not they help learning often depends on the students themselves.

Table 9.3. *What Helped Your Learning?*

Mean	% Didn't Do	Item
		Items that 90%–100% of Students Reported Doing and How Much Each Helped Learning
3.46	0.0	Liking the subject before I take the class
3.45	2.0	Having professor(s)/instructor(s) who seemed to care about my learning
3.43	8.5	My own efforts—reading, studying, doing my homework, going to classes, staying focused
3.40	0.0	Having professor(s)/instructor(s) who were experts in their fields
3.21	9.2	Talking one-on-one with the professor/TA
3.11	3.3	Feeling as though my instructors think I am intelligent and capable
3.09	2.6	Feeling as though my peers think I am intelligent and capable
3.06	5.9	Talking with friends and peers about ideas and values not directly related to class work
3.03	3.3	Thinking for myself rather than being told what is "truth"
3.03	8.5	Emailing the professor/TA
2.77	7.8	Writing papers
2.77	9.8	Learning multiple ways of looking at ideas, events, or experiences from lectures/readings
2.57	9.2	Reading that was challenging
		Items that 66%–89% of Students Reported Doing and How Much Each Helped Learning
3.58	13.1	Having course readings, assignments, lecture notes, or other content materials on the web
3.37	15.7	Having a professor's syllabus on the web
2.98	28.8	Using the Internet to find additional information on a topic, though I was not required to
2.95	23.5	Using the Internet to do required research
2.88	17.0	Asking questions during class
2.78	11.1	Learning about multiple ways of looking at ideas, events, or experiences from discussions with students in class
2.69	33.3	Working with groups on class projects and papers
2.62	31.4	Taking essay exams
		Items that 46%–65% of Students Reported Doing and How Much Each Helped Learning
3.09	40.5	Working with a study group
2.97	35.9	Using the library to do research
2.88	51.6	Doing math problems
2.84	34.6	Being asked to review and assess my own work
2.63	42.5	Taking frequent quizzes
2.52	53.6	Giving an oral presentation
2.26	41.8	Learning about one consistent way to view ideas, events, or experiences
2.05	43.8	Taking multiple-choice exams

Table 9.3 (continued). *What Helped Your Learning?*

Mean	% Didn't Do	Item
		Items that 1%–23% of Students Reported Doing and How Much Each Helped Learning
3.38	99.3	Visiting the math study center
3.17	76.5	Finding a faculty member whom I regard as a mentor
2.98	88.9	Getting one-on-one help from a librarian when doing research in the UW library system
2.98	96.1	Visiting a writing center
2.95	81.0	Joining a club or organization
2.89	92.8	Having instruction in class from a librarian on how to do library/Internet research

Table 9.3 further shows that working in study groups contributed to learning for the 45%–65% of UW SOUL students who had the opportunity to do so. Using the libraries, doing math problems, and being asked to self-assess were also helpful to the students who did those things. This group of students felt that taking frequent quizzes and giving oral presentations did not offer much help to their learning, on average; neither did they find learning about one consistent way to view ideas, events, or experiences helpful. Finally, students reported that taking multiple-choice exams contributed little to their learning. In fact, this item received the lowest average rating of all the items provided to students, suggesting that while multiple-choice exams may help faculty assess what students have learned, students did not believe that taking them contributed to learning.

The last section of Table 9.3 shows the items that the fewest students reported doing. Interestingly, all of the items that the fewest number of students experienced were ranked at about 2.9 or above. These results show the value of one-to-one type experiences, such as getting individualized help in math, writing, and research, that only a few of our students—one out of four, at best—were able to access. Students in this group also reported that finding a faculty member whom they regarded as a mentor was helpful.

It could be a matter of concern that fewer than 24% of the UW SOUL students said that they had experienced faculty mentoring. However, students' responses to an interview question we asked at the end of their third year indicated that a mentoring relationship is only one kind of faculty connection that students consider meaningful. In spring 2002, we asked all the UW SOUL interviewees if they had made a meaningful connection with a faculty member while at the UW. About 63% said yes and 37% said no. Even if they had reported no meaningful connection with faculty, we followed up by asking all students what they meant by a "meaningful connection:" What would/does such a connection look like?

The two groups—those who had formed a meaningful connection to a faculty member and those who had not—defined "meaningful connection" identically. In addition, we analyzed responses by gender and ethnicity and detected no differences across groups. About 43% defined a meaningful connection with a faculty member as a "personal" relationship, in which the faculty member showed an interest in the student's personal life, as well as in her academic life, and remembered the student's name over time. About 19% of the interviewees described "a mentor relationship," similar to a "personal" relationship, but one where faculty members served as guides or counselors, and had a sustained learning relationship with students. About 12% described the connection as a "recommender" relationship, where the faculty member knew the student well enough (and was willing) to write letters of recommendation on his behalf. A few students—4%—described the faculty connection simply as one that encouraged learning. Finally, about 22% provided definitions that were impossible to categorize.

Students' majors and eventual majors were much less of a factor in their ratings of what helped them learn than they were in how much students said they had learned in the areas studied. Only three of the items exhibited significant differences across majors, and, for the most part, these were no surprise, as Table 9.4 shows. Data on quantitative reasoning and information literacy have prepared us for the first two of the results. Regarding the third, we can only speculate that majors in the arts and business learn to view phenomena through very particular lenses.

Focus Group Results on What Helped Learning

Students' focus group responses on what helped their learning were very similar to their survey responses across the years of the UW SOUL. Over all four years, students in the focus groups said that professors who were passionate about their subject areas and who demonstrated that they cared about students' learning were the most helpful to their learning. As the survey results also indicated, students reported that their peers, especially when working together in study groups, were very helpful to their learning. Finally, students in several groups mentioned their own roles in learning.

Table 9.4. *Significant Differences by Area of Major in Survey Responses to "What Helped Your Learning?"*

Item	Years	Highest Rating	Lowest Rating
Doing math problems	Overall and years 1, 2, and 3	Engineering Sciences	Arts Humanities
Using the library to do research	Overall and years 3 and 4	Social Sciences Arts	Engineering Business
Learning about one consistent way to view ideas, events, or experiences	Overall and years 2, 3, and 4	Art Business	Social Sciences Science

Interview Responses to How Faculty Communicate They Care About Students' Learning

In both survey and focus group responses, students said that their learning was helped by faculty who cared about it. The course evaluation system used at UW asks students to rate the "instructor's interest in whether the student learned,"[6] and after hearing a presentation for faculty on UW SOUL, a faculty member in the psychology department asked if we could determine what things professors did that led students to think faculty members cared about student learning. We put that question on our spring 2002 interviews, and 11 clear themes emerged from students' responses, as follows.

Faculty interact with students in class, engaging them in substantive ways. A total of 87% of the students talked about interaction between the professor and the students in class. Their responses could be placed into three closely related subcategories. About 34% said they felt that professors cared about learning when they asked for questions in class, answered them respectfully and completely, and checked to make sure answers and explanations were clear. Two students' quotations illustrate this large group of responses:

> Every time the professor goes over one main point, they have to ask [if we have questions]—not after they go over five. You really don't think they care if their back is to you and they are writing on the board and they never ask. Even if the students never ask any questions when the professor asks if there are questions, his asking makes us think he cares about our learning.

> Also the way they answer questions in class—their attitude about it. There are times when there are stupid questions, but even then, a teacher who cares about your learning will be nice about it.

A second way that faculty interacted with students in class was to monitor whether students were learning through observation or requests for feedback. About 34% of the interviewees mentioned this way of engaging students, as the following quotation illustrates:

> In class, it registers with them more easily if the student is not catching on to the concepts. They have a tendency to say, "I feel that everyone is not completely getting this, so let's go ahead and break this down a little further." They are monitoring in some way.

Finally, about 19% of the students who spoke about substantive interaction in class said that when professors encouraged students to share opinions or contribute to discussion, students knew that faculty cared about their learning. For example:

> In class, they engage us in discussion and not just lecture at us. It's not just, "Here's a bunch of information; test next week." We are called upon to voice our thoughts and perspectives. We are treated more like human beings. We learn to put into words things that we think. Testing is not just based on "Can you remember this concept?" but "Can you think, can you write, can you formulate ideas?" That brings out the better part of students. I feel more acknowledged as an intellectual mind when I get to express myself.

Faculty design lectures/courses that anticipate and reduce barriers to students' learning. UW SOUL interviewees—about 47%—also talked about the ways that a course's structure and the daily lectures communicated faculty concern for their learning. We were surprised at how carefully students paid attention to faculty use of course structure as a guide through the material. One student said this:

> When it's clear they have put a lot of effort in creating a lesson plan that is geared to our needs. By that I mean, I guess, when it's not coming from the perspective of someone who understands all the bases of the logic for that class, especially when you are talking about a technical difficulty. We need to understand the bases—what are your primary assumptions,

things like that, so they start out explaining that first off—kind of a sequential presentation of the material, and coming back to earlier concepts, things like that.

Faculty are accessible in a variety of ways. About 36% of the students interviewed mentioned the importance of encouraging students to come to office hours, of being willing to meet them by appointment and before/after class, and of using email and web sites. This point was also raised in survey results about what helped student learning. In their interviews, some students said that even if they never took advantage of office hours, they were encouraged to learn simply by the professor welcoming them to come speak with him. The following quotation illustrates this group of responses:

> When a professor has a good web site and is accessible by email. When they respond to your emails and are really open to having office hours. When they respond to your needs and are willing to go with your schedule. And when they tell you that in class.

Faculty demonstrate a passion for the subject and are enthusiastic about teaching it. In earlier interviews and in all the focus groups, students spoke of the importance of instructors' enthusiasm for their subjects. The general feeling was that if the faculty member was not passionately interested in her subject, students did not understand why they should care about it. About 26% of the UW SOUL students interviewed spoke about the importance of professors' deep interest in their subjects. The following student's comment serves as an example:

> Their passion about what they are teaching is what makes me want to learn. They don't particularly say that they want us to learn, but their interest in what they are teaching makes you feel that you want to learn more from them. It makes you think that there are things to be learned from them.

The faculty member knows something about students' personal experience or interests and knows some students in the class by name. The importance of personal knowledge was mentioned by 19% of the UW SOUL interviewees. Many of these students said that it did not matter if the professor knew *their* names, but that it was important to know she knew *some* of the students' names. One student's comment illustrates this group:

> When professors learn my name, that really means a lot to me. I want to do better in their class then. I try to introduce myself

to the profs, too. When you raise your hand in class, they call on you by name, or if they write a personal message on your midterm or a paper you get back—it could be either criticism or praise—that communicates they care.

Faculty have high expectations for students' learning; they challenge and stretch students' thinking. About 16% of the students who were interviewed explicitly mentioned the value of taking challenging courses and doing challenging coursework. They saw high standards as a sign of caring. One student in this group put it this way:

> They challenge you. They might ask you to retry or redo something, because they don't think it worked. You don't always get the easy way out—that's a sign they care about my learning.

Faculty provide critical feedback that guides students' learning on assignments. Feedback communicated caring to14% of the UW SOUL interviewees. As one student said:

> Constant feedback. I've had classes where you turn in a home-work assignment and they just check it off and others where they dissect it, like yours was the only one. When they do that, you know that they are not just giving you a grade on it, but they are helping you learn it, learn the information.

Faculty are experts in their fields of study. Eight percent of the UW SOUL interviewees mentioned that their instructors' level of expertise communicated caring about learning. As one student said:

> It's really those aspects of being a credible source, someone who gets up there and knows what they are talking about, someone who presents both sides.

Faculty help students do well on tests. About 7% of the students we inter-viewed said that faculty help in preparing for or understanding the results of exams communicated that professors cared about their learning. When students spoke about this aspect, they often spoke of heroic faculty efforts to ensure that students understood course material. For example:

> In biology last quarter, a couple of my professors had extra review sessions for us to go to. They would schedule them around the time students could take them, even doing some

on Sunday night. That was really nice to know—-that they were willing to spend their extra time, even on the weekends, to help us.

Faculty treat students with respect and understanding. This theme overlaps with others. For example, when professors ask students for their opinions, students interpret that as respectful treatment. Therefore, we counted comments in this group only when students specifically described how they were treated, and about 7% did so. One example:

> I like teachers who treat the students like scholars, who don't talk down to us and ask us stupid questions—stupid questions meaning that they have the answers and we are trying to guess what they are.

Faculty connect course material to real-world applications and events. Several students (5%) believed that linking course content to the world outside academia demonstrated that faculty cared about students' learning.

These 11 themes generated by the responses of the 85 students we interviewed serve as an interesting guide for faculty. In these responses, students not only outlined the ways that faculty members communicated they cared about students' learning, but, according to research on learning (Bransford, Brown, & Cocking, 2000), students' responses also outlined how to *improve* student learning. In other words, if faculty put these methods in place to communicate they cared about students' learning, they would actually increase it. As Light's (2001) research on student engagement at Harvard has shown, students learn more when they are actively engaged in their courses, and they are more engaged when they are asked to respond, write papers, and discuss what they think about course material. Furthermore, in detailing the roles faculty can play, these 11 themes are consistent with our own UW SOUL survey and email responses to what helped students' learning.

Email Responses to "What Advances Your Education?"

In winter 2002 a former dean and faculty member asked us another question about the meaning of an item on our course evaluations, which speaks to the question of what helps students learn. He wondered how students defined a course as "valuable in advancing my education." To answer his question, we sent an email message to 182 UW SOUL participants that quarter, asking them to tell us what the phrase "valuable in advancing my education" meant to them when they filled out course evaluations. It also asked them to describe briefly what they considered valuable and not valuable about two courses they had taken. Seven major categories emerged from their responses.

Assignments. The majority of students who responded (69%) said that the existence and nature of assignments was critical to feeling that their learning had been advanced. About a third of these students specified that assignments that were challenging and designed to teach them something were valuable, and about 29% spoke of the value of assignments that asked them to apply course material to problems, cases, or real-world examples. Students in this group also spoke of the value of certain kinds of assignments, including

- Reading that was well integrated into the course (23%)

- Hands-on work, such as labs, fieldwork, and field trips (18%)

- Writing assignments (18%)

- Homework that helped them learn something and was not repetitious (15%)

- Research (12%)

Many students specifically stated that assignments should not be merely "busy-work," which they defined as work that required little thinking on their part, asked them to regurgitate information rather than use it, and/or asked them to repeat the same set of tasks in order to memorize information. Several students spoke about the critical importance of feedback on assignments—from papers to problem sets—to their learning. Two students' quotations illustrate this group of responses:

> I think "hands-on" or applied learning is the most influential in advancing my education. This can be learning an equation and practicing how to put it to use in a real-life problem or reading a book and demonstrating how it applies to the world around us.

> I do believe that research assignments have contributed great-ly to my ability to articulate ideas.

The importance of assignment in advancing student learning suggests that, in general, students do not consider courses that one student described as "lecture-test, lecture-test" as doing much to advance their learning.

Learning that could be applied to majors, careers, or life. About 55% of the email responses focused on applied learning. Of the students who focused on application, the majority (70%) spoke of learning that had a bearing on their majors and/or on their intended careers. Two students' quotations illustrate students' sense of the value of applied learning:

> When I think of the value of classes in terms of advancing my education, I usually think of it in terms of whether or not it's in my major. If the content of the course directly pertains to my planned major, I consider it valuable.

> "Valuable in advancing my education" would be that I learned something that makes me a better person or a more well-rounded person and I learned something that I could use or want to know later in life—where I actually take something from the class, [rather than] forget everything after the quarter's over.

Aspects of course design. Closely echoing responses to the question about how faculty communicated that they cared about students' learning, nearly half of the UW SOUL participants—47%—spoke about the importance of course design. These students said that interaction, class discussion, and/or working in groups in class advanced their educations. One out of every three said that when the class challenged them to think, rather than focusing solely on memorization of material, they felt it advanced their educations. Finally, about 14% of those students focusing on course design pointed to well-organized courses, describing these as classes where the pieces—such as labs, reading, and other assignments—were clearly integrated. Two students' comments serve as examples:

> My experiences with his class are not soon forgotten, because, since it is a class he teaches WITH the students, there is always a heightened sense of accountability to do the work and share what you are learning. He understands that education is a journey to be traveled together, rather than something we as students are herded into like dumb cattle.

> Active participation is also very valuable because it draws on the wide variety and diversity of student experiences and knowledge in addition to the instructor's.

Professors. About 42% of the respondents said that faculty were the key to advancing their educations. Students focused on three ways professors accomplished this. First, about four out of five of the students who spoke about professors pointed to how they conducted class, including:

- Providing clear, concise, and interesting lectures

- Adding to the required texts (as opposed to just repeating them)

- Using examples, especially those from "real life," to illustrate ideas and concepts

Second, students said that professors advanced their educations when they demonstrated that they cared about students' learning. This group—about a third of those who talked about professors—said that offering help in and outside class, monitoring students' understanding in class, and being accessible before/after class, in office hours, and through email were ways that advanced student learning. Finally, many students said that when a professor was passionate and enthusiastic about her subject area, they were inspired to learn more, and, thus, the professor's own interest advanced students' educations. These responses echoed students' interview comments, reported in the previous section of this chapter, on how faculty communicated they cared about students learning. The following quotation illustrates this set of responses:

> An instructor who shares his/her excitement and knowledge about the class topic(s) is always valuable because s/he can pique students' interest in topics that were of no original interest to them just by being enthusiastic and passionate about the subject, rather than just reading off lecture notes.

Any learning. About 40% of the students said that a course advanced learning when they learned *anything* that they had not known before, including information, methods, and ideas that they believed they would retain, perspectives that changed their thinking or thinking processes, methods or practice in how to be a better critical thinker, or just something new. For example:

> My interpretation is related to how much new insight I gain from a class. I ask myself—did I gain a new perspective on a certain subject? A valuable understanding of it? Was I introduced to a value/conceptual system, which I didn't know before taking this class? Was I given new insights into the subject? But most importantly . . . will this new insight/conceptual system/perspective stay with me one, two, ten years from now? In other words, did I gain a true understanding of something which is valuable [that will] stay with me forever, or was it just a static accumulation of facts/information/disconnected knowledge, which will disappear in a few months?

Students' own actions. About 11% of the respondents mentioned going to class, putting in effort, doing the required work, and taking their coursework seriously as valuable in advancing their educations. As one student said:

> A lot of the work I do is self-driven, and I've found that the many hours (outside of class time) that I dedicate to designing studio projects have been beneficial. Other activities I've also done that have been valuable include library and/or Internet research, as well as going to lectures offered by the College of Architecture.

Interest level. Several students, about 7%, said that classes that were interesting or fun advanced their educations, as this student's response illustrates:

> But there's also those classes that are just plain interesting, even though they aren't in your major.

Responses to the UW SOUL email question on what advanced students' learning confirmed survey, focus group, and interview responses to questions about what helped students learn. Contrary to what some might have predicted, only a few students said that courses that gave them high grades or low grades advanced their learning.

Challenging Courses

Challenging courses helped students' learning. While this result was confirmed repeatedly by our various data sources, specific information about the level of challenge students experienced in the early part of their undergraduate programs came from 230 UW SOUL participants' responses to email questions in 2001. The first of those questions asked students to comment on and provide two examples of the level of academic expectations they were experiencing. The second asked them to note what barriers they had to overcome, if any, to meet academic expectations. In responding to these questions, students indicated that they were experiencing high levels of academic challenge and that several aspects of their courses made them challenging. A list of those we could categorize, as well as the percentage of the students who mentioned them (with students sometimes mentioning more than one), were:

- Level of thinking required to do well (39%)

- Challenging/hard writing assignments (28%)

- Amount and difficulty of reading (12%)

- Time it takes to complete schoolwork (11%)

- The need to learn/work on one's own (10%)

- The focus on learning (8%)

- Good/enthusiastic/clear professors and TAs (5%)

- Level of material presented (5%)

- Unclear, unhelpful professors and TAs (4%)

- Application of course material to real-life contexts (3%)

- The kind of testing (3%)

- A pace that is too fast (2%)

- A large class size (2%)

In the following section we discuss the barriers that students noted as hindrances to their learning.

Similar ideas about the importance of challenging courses can be found throughout the book, particularly in our chapters on critical thinking, writing, and quantitative reasoning. Furthermore, when students were asked in which of their courses they had learned the most and in which the least, they repeatedly said that the courses that presented them with the greatest challenge were the courses they enjoyed the most and learned the most in. Clearly, challenging courses helped students learn, not only because they asked students to stretch, but because challenge, particularly the "tightrope with a net and a spotter" type of challenge, communicates to students that faculty care about their learning.

Conclusions About What Students Said Helped Their Learning

Through all our methods of asking, students told us that what helped their learning the most were faculty. In surveys, focus groups, interviews, and email responses, students described the ways faculty did and could continue to help them learn, and nearly every point that students made is supported by research on learning. Faculty helped students learn when they asked them to think deeply, engaged them in meaningful ways in class, and gave them assignments that were challenging—assignments designed to teach them something; assignments asking students to apply rather than merely repeat knowledge. Faculty helped students learn when they were accessible and respectful, when they were both knowledgeable and passionate about their fields. It also helped students when faculty structured their courses in ways that anticipated what students would need to know next, and when faculty could name at least some students, even in their largest classes.

In addition to the importance of faculty to students' learning, students noted the importance of peers, particularly in the surveys. Students cared about peers' good opinions of them, learned from working in study groups, and got help from each other formally and informally. Finally, students also mentioned some of the things they did to help themselves learn. But those efforts seemed less important to students than the efforts of inspiring faculty and interactions with peers.

What Hindered Learning

We did not want to assume that the opposite of what helped students' learning would hinder it, so we asked students what hindered their learning on the quarterly web-based surveys and in focus groups. As with what helped learning, the picture students drew about what hindered their learning was coherent. However, while faculty received the most credit for helping students learn, the students gave themselves the most credit (or should we say, *blame?*) for hindering their learning. And students had many ways of getting in their own way.

Survey Data on What Hindered Learning

We asked students on quarterly surveys to rate 36 factors that might hinder their learning on a 4-point scale.[7] As we did with students' responses to what helped their learning, we averaged responses for each year, and to help us better understand students' responses, we divided the 36 items as indicating obstacles presented by the following:

- Self/procrastination

- Concerns about personal issues

- Faculty

- Self/feelings of inadequacy/fears

- Course practices

- Institutional structure

As Table 9.5 shows, students believed that what they chose to do and not do presented the most significant barriers to their learning. Four of the six most

Table 9.5. *What Hindered Your Learning?*

Item	Mean	Rank
Self/procrastination		
Wanting to play instead of study	2.84	1
My own procrastination	2.64	2
Poor study habits	2.29	4
Too many fun things to do at the UW and in Seattle besides study	2.12	6
Concerns about personal issues		
Relationship worries—parents, girl/boyfriends, friends	2.30	3
Money worries	2.09	8
The amount of time I had to work for wages	1.91	11
Missing my family and friends	1.67	16
Having English as my second language	1.12	33
Concerns over child-care	1.02	35
Faculty		
Professor(s) or TA(s) who were disorganized, confusing, or unclear	2.25	5
A professor or TA who didn't know me	1.65	18
Having a TA/professor whom I could not understand because of bad handwriting/ language skills	1.63	19
A professor or TA who seemed to dislike me	1.44	26
Being singled out by the professor/TA or my fellow students because of my race, ethnic background, gender, or sexual orientation.	1.12	32
Self/feelings of Inadequacy/fears		
Feeling less well prepared than my peers seemed to be	2.11	7
Not feeling comfortable asking questions or making a point during class	2.04	9
Not knowing anything about the subject before I took the class	1.73	15
Not asking questions during office hours	1.66	17
Feeling underprepared in my writing ability	1.59	21
Feeling as though the level of work demanded was significantly higher than that demanded at my previous educational institution	1.52	22
Feeling unprepared in my math ability	1.47	23
Feeling unprepared to do research	1.46	24
Feeling unprepared in my computer skills	1.30	31
Course practices		
Not being able to take the time to review and assess my own work	1.97	10
Getting a low grade early in the quarter	1.88	12
Frequent homework with no feedback	1.86	13
Homework assigned daily or close to daily	1.74	14
Teachers who gave me theories rather than facts	1.62	20
Only getting one point of view in class	1.52	22
Not being challenged in my classes	1.36	28
Getting a high grade early in the quarter	1.36	28
Getting many points of view in class	1.33	30

Table 9.5 (continued). *What Hindered Your Learning?*

Item	Mean	Rank
Institutional structure		
Not getting the courses I wanted or needed	1.45	25
Lack of community at the UW	1.36	28
Difficulty navigating campus or course requirements because of a disability/ limited access	1.06	34

highly ranked items centered on student procrastination and the attraction of recreational opportunities, and one of the six related to relationship worries. The items, "wanting to play instead of study" and "my own procrastination," were the two most highly rated items by quite a margin. As the table shows, students did not consider the most serious of those obstacles as very significant; only ten hindrances were considered more than "a minor obstacle." Students clearly placed more blame on themselves for failure to learn than they placed on the faculty or university.

The quarterly averages for the item students identified as the most significant obstacle to their learning—"wanting to play instead of study"—revealed a significant eighth order interaction, which is rare in any data set. Figure 9.1 shows a plot of the averages for each academic term, illustrating the effect and revealing an interesting trend. As the figure shows, the temptation to play rather than study increased from fall to winter to spring each year. It is hardly surprising that the urge to play was the least strong, on average, in the fall quarter of each year, a time when many students have resolved to buckle down. The figure shows why students might so resolve, for their desire to play hindered them most significantly *each spring quarter.* The obstacle of wanting to play instead of study was greatest in the last quarter of their fourth year, for which we even have a term—*senioritis*—which sets in after many students have secured jobs and realized that their GPAs will not be affected greatly by final quarter grades.

In addition to information about how students can distract themselves from their studies with procrastination and entertainment, Table 9.5 shows, once again, the significant impact that personal relationships had on students' experience in college, which we saw in Chapter 3. There was no significant trend in students' identification of this item as a hindrance, suggesting that relationship worries remained a salient hindrance to learning throughout students' four years. Another item, which ranked in the top six obstacles students selected, was professors and TAs who were unclear and disorganized. This item was clearly the other side of the coin to students' comments about what helped their learning.

Figure 9.1. *"Wanting To Play Instead of Study" by Quarter*

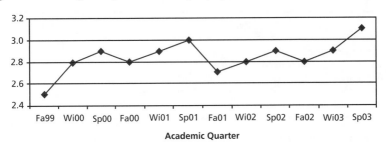

The last four items in the top 10 on this list are also important. Two "comfort-level" questions appear in this group. One identified how well prepared students felt in relation to peers, and illustrated, once again, the importance of peers to students' learning. The other pointed to students' discomfort with speaking in class, a topic we discussed in the previous section of this chapter. Finally, the tenth most frequently chosen obstacle speaks to the importance to students of the need to reflect on and review their work as an aid to their learning. This result indicates that students sense the value of metacognition to their scholarly work, a point discussed in Bransford et al. (2000).

Two other interesting results shown in Table 9.5 include:

- "Getting a low grade early in the quarter" hindered students' learning more than "getting a high grade early in the quarter"—a result that runs contrary to many faculty assumptions and practices.

- Structural issues, such as "not getting the courses I wanted or needed" and "lack of community at the UW"—both of them major concerns among administrators at most large institutions—had considerably lower overall means than other categories of responses.

As noted earlier, students' choice of major had a large effect on what they felt they learned, but little effect on what helped their learning. Similarly, students' areas of major had little impact on what hindered their learning. Only two items were significant for three of the analyses: "homework assigned daily or nearly daily" and "the amount of time I had to work for wages." The areas for which daily homework was rated the greatest hindrance were business and humanities; majors that rated "daily homework" the least hindrance were engineering and sciences. Regarding time needed to work at a job, art and humanities majors determined this need to be a greater hindrance than science and engineering majors.

Focus Group Results on What Hindered Learning

We asked focus groups what hindered their learning in each of the four years of the study. Students' focus group responses were quite similar to their survey responses, with students each year identifying the obstacles they placed in front of their own learning as the most significant hindrances. As they had in the surveys, students noted that faculty could hinder their learning in a variety of ways—for example, by conducting unclear classes, delivering lectures in a monotone, or actually saying they did not care about teaching.

In addition to asking students what hindered their learning in the focus groups, we asked them to identify the one change that the UW could make that would most improve their learning. Table 9.6 shows students' responses over the four years of the study. As the table shows, in all four years, improving the quality of teaching was among students' top three recommendations. In addition, students felt their learning could be improved with smaller classes and greater class availability. It is noteworthy that students recommended reducing class size even in their junior and senior years, the years when most students' classes are the smallest.

Table 9.6. Focus Group Recommendations for the Institution

2000 10 groups	2001 9 groups	2002 9 groups	2003 10 groups
Smaller classes (7)	Improve faculty teaching (5)	Invest in professors who care and can teach (5)	Hire, train, and retain professors who are excellent teachers (6)
More student-teacher interaction (6)		Smaller classes (4)	Smaller classes (3)
Better professors/TAs (5)		Add more classes to improve availability (3)	Greater class availability (2)

Challenging Courses: Barriers

When responding to the second question in the winter 2001 email questions, which concerned barriers to meeting academic expectations, students tended to hold themselves responsible, as they had in their survey reports. Furthermore, while they mentioned a wide range of barriers, none said that the barriers were insurmountable. The most frequently mentioned barriers to meeting academic expectations were as follows:

- Time issues: balancing life/school needs and demands, time management (26%)

- Procrastination (12%)

- Personal problems (such as depression) or financial issues (12%)

- Feeling uncomfortable asking professors and TAs questions in and outside class (10%)

- No barriers (9%)

- Learning how to study (8%)

- Size of the UW and of classes (4%)

- Unclear or unhelpful professors and TAs (3%)

- No letdown time—every assignment and every class counts (2%)

- Had to get serious, put out effort (2%)

- Feeling isolated by age or because of transferring from a community college (2%)

- Difficulty finding and using resources (2%)

Conclusions About What Students Said Hindered Learning

The most important message we received from students' responses about hindrances to their learning was that they felt their own behavior and choices were the primary obstacles to their learning, as shown in Table 9.7, which gives a sample of responses from 20 students. We must note, however, that sometimes barriers to students' academic learning can open paths to other kinds of learning that students valued. Friends, for example, were noted as distractions to learning, but as we said in Chapter 3, students cared a great deal about learning about others and about nurturing their relationships. In addition, peers were considered an important asset to learning, as well a potential hindrance. As Chapter 3 also noted, students considered having wide-ranging experiences while in college part of their definitions of academic success. That meant that their interests in competitive kite flying, biking, movies, and volunteer work may have presented obstacles to academic learning but, at the same time, met their goal of gaining other kinds of knowledge. Also, while it may seem obvious to faculty and administrators that hours of watching TV and playing video games may be unhealthy for academic performance, there may be ways that some of the activities students cited as obstacles benefited classroom learning. Our point, here, is that the ways and reasons students put up barriers to their own academic learning are complex, as are the outcomes of those barriers.

Table 9.7. *20 Barriers to Meeting Academic Expectations*

1)	"My computer. Computer games."
2)	"Napster."
3)	"Living with a person who is not in school."
4)	"The HUB. Socializing there."
5)	"My boyfriend."
6)	"I like TV."
7)	"I miss one class and that makes it easier to miss the next one."
8)	"Time budgeting. I have to shackle myself down to do what I need to do."
9)	"A class so boring it would be less painful to stab a pencil into your leg."
10)	"If you are going to do well, don't make any friends."
11)	"Five hours of commuting a day."
12)	"Personal and family stuff."
13)	"Just getting over the hump of getting started."
14)	"Going shopping on the Internet."
15)	"Parties don't help either."
16)	"The rain."
17)	"Napping at inappropriate times."
18)	"I got sick this quarter. I took my finals with strep throat."
19)	"In some of my really big classes, people talk during the lecture, and it is really frustrating."
20)	"I have to work 40 hours per week to put myself through school."

Less complex seemed to be students' sense that faculty members who appeared unconcerned about students' learning or about their own teaching presented obstacles to student learning. While in a secondary position to students' own choices, the ways faculty members could prevent students from learning were important, and students spoke eloquently of its reverse in the previous section.

Conclusions and Implications

We draw six conclusions from the findings in this chapter, which we discuss here, including assessment and teaching implications.

Learning Comes From Multiple Sources and Is Both Individualized and Uneven

That students know more when they leave college than they knew when they entered has been supported by studies reported elsewhere (Bok, 2006; Pascarella & Terenzini, 1991). Our findings on learning suggest that while all students learned, their advances were individualized as well as heavily influenced by their majors, confirming findings discussed in previous chapters. Without further belaboring this point about the mediating effects of the disciplines on learning, we note that the strength of this finding across all methods and nearly all measures over time argues for more explicit explanations for what we are doing and why in our classes, whatever the discipline. In addition, it argues for assessment of learning that occurs in academic departments, rather than centrally.

Furthermore, our findings on general learning raise questions about what we mean by general education, particularly in institutions with distributive models. It is clear from the results in previous chapters, as well as in this one, that history, chemistry, and sociology courses at the 100-level require that students know how to read and write in those fields, just as they do at more advanced levels. None of the faculty modifies disciplinary content or methods to make their courses generic for the beginning student's consumption. In addition, it is clear from information on general learning that students begin to differentiate into majors very early, adjusting their course choices according to their majors and their eventual majors. For these reasons, in terms of assessment, we agree with Bok (2006) that it is time to get over our "fixation on general education" (p. 46). If we improve learning in the disciplines, we will have improved general education.

In addition to raising questions about general education, our findings on learning in this chapter show that the shape and content of learning is contingent upon many aspects of students' lives while they are in college. All students learn, but our study shows that learning is uneven, with some students making greater strides in certain areas than others. The directions of growth depend in part on students' own inclinations and attachments, in part on the smorgasbord of possibilities that an institution can offer, and in part on the ways that students' majors defined themselves and conveyed themselves to undergraduates. Further complicating the unevenness of students' learning, these aspects of learning interact in individualized ways that we observed but did not directly study.

Regarding teaching implications, faculty should remember the key roles that their disciplines play in students' overall learning and lives, and thus make explicit what students are expected to learn in their courses and disciplines. But we should also remember that our students' learning takes place all over campus, as well as in places far away from it. This makes assessment of student learning daunting, if we are interested in assessing real learning in all its complexity, rather than in overly simplified, compartmentalized bits of learning. How can we assess Jeremy Nolan's learning (Chapter 1) against Fiona O'Sullivan's (Chapter 3), or Trevor McClintock's (Chapter 5) against Julianne Guest's (Chapter 6), for example? Even when looking at a single aspect of learning, how can we meaningfully compare what Carl Swenson and Jennifer Oswald learned about diversity? Given the complexity of the learning that we observed in the UW SOUL, we believe that assessment of student learning must be departmental. However, centrally located assessment can be a powerful partner to departmental assessment, if it is designed to gather information about how students experience college, if it makes room for student definitions of learning, and if it recognizes differences across students and disciplinary practice.

Faculty Are the Key to Students' Learning

No technology, no study group, no pedagogical technique can replace the effect of faculty members who care intensely that students learn about a subject that is dear to their hearts and minds. Again and again, students reported developing a sudden interest in topics they had never cared about before—rocks, the gastric system, Duke Ellington, quadratic equations, Tony Morrison, the Kung!, juvenile delinquency, operant conditioning, the history of science—and nearly always they attributed these sudden fascinations to faculty. Sometimes students attached themselves to majors because of these experiences, and sometimes they did not. But every time students experienced something unexpected that commanded their intellectual attention, their minds were opened to the next experience. With regard to the importance of faculty, we must note that students also pointed to graduate teaching assistants as central to their learning. Their TAs often walked them through learning step by step. One example is Fiona O'Sullivan's history TA, who taught Fiona how to write in her major.

Institutions need to hire, reward, and train excellent teachers and find ways to enhance faculty-student interaction. Institutions need to focus attention on helping graduate students become excellent teachers, even though these investments will not be fully returned to the institutions that make them. Innovation in educational technology should be viewed as an aid to foster meaningful interaction, rather than a substitute for it. Institutions also need to foster and reward multiple approaches to teaching and learning assessment. These assessments must include the learning outcomes that faculty and departments care about, rather than learning outcomes that others think they should care about.

Students Take Responsibility for Hindering Their Own Learning

Faculty are often surprised to learn that students most often blame themselves for failure to learn. While students also point to faculty who are difficult to understand, who do not seem to care about their learning, or whose courses are disorganized or unclear as hindrances to learning, they most frequently cite their own behavior as barriers. However, it is important to note that some of the "personal behaviors" that students described as obstacles actually represent nonacademic goals that students have for their own learning. This conclusion leads us to be gentle in our judgments of student behavior. Even in their political science classes, even as they evaluate each other's short stories or poems, even as they complete an environmental science lab, they are working on the development of their whole selves.

Students Want To Be Intellectually Challenged

Students valued courses that required them to think and asked them to demonstrate that thinking in more than one way. They did not value courses that were easy or that made few intellectual demands on them. Students also wanted to be *taught* to do the thinking required, rather than merely being *required* to do that thinking. They often described ineffective teaching as "teaching by assigning"—an approach in which students were asked to take intellectual leaps or stretch their abilities in assignments and on exams in ways that they had no instruction for doing.

The implications this finding has for teaching are simple in principle though more difficult in practice: we need to ask students to do intellectual work that is challenging, and we need to provide them with instruction for doing it. In addition, we need to help students practice making inferences before we ask them to take such leaps on exams. Furthermore, asking students to demonstrate their thinking in several ways provides classroom faculty and TAs with information about how well we have stepped into the gap with instruction and where we need to do more. In other words, we can assess how well students understand our teaching by including large and small opportunities for them to demonstrate learning in our courses. This kind of classroom-based assessment is the work of faculty members and TAs, rather than departments. There are many good books available on classroom-based assessment, starting with Angelo and Cross's (1993) important book, *Classroom Assessment Technique*.

Demonstrating Caring for Students' Learning Will Improve Their Learning

Students preferred courses that stretched them over courses that did not. In addition, nearly every student we asked said that engaging them in substantive ways in class—asking what they thought, responding to their answers, monitoring their understanding, making room in class for their questions—indicated that faculty cared about their learning. Even though welcoming the opportunity to participate meaningfully in their classes, many students reported that they were embarrassed to ask questions in class, and many also hesitated to ask questions outside class. Even classes that we consider "small"—30–50 students—presented problems for some students who had questions. Faculty who are seen to care about students' learning make questions and responses a normal part of class time and respond respectfully and appreciatively to student questions. They show that higher education is in the question-asking business and that the classroom—however large—is a place where students' questions are not only welcomed but part of an enterprise that requires them to ask questions.

These findings challenge the arguments that students only like "easy" instructors and that course evaluations are "just a popularity contest." UW SOUL students showed little respect for easy classes or easily earned grades, and popular faculty members were those who demonstrated that they cared about students' thinking and learning in ways that appear to guarantee their learning (as also indicated by Bransford et al., 2000).

The teaching implications of this conclusion take us back to the section in this chapter where students described what faculty did to demonstrate that they care about students' learning and what advanced their learning. These two sets of results present a teaching blueprint for faculty members who want to improve student learning.

Students Learn From Each Other

Next to faculty, students name peers, either separately or in the form of study groups, as most helpful to their learning. Regarding teaching, this conclusion suggests that faculty need to build study groups, peer review, small group work, and shared projects into courses whenever possible. Not only is it true that students learn from each other; it is also true that nearly all people work in collaboration with others after school is over. Therefore, faculty provide a service to students by putting them in meaningful relationships with each other over shared needs. In addition, asking students to work together can enhance the social side of a diverse education and address a nonacademic goal that students have for their own learning—the development of social skills.

However, students must be taught about effective collaboration directly and through modeling. A student in a focus group pointed out an interesting fact. He said that students in today's classrooms are being asked to practice teamwork skills by faculty who have never been taught how to be effective team members themselves. He was right; as college students, many of us were rarely asked to work on projects with peers, especially in the arts and humanities. That lack of knowledge and experience causes many of us to "teach" students about working in groups by assigning them to do so—the "teaching by assignment" approach mentioned earlier. However, the power of peers in helping each other learn and the importance of giving students experience in collaboration as a preparation for life after college demand that we make efforts to learn how to teach students to work effectively in groups.

Endnotes

1) 1 = *zero,* 2 = *a little,* 3 = *a moderate amount,* 4 = *a lot*

2) We used one way analyses of variance and the Eta Squared statistic, which indicates the proportion of total variance accounted for by differences among levels of the independent variable.

3) $P < 0.05$

4) One item, "Challenging a theory, conclusions, arguments, or results of an authority in a discipline," was added after the first-year surveys.

5) *Didn't do,* 1 = *wasn't helpful,* 2 = *a little helpful,* 3 = *somewhat helpful,* 4 = *very helpful*

6) *See* www.washington.edu/oea/services/course_eval/index.html

7) 1 = *not an obstacle,* 2 = *minor obstacle,* 3 = *moderate obstacle,* 4 = *major obstacle*

Summary and Last Words

There is no way that a person can be fully prepared for the freedom, the temptations, and the challenges that lie ahead of them as they leave high school. It is part of growing up to make mistakes, fall flat on your face, and learn from it all. In my four years, I have done all of these things. If there is any advice I can give to a future college student, it would be the following:

- *Study something YOU enjoy, not something that your parents want you to enjoy.*

- *Credit cards are bad.*

- *Friends will get you through hard times.*

- *You can survive on Top Ramen for four weeks, if needed.*

- *If you choose to drink alcohol, take it in moderation, and no matter what anyone ever says, it is not cool to drink and drive.*

- *There is nothing better than a home-cooked meal, so enjoy it now.*

- *BS may work in high school, but it is seen for what it is in college.*

- *Make friends with at least one professor.*

- *A nice car can wait.*

- *Above all, enjoy it, because before you know it, you will be done. This is the last time in your life when it is okay to be broke, you can sleep in, you get two weeks off for Christmas and one week in the spring, and you still have limited responsibilities.*

Good luck and have fun! I know I did!

During the data collection phase of the UW SOUL, our offices were moved from an ugly concrete building built in the 1960s to a shiny, new, 21st-century, brick building. The building we left sits on the western edge of the campus, and from that building, our fourth-floor windows offered a fascinating view of diverse commerce and human life moving along the colorful street adjacent to campus, the street known as "the Ave." In contrast, our new fourth-floor windows face a yellow brick office building exactly like ours, separated from ours only by the width of an alley. In moving, we went from a busy, ever-changing view of people in motion to a view of an unchanging wall of perfectly spaced, perfectly still bricks, punctuated by regularly spaced windows occasionally framing the anonymous face of an insurance company worker. Or so we thought, before we discovered the time we eventually called "brick magic."

Every bright day at noon, the overhead sun creates depth through shadows, and the seemingly flat brick wall across the alley from our office windows gives up its secret. Though competently laid, the bricks in this wall are neither exactly the same size nor perfectly placed. The severely angled light and shadows reveal curves in the bricks, color variations, waves in the mortar—planes and depths in what appeared to be a flat surface. For no more than 15 minutes, these shadowy patterns display themselves, make their subtle adjustments, and reveal what they reveal. Then the sun passes the narrow crack between the buildings, the shadows disappear, and the bricks across the alley become flat and nearly indistinguishable from one another once more.

On a campus the size of the University of Washington, it is possible to look out over the thousands of undergraduates and think of them as something like our brick wall at 11:00 a.m., when each brick seems bright but uniform. Indeed, even in our own work in the UW SOUL, when we have had the pleasure of seeing many students in full light, we have often spoken here of their uniformity and sameness.

Our wall gives us two lessons. If the bricks were uniform and if the mortar were perfectly even with the front surfaces of the bricks, there would be no magic time. It is difference and the accident of light that creates magic. The second lesson is that magic times are often fleeting. For our wall that time is only 15 minutes in 24 hours, and then only if the sun is not obscured by clouds and only if we are not sitting in a meeting somewhere else.

In this book, while we have presented the whole "wall" of students, we have also tried to illuminate our undergraduates in such a way that their unique colors, patterns, textures, shadings, and placements are visible over time. This chapter summarizes that work. It includes a discussion of the effects of the UW SOUL on the students who participated in it, an overview of the conclusions drawn in previous chapters, and a final case study, which is a follow up with Jeremy Nolan, the student whose story began this book in Chapter 1. This chapter concludes with a complete list of UW SOUL conclusions and their teaching and assessment implications.

Effects of UW SOUL on Participants

In this section, we discuss student perceptions of the effects of participating in the UW SOUL and effects of the study on retention and four-year graduation rates.

Participation in UW SOUL and Students' Learning

The majority of our UW SOUL students, both those in Group 1 and in Group 2, reported that participation affected their educational experience. At the end of the study or earlier, when individuals were about to graduate, we asked via email what effects, if any, participation in UW SOUL had on their educations. Possibly because they had completed their parts in the study and we had no carrots on sticks to motivate response, not all students responded to the question. Of the 159 participants (69% of those eligible) who answered the question, 75 (47%) of them were from Group 1, the group which had a great deal of personal contact with researchers, including face-to-face contact via interviews, yearly focus groups, and the process of turning in portfolios. The remaining 84 (53%) were from Group 2, the group that had no face-to-face contact with our office and knew us only through email and survey responses.

Overall, 76% of the respondents said that their participation in the study had positively affected their educations. About half of the remaining 24%, as well as a number of students in the previous group, said that they had appreciated participating, because they believed their participation could contribute something of value to future undergraduates, as these two quotations illustrate:

> Although this study did not have any direct effect on my education, I strongly believe that this will help students in the future. Through this study, students who are participating are given the opportunity to share their experiences and express their inner thoughts (about any aspect of UW education) freely. Future students will someday face struggles that we've encountered here and find the results of this study helpful.

> The biggest effect is that I feel better connected to the university. I'm here taking classes and learning, but I also feel like I'm giving back to the school. Getting to express my likes and dislikes might improve things for future students.

We compared the responses of transfer students with those of freshmen and the responses of students in Group 1 with those in Group 2. Slightly more transfer students said that their experience in the study had contributed to their educations, but these differences were not statistically significant. A slightly higher percentage of Group 1 students than Group 2 students said that their educations had been affected by study participation, but that difference was not statistically significant either.

Regarding the nature of change, 58% said that participation in the UW SOUL had caused them to reflect on and think critically about their undergraduate experience. Many of these students said that this reflection had guided decisions about courses or academic direction. Some spoke of the reflective process as helping them engage more actively in their own academic experience. Others said that reflection helped them synthesize that experience, and still others said that through the reflective process, they had learned something about themselves. The following quotations illustrate this category of response:

> I do think that participating in SOUL affected my education. It made me think about aspects of my learning that I would not have considered. The end of quarter questions and the end of year interview really made me consider what I am actually getting out of my education. If I noticed through the surveys that I wasn't using my resources enough (e.g., using office hours, asking questions during class), then I tried to make an effort the next quarter to correct that. I think that participating in SOUL altered the way I learned and changed the amount of learning that actually occurred from quarter to quarter.

> Participating in SOUL has helped tremendously in examining what I need to do to increase my education and learning practices while in school, and I feel that I will be able to take this examining process with me into my next job or endeavor.

> Participating in the UW Study of Undergraduate Learning has had an effect on my education, because it has asked me to question what I am doing at the UW and why I am doing it at every step of the way. Having to constantly reflect on my experiences has made me analyze whether or not my chosen path/career is still fitting with who I am.

> In all honesty, I think this study has affected my education. This study has forced me to reflect on the classes I have taken,

the experiences I have had, and face certain truths (like my own procrastination) that I might have ignored.

While we asked no other direct questions about the impact of participation on students' experience, throughout the course of the study students often mentioned that they were grateful to be a part of it. These two students' unprompted comments from their interviews serve as illustrations:

> I want to say thank you for giving me the opportunity to participate in this study. It always provided some way for me to formally put together what I have been through, and I think that was a healthy process for me. It is in a lot of young people's best interest to answer some of the questions I have been answering—where do you think you are, where are you going, what experience stands out to you? These questions help solidify your identity and your confidence and help both of those grow.

> I think this study is really cool. It allows me to analyze, to look back, and that has been really good for me. It gives me perspective. You don't know where you are unless you look back and see where you came from, and doing that each year—looking back at papers, at my grades, at courses I took before—that has taught me a lot. It makes me a more whole person. I look around at my friends, and I see that they don't have that same kind of perspective. I don't think I would have done that on my own as much.

In addition, although we made no systematic effort to contact study participants after 2003, several contacted us. Their comments suggested that the reflective value many students spoke of may have continued after the study's end. For example, two years after the study ended, one of the participants, an engineering major, sent this email message:

> I was just going through some old emails and I ran across some of our correspondence. I just wanted to write and say thanks for that survey. While the money was nice, some of those questions you asked me have stayed with me and I believe will for a long time. You really helped me learn how to stop and think about things more. Just wanted to say thanks.

In addition to the large group of students who spoke about the contribution of self-reflection to their learning, about 6% said that their participation in the study contributed to their sense that the university cared about their learning, as this student's quotation suggests:

> Just the fact that there is a study being done in efforts to improve the quality of teaching made me feel more confident in the university. In a school that's as huge as the UW, taking an interest in individual students (me!) was really nice.

Finally, another 6%, all of them in Group 2, said that they had become more aware of what they were missing in their education by reading questions on the web-based survey each quarter. This student's quotation illustrates this category of responses:

> The questions about having a mentor or a professor that I looked to affected me. I never did have one but it made me wonder how things would have been different if I had.

The remaining responses specified benefits that were highly individualized and, therefore, could not be categorized.

One of the current conversations in the assessment community concerns whether students who are playing a role in the assessment of institutions and classes should benefit from that process. For example, is it legitimate to administer a performance-based standardized test on quantitative reasoning that measures students' learning in this area, if we never intend to report results to the individuals who took the test? Students' responses to the question about what they learned by participating in the UW SOUL clearly indicate that participants benefited from the assessment process. Furthermore, the amount of interaction students had with the assessment process did not seem to make a difference in their sense of what they gained from it; comments from students in Groups 1 and 2 were similar in content. Most of them felt that they had gained insight into their own experience, which Bransford, Brown, and Cocking (2000) assert is a major benefit to students' learning.

Participation in UW SOUL, Retention, and Four-Year Graduation Rates

Students' open-ended responses about their participation in the UW SOUL noted the study's effects on their undergraduate experience. In addition, comparisons of retention and four-year graduation rates, introduced in Chapter 2, raise the question of whether participation in UW SOUL had an intervening effect on students' movement through college.[1] Table 10.1 presents a comparison of graduation, retention, and withdrawal rates for UW SOUL participants who had taken the Entering Student Survey, non-SOUL students who had also taken the Entering Student Survey, and non-SOUL students who had not taken the survey.[2] The differences in Table 10.1 are highly significant,[3] with UW SOUL participants having a four-year graduation rate and a lower withdrawal rate than those of either comparison group. Table 10.2 presents the same comparison for Group 1 and Group 2 students. The differences were not significant. Thus, increased graduation and retention rates were observed for participants in both Group 1 and in Group 2, although the amount of face-to-face contact the groups had with researchers varied greatly.

Table 10.1. *Graduation, Retention, and Withdrawal Rates for UW SOUL Students, Other Entering Student Survey Takers, and Students Who Did Not Take the ESS*

	In SOUL[4]	Not SOUL, ESS	Not SOUL, Not ESS
Graduated	63.5	53.0	52.7
Enrolled	24.0	29.9	26.7
Withdrawn	12.5	17.1	20.6

Table 10.2. *Graduation, Retention, and Withdrawal Rates for Group 1 and Group 2 Students*

	Group 1	Group 2
Graduated	59.9	66.7
Enrolled	26.1	22.2
Withdrawn	14.1	11.1

What caused this difference in graduation and retention rates between study and non-study students? As discussed in Chapter 2, UW SOUL students entered the UW with somewhat higher entrance test scores and high school GPAs than those of other students, and this academic difference may have influenced graduation and retention rates. However, graduation and retention rates for other entering student survey takers, whose entering GPAs and test scores were similar to those of UW SOUL participants, argue otherwise. In contrast to graduation and retention rates for the UW SOUL participants, the rates for the other ESS takers were more like the rates for non-SOUL students than those for SOUL participants (see Table 10.1). Perhaps the study acted as an intervention. A positive effect of participation in UW SOUL on gradation and retention would support Tinto's (1993) argument about the relationship between meaningful connections with faculty/staff and retention. In addition, these positive results may confirm the participants' own perceptions about the relationship between self-reflection and their educational choices.

Unfortunately, we did not design the UW SOUL as an intervention study, nor did we study intervention effects in any detail. Therefore, we cannot draw strong conclusions about causal relationships between connection or self-reflection and retention or four-year graduation. This area needs further study.

Study Conclusions

Our focus on the six areas of learning led us to the conclusions, represented in the final section of this chapter. Of those conclusions, six appear to cross areas of study. This section summarizes those six areas.

There Are Significant Gaps Between High School and College Learning Experiences

Gaps between high school and college experiences are most frequently noted in students' quantitative reasoning and writing experiences, but they were mentioned in other areas, as well. In terms of quantitative thinking, the gap that students reported was between plug-and-chug equations and using quantitative methods to think and analyze in a wide range of settings, including math courses. In terms of writing, the reported gap was between writing for English courses in high school and writing arguments in the disciplines in college. In other areas, students reported doing thinking, accessing information, and using technology in ways unlike any they had been asked to do in their high schools; however, students were not as explicit about the problems inherent in these differences as they were about differences between high school and college quantitative reasoning and writing. These gaps remind us that 100- and 200-level courses must teach explicitly into the gap so that students do not get lost there. The gaps also point out the importance of substantive connections between high school and college faculty.

All Academic Learning Is Mediated by the Disciplines

As UW SOUL findings made clear, learning in college is mediated in all areas by the disciplinary context in which it occurs. This mediation is not only true for learning in the major, but also for the courses identified as "general education." Students writing papers for 100-level history courses are expected to adhere to argumentative practices and critical thinking strategies that differ from the papers they may write for 100-level philosophy or 100-level chemistry classes. This reality was so pronounced that when students completed their majors, they identified critical thinking with the practices of the disciplines in which they had been immersed for two or more years. An earlier study on writing at the UW (Beyer & Graham, 1994a) found the same to be true for students' conceptions of "good writing."

Responses of UW SOUL participants suggest that although students who came to the university directly from high school may have had some experience with the disciplinary nature of knowledge—writing lab reports for chemistry classes, for example, that were different from papers they wrote for English courses—they did not understand these differences as disciplinary. Furthermore, as we discussed earlier, disciplines that students took in high school were often quite different from their college counterparts. Our students' high school history courses, for instance, appeared to be focused on learning generally accepted narratives of events, while college history was often focused on making and supporting arguments about why things happened as they did.

Even students who came to the university from community colleges sometimes had little experience with the force of disciplinarity on shaping the boundaries, the content, the methods, and the paths of fields of knowledge. However, UW SOUL transfer students from community colleges often entered directly into majors, where they were immediately immersed in the language and thinking practices of those fields. In contrast, students entering the UW from high schools often floundered in their first two years, because they were unaware that movement from courses in one discipline to those in another was movement from one set of practices to another. This lack of awareness was exacerbated by the fact that faculty and staff are often not explicit about disciplinary practices and purposes, particularly in the early courses students take.

Assessment Must Be Centered in Departments

Because academic learning is a disciplinary act, the assessment of that learning must be designed, implemented, and reported by departments. Furthermore, the focus of that assessment must be on learning in the major. The work of centrally housed assessment professionals, such as ourselves, must be to help departments think about their learning goals (for majors and for undergraduates taking their courses who are not majors), design strategies for assessing them, work with faculty on classroom-based assessment, assist in the creation of assessment tools, and join faculty in conducting assessment work. Central assessment offices can also create and administer university-wide practices, such as course evaluation systems and alumni surveys, and conduct studies aimed at broader questions—such as the UW SOUL—that can inform and shape departmental assessment and institutional policy and practices. However, judgments about student learning must be made by those who can understand and interpret such learning. At most colleges and universities, those people are departmental faculty.

Learning About Others and Oneself Is a Central Part of the College Experience and May Be Affected by the Disciplines of Students' Majors

College changes students. Almost without exception, undergraduates learned who they were, what they hoped to achieve, what they believed, and how they might accomplish their goals. The impetus for these changes did not reside only in the classroom, but was found in every corner of students' experience. Often such change was the result of interaction between classroom learning and outside experience. The contribution of study abroad, undergraduate research, internship, service-learning, volunteer work, and paid work experiences to students' self-knowledge, self-confidence, and self-awareness cannot be overstated. Perhaps because they were coupled with classroom learning that often challenges students' thinking, sense of themselves, and understanding of others at the same time, these experiential learning opportunities helped students meet both academic and personal learning goals. In looking at the interactions between experiential learning, classroom learning, and self-knowledge, we could see clearly the connection between Arnett's (2000) concept of emerging adulthood and its relationship to a time of exploration.

Another significant contributor to personal growth was self-reflection, as seen in students' responses to questions about the study's impact on their learning. And a third contributor was likely students' majors. Students in majors that engaged them in ethical questions, social issues, conversations about diversity, and conflicting viewpoints may have fostered personal growth more than majors that primarily transmitted a body of knowledge and practices. However, this possibility needs further study.

We saw no evidence in the UW SOUL that student growth was linear or staged. Furthermore, we saw no evidence that personal or intellectual growth was a consistent response to new challenges in which students experienced instability. While often such challenges motivated change, they sometimes led to withdrawal and retreat. Students' responses to such challenges depended a great deal upon the contexts in which they occurred—for example, whether students' felt safe to fail—as well as on the students' interests and backgrounds.

Students Want To Be Intellectually Challenged

Students told us again and again that they wanted to be challenged. It is important to note that challenges that represented too great a leap—or perhaps more to the point, too great a leap without a safety net—sometimes killed students' interest in subjects. However, students welcomed challenging courses and assignments, even when only modest amounts of help in meeting those challenges was offered. Many students easily succeeded in high school, and they came to the university hoping that their instructors would no longer permit them to cruise through their courses and assignments with little thinking or engagement. They told us in focus groups, email, and interviews that they appreciated having to grapple with difficult tasks and ideas. This, of course, is understandable; a sense of accomplishment only comes with the completion of challenging tasks. Most community college students did not describe this need to be "tested," probably because they had already proven to themselves that they could succeed in the rigorous climates of their community colleges. While they were sometimes annoyed about having to start over in demonstrating their capabilities, they welcomed the challenges their majors presented.

Often the majors students eventually selected coincided with the thinking they described as their most challenging in their first and second years at the UW, and students told us again and again that the classes that asked them to think were the ones in which they learned the most and did the best. In focus groups through all four years of the study, UW SOUL participants universally expressed contempt for classes that were easy.

The key difference between challenges that students valued and those they did not was the support students felt they received for trying to meet these challenges. If they had support—for example, explicit instruction, access to faculty and teaching assistants, the ability to work with peers—then these challenges were exhilarating. If they felt they had no support—for example, if they were presented with a new challenge on a final exam—then they often felt set up to fail.

Students' Learning in College Comes From Many Sources and Their Interaction, But Faculty Are the Key

As stated earlier, student learning came from a wide range of sources, inside and outside the university. The key element to learning in college was clearly faculty. Students wanted direct interaction with faculty, and the most significant changes in students were covered with faculty fingerprints. Students said that they also learned from their peers, and it was clear that often learning from peers was structured by faculty. In addition, students learned about academics from experience, and they placed a great deal of value on hands-on, experiential learning of all kinds, from lab experiments to assignments that required them to gather the real-life experiences of others. Hands-on experiences were considered valuable for what they contributed to academic learning and vice versa. The interaction of the two seemed to be key.

Students Have Complex Definitions and Multiple Goals for Learning; to a Great Extent, They Meet Those Goals

UW SOUL participants' sense of what it meant to be educated was complex when they arrived at the university in 1999, and it remained complex when the study ended in 2003. While they became more focused on their own academic goals (usually at the start of their second year) than they were on entry, they still retained complex definitions of what it meant to be successful in college. Furthermore, at the end of their time at the UW, they generally felt that they had met many of these goals, even though the focus of the university was academics. We believe that with increasing emphasis on active learning strategies, peer-learning groups, and student self-assessment—all approaches that research shows contribute to learning—higher education plays into students' nonacademic learning goals. In other words, by using methods that are the best for teaching students academic skills and content, faculty can advance students' complex learning goals.

Last Words: Jeremy's Path

It seems fair to let a student have the final words in a book that has attempted to capture so many of the students' words. Thus, we return to Jeremy Nolan, the student whose case study began this book. As we noted, Jeremy graduated in March 2004 with B.S. degrees in biology and psychology and academic minors in anthropology and quantitative science. In late autumn 2005, he graciously agreed to submit to a phone interview to fill us in on what he was doing and what he then felt about his undergraduate experience.

Jeremy told us that after he graduated, he took a trip to Thailand and Laos, checking out a field site in northern Thailand, a wildlife sanctuary run by the State University of New York–Stony Brook. Those at the site were looking for field researchers and had research interests similar to Jeremy's, but he said he "didn't feel like dropping everything at that point and doing a field apprenticeship so soon after college." So Jeremy returned to Seattle and took a full-time job as a research technologist in the UW's primate center, the same lab he had worked in since 2001. While there, he worked with a postdoctorate faculty member, who was soon hired by a major research university in the southern

United States. The professor wanted to start a lab there, and he took Jeremy with him to set it up.

Jeremy's work at the new university was complex. He was responsible for the physical and psychological well-being of two rhesus monkeys whose diet and fluid intake needed careful monitoring. In his new job at the animal research center, Jeremy trained the monkeys to perform cognitive tasks, identified and implemented procedures to keep the monkeys happy, kept the laboratory well organized and well stocked, designed systems for detailed tracking of animal care procedures, and oversaw and managed surgical procedures. He described his work at the lab as both challenging and fun:

> It's always amazing what you learn from a monkey. Learning and teaching two brand new monkeys, Bob and Matt, [was hard]—training them, for example, how to come out of their cages and sit in their chairs, stuff that I took for granted in Seattle because those monkeys were already trained. There have been so many firsts in starting this job. The first time a monkey got loose, for instance. We've been using hand-me-down cages, these old baboon cages that seem like they're from the 1960s. You could just see the original NASA space guys keeping their chimps in them. We had to train Bob and Matt to be walked out and sit in their chairs. The doorways to these old cages slide up and down, and I opened the door too much and Bob came running out. I remained calm—but the principal investigator let out a sharp scream and ran out of the room.

While continuing to work with Bob and Matt, Jeremy made plans for his future. He said that he hoped to take the Graduate Record Exam (GRE) soon after he finished revising a manuscript for *Primates,* a peer-reviewed journal. Jeremy had postponed taking the exam primarily because, although he has had one success after another in college, he was afraid of not doing well on it. As he put it:

> It's a big test like the SATs and getting into grad school makes or breaks your career. I am such a perfectionist, and I hate doing stuff like this and especially when you have to study in your own time. I'm just afraid of not doing it 100%.

Jeremy also said that he may take a biological anthropology class spring semester, when his free-class benefit at his place of employment kicks in. He is considering the possibility of working on a master's degree in anthropology at his new institution, but his bigger goal is to complete a Ph.D.:

I think I want to be a professor in behavioral ecology and monkey economics. Behavioral ecology is the interaction of primate behavior and the environment—how the ecology shapes or affects their behavior. I want to do field work in behavioral ecology. It's interesting, and the rapid deconstruction of natural forests and resources means there's not much time to study this stuff in the wild and there's so much that we don't know yet. It's important that we study this now while we have a chance to. We can better understand the evolution of humans and human behavior by understanding what primates do—understanding where we came from. Monkey economics is a train of thought in the neural field right now. [Recent research has shown] that when monkeys are making decisions, they are using a cost-benefit analysis. I don't know a lot about this, but I think it's interesting and the beginning of a bridge between the neurological sciences and the ecological sciences.

When asked if he felt he had changed in any way since he had been away from the UW, Jeremy said:

The whole moving experience has made me grow up a lot. Living in Seattle where you were born and raised for 23 years and moving to a place where you only know one person who's your boss, having to really budget because you know that your salary is all the money you are going to get—I feel more grown up now. I can't drive to my mom's house if I don't have a lot of money and convince her to take me out to dinner. I don't have that option. This makes me feel like the next step is easier, too.

In addition, like many people his age, Jeremy said that he felt old:

I feel terribly old. The age of 24 did it. You are no longer in that college age. It was also my first birthday away from home. And the funny thing is that here people are always asking me how I'm liking school this semester—and I have to tell them I'm not a student. Luckily I can see three more stages in my life—grad school and becoming a student again, the stage of postdoc, and the stage of faculty. What is great about my situation is that I know that there are things to still be done. There are so many places I want to travel. I want to go to India. I really want to

explore the South Pacific, Europe. I've been really wanting to go
to Rwanda and see the mountain gorillas.

Looking back at his time as an undergraduate, Jeremy said that the education he received was "top-notch:"

> My life at the UW was such a significant and substantive time
> in my life—it just shaped me into who I am today—how I
> critically think about things, how I manage time. I honed
> those skills while I was at the UW. I don't think I'd be the same
> person if I had never attended the UW. I went to college want-
> ing to be a stockbroker, and at the UW I met the right people
> who encouraged me to follow a different path. I was exposed
> to new things that I wouldn't have been exposed to before.
> Let's say I went to some place other than the UW; I probably
> would have ended up in business school, like I had planned.

In addition, we asked Jeremy how he felt about what he had learned about writing, thinking, quantitative reasoning, and research. He said:

> I definitely learned how to write in college, evident in the fact
> that I just sent off a manuscript to a peer-reviewed journal,
> and it didn't get turned down. I won a "paper of the year"
> award from the psych department, and that was an indication
> of learning how to write, but the fact of not having a Ph.D.
> and sending off a paper to a scientific journal and not getting
> flat-out denied says a lot about where my writing ability is. I
> think it was just the program of my studies that helped shape
> my writing ability. And I worked on writing because I knew I
> wanted to pursue an academic career.
>
> I also learned quantitative skills in college. I attribute all
> my quantitative skills to the Center for Quantitative Sciences.
> It was effective because it was applied to my discipline; it was
> very student oriented; and it had an office with a lot of text-
> books and resources that you could check out. And also in
> choosing the faculty, the director sought out faculty who had
> unique ways of reaching and teaching students. They had high
> student focus. Each course I took was taught in effective ways.
> In the 400-level stats classes, it was more than just learning the
> theory of stats but also learning practical applications—how

to do it yourself. And that affected my ability to understand my own data for my own research.

I [learned to] think about things more critically—more from a scientific perspective. I don't take things for how they are, but I question how they are the way they are and how someone came up with that conclusion. In high school, I never had to think about anything. Everything came too easy for me. It wasn't till college that I was actually challenged with something.

I learned everything about research at the UW. If you are doing research in high school, you just have to find a book in a public library somewhere. I learned that the UW library system is excellent. It was easy to find things and here, it is a bit more difficult. I'm basically still using what I learned at the UW about research design, methodology, and analysis and applying it to here.

When asked what advice he might give new students, Jeremy said:

Here's what I've always told people: by the end of the first week of the quarter, make sure the professor knows your name. I did that and doing that the first couple of quarters really helped. Down the road it really does benefit you. It's okay to sit up front. It's okay to ask questions. It's okay to look like a suck-up. It's okay to be interested in school.

Finally, we asked Jeremy to review the list he wrote in 2002 of the 11 things he hoped to do after he graduated. He said:

- Work in Antarctica (sp?). *Not enough time!*

- Capuchin field site in Costa Rica. *That was more an opportunity to do before graduate school, but now I feel I don't need another year doing someone else's research before I get started on my own.*

- Teach English in foreign country. *No, I was looking at that as an opportunity to go travel and figure out what I wanted to do, and I pretty much know what I want to do now.*

- Trek through Africa/climb Mt. Kilaminjaro. *This one's still on my list.*

- Scuba instructor in Thailand. *Maybe when I retire.*

- Ph.D. *Still on the list.*

- EMT. *I don't want to do this any more. It doesn't fit in with my plans.*

- Skydive. *I still want to do it.*

- Bungee jump. *And I still want to do this.*

- Snowboard. *I want to learn to do this eventually. There's not a lot of snow or mountains around here. That's something I really kick myself for not doing while I was in Seattle.*

- See Mt. Everest (possibly climb . . . ?) *Yeah, I want to continue to travel, to become a citizen of the world by traveling.*

While Jeremy Nolan's experience as an undergraduate in college was unique, much of it was marked by the same things that marked the lives of other students. Like them, he moved away from an easier life in high school into the greater demands presented by college. He found a community of friends. He worked hard at jobs outside class. He used his credit card to finance some of his education. He was a son and a brother to people who cared about him, and he had a wide array of friends who demanded his time. He watched TV. He had moments of self-doubt, frustration with what he did not understand, and irritation with faculty members and staff who made things unnecessarily difficult. He learned that he had abilities, interests, talents, and capacities that he had never dreamed he possessed before he came to college. His classes, professors, and fellow students helped him open these doors into himself so that he could discover who he really was and what he might be capable of doing. He is by nature a happy person, unpretentious and grateful for his life. We wish him and his fellow travelers, human and otherwise, a joyful journey.

Summary of UW SOUL Conclusions and Implications for Teaching and Assessment

Personal Growth

Students Enter and Exit the University With Complex Ideas About Learning

Conclusion. Undergraduates defined academic success in multidimensional ways. They saw college as a place that offered them the chance to learn about many things and, to a large extent, they measured their own academic success by how many learning experiences they tapped into.

Teaching implications. Faculty can and often did take advantage of students' multidimensional definitions of learning by providing them with opportunities to interact with peers, especially peers unlike themselves; to engage in active and experiential learning; to think reflectively about their own learning; and to engage with them in the study of topics that fascinate them.

Assessment implications. Assessment of learning must include social, personal, and academic learning if it is to match students' goals for their own educations.

Academic Difficulty Can Be Productive, But It Does Not Always Foster Growth

Conclusion. Most students experienced some kind of academic disappointment ("the hammering"), particularly in their first year. While this experience was often beneficial to students' growth, it also sometimes stopped learning.

Teaching implications. Faculty, particularly those teaching 100- and 200-level courses, need to remember that students are experiencing processes that are often simultaneously generative and difficult. Faculty can help students manage effects of the hammering by identifying it as a natural part of the learning process.

Assessment implications. We need to continue to track how students respond to academic failures, paying particular attention to how differing groups respond. For example, do women respond differently than men? Does a low grade on an exam mean something different to underrepresented minority students than it does to students in the majority?

Students Change Intellectually, Socially, and Personally While in College

Conclusion. While students experienced varying opportunities for personal growth within the structures of majors, all students experienced some growth and change. They gained in personal and intellectual independence in their first year. In the second year, they gained direction and focus, and in their majors, they gained expertise and often a community of like thinkers.

Teaching implications. Seniors are different people than they were as freshmen. Often, the way we teach upper-level courses—allowing students greater intellectual freedom and requiring them to work independently—already acknowledges this reality. If we build opportunities for self-reflection, intellectual freedom, and social interaction into students' earliest learning opportunities, we will better prepare them to meet the academic demands ahead.

Assessment implications. Assessment research should include longitudinal studies so that we can better understand the process and the nature of change that students experience.

Diversity

Recruitment and Retention of Diverse Students Are Important to Learning

Conclusion. Diversity in all its forms contributed to the learning of all students, and most students valued that contribution. We need to understand what makes a campus a welcoming environment for all students and provide that.

Teaching implications. When faculty make use of small group work, it is beneficial if students have opportunities to work in more than one group during the course, so that they can experience as much diversity in students and ideas as possible. This may be particularly important in 100- and 200-level courses.

Assessment implications. Institutional study needs to focus on the demographics of both student and faculty populations, perceptions of climate based on ethnicity and gender, and attitudes toward diversity. In addition, we need to continue to examine the effects of diversity on student learning.

Student Learning Regarding Diversity Is Disciplinary

Conclusion. Efforts to integrate diverse content into appropriate courses pay off. However, students in some disciplines learn less about diversity in their normal course of study than do others.

Teaching implications. Faculty need to integrate instruction on diversity issues where it fits into the curriculum of their fields.

Assessment implications. Departments should think about learning goals for diversity that naturally emerge from disciplinary content and methods, as well as the ways they might assess whether they are meeting those goals.

Institutions Need To Build Structures for Interaction That Cross Disciplines and Ethnicity

Conclusion. In general, entering students valued and desired interaction with diverse others, but at some point in their first two years, they become less willing to be proactive in seeking it out. Students need structures that do not allow them to avoid interacting with those who are different from themselves, as well as structures that allow students to experience others like themselves.

Teaching implications. As stated earlier, when faculty make use of small group work, it is beneficial if students get opportunities to work in more than one group during the course so that they can experience as much diversity in students and ideas as possible. This may be particularly important in 100- and 200-level courses.

Assessment implications. Once they are created, structures that foster interactions among diverse students need to be institutionally evaluated. Institutions need to remember that it is also essential for students of color to interact with students from ethnic backgrounds like their own and provide paths for such interaction. Institutional tracking of retention and attrition rates among ethnic groups and of the campus climate for students of color, as well as for other students, should be routine.

Critical Thinking and Problem Solving

Critical Thinking and Problem Solving Are Disciplinary

Conclusion. Generic models of critical thinking and problem solving, though perhaps accurate at some high level of abstraction, are fairly useless in helping us (and our students) understand what students must actually do when they are asked to think critically or to solve problems in specific contexts. In college the contexts are academic, and critical thinking is disciplinary.

Teaching implications. Faculty in the disciplines need to be explicit in teaching their students how to do the kinds of thinking they require, particularly in 100- and 200-level courses. Recognizing that effective pedagogy for teaching critical thinking may also be discipline-specific, faculty in the disciplines need to be given support to determine the most effective disciplinary strategies to teach students what it means to think in their fields.

Assessment implications. Disciplines, departments, and programs must define, articulate, and identify examples of critical thinking and problem solving internally; identify their learning goals for students in these areas; and assess how well their students meet them.

Students' Abilities To Think Critically and Problem Solve Increase While in College

Conclusion. Students' discussion of their critical thinking and problem solving, as well as the tasks they described, increased in complexity and specificity.

Teaching implications. Faculty need to determine if the critical thinking and problem solving gains students make in their disciplines are "enough."

Assessment implications. To determine if aggregate increases we detected are sufficient, disciplines and departments will need to determine what paths they want their students to take, and how best to measure success among their majors.

Students Gradually Adopt the Definitions of Critical Thinking and Problem Solving That They Perceive in Their Majors

Conclusion. As seniors, students' definitions of critical thinking are similar to those they attribute to their majors. These gains in expertise in the disciplines of their majors likely brought with them losses in awareness of how other disciplines may think or what they value.

Teaching implications. Inability to remember our own paths to expertise makes it difficult to design curricula and pedagogy that bring novices into our fields of study as full participants. Faculty need to remember their own time of unknowing, to make use of self-reflection, and to use a variety of classroom assessment techniques that help them understand what students are and are not learning and that also advance students' learning.

Assessment implications. The blinding effects of one's discipline make it imperative that people from inside the disciplines evaluate students' learning in those fields. Design of longitudinal assessment studies like UW SOUL should include active participation of disciplinary faculty. Faculty should receive help in integrating course-based assessment into their classes.

Writing

There Is a Gap Between High School and College Writing and Students Falter in That Gap

Conclusion. In contrast with high school writing, writing in college was argumentative, rooted in disciplinary practices, and reliant on sources outside the self for support. The focus was not on what the student thought about X but on what the student thought about what others think about X.

Teaching implications. Instruction that makes the writing practices of the discipline explicit to students and includes examples of good student writing helps students navigate early writing demands. Frequent opportunities for feedback on required drafts of papers help students understand disciplinary writing practices and improve writing skill.

Assessment implications. We need to help students understand the limitations of standardized assessments of writing. College and high school faculty need to discuss the writing differences students find when they enter college.

Writing Is a Disciplinary Act From Students' First Classes at the UW to Their Last

Conclusion. All writing is mediated by the disciplines. In their first two years, students must figure out and implement the writing practices of several disciplines, usually simultaneously. When they become immersed in the disciplines of their majors, they learn to write in those fields.

Teaching implications. We need to provide students with more explicit writing instruction—instruction that includes disciplinary methodology as well as information about content and correct format. In addition, we need to provide students with opportunities to draft, get feedback on those drafts, and revise them.

Assessment implications. Assessment of student writing in college should be conducted by faculty in the departments of students' majors.

Challenging Writing Is Argumentative and Research Based

Conclusion. The writing students found the most challenging involved arguments that required them to formulate their own hypotheses, use good evidence in support of those arguments, and conduct research effectively in the discipline.

Teaching implications. Paper lengths should match purposes. For example, short papers can help students learn concepts. Longer papers can help students learn to sustain resource-based, complex arguments. Faculty need to help students learn effective argumentation within their field.

Assessment implications. Departments must conduct writing assessment of their majors. Departmental assessment should include examination of students' responses to complex writing assignments that ask them to formulate and support researched arguments.

Quantitative Reasoning

There Is a Gap Between High School and College QR and Students Falter in That Gap

Conclusion. In contrast to high school QR, college level QR was perceived to be harder, more complex, and more focused on application, both in math courses and in courses across the curriculum. College-level QR required more thinking than high school QR required.

Teaching implications. Faculty across the curriculum who require students to use quantitative reasoning skills need to understand that they are asking students to do something they have had little experience with, and they need to teach across that gap.

Assessment implications. Students' success in high school math courses may not predict an easy time with quantitative reasoning at the college level. Students need to be informed about differences between high school math and college QR.

Most Students Are Comfortable With Their QR Abilities, But . . .

Conclusion. No matter what their actual QR abilities were, most students were comfortable with them. However, this result was at odds with commonly held faculty views that students were not well prepared to do QR.

Teaching implications. Students need more instruction in how to apply mathematical concepts in disciplines that require such application.

Assessment implications. Classroom-based assessment would help faculty track how well students are learning.

Students' Learning Paths in QR Depend on Their Majors

Conclusion. Math and QR instruction were front-loaded in the undergraduate curriculum at the UW. Beyond that, the QR paths students took were highly variable depending on their majors and sometimes even within them.

Teaching implications. As with other kinds of learning, students' success with QR required that faculty be explicit in their teaching about how to use QR, especially at the 100- and 200-levels. In addition, students needed help in understanding the value QR adds to any discipline.

Assessment implications. Departments must conduct QR assessment of their majors. Centralized administration of a standardized test is unlikely to capture the necessary QR abilities of any major. However, some majors may feel no need to measure QR unless the institution has a learning goal that includes numeracy.

Information Technology and Literacy

Information Technology and Literacy Are Disciplinary in Nature

Conclusion. All students use computers to locate information, and they use the university libraries' interface to access the titles, abstracts, journal articles, and the locations of books and journals. However, preferred library resources, as well as specific websites, were unique to disciplines. In addition, the technology students used in order to use information, where one might locate information, how one ought to evaluate and use it, and the purposes for its use varied quite a bit across disciplines. Even definitions of information technology varied by discipline.

Teaching implications. Different disciplines have different criteria for evaluation of sources. Faculty need to be explicit in their teaching about how one goes about finding information that is credible in their fields, how one can tell if the information is credible, and how to incorporate such information within one's own work.

Assessment implications. Assessment needs to be done within disciplines, because accessing, evaluating, and using information is related to disciplinary practice. Even so, assessing information literacy is difficult because so much of information literacy—the decisions a student makes as she moves through an information gathering/using process—is internal.

An issue that remains for both teaching and assessment is whether faculty and administrators are knowledgeable enough about the most recent technologies to teach students how to use them and to assess that use.

Nearly All Students Are Adding to the Knowledge That Assignments, Lectures, and Research Impart

Conclusion. Students have become independent researchers, constantly gathering information, both academic and personal. Accessing information online was not simply a way to gather information; it was also a way to learn.

Teaching implications. It seems likely that this new reality where students are engaged in self-initiated research could create amazing new teaching opportunities for faculty.

Assessment implications. Classroom assessment is likely not capturing the learning that students gain via unrequired research that is course related. ITL assessment plans should have student input. The nature of the new opportunities will determine how they can be assessed.

General Learning

Learning Comes From Multiple Sources and Is Both Individualized and Uneven

Conclusion. All students learned, but their advances were individualized—in large part based on their majors. The idea of general education where all students share the same educational outcomes, is unlikely.

How much students learned was affected by how much exploration they did—taking a variety of courses, studying abroad, making friends with students from differing cultures, becoming involved in internships, volunteer work, or research with faculty, and so on.

Teaching implications. Regarding teaching implications, faculty should remember the key roles that their disciplines play in students' overall learning, and, thus, make explicit what students are expected to learn in their courses and disciplines. But we should also remember that our students' learning takes place all over campus, as well as in places far away from it, making assessment of student learning daunting if we are interested in assessing real learning in all its complexity.

Assessment implications. We believe that, given the complexity of the learning that we observed in the UW SOUL, assessment of student learning must be departmental. However, centrally located assessment can be a powerful partner to departmental assessment if it is designed to gather information about how students experience college, makes room for student definitions of learning, and recognizes differences across students and disciplinary practice.

Faculty Are the Key to Students' Learning

Conclusion. Faculty members who are passionate about their subjects, who are experts in those areas, and who communicate that they care that students learn about those subjects contributed the most to students' learning. Such faculty can inspire students to learn about subjects they had no interest in and to major in subjects they had never heard of before entering college.

Teaching implications. Innovation in instructional delivery via technology should be viewed as an aid to foster meaningful faculty-student interaction, rather than as a substitute for it.

Assessment implications. A key measure of the effectiveness of any college or university must be how well that institution fosters, sustains, and rewards excellence in teaching. Regarding rewarding excellence in teaching, administrators need to remember that faculty teach in a wide range of settings, in addition to the classroom.

Students Take Responsibility for Hindering Their Own Learning

Conclusion. For the most part, students blamed themselves for failure to learn. However, they also noted the ways that poor organization of course material, faculty who appear not to care about their learning, and not being asked to think hindered learning.

Teaching implications. Learning is a two-way responsibility, and students are aware of their responsibilities in that relationship. They know that faculty are not responsible for the powerful draw of the *World of Warcraft* or of someone's winsome boyfriend.

Assessment implications. As always, we need to assess what we can control and understand what we cannot.

Students Want To Be Intellectually Challenged

Conclusion. Students' responses to a variety of questions showed that students valued courses that required them to think and asked them to demonstrate that thinking in more ways than one (i.e., not only via exams). Students also wanted instruction in how to do the thinking we require, rather than merely be required to do that thinking. Students did not value courses that were easy or that made few intellectual demands on them.

Teaching implications. We need to ask students to do intellectual work that is challenging, and we need to provide them with instruction for doing it.

Assessment implications. We can assess how well students understand what we hope we are teaching by integrating large and small opportunities to demonstrate understanding into our courses. This kind of classroom-based assessment is the work of faculty members and TAs, rather than departments.

Demonstrating Caring for Students' Learning Will Improve Their Learning

Conclusion. Nearly every student we asked said that engaging them in substantive ways in class—asking what they thought, responding to it, monitoring their understanding, making room in class for their questions—indicated that faculty cared about their learning. Research on learning suggests that such active learning approaches improve student learning.

Teaching implications. Teaching implications of this conclusion take us back to the results reported in Chapter 9, where students described what faculty did to demonstrate that they cared about students' learning and what advanced their learning. These two sets of results would be helpful for faculty members who want to improve student learning.

Assessment implications. Course evaluations may want to take into account students' thinking on what advances their learning in the questions they raise.

Students Learn From Each Other

Conclusion. After faculty, students say that peers—often in the form of study groups—help their learning.

Teaching implications. Faculty can help students benefit from the knowledge peers possess by asking students to work together on small and large projects. Working with peers helps students learn, and such interaction also helps students accomplish a goal that matters to them—social development.

Assessment implications. It is helpful to students when assessment of group projects includes assessment of individual contributions, as well. If departmental assessment includes evaluation of collaboration or team skills, we may want to learn how to teach those skills.

Asking Students To Reflect on Their Learning Increases Their Learning

Conclusion. The importance of metacognition to learning is well established, and students in the UW SOUL reported that participation in the study made them more reflective and that such reflection increased their learning and clarified their direction.

Teaching implications. Self-assessment should be a component of all classrooms. Asking students to self-assess helps them know what they know, see where they have come from, identify the significant markers along the way, and review where they hope they are headed. Self-assessment is a workplace skill, as well as life skill, and we need to do a better job of building self-assessment opportunities—large and small—into our academic environments.

Assessment implications. Self-reflection should be a component of all assessment activities. It is possible to integrate student reflection at the institutional level in smaller ways than we did in the UW SOUL. For example, administrators could announce that a sample of students would be contacted each quarter by email to respond to questions about their experience. Continued over time, this practice would become familiar to students, and their responses would provide valuable information to the institution and serve as an impetus for student reflection.

Endnotes

1) Our results on why students left the UW were unsurprising. Their reasons for leaving the UW were often highly individual—a girlfriend in another city becoming pregnant, a commute impossible to manage for very long, the need to work too many hours to leave enough time for studying. Occasionally, students' reasons for leaving were related to disappointment with their experience at the UW—classes that were too big for students to feel they were learning or the structure of majors too rigid for students to be able to do what they had hoped, for example. Most often, students' reasons for leaving focused on not getting into majors they wanted, and many of those students transferred to institutions that allowed them to complete those majors—most often computer science engineering, business, or nursing.

2) This third group represented the majority of students entering in 1999.

3) $X^2 = 29$, p < 0.00001

4) This category represents students who participated in the UW SOUL for longer than one academic quarter.

Bibliography

AASCU/NASULGC Enrollment Report. (2002). *Findings and trends: Fall 1990–Fall 2000.* Retrieved November 29, 2006, from: www.nasulgc.org/publications/NASULGCAASCU2002_enrollment.pdf

Allen, W. R. (1992). The color of success: African-American college student outcomes at predominantly white and historically black public colleges and universities. *Harvard Educational Review, 62*(1), 26–44.

Angelo, T. A. (1999, May). Doing assessment as if learning matters most. *AAHE Bulletin, 52,* 3–6.

Angelo, T. A., & Cross, K. P. (1993). *Classroom assessment techniques: A handbook for college teachers.* San Francisco, CA: Jossey-Bass.

Appel, M., Cartright, D., Smith, S. G., & Wolf, L. E. (1996). *The Impact of diversity on students: A preliminary view of the research literature.* Washington DC: Association of American Colleges and Universities.

Arenson, K. W. (2006, February 9). Panel explores standard tests for colleges. *New York Times,* p. A20.

Arnett, J. J. (1997). Young people's conceptions of the transition to adulthood. *Youth and society, 29*(1), 3–21.

Arnett, J. J. (2000). Emerging adulthood: A theory of development from the late teens through the twenties. *The American Psychologist, 55*(5), 469–480.

Association of College and Research Libraries. (2000). *Information literacy competency standards for higher education.* Chicago, IL: American Library Association.

Astin, A. W. (1993a). *What matters in college: Four critical years revisited.* San Francisco, CA: Jossey-Bass.

Astin, A. W. (1993b). Diversity and multiculturalism on the campus: How are students affected? *Change 25*(2), 44–49.

Banta, T. W., Lund, J. P., Black, K. E., & Oblander, F. W. (1996). *Assessment in practice: Putting principles to work on college campuses.* San Francisco, CA: Jossey-Bass.

Barr, R. B., & Tagg, J. (1995). A new paradigm for undergraduate learning. *Change, 27*(6), 12–25.

Baxter Magolda, M. (1992). *Knowing and reasoning in college.* San Francisco, CA: Jossey-Bass.

Bazerman, C. (1981) What written knowledge does: Three examples of academic discourse. *Philosophy of the Social Sciences, 11*(36), 1–382.

Bazerman, C. (2000). *Shaping written knowledge: The genre and activity of the experimental article in science.* Madison, WI: University of Wisconsin Press.

Bazerman, C., & Russell, D. R. (1994). *Landmark essays on writing across the curriculum.* Davis, CA: Hermagoras Press.

Becker, L. (1999). *Measures of effect size (strength of association).* Retrieved November 29, 2006, from: http://web.uccs.edu/lbecker/SPSS/glm_effectsize.htm

Beecher, T., & Trowler, P. R. (2001). *Academic tribes and territories: Intellectual enquiry and the culture of disciplines.* Suffolk, U.K.: St. Edmundsbury Press.

Belenky, M. E., Clinchy, B. M., Goldenberger, N. R., & Tarule, J. M. (1986). *Women's ways of knowing: The development of self, voice, and mind.* New York, NY: Basic Books.

Beyer, C. H. (1997). *The freshman/sophomore writing experience: 1994–96* (OEA Rep. No. 97-2). Seattle, WA: University of Washington, Office of Educational Assessment.

Beyer, C. H., & Graham, J. B. (1990). *The link between high school and first-term college writing.* Seattle, WA: University of Washington, Office of Educational Assessment.

Beyer, C. H., & Graham, J. B. (1992). *The freshman-sophomore writing study: 1989–91.* Seattle, WA: University of Washington, Office of Educational Assessment.

Beyer, C. H., & Graham, J. B. (1994a). *The junior/senior writing study: 1991–93* (OEA Rep. No. 94-2). Seattle, WA: University of Washington, Office of Educational Assessment.

Beyer, C.H., & Graham, J. B. (1994b). *Portfolio assessment of student writing at the rising-junior level* (OEA Rep. No. 94-6). Seattle, WA: University of Washington, Office of Educational Assessment.

Beyer, J. L. (2003). *2002 Undergraduate Research Study.* Unpublished report, University of Washington, Office of Undergraduate Education.

Bickman, L., & Rog, D. J. (1998). *Handbook of applied social research methods.* Thousand Oaks, CA: Sage.

Biglan, A. (1973). The characteristics of subject matter in different academic areas. *Journal of Applied Psychology, 57*(3), 195–203.

Block, N. (1999). Ridiculing social constructivism about phenomenal consciousness. *Behavioral and Brain Sciences, 22*, 199–201.

Bloom, B. S. (Ed.). (1984). *Taxonomy of educational objectives: The classification of educational goals.* New York, NY: Longman.

Bok, D. (2006). *Our underachieving colleges: A candid look at how much students learn and why they should be learning more.* Princeton, NJ: Princeton University Press.

Bransford, J. D., Brown, A. L., & Cocking, R. R. (Eds.). (2000). *How people learn: Brain, mind, experience, and school.* Washington, DC: National Academy Press.

Campbell, D. T., & Stanley, J. C. (1971). *Experimental and quasi-experimental designs for reseach.* Chicago, IL: Rand McNally.

Chickering, A. (1969). *Education and identity.* San Francisco, CA: Jossey-Bass.

Cross, W. E., Jr. (1991). *Shades of black: Diversity in African American identity.* Philadelphia, PA: Temple University Press.

Dannefer, D. (1984). Adult development and social theory: A paradigmatic reappraisal. *American Sociological Review, 49,* 100–116.

Donald, J. G. (2002). *Learning to think: Disciplinary perspectives.* San Francisco, CA: Jossey-Bass.

Dwyer, C. A., Gallagher, A., Levin, J., & Morley, M. E. (2003). What is quantitative reasoning? Defining the construct for assessment purposes. *ETS Research Report.* Princeton, NJ: Educational Testing Service.

Emig, J. (1977). Writing as a mode of learning. *College Composition and Communication, 28,* 122–28.

Erikson, E. (1968). *Identity, youth, and crisis.* New York, NY: W. W. Norton.

Ewell, P. (1997, December). Organizing for learning: A new imperative. *AAHE Bulletin, 50*(4), 52–55.

Fisher, A., Beyer, C., & Gillmore, G. M. (2001). *Spring 2000 interviews: Critical thinking and problem solving* (OEA Rep. No. 01-18). Seattle, WA: University of Washington Study of Undergraduate Learning, Office of Educational Assessment.

Fullan, M. (1997). Emotion and hope: Constructive concepts for complex times. In A. Hargreaves (Ed.), *1997 Association for supervision and curriculum development (ASCD) yearbook* (pp. 14–33). Alexandria, VA: Association for Supervision and Curriculum Development.

Gilligan, C. (1982). *In a different voice: Psychological theory and women's development.* Cambridge, MA: Harvard University Press.

Gillmore, G. (2003). *The evaluation of general education: Lessons from the USA State of Washington Experience.* Retrieved November 29, 2006, from: www.washington.edu /oea/pdfs/reports/OEAReport0310.pdf

Gurin, P. (1999). *New research on the benefits of diversity in college and beyond: An empirical analysis.* Retrieved November 30, 2006, from: www.diversityweb.org /Digest/Sp99/benefits.html

Gurin, P., Dey, E., Hurtado, S., & Gurin, G. (2002). Diversity and higher education: Theory and impact on educational outcomes. *Harvard Educational Review, 72,* 330–366.

Hartzler, R. (2002). *Final report on interviews with department chairs about the quantitative reasoning (QR) needs of undergraduates.* Unpublished report, University of Washington, Office of Educational Assessment.

Hurtado, S., Dey, E., & Trevino, J. (1994). *Exclusion or self-segregation? Interaction across racial/ethnic groups on college campuses.* Paper presented at the annual meeting of the American Educational Research Association, New Orleans, LA.

Hurtado, S., Milem, J. F., Clayton-Pedersen, A. R., Walter R., & Allen, W. R. (2000). *Enacting diverse learning environments: Improving the climate for racial/ethnic diversity in higher education.* San Francisco, CA: Jossey-Bass.

Hutchings, P., & Shulman, L. (1999). The scholarship of teaching: new elaborations, new developments. *Change, 31*(5), 10–15.

Kirk, R. E. (1982). *Experimental design: Procedures for the behavioral sciences* (2nd ed.). Belmont, CA: Brooks/Cole.

Kitchener, K., & King, P. (1981). Reflective judgment: Concepts of justification and their relationship to age and education. *Journal of Applied Developmental Psychology, 2,* 89–116.

Kvavik, R. B., & Caruso, J. B. (2005). *ECAR study of students and information technology, 2005: Convenience, connection, control, and learning.* Boulder, CO: EDUCAUSE.

Lazerson, M., Wagener, U., & Shumanis, N. (2000). What makes a revolution? (movement to improve quality of higher education). *Change 32*(3), 12–19.

Light, R. (2001). *Making the most of college: Students speak their minds.* Cambridge, MA: Harvard University Press.

Maki, P. L. (2002). Developing an assessment plan to learn about student learning. *Journal of Academic Librarianship, 28,* 8–13.

Mathematical Association of America. (1998). Part II: Quantitative Literacy: GOALS. In *Quantitative reasoning for college graduates: A complement to the standards.* Retrieved November 30, 2006, from: www.maa.org/past/ql/ql_part2.html

Matthews, J. (2004, September 21). How to measure what you learned in college. *The Washington Post.* Retrieved November 30, 2006, from: www.washingtonpost.com /wp-dyn/articles/A37990-2004Sep21.html

Mazur, E. (1997). *Peer instruction: A user's manual.* Upper Saddle River, NJ: Prentice Hall.

McGhee, D. (2000). Entering student survey, 1999: Representativeness of the respondent sample. *Office of Educational Assessment Report.* Retrieved November 30, 2006, from: www.washington.edu/oea/pdfs/reports/OEAReport0004.pdf

Merriam, S. B. (1998). *Qualitative research and case study applications in education.* San Francisco, CA: Jossey-Bass.

Nagda, B. A., Gillmore, G. M., Schmitz, B., & Silas, K. A. (1997). *Does taking diversity courses make a difference?* Unpublished manuscript.

Nathan, M. J., & Petrosino, A. (2002, October 23–26). *Expert blind spot among pre-service mathematics and science teachers.* Paper presented at the annual meeting of the International Conference of the Learning Sciences, Seattle, WA.

National Research Council. (1989). *Everybody counts: A report to the nation on the future of mathematics education.* Washington, DC: National Academy Press.

Pace, D., & Middendorf, J. (Eds.). (2004). *Decoding the disciplines: Helping students learn disciplinary ways of thinking.* San Francisco, CA: Jossey-Bass.

Pascarella, E. T., & Terenzini, P. T. (1991). *How college affects students.* San Francisco, CA: Jossey-Bass.

Paul, R. W., & Elder, L. (2002). *Critical thinking: Tools for taking charge of your professional and personal life.* Upper Saddle River, NJ: Financial Times/Prentice Hall.

Perry, W. (1970). *Forms of intellectual and ethical development in the college years: A scheme.* New York, NY: Holt, Rinehart & Winston.

Perry, W. (1981). Cognitive and ethical growth. In A. Chickering & Associates, *The modern American college: Responding to the new realities of diverse students and a changing society.* San Francisco, CA: Jossey-Bass.

Pike, G. R. (2004). Measuring quality: A comparison of U.S. News Rankings and NSSE benchmarks. *Research in Higher Education, 45*(2), 193–206.

Rimer, S. (2002, November 12). *Colleges find diversity is not just numbers.* New York Times, p. A1.

Russell, D. R. (2002). *Writing in the academic disciplines, a curricular history.* Carbondale, IL: Southern Illinois University Press.

Sanoff, A. P. (2006, March 10). What professors and teachers think: A perception gap over students' preparation. *The Chronicle of Higher Education, 52*(27), B9.

Searle, J. (1995). *The construction of social reality.* New York, NY: The Free Press.

Shulman, L. S. (1986). Those who understand: Knowledge growth in teaching. *Educational Researcher, 15*(2), 4–14.

Shulman, L. S. (1987). Knowledge and teaching: Foundations of the new reform. *Harvard Educational Review, 57*, 1–22.

Shulman, L. S. (2002). Truth and consequences? Inquiry and policy in research on teacher education. *Journal of Teacher Education, 53*(3), 248–253.

Smart, J. C., Feldman, K. A., & Ethington, C. A. (2000). *Academic disciplines: Holland's theory and the study of college students and faculty.* Nashville, TN: Vanderbilt University Press.

Smith, D. G., Moreno, J., Clayton-Pedersen, A. R., Parker, S., & Teraguchi, D. H. (2005). *"Unknown" students on college campuses: An exploratory analysis.* San Francisco, CA: The James Irvine Foundation.

Tatum, B. D. (1997). *Why are all the black kids sitting together in the cafeteria?* New York, NY: Basic Books.

Tinto, V. (1987). *Leaving college: Rethinking the causes and cures of student attrition.* Chicago, IL: University of Chicago Press.

Tinto, V. (1993). *Leaving college: Rethinking the causes and cures of student attrition* (2nd ed.). Chicago, IL: University of Chicago Press.

Tsoukas, H. (2000). False dilemmas in organization theory: Realism or social constructivism? *Organization, 7*(3), 531–535.

U.S. Census Bureau. (1999). *School enrollment in the United States—Social and economic characteristics of students.* Retrieved November 30, 2006, from: www.census.gov /prod/2001pubs/p20-533.pdf

University of Washington. (1998). *Regents statement on diversity.* Retrieved November 2, 2006, from: www.washington.edu/diversity/archive/policies/regents.html

University of Washington. (2006). *SOC 220: Introduction to sociological methods.* Retrieved November 17, 2006, from: www.washington.edu/students/crscat /soc.html#soc220

University of Washington Office of the President. (2004). *University of Washington diversity compact.* Retrieved November 2, 2006, from: www.washington.edu/president /10_21_00-Diversity_Compact.htm

Villalpando, O. (1994, November 10–13). *Comparing the effects of multiculturalism and diversity on minority and white students' satisfaction with college.* Paper presented at the annual meeting of the Association for the Study of Higher Education, Tucson, AZ.

Washington Council of Presidents and State Board for Community College Education (1989). *The validity and usefulness of three national standardized tests for measuring communication, computation, and critical thinking skills of Washington State college sophomores.* Bellingham, WA: Western Washington University Office of Publications.

Willets, J. B. (1988). Questions and answers in the measurement of change. *Review of Research in Education, 15,* 345–422.

Wineburg, S. (1991). On the reading of historical texts: Notes on the breach between school and academy. *American Educational Research Journal, 28*(3), 495–519.

Index